Aristotle's Theory of Language and Meaning

This is a book about Aristotle's philosophy of language, interpreted in a framework that provides a comprehensive interpretation of Aristotle's metaphysics, philosophy of mind, epistemology, and science.

The aim of the book is to explicate the description of meaning contained in *De Interpretatione* and to show the relevance of that theory of meaning to much of the rest of Aristotle's philosophy. In the process Deborah Modrak reveals how that theory of meaning has been much maligned.

This is a major reassessment of an underestimated aspect of Aristotle that will be of particular interest to classical philosophers, classicists, and historians of psychology and cognitive science.

Deborah K. W. Modrak is Professor of Philosophy at the University of Rochester.

Aristotle's Theory of Language and Meaning

DEBORAH K. W. MODRAK
University of Rochester

CAMBRIDGE UNIVERSITY PRESS
Cambridge, New York, Melbourne, Madrid, Cape Town, Singapore, São Paulo, Delhi

Cambridge University Press
The Edinburgh Building, Cambridge CB2 8RU, UK

Published in the United States of America by Cambridge University Press, New York

www.cambridge.org
Information on this title: www.cambridge.org/9780521103985

© Deborah K. W. Modrak 2001

This publication is in copyright. Subject to statutory exception
and to the provisions of relevant collective licensing agreements,
no reproduction of any part may take place without the written
permission of Cambridge University Press.

First published 2001
This digitally printed version 2009

A catalogue record for this publication is available from the British Library

Library of Congress Cataloguing in Publication data
Modrak, Deborah K. W.
Aristotle's theory of language and meaning / Deborah K. W. Modrak.
p. cm.
Includes bibliographical references and index.
ISBN 0-521-77266-4 (hardcover)
1. Aristotle – Contributions in philosophy of language. 2. Language and languages – Philosophy – History. 3. Aristotle – Contributions in philosophy of meaning. 4. Meaning (Philosophy) – History. I. Title.
B491.L3 M57 2000
121′.68′092 – dc21

99-056850

ISBN 978-0-521-77266-2 hardback
ISBN 978-0-521-10398-5 paperback

In Memoriam

Carolina Shubrick Hart Ward

1915–1990

Charles Nathaniel Ward

1908–1986

Contents

Acknowledgments

Many of the topics covered in this volume were originally broached in talks. I would especially like to thank the audiences and commentators at Boston University, Chapel Hill Colloquium, Graduate Center of the City University of New York, Society for Ancient Greek Philosophy, University of Edinburgh, and Central and Pacific Division meetings of the American Philosophical Association for stimulating comments and queries. I would also like to thank the graduate students in the Aristotle seminars I taught in 1993 and 1997 at the University of Rochester; our discussions were very helpful. Finally, I would like to thank Robin Smith and the other, anonymous reader for Cambridge University Press for their very thoughtful and careful reading of the penultimate version.

Introduction

This book began as a paper on *De Interpretatione* 1, 16a3–8:

Spoken words then are symbols of affections of the soul [τῶν ἐν τῇ ψυχῇ παθημάτων] and written words are symbols of spoken words. And just as written letters are not the same for all humans neither are spoken words. But what these primarily are signs of, the affections of the soul, are the same for all, as also are those things [πράγματα] of which our affections are likenesses [ὁμοιώματα].[1]

This description is Aristotle's only explicit attempt to define meaning, and it has been, as a recent commentator remarked, "the most influential text in the history of semantics."[2] Notwithstanding, the account of meaning found in these lines was dismissed by John Ackrill as inadequate, and Aristotle has found few defenders in more recent literature.[3] Suspecting that the negative assessment had been too hasty, I set out to discover whether Aristotle might, after all, be right about meaning.[4] Framing the issue in this way proved jejune, and my initial query was replaced by a series of questions: What position is Aristotle taking here? Is it an account of meaning in the modern sense? Is this account one that he tries out in a relatively early work and later rejects? Does the conception of language embodied in these lines help us better understand the linguistic and ontological notions of definition and universals that are key players in Aristotle's epistemology and metaphysics?

1 Unless otherwise indicated the translations will be mine.

2 Kretzmann (1974, p. 3).

3 Ackrill (1963). Kretzmann (1974) defends Aristotle by denying that Aristotle intended to frame a general theory of meaning in *De Interpretatione* 1; Irwin (1982, pp. 241–66) distinguishes between a theory of meaning and a theory of signification and attributes the latter to Aristotle.

4 The negative assessment, whether hasty or not, is ubiquitous. It is not only found in commentaries on Aristotle but is often used by philosophers of language to preface the presentation of what they take to be a far better approach to meaning. A striking example of this use of criticism of Aristotle's theory of meaning is found in papers by two contemporary philosophers, who agree about little else: Dummett (1978, p. 95); and Putnam (1988: reprinted in Goldman 1993, p. 597).

Granted, the theory of meaning expressed in these lines is puzzling. Two troublesome relations are posited – one between a significant sound and an internal state and the other between that state and the external object of the state. Is the internal state an intentional content, a meaning, or is it a psychological state, an image? Is the thing of which the state is a likeness to be construed as the external referent of the internal state? If the internal state explains how phonemes bear meanings, why does the problem of skepticism not arise for Aristotle? If there is a necessary connection between the internal state, the meaning, and the external referent that determines the content, why does this not make the content inaccessible to the subject? The effort to answer these questions led me to divide the passage into three parts: the nature of words and the relation between the word and the mental state it signifies; the nature of the object that ultimately grounds the significance of the term; and the nature of the relation of likeness that obtains between the mental state and the object. These three parts provide the skeleton of the present study. The first is covered in Part I, which consists of four chapters about semantic, logical, and epistemological issues; the second is addressed in Part II, which consists of two chapters about ontology; and the third corresponds to Part III, which consists of two chapters about the cognitive capacities involved and a concluding chapter.

Far from being inadequate, *De Interpretatione* 16a3–8 summarizes a theory of meaning, I shall argue, that served Aristotle well throughout his career. The objectives of the present study will be three: first, to explicate the *De Interpretatione* description of meaning; second, to show that far from being of little relevance to other parts of Aristotle's philosophy, the theory of meaning summarized in these lines is of precisely the right sort to meet the requirements of his epistemology and metaphysics; and third, to argue that his theory of meaning has been much maligned. Part of my strategy will be to show that the *De Interpretatione* theory of meaning is one that meets a number of desiderata from Aristotle's perspective. First, it is simple, comprehensive, and internally consistent. Second, it provides a semantics for an epistemically adequate language. Third, it supports his analysis of definition in the *Analytics* and *Metaphysics*. Fourth, it is consistent with his account of the acquisition of basic concepts. This strategy results in an interpretation of Aristotle's theory of meaning in the context of his epistemology and ontology. This has several advantages. Chief among these are a deeper understanding of the empirical basis of concepts and successful articulation of the connection between meaning as a characteristic of the terms of a natural language and real definition as employed by the demonstrative sciences.

It must be admitted that the description of meaning in *De Interpretatione* 1 is, to say the least, highly compressed and elliptical. The crucial elements in Aristotle's summary are the word, the meaning-bearing mental state (*pathema*), and the object in the world (*pragma*) that is the referent of the word; the crucial relations are the relation between the word and the mental state and the relation between the mental state and the object in the world. Each of these elements and relations will be examined below in order to explicate Aristotle's theory of meaning. In the course of this examination, the relevance of the theory of meaning to Aristotle's epistemology and ontological theory will become apparent. This in turn will engender further insight into Aristotle's reasons for rejecting Platonic intuition and Platonic transcendent Ideas in favor of a conception of knowledge firmly rooted in the world of physical objects and sentient knowers.

In Part I, the *De Interpretatione* passage is interpreted in the context provided by the logico-semantic and epistemological doctrines found in the *Organon*. There, the basic entities are simple subjects and their characteristics. For language and logic, the basic items are simple subjects and predicates. For epistemology and ontology, the basic units are simple substances and their properties and relations. Throughout, Aristotle assumes that the basic categories of language, knowledge, and reality are structural equivalents.

In the *Categories* and *De Interpretatione,* Aristotle develops an account of language adequate to the expression of demonstrative knowledge. Meaning and truth are critical features of language viewed from this perspective. Aristotle looks for the linguistic elements that are the basic units having meaning and truth, and he finds them, respectively, in words having reference and simple assertions. Fleshing out Aristotle's conceptions of reference and truth is the goal of the first two chapters of Part I. The remaining two chapters of Part I continue the investigation of Aristotle's theory of meaning by situating it in the epistemological context provided by the *Posterior Analytics.* Aristotle's intent, I shall argue, is to give an account of language and its relation to the world that supports, inter alia, the realist epistemology of the *Posterior Analytics.* Two topics covered in the *Posterior Analytics* bear directly on the explication of Aristotle's theory of meaning. Definition is discussed at some length, as is the acquisition of universal concepts. These texts provide a test for the interpretation of Aristotle's theory of meaning developed in the preceding chapters. In addition, once consistency is established, they will prove useful aids in the effort to fill in the details of Aristotle's theory of meaning.

Chapter 1 examines Aristotle's handling of the issues surrounding meaning and reference in the *Categories* and the *De Interpretatione.* The philosophical context in which Aristotle addresses these issues is provided by his predecessors, most importantly by Plato, and thus the first order of business is to look at Plato's *Cratylus* on meaning and reference. The *Cratylus* is a sustained attack on the theories of meaning that were currently in vogue. Two theories are canvassed there and shown to be inadequate. These theories, moreover, would appear to exhaust the possibilities: either words are conventional signs and meanings are assigned by human beings and can be changed at the whim of the language user(s), or words are natural signs. Naturalism is shown to be required in order to give an adequate account of truth; conventionalism, however, is shown to provide a more satisfactory account of the way in which the words of a natural language acquire, maintain, and change their meanings. In the *De Interpretatione,* Aristotle chooses to negotiate a compromise between the two rejected alternatives. The relation between written and spoken words is conventional, as is the relation between spoken words and the mental states that are the vehicles of meaning; different languages correlate different sounds with the same intentional content and the same sound with different contents. Notwithstanding, the relation between the mental state and the object it represents is natural – the same for all humans – and reference is secured by resemblance.

The discussion of the *Cratylus* is followed by a discussion of Aristotle's views on predication and an argument to show that significant terms refer to real objects. In order to understand Aristotle's conception of words and the mental states words signify, I turn to his analysis of language into basic linguistic units and rules governing the generation of complexes out of these elements. Subjects are primary, both grammatically and ontologically, and this fact has significant consequences for Aristotle's theory of meaning and his construal of definition. A referential term denotes a subject existing in the world. The meaning of the term is determined by its referent. By making subjects primary, Aristotle makes the meanings of all terms ultimately dependent upon their relation to extralinguistic subjects. Moreover, the distinction between nominal and real (scientific) definition that figures importantly in Aristotle's epistemology derives its importance from the real definition's successful reference to actual objects whose essence it articulates.

The notions of truth and necessity as employed by Aristotle are the subject of Chapter 2. Both are predicates of sentences and their correct application is a function of the relation between the sentence and the extralinguistic state of affairs expressed by the sentence. Despite some initial hesitation, Aristotle opts for a correspondence theory of truth and an externalist account of necessity. Because meaning is a function of reference in the *De Interpretatione,* the relevance of truth conditions to meaning is evident, and one might expect Aristotle promptly to define truth. This expectation is not met, because Aristotle tends to view truth as an unproblematic notion. Neither the *Categories* nor the *De Interpretatione* explicitly defines truth, although the notion figures importantly in arguments found in these works. Because Aristotle has more to say about truth in the *Metaphysics* and because, as I shall argue, these remarks are consistent with the conception of truth found in the *Organon,* Chapter 2 also examines relevant texts from the *Metaphysics.*

Since Aristotle has many things to say about truth but leaves the notion undefined, an instructive way to approach his conception of truth is to ask what type of theory of truth is implicit in what he does say. That Aristotle accepts a correspondence theory of truth is well supported by his writings. A coherence theory of truth, however, seems to be implied by the strategy he adopts for defending the Law of Noncontradiction in *Metaphysics* IV, and the author of a recent influential study has defended the attribution of a coherence theory to Aristotle. I shall argue against that interpretation. Overall, *Metaphysics* IV supports the attribution of a correspondence theory of truth to Aristotle. This finding provides further evidence of the semantic importance of reference to mind-independent objects. Aristotle appears, for quite different reasons, however, to be committed to two notions of truth, namely, truth in the familiar sense, where the truth predicate applies to assertions in speech and thought, and a second sense of truth appropriate to the apprehension of an indivisible object of thought. Aristotle seems to be ambivalent about calling the correct apprehension of a simple essence 'true'; he avoids that description in *De Anima* III 6 but uses it in *Metaphysics* IX 10; yet in both texts he describes a second sort of object that the mind must get right in order to have knowledge. Aristotle's two notions of truth, I shall argue, express the same metalevel conception of truth as correspondence.

As in the case of truth, Aristotle construes necessity (also possibility) as a property that a statement has in relation to what it asserts. Necessity is of special interest to Aristotle, because it is central to his conception of knowledge. Just as the meaning of a sentence in ordinary language determines (and is determined by) its truth conditions, the meaning of a sentence in scientific discourse is a function of its specialized truth conditions. From the *Organon* to the biological treatises, Aristotle requires the sentences providing the foundation of a science to express necessary truths; such sentences ensure the timeless character of knowledge. The *De Interpretatione* conception of necessity as a predicate of sentences, I shall argue, is developed in the scientific treatises in a way that in effect yields a specialized truth predicate, necessarily true, that applies to the first principles of any science.

In Chapter 3, the relation between word and object is situated in the broader background theory of the requirements for knowledge. Demonstrative knowledge is knowledge par excellence. Demonstration is a method, not a subject matter. Demonstrative sciences are those that meet a demanding set of formal and epistemic requirements that Aristotle spells out in the *Posterior Analytics.* For every demonstrative science, there is a set of basic objects, the definitions of which are first premises. Aristotle's treatment of definition in epistemic contexts provides a wealth of material for the interpreter seeking to understand his views about meaning and reference. Aristotle draws a contrast between definition in the strict sense, the sort of definitions required for demonstrative knowledge, and lexical definitions, about which he otherwise has very little to say. In the *Posterior Analytics,* Aristotle discusses definition at length and recommends a method for producing the right sort of scientific definition; that method, however, like demonstration as a whole, is based on the presupposition that unmediated knowledge of basic objects is possible. Aristotle takes several stabs at describing the way in which universals, the building blocks of language and knowledge, are acquired by human beings – in *Posterior Analytics* II 19, *Physics* I 1, and *Metaphysics* I 1–2. At first reading, these descriptions appear inconsistent. In both *Posterior Analytics* II 19 and *Metaphysics* I 1, the cognitive movement is from particulars to universals, but a different cognitive process seems to be involved in the articulation of concepts as described in *Physics* I 1, where the cognitive movement seems to go from universals to particulars. The careful reading of these passages here, however, yields an interpretation that absolves Aristotle from the charge of inconsistency.

In *Posterior Analytics* II 19, Aristotle offers this sketch: the human mind is so related to the world that the mind is able to grasp the basic categories of reality. Looking at Callias, the perceiver sees a man, and this enables her to grasp the concept 'man'. Bringing this passage to bear on the *De Interpretatione*'s account of meaning yields the following picture: existing in the world, the mind apprehends its structures – the types of natural objects and the modes in which entities exist as basic subjects or their characteristics. The impact of the world on us through our senses and intellect produces the concepts, which provide the foundations of knowledge and language, for not only are empirically produced concepts the basis of science, they also serve as the intentional content of the internal states that words symbolize. When one acquires a natural language, one acquires a classification scheme that is embodied in these internal states and is isomorphic with the things that are. Since these objects have stability, senses of words are stable and, for general terms, reference is fixed by sense, so that human beings equipped with a language are able to refer to and describe real objects.

Chapter 4 develops this line of interpretation further by examining the three types of theoretical science, namely, metaphysics, physics, and mathematics. The epistemological theory set out in the *Posterior Analytics* is a version of foundationalism that envisages first premises that are definitions of real objects. Aristotle fills out the details of this picture elsewhere. Examining the grounds for the distinction between the three types of theoretical science as formulated in the *Metaphysics* brings Aristotle's conception of the basic definitions required by a demonstrative science into sharper focus. Once it is recognized that the primary definitions belonging to each type of theoretical science refer to physical objects or their properties or (in the case of abstraction) to objects derived from them, it is possible to articulate the conditions that the terms and definitions to be employed in a science must satisfy. Together, Chapters 3 and 4 establish a criterion of adequacy for an Aristotelian theory of meaning, and this criterion is internal to his semantics and epistemology.

The investigation undertaken in the first four chapters establishes that Aristotle is committed to a particular conception of language, according to which, terms refer to real entities that are definable. Definitions of the basic objects falling under the domain of a science are the foundational premises of that science. In Part II, Aristotle's ontology of substance in the central books of the *Metaphysics* is examined to determine whether it meets the ontological requirements of his semantic theory and epistemology as described in Part I. Part II is divided into two chapters: Chapter 5 examines the notion of essential definition developed in the *Metaphysics;* Chapter 6 looks at Aristotle's conception of essence. In *Metaphysics* VII–IX, Aristotle ultimately identifies the basic objects (primary substances) with forms that exist in matter and are apprehended by the mind. The existence of stable, extramental and intelligible objects is critically important to Aristotle's explanation of meaning and knowledge – for reasons that are clearly stated by Plato in the *Theaetetus* and accepted by Aristotle. Notwithstanding, Aristotle believes that Plato's ideal objects are an ontological complication that can be avoided by a proper analysis of the empirical basis for knowledge. To explicate the relation between essence, definition, and substance is Aristotle's primary objective in *Metaphysics* VII. The distinction between nominal and real definitions in the *Posterior Analytics* is developed further in the *Metaphysics* to make the real definition the expression of an essence of an extramental object. In order to secure the unity of the definition and establish the intelligibility of the individual substance, Aristotle attributes to the *logos* (formula) that is asserted by the definiens the very same form as the *logos* that is realized in matter. The sameness of the *logos* grasped in thought and the form of the concrete substance provides the missing link in the account of the acquisition of basic concepts in *Posterior Analytics* II 19. Because the mind is such that it is affected by the external *logos* presented in perception, the *logos* that is grasped at the end of the inductive process is, in the favored cases, the real essence of the substance in question.

Useful as this notion of definition proves in the *Metaphysics,* it presents a challenge for Aristotle's theory of meaning. Ordinary language depends upon words having meanings, and these meanings may be expressed in (nominal) definitions. For every significant term, there is a definition of this sort available. Aristotle seems to dismiss such definitions in the *Metaphysics,* where he equates them with mere synonymous strings of words. This prompts the question in Chatper 5: Has Aristotle given us an account of definition in the *Metaphysics* that is of little help in understanding meaning in the context of ordinary language? I argue that despite the obvious tensions between the requirements for linguistic and real definition, there is common ground, and, moreover, that Aristotle exploits this feature in the methodological discussions in the scientific treatises.

Meaning requires an intelligible essence; knowledge requires a unified essence (to block a potential regress of basic objects). Aristotelian forms have the requisite character, as will become clear in Chapter 6. Forms exist in the world, make physical objects what they are, and are accessible to human minds. The ability to apprehend forms is the source of the definitions of essence that are fundamental to Aristotelian science; it is also the basis for Aristotle's analysis of language where terms have empirically based meanings. In the favored case, the meaning of a term for a natural kind will be the articulation of the species form that is realized in the individuals belonging to the kind.

Thus, the account of definition and essence in *Metaphysics* VII–IX provides the ontological underpinning required by the analysis of language in the *Organon*, as will be established in Part II. By the end of Part I, Aristotle's conception of language will have been examined, and within the context of his semantics, the importance of extralinguistic referents to determine meaning and warrant truth ascriptions will have been established. Part II picks up where Part I leaves off by turning to the ontological requirements of the semantics and epistemology detailed in Part I. By the end of Part II, only one task remains – to explicate Aristotle's claim that the mental state signified by a linguistic expression is a likeness of an extramental object.

In Part III, in Chapters 7 and 8, Aristotle is taken at his word that the explanation of the role likeness plays in securing reference in his theory of meaning is to be found in the psychological treatises. Chapter 7 weighs the considerations in favor of, and the considerations against, identifying the internal state in the case of meaning with an exercise of *phantasia* (imagination). Several factors favor this identification. *Phantasia* is mentioned by Aristotle in connection with human language and the *phantasma* (image) seems well suited to play the role of a likeness of an external object. *Phantasia* is the cognitive ability to use sensory contents to represent objects; these representations may be of objects in the subject's immediate environment, if conditions do not favor veridical perception of these objects, or of objects that were perceived on a prior occasion, or of objects that are constructions out of sensory contents that were previously acquired. A careful study of Aristotle's analysis of *phantasia* in the *De Anima*, however, establishes that *phantasia* alone is not powerful enough or versatile enough to support a satisfactory account of reference.

Chatper 8 looks for a way out of this difficulty by identifying the internal state with an exercise of the rational faculty. This stratagem (while yielding a more adequate account of meaning) appears to be at odds with Aristotle's appealing to likeness to explain reference. The role *phantasia* plays in thinking will then be marshaled in support of an explication of the cognitive component of Aristotle's theory of meaning that resolves this problem. Aristotle, I shall argue, construes sensory representation in a way that allows images to represent universals. Once this piece of the puzzle is in place, the cogency of his theory of meaning is secured. The meaning, as it turns out, is a way of conceptualizing the content presented in the *phantasma*. When the internal state is the recognition of an essence, the mental object is the same *logos* as the *logos* embodied in the external object. The challenge is then to explain why Aristotle believes that under these conditions, the *logos* qua cognitive object, which is a meaning, resembles the object to which the uttered sound refers. The answer is found in his claim (investigated in Part II) that the essence (*logos*) of the external object is the same *logos* as the one grasped in thought. Under ideal circumstances, using the *phantasma* of a concrete particular as a representation of a token enables the thinker to recognize the essence of the type to which the token belongs. In such cases, the *pathema* qua *phantasma* is like a token of the type and the *pathema* qua meaning is also properly described as a likeness of the *logos* realized in the concrete token.

Chapter 9 opens with a review of the findings of the preceding chapters. By this point, the explication of the *De Interpretatione* description of meaning will have led to a construal of this theory, which places it squarely within the broader context of Aristotle's epistemology and metaphysics, and the cognitive theory of the *De Anima* will have been shown to support a more sophisticated account of reference than at first meets the eye. In the final part of Chapter 9, I shall evaluate the overall cogency of Aristotle's theory of meaning and explore some of the common ground between Aristotle's views and modern philosophy of language.

Since several of the methodological assumptions that shape this work are somewhat controversial, let me give a brief defense of them here – even though I believe that their final justification rests with their fruitfulness in the course of the analysis to follow. First, I look at a number of treatises in the course of this study; some of these, like the *De Interpretatione*, are believed to belong to Aristotle's early writings and others that figure importantly here belong to Aristotle's mature writings. There is, on the one hand, a legitimate worry about anachronism when one uses a later doctrine to interpret an earlier one. On the other hand, it is important to remember that the treatises at issue were not published during Aristotle's lifetime and quite likely were reworked throughout his lifetime, so for an interpreter to adhere rigidly to a particular chronological scheme also seems misguided. It is my hope that I can steer a course between the two dangers by being sensitive to changes in Aristotle's positions over time and by still availing myself of doctrines spelled out in later writings to interpret earlier ones where there is a demonstrable continuity of thought.

Second, I assume that Plato's positions are seldom far from Aristotle's thoughts. There is considerable textual support for this view. Aristotle frequently refers to Plato or Plato's writings, and even in the absence of such references, in many other places in Aristotle's works there are so many similarities in vocabulary and issues raised that there should be little doubt about Plato's influence. In view of this evidence, Plato's writings should, I believe, be appealed to (when appropriate) in order to clarify the context in which Aristotle addresses specific philosophical issues. Typically, Aristotle's explicit references to Plato occur when he wants to differentiate his own positions from Platonic ones, and this supports the view taken here that for the most part Aristotle accepts the way philosophical questions have been framed by Plato but rejects Plato's answers.

PART I

Language and Knowledge

1
Meaning

Aristotle grapples with the topic of meaning head-on in only one place – at the beginning of the *De Interpretatione.* As already noted, this text is, on the most charitable reading, compressed and elliptical.

Spoken words then are symbols of affections of the soul [τῶν ἐν τῇ ψυχῇ παθημάτων], and written words are symbols of spoken words. And just as written letters are not the same for all humans, neither are spoken words. But what these primarily are signs of [ὧν μέντοι ταῦτα σημεῖα πρώτων], the affections of the soul, are the same for all, as also are those things [πράγματα] of which our affections are likenesses [ὁμοιώματα]. (16a3–8)

Confronted with a summary statement of this sort, an interpreter must try to situate Aristotle's words in a broader context in order to understand their import. The *Categories* and the remainder of the *De Interpretatione* provide the context in which Aristotle's conception of significant terms will be explored in this chapter.

The problem of meaning as framed by Plato in the *Cratylus* will also be briefly discussed, because it sets the stage for Aristotle's account. Aristotle believes the relation between a phoneme and a meaning is conventional (16a20–29). The meaning is the intentional content of the psychological state for which the word stands. He holds, nevertheless, that the relevant mental states (meanings) are the same for all humans and are likenesses of extramental states of affairs. The crucial contrast here is between convention as the explanation of how sounds carry meaning and a natural relation, the same for all humans, rooted in the likeness between a meaning and a reality. This same contrast plays a pivotal role in the *Cratylus.* Aristotle is apparently directing his answer to the question about meaning to an audience familiar with the problem of meaning as that problem is formulated in the *Cratylus.*[1] There Plato seems to draw a

1 As often is the case, when Plato's influence on Aristotle is at issue, it is impossible to know whether Aristotle is addressing a group of questions about meaning that were under discussion in the Academy during his tenure there or whether he is responding to a pub-

skeptical conclusion about the possibility of a theory of meaning, and this conclusion is the hurdle that Aristotle intends his account to clear – as is obvious from Aristotle's terminology and the advantages he claims for his own theory.

1 Plato's Challenge

Plato's *Cratylus* is a sustained attack on the theories of meaning that were currently in vogue.[2] Two theories are canvassed and shown to be inadequate. These theories, moreover, would appear to exhaust the possibilities: either words are conventional signs and meanings are assigned by human beings and can be changed at the whim of the language user(s). Or, just as smoke is a natural sign of fire, a word is a natural sign such that the word indicates an extralinguistic object. Clearly, both conventionalism and naturalism can be developed in a variety of ways, some of which are more plausible than others.[3] The versions of their respective theories that the two protagonists in the *Cratylus,* Hermogenes and Cratylus, choose to defend are quite radical. Hermogenes not only holds that there is no other arbiter of the correct use of a word besides convention and agreement (συνθῆκη καὶ ὁμολογία) among the members of a linguistic community, but he also believes that any individual may privately assign a name to a class of objects, for example, 'man' to horse. If an individual does assign a class a unique name, then that name is correct for him, even when it conflicts with common usage in his community (384c–385a). Cratylus, by contrast, believes that a correct name, whether it is a proper name or a common noun, correctly describes its referent. Thus, according to him, the name 'Hermogenes' is not the correct name for Hermogenes who lacks skill in business matters (383b).[4] From a modern perspective, both positions seem confused. No effort is made to distinguish

lished work by Plato. I am satisfied, however, that the *Cratylus* states the problem Aristotle is addressing. Since my concern is to understand the problem of meaning as Aristotle understood it and since we have access to the *Cratylus* but not to debates within the Academy, the *Cratylus* will be my source. Cf. Kretzmann (1974 p. 13).

2 While no doubt Plato tailored these positions to fit the argumentative strategy of the *Cratylus,* it is likely that variants of both positions did have historical proponents; otherwise Socrates' ironic comment (384b–c) that Prodicus promised to teach the truth about the correctness of names in his fifty drachma lecture would fail to hit its intended target (cf. 391bc, 396d).

3 There is a broad scholarly consensus that conventionalism and naturalism are the two approaches to meaning examined in the *Cratylus.* Whether at the end of the day Plato favors one or the other, or both or neither, is still debated. Among the scholars who argue that Plato opts for conventionalism are Robinson (1969a, 1969b) and Schofield (1982). Kretzmann (1971, pp. 126–38) gives a particularly compelling argument for attributing naturalism to Plato. By contrast, Lorenz and Mittelstraus (1967, pp. 1–20) argue that Plato rejects both naturalism and conventionalism.

4 Hermes, the messenger of the gods, was also the deity of business deals and merchants.

between proper names and common ones, or between reference and meaning, nor does either man consistently acknowledge the communicative function of language. Up to a point, Plato seems to have recognized these shortcomings, insofar as Socrates exploits the internal tensions in each man's position in his critique. Notwithstanding, both positions are instructive, because on different stories about meaning and reference, each position is consistent with a philosophically respectable story.[5] On a causal theory of reference, an initial baptism is required that attaches the word to its referent, and it makes no difference whether the baptism is by an individual or a community; for a speaker to use the word as a referring expression all that is required is that one historical chain or another connect the speaker to the original baptism.[6] Hermogenes would find this theory quite congenial. On the descriptive theory of names, a name is a disguised definite description, and the successful use of a name requires that both the speaker and the listener agree on at least some of the elements of the definite description.[7] The speaker, for instance, might know many things about Socrates and thus have a very rich description by which to fix the referent of 'Socrates', whereas the listener might have a very meager one, for example, 'the philosopher who drank hemlock'; nevertheless, the speaker and the listener would agree about the object referred to by 'Socrates'. If a name is a disguised description, then one might believe, as Cratylus does, that the same requirements for correctness hold both for names and for descriptive terms.

The *Cratylus,* one of the more difficult dialogues in the Platonic corpus, displays the complexities of language by playing with words and their referents. The assumption throughout, as Socrates develops and challenges Hermogenes' and then Cratylus's account of names in turn, is that, unlike pragmatic value, correctness is a function of the relation between the name and the extralinguistic nominatum.[8] While agreement among the users of a name is sufficient to secure its use as a referring expression, the name is correct just insofar as it is a tool for distinguishing things according to their essences. The latter is best accomplished by words that accurately describe the object that the word names (refers to)

5 In the subsequent discussion, I appeal to slightly modified versions of the two theories of reference that have dominated the discussion in philosophy of language in the past two decades. Needless to say, Plato did not have these theories in mind; however, the fact that the positions he developed can be usefully discussed in the framework provided by modern theories should lay to rest the suspicion that the *Cratylus* is a tedious philosophical joke. Hermogenes' and Cratylus's theories of meaning, while extreme, can be shown to be plausible, if their proponents are allowed to appeal to appropriate theories of reference, and this makes their accounts worthy of serious attention today.

6 Kripke (1972, pp. 253–355); Donnellan (1966, pp. 281–304; 1968, pp. 203–15; 1972).

7 Russell (1956a).

8 Cf. Kahn (1973, pp. 152–76).

and when the meaning of the elements of a word accords with the nature of the referent of the object(s) named by the word. The first interlocutor, Hermogenes, initially attempts to combine a radically subjective conventionalism that licenses idiolects with an objective account of the truth of sentences. He claims that all meanings are established by agreement among speakers or when only one speaker is involved by fiat. Socrates, according to Hermogenes, may use 'horse' for a man, if he chooses, and his usage will be as correct as it would be were he to use 'man' for a man.[9] There are no constraints on a speaker to use one sound instead of another in order to make an assertion or name an object. Hermogenes, however, agrees with Socrates that sentences and their components are true, and that a true sentence asserts that which is the case (385b–d).[10] When pressed for a definition of truth, Hermogenes refuses to embrace Protagorean relativism and opts instead for an objective account. The problem posed by idiolects for an objective theory of truth is that the sentence 'Snow is white' in my idiolect might mean the same thing as 'Snow is black' in yours, in which case the two idiolect sentences would be true under the same conditions. If, like Aristotle, one believes that knowledge can be verbalized, one idiolect or the other would have to be assigned a privileged status, but this would be inconsistent with the initial hypothesis that any idiolect is as good as any other. Another solution, which is suggested by Socrates' closing remarks in the *Cratylus,* is to posit truths that are grasped by the mind without the mediation of language (439b). Notwithstanding, in the opening foray of the dialogue, Socrates makes short work of establishing the incoherency of Hermogenes' position, which combines incompatible theses about meaning and truth (385b–386e). Moreover, actions have fixed essences, both men agree, and uttering a particular word or string of words is an action (387a–c). If what a word symbolizes is determined by the speaker or a group of speakers, the same string of words uttered by two different speakers might express different propositions and thus the same action would have two distinct essences.

Having persuaded Hermogenes to reject the radically subjective element of his theory in favor of the view that words have correct and incorrect usages, Socrates then explores with him the cogency of a modified conventionalism where the original meanings of words are given by

9 Although not developed in the dialogue, Plato is implicitly differentiating semantics from pragmatics; an English speaker's intent to communicate with another English speaker would constrain him or her to use 'human' not 'horse' for a human being except in cases where the context made the unusual usage intelligible to the listener.

10 One of the first things Aristotle does in the *De Interpretatione* is restrict truth and falsity to statements (16a11–18). Another crucial feature of Plato's argumentative strategy in the *Cratylus* is making the components of significant words themselves significant. In tacit acknowledgment of Plato's criticisms, Aristotle makes the whole name, not its parts, the minimal unit for meaning (16a19–29).

human beings but where correctness depends upon whether a term successfully describes the object it names (391a–427d). Socrates' initial examples, namely, proper names drawn from Homer and ordinary practice, seem to provide support for this theory, all the more because many of these names contain descriptive elements and thus seem to be disguised descriptions (392d–395e). For instance, Astyanax (Ἀστυάναξ), the name of Hector's son, is composed of the word for city (ἄστυ) and the word for ruler (ἄναξ).[11] As the discussion progresses, however, the examples become more and more fanciful as Socrates shows that the words naming moral virtues and the arts and even 'man' and 'woman' are derived from other words indicating change and motion. This virtuosic display of verbal ability suggests the importance of looking for common roots of words and prompts Socrates to apply the same technique to the syllables making up words and ultimately to the letters. The primary names, he explains, must make the things that are (τὰ ὄντα) apparent, and the primary names (roots) are themselves analyzable into syllables and these into letters. The sounds of letters are found to indicate motion by resemblance (423a–427d). Needless to say, this reductio ad absurdum of the position they are considering causes Socrates and Hermogenes to abandon the defense of a conventional account of naming combined with a descriptive account of names.

This pleases Cratylus, who now steps forward urging the case of naturalism. Deftly avoiding the first pitfall Hermogenes stumbled into, Cratylus denies that names are false; there are failures of reference, in which case the name is as meaningless as a nonsense syllable, but it is not false.[12] A genuine name is a natural sign, according to Cratylus, in that the word resembles that which it represents. Plato's Socrates argues convincingly that the naturalist cannot tell a plausible, nonarbitrary story that justifies the claim that the words of a natural language resemble the extralinguistic world. In the first place, how do we know that the original name giver had the knowledge required to craft a term that resembles the reality it reports to represent? In the second place, even if the original word is an adequate likeness, since words are subject to change over time, the word as currently used might fail this test. This leads Socrates to suggest that perhaps knowledge relies upon a direct apprehension of reality, unmediated by words.[13]

11 No doubt there is an element of Socratic irony displayed in the etymology of Astyanax. At birth, the infant might have seemed aptly named; however, shortly thereafter, according to legend, he was hurled from the walls of Troy.

12 Cf. Palmer (1989), who appeals to the descriptive content of a name to explain why Cratylus makes this claim.

13 Insofar as Aristotle takes the challenge in the *De Interpretatione* to be one of formulating a theory of meaning that has the strengths of each of the rejected alternatives in the *Cratylus*, he ignores Socrates' final suggestion that a nonlinguistic apprehension of basic objects may be required for meaning. This Platonic position may prove of more con-

In spite of the rejection of both conventionalism and naturalism, the dialogue has affirmed a number of theses about language that go unchallenged. Words are tools that enable us to distinguish between objects. All languages that carve up reality correctly will have the same deep structure (389d).[14] Such languages will differ only at the phonetic level, where different sounds will indicate the same object. A correct name indicates the nature of the thing named (426d), and it is a verbal representation (δήλωμα) of its referent. Plato has, in addition, demonstrated the speculative and suspect nature of appealing to a resemblance between word and object to explain meaning, because employing this method, he was able to generate incompatible accounts of the same Greek words; most notably, *episteme* is initially shown to imply motion (412a) and subsequently cessation of motion (437a).[15]

In sum, conventionalism has been rejected on the grounds that if language is a tool for marking real distinctions in the nature of things, it is not merely a matter of convention, for there is a fact of the matter as to whether the language divides reality up at its proper joints.[16] Radical subjectivism has been rejected on the grounds that what a particular sequence of sounds uttered by a member of a linguistic community means is determined by public, interpersonal criteria, not by the whims of the speaker. Naturalism has been rejected because it has proven too difficult to tell a satisfactory story about the connection between a word and the object it represents in light of the historically conditioned nature of language. It is worth noticing that Plato's attack on naturalism is aimed at ordinary Greek words and not at the deep structure of language, where the same name (category) is expressed by different words in different languages. [17]

Despite the dialogue's outcome, an enterprising student of Plato such as Aristotle might not lose heart about the prospects for formulating a satisfactory theory of meaning. Plato makes a strong case for the epistemic requirement for universal concepts of natural kinds and the importance of objective standards for correctness. Aristotle accepts Plato's positive findings, and he tries to find a middle ground between Hermogenes' and

sequence to Aristotle's thinking about the role of *nous* in the apprehension of first principles, and thus this issue will be revisited in Chapter 3, sections 3–4.

14 Cf. 299d, 390e, 393c, 409d–e.

15 Transliterations will be used throughout instead of Greek for terms that are frequently used in this work, such as *episteme* (knowledge).

16 It is risky to summarize an argument as intricate and fascinating as that of the *Cratylus*, which has been variously interpreted by numerous commentators. Besides the interpreters already mentioned, see Gold (1978, pp. 223–52); Ketcham (1979, pp. 133–47); Penner (1987); Spellman (1993, pp. 197–210).

17 The difference between the phonetic level and deep structure of a language is explicitly recognized by Plato at 389d–e; it is also implied by the claim attributed to Cratylus by Hermogenes that there is an inherent correctness in names that is the same for all humans (383a).

Cratylus's positions that will enable him to fend off the objections that Plato raises to each position individually. Moreover, Aristotle must meet the underlying challenge of the *Cratylus* to show that the dynamic character of language as artifact does not undermine its ability to serve as a vehicle for truth in word and thought. Socrates exploits the apparent tension between the dynamism of a natural language and the stability of truth in his arguments against both Hermogenes and Cratylus. The dialogue ends with the suggestion that language cannot serve as a vehicle for truth. Aristotle's strategy in the *Categories, De Interpretatione,* and *Prior* and *Posterior Analytics* is to develop step by step an account of linguistic items and their extralinguistic correlates that will dispel any reservations we might have about the usefulness of language as a tool for expressing truths. The conclusion that Aristotle draws from the arguments of the *Cratylus* is that an adequate philosophy of language would distinguish between the language of thought (universal concepts) and the spoken language (particular sounds); and the claim of natural language to be a tool for understanding the world would be explicated in a way that allowed for the historical phenomenon of language change and growth.

2 Meaning and the *De Interpretatione*

The task of the philosopher of language, as Aristotle construes it in the *De Interpretatione,* is to acknowledge the plasticity of natural language (the variety of languages, the many functions of utterances, etc.) while making sense of the use of words to express the unchanging truths of art and science (see, for instance, 17a1–8). In *De Interpretatione* 1, he advocates conventionalism with respect to the relation between a phoneme and the meaning it bears, and naturalism with respect to the relation between meaning and reference. This is Aristotle's response to the problem of meaning raised in the *Cratylus.* Unlike Cratylus, Aristotle grants that the relation between the written word and the spoken word and the relation between the spoken word and the psychological state (*pathema*) the word signifies is determined by social practice (συνθήκη) (see 16a20–29).[18] The speakers of a particular natural language might have chosen to adopt a different practice with respect to the written or spoken sign or with respect to the correlation of these with the idea that makes them meaningful. By contrast, the relation between the notion and the thing it represents is natural; a mark of its being a natural relation is that this relation is the same for all humans.[19] The divergence of the two relations is indi-

18 Cf. Hermogenes' remark that there is no other criterion of correctness for names except *suntheke* and *homologia* (Plato, *Crat.* 384c–d).

19 Plato also seems to believe that at the deep structure all properly formed languages would be the same (*Crat.* 389d–e).

cated at 16a3–8 by Aristotle's use of σύμβολον and σημεῖον to explicate the relation between the word and the associated mental state (πάθημα) and his use of ὁμοιώματον to explicate the relation between the mental state and its intentional object (πρᾶγμα).

Spoken words then are symbols [σύμβολα] of affections of the soul and written words are symbols of spoken words. . . . But what these primarily are signs of [ὧν μέντοι ταῦτα σημεῖα πρώτων], the affections of the soul, are the same for all, as also are those things [πράγματα] of which our affections are likenesses (ὁμοιώματα). (16a3–8)

Σύμβολον and σημεῖον, two terms for sign or token, have well-established senses as signs by convention, agreement, or social practice; for instance, the custom among parties to a contract was to break a coin between them, and the pieces of the coin were called σύμβολα. Greek usage and a long tradition of commentary on this passage supports treating σύμβολα and σημεῖα as synonyms here. N. Kretzmann argued against the tradition and urged a distinction between the two.[20] While Kretzmann was surely right to call attention to the conventional connotations of σύμβολον (cf. 16a28), a cautious attitude should be adopted with respect to his further claim that σημεῖον should be read as symptom in this context. Aristotle's preferred term for signification is σημαίνω, and he frequently uses σημεῖον as a cognate. If words are signifiers of mental contents rather than symptoms of mental states, then these lines do express a semantic theory, however elliptically or inadequately. That this is so is supported by the claim that the mental state resembles (stands in the relation of likeness to) the *pragma.*

Pragma is Aristotle's term for the actually existing object, event, or situation that a word, a sentence, or a belief refers to or describes. This is clear from his characterization of truth. The truth value of a sentence or a belief is determined by the *pragma.*[21] 'Callias sits' is true just in case the *pragma* is so disposed, that is, just in case Callias's body is in a certain position.[22] *Pragmata* exist in their own right. The mind apprehends them but does not, unless certain mental dispositions are at issue, create them. In *De Interpretatione* 1, the mental states corresponding to the *pragmata* are described as *pathemata* and ὁμοιώματα (likenesses). Resemblance depends upon features that are possessed by the objects that resemble each other. If the relation of likeness obtains, both the mental state and the *pragma* exist.[23] Moreover, they possess some characteristics that are common to both. This is most easily understood on a model that construes

20 Kretzmann (1974, pp. 3–9).

21 Cf. Plato, *Sophist* 263b: "The true ⟨sentence⟩ states about you the things that are as they are." Cf. also *Crat.* 385b; *De Int.* 19a33–34.

22 Cf. *Cat.* 4a21–4b2.

23 The claim that likeness in the case of a representational state is a two-place relation between an extramental object and the representation is also defended by Everson (1997, chap. 5).

the mental state as having an intentional object that is similar to the extramental object. By describing the mental state as a *pathema* (literally, the result of some action on the mind), Aristotle emphasizes its origin in some antecedent cause. A likely surmise about the origin of these particular *pathemata* is that they are caused by the *pragmata* they resemble.

Let us canvass all the possibilities if (a) the *pathema* is caused by the object it resembles: (a1) (a) and the object it resembles just is its intentional content; (a2) (a) and the object it resembles is typically an extramental object; (a3) (a2) and the *pathema* is an intentional state, and its intentional object is its cause. Notice that (a) is consistent with Kretzman's symptom interpretation as well as semantic interpretations of the passage. Interpretation (a1) offers a narrow construal of the *pathema* as a linguistic item that need not stand in any relation to any nonlinguistic state. Interpretations (a2) and (a3) posit a relation between the *pathema* that a word signifies and an object external to the mind. Under interpretation (a3), the mental state is directed at (has as its content) the object causing the mental state. Under (a3), the mental content for which the spoken word stands mediates the relation between the word and the object to which it refers, and the object determines the mental content or meaning. Interpretation (a3) thus has the greatest potential for yielding an adequate semantics. Still there are obstacles.

In a semantic context, the notion of likeness is troubling. About the only positive thing that can be said for it is that resemblance might be used to explain reference. The fact that the object in the world is like the mental state could be exploited in order to address two difficult questions that have been much discussed by modern philosophers of language. The questions are: How does the object in the world act as a constraint on the cognitive content of a word? How does the thought refer to a mind-independent object? A similar concern is voiced by Aristotle in the *Posterior Analytics* when he asks, what makes the definition of a circle its definition rather than the definition of mountain copper (92b20–22)? While the possibility of answering these questions is afforded by the notion of likeness, the obstacles to success seem almost overwhelming. On the face of it, likeness seems completely inadequate to explain the relation between words and the world, between meanings and extralinguistic realities. How can something mental resemble something in the world? The most obvious candidate is an image of the thing. Aristotle seems to agree; elsewhere he mentions *phantasia* in connection with meaning (*De An.* 420b30–33).[24]

In some instances, there is a plausible story to tell about how a speaker might learn to use a word by coming to associate the word with a partic-

24 Spellman (1993) argues that in the *Cratylus,* Plato envisages a language of thought consisting in images. If she is right, then Plato may have influenced Aristotle's thinking here as well.

ular image and then applying the word in the future in accordance with the image. A young child seeing Socrates wandering about the streets of Athens might learn to associate 'Socrates' with Socrates on the basis of stored images of Socrates. A child who initially learned the term 'cup' by ostensive definition might come to associate that sound with the image of a cup and as a result understand 'cup' when it occurred in discourse. Perhaps the child learns what *anthropos* means in the same way. Already the plausibility of the account is greatly reduced, for it assumes that the child learns a concept that includes all human beings on the basis of a very limited sample. This sample is typically also limited with respect to nationality and race. These limitations would suggest that at best the child's concept resembles a particular human being or a generic representative of a subclass of human beings. Suppose it is the first, and the child uses *anthropos* in accordance with an image of Socrates; this image would seem to be of little help in enabling the child to apply the concept to any person whose physical characteristics were quite unlike Socrates'. Suppose instead of distinct images of one or more individuals, the child has a generic image of some sort. As Berkeley pointed out against Locke's general ideas, it is hard to see how images of specific humans could coalesce into an image corresponding to the general concept.[25] Even if the images did coalesce, the result would most likely be wholly unintelligible and of no help to a speaker in search of the meaning of *anthropos*. There are, moreover, many words in our vocabulary that do not seem to connect even in this very attenuated sense with specific objects capable of producing images in the speaker that resemble the object. The abstract ideas of ethical and mathematical objects that fascinated Plato do not seem to resemble specific concrete individuals. Syntactic terms also seem very problematic; there is no object in the world for the meaning of 'or' to resemble. The last difficulty, while not addressed in the *De Interpretatione*, is met in *Poetics* 20 by differentiating between syntactic terms that are without significance (ἄσημος) and other terms (1456b37–1457a10).

It would be premature, at this stage of our investigation, to decide that Aristotle's account of meaning is hopelessly flawed, because he appeals to likenesses in the mind. Aristotle may be able to meet our objections by exploiting the notion of form developed in the *Metaphysics* and by invoking the analysis of cognition developed in the *De Anima*. These aspects of his philosophy will be explored in Parts II and III. For the present, let us grant that the sound represents the object through the mediation of the internal state and that an utterance is significant just in case the sound stands in a particular relation to an object, namely just in case the sound stands for an internal state that resembles the object. Even so, a number

25 Commentators sometimes find evidence for this position in Aristotle at *Met.* 981a5–7; but see Modrak (1987a, chap. 7).

of questions remain unanswered. These concern the role of meaning in mediating the relation between word and object and how reference is determined.

Before turning to these questions, however, an even more fundamental question must be answered: In what sense, if any, can Aristotle be rightly described as having a theory of meaning? There are several issues here – the implications of using 'theory' to describe the elliptical account of meaning found in *De Interpretatione* 1 and the implications of using 'meaning' instead of 'signification' to describe Aristotle's topic. First, it should be noted that Aristotle does not have a theory of meaning, if by 'theory' is meant the specification of necessary and sufficient conditions for a sound to have significance for persons sharing a common language.[26] If by 'theory' is meant a general account of this phenomenon, then Aristotle does, or so I shall argue, have a theory of meaning. Three sorts of entities are posited at 16a3–8: words as expressed in written and spoken tokens, mental states, and mind-independent objects. The relations between the three explain the phenomenon of human languages, systems of representations by means of linguistic signs. This picture cannot be easily assimilated to certain modern theories of meaning, and so there has been an understandable tendency among commentators to find it wanting. If modern theories of meaning that analyze meaning in terms of criteria of application or criteria of synonymy exhausted the philosophical understanding of meaning, then to describe Aristotle as having a theory of meaning would be eccentric at best and misleading at worst. Happily, there are other candidates. Meaning identified with an intention or mental content is consistent with Aristotle's conception of a *pathema* that is common to speakers and is the content of which the sound is a sign. Moreover, the question Aristotle addresses is what makes a linguistic sign, written or spoken, useful in a system of representations, and this is a question about meaning. This query is at the core of Aristotle's semantic theory. Ultimately, it will be answered by an appeal to truth; meanings are required in order for linguistic entities, sentences, to represent what is actually the case.

Unlike a modern linguistic philosopher, Aristotle is not interested in generating an analysis of meaning for any possible language. He is interested in explaining meaning in the context of actual languages and in particular in explaining meaning in the context provided by a language that is adequate to the task of describing the external world. Since the test of adequacy here will be getting it right about the world, meaning is explicated by Aristotle in terms of a relation between words and external

26 That Aristotle does not have a theory of meaning in this narrow sense may prove a strength rather than a weakness. Recently a well-known philosopher of language, T. Burge (1992, pp. 3–51), has suggested that the notion of a theory of meaning as contrasted to meaning may be singularly unhelpful in the modern context.

objects that enables a speaker to use words to construct statements expressing true beliefs about the world. In this respect, Aristotle's theory of meaning is far more limited in its range of application than modern theories, and in this respect Aristotle's theory is arguably less satisfactory. Yet by restricting his account of meaning to actual, epistemically adequate languages in the *De Interpretatione*, Aristotle keeps the discussion where he wants it to be, namely, on the use of language as a tool for understanding.

Second, the differences between Aristotle's handling of the notion of signification in the *De Interpretatione* and modern discussions of meaning seem to count against taking Aristotle's topic to be meaning. Having construed Aristotle's remarks about signification in the *De Interpretatione* as an attempt to frame a theory of meaning, Ackrill viewed it as a failed attempt.[27] He faulted Aristotle's account on numerous grounds; not only had Aristotle appealed to images in the mind, but Aristotle had also made a number of other elementary mistakes, including confusing use and mention.[28] Terence Irwin was more sympathetic to Aristotle but saved him at a price. Irwin distinguished between Aristotle's theory of signification and the modern notion of meaning in a way that left the relevance of Aristotle's approach to modern concerns in doubt.[29] While it would be impetuous to decide the broader question of relevance in Aristotle's favor now, we should consider the narrower question of whether it is appropriate to talk about a theory of meaning in Aristotle's case.

Irwin argues that several of Aristotle's claims about signification become problematic, if read as claims about meaning, and moreover, that meaning in our sense and signification in Aristotle's sense are distinct, in that meaning the same thing is neither necessary nor sufficient for signifying the same thing.[30] Aristotle claims that negative predicates such as 'not-man' signify something indefinite, whereas positive predicates such as 'man' signify something definite (16a29–31, b11–15, 19b9). Irwin cites this case as one piece of evidence for his interpretation because (according to him) insofar as meaning is at issue there is no difference between these two types of predicates; both have perfectly straightforward meanings.[31] Granted, certain statements that Aristotle makes about negative predicates and nonreferring terms appear to be problematic,

27 Unlike Ackrill and in contrast to a long tradition of commentary on *De Interpretatione* 1, Kretzmann (1974) does not find a general theory of meaning in Aristotle's remarks at 16a3–8, which in his opinion were designed to meet the narrow objective of showing that spoken sounds are significant by convention.

28 Ackrill (1963, pp. 113–15).

29 Irwin (1982). Irwin's account of signification is challenged by Bolton (1985, pp. 153–62).

30 The relation between the meaning of a word in a natural language and the real definition of a term employed in a demonstrative science will be discussed in Chapter 5.

31 Irwin (1982, p. 245).

when interpreted as remarks about meaning. If one accepts that meaning is "what is entered in a dictionary" (the use conception of meaning), then the difficulties advanced by Irwin do indeed arise.[32] The use conception of meaning is not the only one found in recent philosophical treatments of meaning, however. If meaning is construed as an intentional property, then we can make sense of Aristotle's examples of the signification of negative predicates (e.g., not-man) or nonreferring terms (e.g., manandhorse, goatstag, etc.) as claims about meaning. The content of the *pathema* that 'not-man' signifies (its meaning) is indefinite, in that it fails to articulate all the different objects of which 'not-man' could be correctly predicated; 'man', by contrast, signifies a concept that delimits the extension of 'man' by specifying the actual (positive) characteristics of humans. Indefinite names have signification in a way (ἕν πως σημαίνει), Aristotle says (19b9), and he is tentative for good reason, because on his account of meaning, the coherence of the mental content (its expressing one notion) is one necessary condition for signification, but standing in a relation of likeness to an external *pragma* is another. In the case of negative names such as not-man, the first condition is satisfied, but in a way that makes the satisfaction of the second condition indefinite rather than determinate. Indefinitely many, arbitrarily selected individuals will satisfy the concept not-man; these individuals need not have any positive characteristics in common. There is no definition (ὁρισμός) or definable class under which they all fall; the group consisting of them is without determinate conceptual boundaries; it is ἀόριστον (indefinite).

According to Aristotle, the simple sentence, 'A manandhorse is white', is either meaningless or equivalent to the compound sentence, 'A man is white and a horse is white' (18a18–25). Treated as a single term, 'manandhorse' is nonreferring and signifies nothing. Irwin argues that 'manandhorse' has a single meaning just like 'man' and thus this case also displays the difference between Aristotle's notion of signification and meaning. Again the difference between two modern conceptions of meaning provides a way out for Aristotle. 'Manandhorse' fails to correspond to a concept expressing a single real essence; interpreted as a compound of two subject terms, it corresponds to two such essences. There are simply no actual individuals that satisfy the concept 'manandhorse' unless it is treated as a complex notion picking out at least one individual from each of two distinct kinds (humans and horses).

The superficially similar term 'goatstag,' however, signifies something (i.e., produces a determinate *pathema*), because it has a nominal definition, albeit one that is not satisfied by any actual existent (cf.

32 Irwin (1982, p. 242) defines meaning in terms of use and translation manuals. For a recent defense of the use conception of meaning, see Horwich (1995, pp. 355–68).

16a16–18).[33] For Aristotle, the significant difference between 'manandhorse' and 'goatstag' is whether there is a context that would allow a hearer to form a precise mental concept corresponding to a nonreferring term or a sentence in which a nonreferring term occurred.[34] In the case of 'A manandhorse is white', the listener lacks such a context in contrast to a listener who is familiar with the mythical creature that is half goat and half stag. (Aristotle arbitrarily assigns the name 'garment' [ἱμάτιον] to the putative concept of 'manandhorse' at 18a19, thus making it clear that this example is not about a centaur [κένταυρος] a mythical creature that is half horse and half man. Unlike the example, 'centaur' does have a nominal definition.)[35] This is not to say that treating 'goatstag' or 'centaur' as significant terms is not troublesome for Aristotle. The mythic context supplies a context in which to construe the concept; in this context, the name of a mythic creature functions as a referring term. However, in order to satisfy the second condition on signification actual referents seem to be required, and thus when Aristotle turns his attention to such terms he solves this problem by distinguishing between terms having genuine definitions (signification in the strict sense) and terms having only nominal definitions.

These examples suggest that Aristotle's account of signification is concerned with ontological presuppositions in a way that many modern theories of meaning are not.[36] Irwin's examination of Aristotle's claim that both the word and its definition signify the same thing, namely, a real essence, points to the same conclusion. None of these examples show that a theory of signification is not a theory of meaning as intension supplemented by a metaphysical thesis about the ontological correlates of meaningful terms. Since, as Irwin recognizes, many of Aristotle's remarks about signification are consistent with the identification of signification with meaning, it seems better to adopt an interpretation according to which the analysis of meaning is an important component of a theory of signification.[37] This is precisely what I propose to do – to talk about meaning and about ontology.

Words represent mind-independent objects in virtue of signifying

33 See Chapter 5 for more discussion of nominal and real definitions. Here I use 'nominal definition' for the item Aristotle calls the definition of the name. Other commentators have restricted the range of nominal definitions to definitions having existential import. E.g., Bolton (1976, pp. 514–44); and DeMoss and Devereaux (1988, pp. 133–54).

34 Cf. *De Int.* 16b19–21.

35 Aristotle uses κενταύροις at *De Insomn.* 461b20 for the mythical creatures.

36 Bolton (1985, pp. 154–8), argues against Irwin that signification is always a matter of convention, even though some names signify real essences.

37 Irwin differentiates between signifying for us and signifying by nature, where the former is not a component of the latter, because some terms, e.g., 'goatstag', have significance in the former sense but not in the latter. This is a helpful way to look at Aristotle's distinction between nominal and real definitions; it is less helpful as a way of explicating Aristotle's views on meaning because in this context Aristotle assigns the terms and

mental contents. As described in *De Interpretatione* 1, signification is a relation that holds between words and mental contents, but this relation has a counterpart in the relation between the mental content and the extralinguistic state of affairs (*pragma*). Elsewhere Aristotle uses 'signifies' to describe the latter relation as well. This is the reason for saying that signification is a broader notion than meaning; but we should not lose sight of the fact that, according to Aristotle, words signify mental contents and it is in virtue of this relation that a sound is meaningful. Again a caveat is in order – these are preliminary considerations in support of attributing a theory of meaning to Aristotle and adopting the hypothesis that he does have a theory of meaning in order to investigate his conception of language further.

The passage at 16a3–8 supports the following theses about meaning: the question of meaning is primarily a demand for an explanation of how the vocal and graphic signs of a natural language function in representations of objects and states of affairs (*pragmata*). It is of concern to Aristotle because linguistic systems are cultural artifacts, yet the representational systems in which they figure make claims to truth. The association of a particular linguistic sign with a particular meaning is conventional. The meaning, however, is an intentional state, a *pathema,* that is a likeness of the extralinguistic object, the *pragma,* to which the intentional state refers. The *pragma* has a definite character and the *pathema* as its likeness shares this character. Meaning is a function of reference.

The philosophical importance of *De Interpretatione* 16a3–8 has been queried on other grounds. It has been claimed that this text is unique in the Aristotelian corpus in its treatment of language in terms of intentional states. One version of this challenge argues that the three-tiered description of language, meaning and the world found at 16a3–8 is about psychology, not theory of language, and plays no further part in the *De Interpretatione.*[38] The best answer to this objection is to show by a careful examination of the *De Interpretatione* the coherence between the description of language at 16a3–8 and the remainder of the work and to establish the relevance of the *De Interpretatione*'s conception of language to other parts of the corpus. This I hope to do in the following pages.

3 Categories and Linguistic Units

To return, then, to Aristotle's conception of meaning and reference: his position on these topics can, I believe, be partially reconstructed by in-

sentences that express knowledge a normative role – a practice that has a counterpart in several influential twentieth-century philosophies of language.

38 Sedley (1996) argues that the "*De Interpretatione* is . . . the most seriously misunderstood text in ancient semantics" and that its central theme is not semantics at all but the nature of contradiction. Cf. Whitaker (1993; 1996).

terpreting *De Interpretatione* 1 in light of the *Categories.* The theory of meaning uses a symmetrical relation (likeness) to explain reference and to indicate how the world determines the meanings of words. That such a symmetry exists is one of the tacit assumptions of the *Categories,* a work that provides valuable insights into the relation between terms and things as understood by Aristotle. *De Interpretatione* 1 speaks of a significant sound, the internal state (*pathema*) it signifies, and an external state (*pragma*) that the internal state represents by resemblance. *Categories* 1 speaks of the word (*onoma*), its definition (*logos*), and what the word is predicated of. Setting aside questions about the psychological nature of the *pathema,* it seems reasonable to suppose that the internal state is constitutive of the *logos* and thus that the two passages are describing the same three items from different perspectives. The definition (*logos*) of a significant sound determines its objective correlate and the items of which the word can be correctly predicated. The *Categories,* moreover, is a work that claims both to provide a classification scheme for predicates and to articulate the ontological framework that holds true not only of language but of the world.[39] Aristotle begins with names – simple names and names in various combinations. Then he turns from the things that are said (τά λεγομένα) to the things that are (τὰ ὄντα). These are divided into ultimate subjects and things that are said of or present in them; that is, the kinds of existents separate naturally into ontological subjects and predicates.[40] The remainder of the *Categories* discusses the types of predicate, construed as what is signified by an uncombined expression and its ontological correlate.

For the sake of simplicity, in this chapter the *logos* (literally, account or definition) of a simple expression will be identified with the meaning of the term.[41] This practice arguably trivializes the difference between a string of words specifying the conditions of use for a term and the intentional object that enables both speaker and listener to understand the term. There is, however, a certain ambiguity in Aristotle's use of *logos.* On the one hand, he would no doubt agree that a Greek speaker would use different words to express the *logos* of *anthropos* than a barbarian (a non-Greek speaker) would use. Moreover, much that Aristotle says about ra-

39 Cf. Ackrill (1963, pp. 71–6); Ferejohn (1991, pp. 75–83).

40 This conception of basic subjects and predicates is found throughout Aristotle's writings and is applied in a number of different contexts. See, for instance, *Physics* I 7, 190a34–37, and III 1, 200b32–201a9, for its implications for theories of change; *Metaphysics* VII 1, 1028a13–30, for its implications for the study of being; *Nicomachean Ethics* I 6, 1096a23–29, for its implications for ethical theory.

41 *Logos* is by far the favored term for definition in the *Organon.* Aristotle has other more technical terms for definition, namely, *horismos* and *horos,* yet when he defines them, he uses *logos.* See, e.g., *Topics* I 5: a definition (ὅρος) is a *logos* signifying essence (τό τὶ ἦν εἶναι).

tionality seems to fit the internalized speech model of thought he inherited from Plato, for whom thought is internal discourse (*Sophist* 263e). Not only is *anthropos* significant by convention, but so too is the definition the Greek speaker uses to express its meaning. On the other hand, the insistence on the universality of the *pathema* of which the word is a sign suggests that for Aristotle the linguistic structures underlying the *logoi* expressed in the native language of the thinker are ones that are common to all speakers using synonymous terms. In the final analysis, these underlying structures are the units of meaning. Just as the spoken word stands to the surface *logos,* the verbalized *logos* must stand to the common *logos.*

Aristotle's notion of a universal *pathema* is the counterpart of Plato's conception of the universal name that is the same for all speakers.

> Accordingly you will consider the legislator, the one here or the one among barbarians, as long as he gives the proper form of the name in each case in whatever syllables, no less a legislator whether here or anywhere else, will you not? (*Crat.* 390a)

Moreover, for both Plato and Aristotle, the internal units of meaning are not merely products of the human mind, they also correspond to an objective reality. Plato takes it as obvious that this reality must be ideal. Aristotle, by contrast, believes that the objective reality is constituted by physical objects and their properties and that external (nonideal) *pragmata* determine the character of the universal *pathemata.*

The first chapter of the *Categories* defines homonymous, synonymous, and paronymous uses of names. Although Aristotle's way of describing homonyms and synonyms makes it sound as if he is talking about the referents of the names instead of words, it becomes clear as the discussion progresses that he is interested in the application of terms to things. If a single term is used to refer to items with different natures, the items are said to be homonymous. When I point to my cat and say 'cat' and when I point to her picture and say 'cat', the term 'cat' is being used homonymously, because the definitions corresponding to 'cat' in the two instances are different (cf. 1a1–3). When I say, however, that my cat is an animal, as is the neighbor's dog, I use 'animal' synonymously, for 'animal' refers to the common nature shared by the cat and the dog. The relation between paronymous things is more elusive, and Aristotle appeals to the relation between linguistic expressions to elucidate it.

> Things which have their names from another with a difference in ending are called paronymous as is the grammarian from grammar and the brave from bravery. (1a12–15; cf. 10a27-b1)

All three explanations of what from one perspective are linguistic categories, homonyms, synonyms, and paronyms turn on the way extralinguistic objects determine the meanings (definitions) of the terms and govern their usage.

In the second chapter, Aristotle divides the things that are (*onta*) into four kinds:

> (a) some are said of a subject but are not in any subject. For example, man is said of a subject, the individual man, but is not in any subject. (b) And some are in a subject but are not said of any subject. . . . For example, the particular knowledge of grammar is in a subject, the soul, but is not said of any subject; and the particular white is in a subject, the body . . . but is not said of any subject. (c) Some are both said of a subject and in a subject. For example, knowledge is in a subject, the soul, and is also said of a subject, knowledge of grammar. (d) Some are neither in a subject nor said of a subject, for example, the individual man or individual horse – for nothing of this sort is either in a subject or said of a subject. (1a20–1b6)[42]

According to the traditional construal of this classificatory scheme, the four kinds of beings are (a) universal substance, (b) particular attribute, (c) universal attribute, and (d) particular substance.[43] (Below I shall use 'primary' and 'secondary' instead of 'particular' and 'universal', because Aristotle uses these terms in the case of substance in the fifth chapter, and because these terms highlight the dependence of general features of the world on particular exemplifications of these features.)[44] The objects described in (b) and (d) are said to be individual (ἄτομα) and one at 1b6–8. Aristotle, however, does not use proper names or arbitrary names in his examples; instead he uses a phrase consisting in a definite article, an indefinite pronoun, and a general term (ἡ τὶς γραμματική, τὸ τὶ λευκόν, ὁ τὶς ἄνθρωπος, ὁ τὶς ἵππος). The function of the ὁτις phrase is to restrict the application of the universal to a particular instantiation of the universal. Unlike an arbitrary name, for instance 'A', the phrase Aristotle uses both serves to pick out a particular and to include the particular in the extension of a universal.

Considerable agreement exists among recent interpreters of *Categories* 2 about the characteristics of (d) primary substances, (a) secondary substances, and (c) secondary attributes. Disagreements concern the defining characteristics of (b) primary attributes, those entities that are present in but not said of anything else. Even here there has been widespread agreement that primary attributes are nonsubstantial individuals.[45] Ack-

42 As Matthews (1989, pp. 91–104) points out, "Perhaps no passage in Aristotle has excited more attention in recent years, or aroused more controversy, than the second paragraph of Chapter 2 of the *Categories*."

43 Ammonius, *Commentaria in Aristotelem Graeca*, vol. iv.4 (1895, 25.9–14).

44 While not found in this chapter, the terms, 'primary substance' and 'secondary substance' as used in *Categories* 5 are obviously the same entities as the ultimate subjects and the things said of but not present in a subject of *Categories* 2.

45 One notable exception is Anscombe and Geach (1961, pp. 8–9), who believe that Aristotle reserves 'individual' for substances.

rill construed nonsubstantial individuals in a way that made their existence dependent on their bearers; according to him, to be in a subject *x* was defined by these conditions: in *x*, not as a part of *x*, and could not exist apart from *x*. This reading was disputed by G. Owen and also by Michael Frede, who both argued for a less restrictive definition of 'in a subject' that would allow for generalized dependence, for example, of white on body.[46] The criteria for being in a subject were correctly expressed, Frede argued, by: *X* is in something, if there is a *y* such that *X* is not a part of *y*, and *X* cannot exist independently of *y*.[47] The crux of the argument between these commentators is whether a primary attribute – for example, the pallor of Socrates – could recur in some other bearer. On Ackrill's reading, it could not; the generalized attribute of pallor (the shade of Socrates' skin) recurs (or could recur) but not the primary attribute of pallor that is in Socrates; for Owen and Frede, there is nothing intrinsic to a primary attribute that rules out recurrence. What distinguishes a primary attribute from a secondary attribute is that the former cannot be predicated of anything else; it does not, according to Frede, have subjective parts. Viewed from the vantage point of the definition of meaning in *De Interpretatione* 1, the impact that these different treatments of primary attributes would have is marginal but instructive. If Ackrill is right, then singly occurring, primary attributes of pallor would have to be such that a general notion (*logos*) of pallor would be like each primary attribute. The basis for asserting that the particular pallor that exists in an individual body at a particular time is like the pallor that is predicable of body in general would be left wholly unexplained. If Owen and Frede are right, then the conceptual link between a general notion of an attribute and the particular occurrences of the attribute would be less mysterious. What this suggests is that certain conceptual considerations developing out of the theory of meaning would push Aristotle toward the latter position. This is not the end of the story, however, because Aristotle also has good, epistemological reasons, as we shall discover in Chapter 3, to make primary attributes dependent on their individual bearers' existence. On the other hand, Aristotle may be wary of any proposal that differentiates between the ultimate referents of words and the objects present to the knower through sense perception. If the primary attribute is a nonrecurrent individual, it would be present to the percipient in exactly the same way as a primary substance.

The secondary substance 'human' is predicated of Socrates and the secondary attribute 'pale' is predicated of his skin. In order for these predications to be true, it is necessary that the general term 'man' have

46 Frede (1987, 49–71); and Owen (1965, 97–105). For a review of the history of recent interpretations and a new proposal, see also Wedin (1993, pp. 137–65).

47 Owen (1965, p. 104) offers a less formal version of the same criterion for being in a subject.

reference to an individual man who happens to be Socrates, and it is necessary that the general term 'pale' have reference to the pallor instantiated by Socrates' skin. The secondary substances and attributes are dependent on the existence of primary substances and primary attributes. General terms ascribe the characteristics of a secondary substance or a secondary attribute to concrete individuals, which are either individual substances or their particular attributes. Aristotle says that knowledge is in the soul but said of grammatical knowledge (1b1–3). The interpretation of this example by a given commentator will, of course, reflect that commentator's conception of primary attributes, and thus there exists considerable disagreement. At first blush, the example suggests that what a secondary attribute is in is not the same as what it is said of.[48] By making soul the subject in which knowledge inheres, Aristotle acknowledges the ontological dependence of the secondary attribute on the primary subject in which the primary attribute inheres without thereby subsuming the primary subject under the secondary attribute. The secondary attribute, like the secondary substance, is said of instances of itself. Whether the grammatical knowledge of which knowledge is said should be identified with a primary attribute (Socrates' grammatical knowledge) or with a secondary attribute (grammatical knowledge) is not clear in *Categories* 2. In *Categories* 5, however, Aristotle appears to argue that the secondary attribute is present in the primary substance in which the primary attribute inheres.

> Again, color is in body and therefore also in an individual body; for were it not in some individual body it would not be in body at all. Thus all the other things are either said of the primary substances as subjects or in them as subjects. (2b1–5; Ackrill trans.)

Aristotle, it seems, wants to make all secondary attributes present in primary as well as secondary subjects. It is another question whether he should have taken this position. If *Categories* 2 is interpreted in a way that yields a two-tiered ontology of particulars and universals, then the claim that the universal is in the particular if interpreted to mean that the universal could not exist if that particular did not exist is obviously false. Thus Ackrill argued that what Aristotle said was "compressed and careless" for he should have said that every instance of color is in an individual body (p. 83). There are reasons apart from Ackrill's interpretation of *Categories* 2 to be troubled by 2b1–3. Aristotle seems to construe the said of a subject condition in a way that divides simple beings into two groups, a base level consisting of substantial and nonsubstantial individuals and a second-tier ontological level consisting of predicates. If this is his position,

48 On certain accounts of the locution 'in a subject', this possibility is unintelligible. Fortunately, Frede (1987) has given a perspicuous interpretation of the locution that makes perfect sense of Aristotle's remarks.

then he needs to explain how and in what sense items on the second level are in individuals on the base level. There is a tension in Aristotle's thinking here that is evident in the treatment of attributes in *Categories* 2 and 4. In the case of primary attributes, Aristotle wants to make the present in a subject condition very strong in order to ensure the dependence of the primary attribute on its bearer.[49] This same condition applied to secondary attributes, however, threatens to constitute a fundamental ontological relation that holds between universals alone. The problem arises because while Aristotle assumes throughout the *Categories* that the conceptual structure of language mirrors the structure of reality, he is not yet completely clear about how to construe the relation between the ontological base of a language and its conceptual structure.

The fourfold classification of *onta* has important consequences for Aristotle's handling of meaning and reference. With the exception of proper names, the expressions of a natural language are general terms. The meanings of these terms are universals, yet the extralinguistic world seems to consist in concrete particulars. This recognition no doubt drives the distinction between primary substances and secondary ones in the *Categories*. Do general terms refer to primary substances and properties? Or do they refer to secondary substances and properties? If the former, then reference would be construed as reference to any member of a class defined by the essence of the substance or property in question. For instance, *anthropos* (ἄνθρωπος) would refer to any member (any primary substance ἄνθρωπος) of the class defined by the secondary substance ἄνθρωπος. The *pathema* would be a likeness of one or more human individuals. If the latter, then the term ἄνθρωπος would refer to the secondary substance ἄνθρωπος that is said of the individual. This is a simpler picture of reference than the former, and it is supported by Aristotle's willingness in the *De Interpretatione* to speak of universal *pragmata* as well as particular ones and to use species as examples of universals (17a38–39).

The drawbacks to the second approach are several, however. First, there is the question of the ontological status of the universal referents. One solution, the one adopted by Plato, would be to posit extralinguistic, ontologically independent universals to serve as the ultimate referents of general terms and the paradigms for the intentional states of language users.[50] Another solution would be to make universals ontologically dependent upon particulars. *Categories* 2 hints at this solution, and it is explicitly adopted in *Categories* 5. Equipped with the ontology of the *Categories*, Aristotle is able to make sense of general terms that apply to individual substances and individual attributes existing in the world.

49 Frede (1987) and Wedin (1993) offer formulations of this condition that are consistent with taking 2b1–5 to assert just what it says; i.e., color is in an individual body.

50 See Plato, *Crat.* 438d–439d; Aristotle, *Metaphysics* 987b4–11.

Universal terms naming kinds of individuals, properties, and relations are grounded in the world of concrete individuals. At the most basic ontological level, there are individual substances and individual properties; at the next ontological level, there are the things said of these individuals. Corresponding to the ontological levels are linguistic levels; indexicals (this particular man, ὁ τὶς ἄνθρωπος) and proper names refer to objects at the most basic level; general terms refer to objects at the next level, ἄνθρωπος as said of individuals. Second, the meaning of the word ἄνθρωπος is the intentional content of the *pathema* that is a likeness of individual humans. This raises a puzzle about the relation between the individual human of which the secondary substance is predicated and of which the meaning is a likeness and the secondary substance ἄνθρωπος that serves as a universal referent of the term – a problem that must await the *Metaphysics* (and Part II of this volume) for a fully satisfactory resolution. For the moment, on the basis of the *Categories* and *De Interpretatione*, it seems correct to say that reference to secondary substances and attributes is parasitic on reference to primary substances and their attributes (cf. 2a35–2b5).

Having made the case for a fourfold ontology in the second chapter, Aristotle returns to the issue of predicates in *Categories* 3 and 4.

> Of expressions said without any combination, each signifies either substance [οὐσίαν] or quantity or qualification or a relative or where or when or being-in-a-position or having or doing or being affected. (1b25–27; trans. follows Ackrill)

The classification of predicates in *Categories* 4 results in a correlation of terms with categories of existents, because uncombined terms are differentiated according to the kinds of entities they signify. A similar list is found in *Topics* I 9. In *Topics* I 5, Aristotle lists four types of predicables – namely, definition, genus, property, and accident – and in the ninth chapter he asserts that the predicates falling under these four types belong to ten categories.[51] The categories named are the ones at *Categories* 4, 1b25–27 with only one difference: *ti esti* replaces *ousia* on the list (103b24).[52] As discussed in *Categories* 5–9, the ten categories classify predicates according to the kinds of entities they indicate. This is especially clear in the analysis of the category of substance in the fifth chapter. There Aristotle begins with primary substance as defined in *Categories* 2, as that which is neither said of a subject nor in a subject (2a11–14). He goes on to explain that in the case of secondary substance both the name

51 Frede (1981) argues that at *Topics* I 9, 103b25 Aristotelian categories are kinds of predications, whereas in the *Categories* they are ultimate genera of what there is. My own view is that in both the *Categories* and *Topics* I 9, the kinds of categories simultaneously classify predicates and the entities signified by the predicates.

52 *Topics* 103b27, Aristotle remarks that '*to ti esti*' may indicate *ousia* or one of the other categories, thus implicitly acknowledging that *ousia* is a more precise name for the substance category than *ti esti*.

and the definition (*logos*) are predicated of the subject (2a19–26). That Aristotle distinguishes between the name of a secondary substance and the secondary substance indicates that not even secondary substance that is said of a subject should simply be identified with the general term naming the substance or the term's meaning.

Any meaningful, simple utterance signifies (σημαίνει) an item falling under one or the other of the ten categories according to *Categories* 4, but according to the *De Interpretatione* 1 any utterance signifies (σημαίνει) an internal state, a mental *pathema,* that resembles an external state (*pragma*). This raises the question of the relation between the category, the *pathema,* and the *pragma.* Presumably, the content of the *pathema,* the *logos* (meaning) of the term, secures the reference of the term to an entity (*on*) that falls under one or another of the categories. For instance, 'in the Lyceum' will denote a place, as will 'in the Agora', which place is determined by their respective *logoi.* As Aristotle's examples make clear, what counts as a simple expression in this context is not determined solely by reference to surface grammar. 'In ⟨place name⟩' is treated as a linguistic unit, because 'in' is incomplete; without an object, 'in' does not refer to an extralinguistic entity.[53] All simple expressions function in this way. Aristotle uses infinitives for the seventh, ninth, and tenth categories, namely, to be in a position, to have, and to act or be affected. He also gives third person singular forms of verbs as examples of the categories of position ('lies') and having ('has armor on'). Verbs function much like other parts of speech for Aristotle; the true ascription of a verb depends on features of the world like any other ascription. For this reason, presumably, Aristotle uses verb forms to illustrate the four categories named by infinitives (verbal nouns). *Categories* 4 ends with the remark that "none of the things said without combination is either true or false, for instance, man, pale, runs or conquers."

At this point, a certain picture has emerged of the basic existents and, by implication, of the extralinguistic referents of terms, the *pragmata* of the *De Interpretatione* definition. If words stand for internal states that represent states of affairs (*pragmata*) by resemblance, then irrespective of grammatical form, a particular significant expression will stand in a referring relation to a particular *pragma.* The word 'lies' may be used with the same meaning (*logos*) on any number of different occasions (cf. 3b15–17). The *logos* of 'lies' determines the range of conditions falling under the denotation of the word. A new wrinkle, however, is introduced in *De Interpretatione* 3, when Aristotle differentiates between subject terms and verbs. Verbs are said to be names that signify something (*ti*) but do not signify *pragmata* (16b23).

53 *Poetics* 20 lists, besides the parts of words, several types of words as nonsignificant sounds (φωνὴ ἄσημος); these include particles, conjunctions, and articles (1456b37–1457a10).

For not even are 'to be' and 'not to be' and the participle 'being' a sign of any fact [πράγματος], unless something is added; for they do not themselves indicate anything, but imply a copulation, of which we cannot form a conception apart from the things coupled. (16b22–25; trans. follows Edghill)[54]

Every simple sentence then corresponds to a putative, extralinguistic *pragma*.[55] The verb by itself is incomplete; combined with a subject, it expresses a complete thought corresponding to an extralinguistic *pragma*. The primary vehicle for meaning would seem to be the sentence not the simple term. The cognitive content of several simple terms making up a complete thought refers to a *pragma*, and thus Aristotle identifies *pragmata* with extralinguistic states of affairs expressible in affirmative and negative sentences.

The *De Interpretatione* provides further evidence that the *pragma* takes precedence over the grammatical structure of an utterance in determinations of its simplicity or complexity.

To affirm or deny one thing of many, or many of one, unless one thing is made up of many things, is not one affirmation or negation. I do not call them one if there is one name if there is not some one thing made up of them. For instance, man is perhaps an animal and two-footed and tame, and still these do make up some one thing; whereas white and man and walking do not make up one thing. (20b12–19)

The primacy of the *pragma* is well attested to in the *Categories* and the *De Interpretatione*. In several contexts, Aristotle points out that whether the *pragma* obtains or not determines the truth of the sentence and not conversely (4a36-b10, 7b25, 14b19–20, 19a23).

The challenge facing Aristotle is to give an account of meaning that accommodates both the *Categories*' classification of terms with respect to the entities they signify and his analysis of sentence structure and truth in the *De Interpretatione*. The former leads us to expect terms to be the primary vehicles of meaning and reference, and this would support construing '*pragmata*' in the definition of meaning as the sorts of entities described in the *Categories*. The latter analysis would incline us to believe that sentences are the primary vehicles of meaning and that the *pragma* of the definition is a state of affairs expressed by a sentence. It would not be impossible to bridge the distance between these two pictures. How distant the two conceptions of *pragmata* are from each other will in large measure be a function of how states of affairs are construed. If the state of affairs expressed by a sentence is construed as an abstract object, a proposition, it will be much harder to bring this conception in line with the *Categories*' account of basic *onta* than if the state of affairs in question is simply a concatenation of subject and attribute(s) existing in the world.

54 I adopt the manuscript variant οὐδέ in place of οὐ at 16b22.

55 Every true sentence corresponds to an actual *pragma* (14b18–22; 19a33; cf. 4a34–b10).

On the latter interpretation of the *pragma* expressed by a sentence, Aristotle could unproblematically hold that the *onta* of the *Categories* are the components of extralinguistic states of affairs just as simple terms are components of sentences. A fully satisfactory resolution of this tension is not possible within the framework provided by the *Categories* and *De Interpretatione,* where Aristotle sometimes uses *pragma* for the referent of a simple term and yet elsewhere restricts the use of *pragma* to the state of affairs corresponding to a complete thought or assertion.[56]

4 Referring Expressions

In *Categories* 1–9, Aristotle seems to treat all predicates as referring expressions. All simple predicates signify items falling under one or another of the ten categories. Consider, for instance, two simple statements about Socrates: (1) 'Socrates is a man' and (2) 'Socrates is pale'. The first differs from the second, Aristotle says, in that the *logos* of 'man' applies to Socrates but not the *logos* of 'pale' (2a19–34). The *logos* of a term is its linguistic definition; it is the account that spells out the meaning of the term.[57] 'Man' refers to any *x* satisfying the definition of 'man' and hence to Socrates. 'Pale' may be truly predicated of Socrates but, on Aristotle's account, 'pale' does not refer to Socrates, because Socrates does not satisfy the definition of 'pale'. Notwithstanding, there is something in Socrates that warrants the ascription of pale, and this something functions as the extralinguistic referent of 'pale'. The challenge then is to explain how 'pale' in (2) and by extension all other predicates in the nonsubstance categories connect with the world. Several answers are possible: (a) 'pale' in (2) refers to a primary quality that Socrates happens to possess whereas 'man' in (1) refers to a primary substance that Socrates happens to be; (a′) 'pale' in (2) ascribes a property (pallor) to Socrates; (b) 'pale' in (2) refers to a pale thing ("a kooky object") and Socrates happens to be a pale thing, but this particular pale thing is not identical to Socrates.[58] While (a′) seems to be closer to the modern analysis of attributive and predicate adjectives, (a′) ignores Aristotle's distinction between primary and secondary attributes and cannot readily accommo-

56 The tension here is not simply a difference between the *Categories* and the *De Interpretatione.* In the latter work, there are several passages (17a38–b3, 21b28) where '*pragma*' is used for the referent of a term.

57 Elsewhere, Aristotle distinguishes between definitions expressing essence (*horismoi*) and other sorts of *logoi.* A linguistic definition provides a sufficient condition for the application of the term; a definition of essence, necessary and sufficient conditions. See Chapters 3 and 5.

58 Interpretation (b) as developed here extends a thesis about Aristotelian ontology that has found considerable support in recent literature on Aristotle's treatment of various topics, including contingent identity and relatives. Aristotle posits, several commentators believe, substance-like objects, often called kooky objects, to serve as the referents of contingent definite descriptions of one sort or another.

date his use of substantivized adjectives. For these reasons, I shall discuss only (a) and (b) in detail.

The first answer (a) is consistent with taking 'man' and 'pale' to name items in different categories, namely, a substance and a quality. It does, however, seem at odds with the doctrine that items falling under categories other than that of substance are ontologically dependent upon substance. Suppose the categories of substance and quality were established by analyzing the sentence 'Socrates is pale'. On the first interpretation (a), the analysis produces one term, 'Socrates', that refers to a primary substance and another, 'pale', that refers to a primary quality; the categories of substance and quality seem to be coordinate. Each is needed to justify the sentence's claim to combine two significant linguistic units into a significant assertion. Aristotle apparently reasons as follows about the three terms figuring in the two simple sentences under discussion: 'Socrates' names an individual substance, the predicate '*anthropos*' expresses just what Socrates is, and the predicate 'pale' names one of Socrates' attributes, namely, Socrates' paleness. The last cannot exist without Socrates, whereas Socrates can exist without being pale but not without being a human. By simultaneously providing all nonsubstance predicates with referents that are in subjects and by denying these features ontological independence, Aristotle forestalls the Platonist outcome that the subsequent analysis of predicates would otherwise yield, namely, placing the ontological correlates of all predicates on an equal footing. This is the object of the fourfold classification scheme in *Categories* 2. At the level of basic ontology, there are *onta* that are neither present in nor said of anything else and hence are fully independent (viz., primary substances) and *onta* that are present in but not said of anything else (viz., primary attributes); these are the subjects of which other terms are predicated and to which they refer. Primary substances and primary attributes are individuals existing in the world as subjects or things present in subjects; secondary substances and secondary attributes are kinds and properties under which the primary substances and attributes fall. General terms name secondary substances and secondary attributes, and their definitions determine the reference class of objects to which the terms correctly apply.

A critic of this line of interpretation would undoubtedly point out that it seems to work best for qualities and, perhaps, is most vulnerable to objection when applied to relatives. The discussion of relatives in *Categories* 7 has often puzzled commentators. Relative terms, not relations, are the topic of this chapter. Relatives, according to Aristotle, typically have correlates; for instance, the double is the double of the half, the slave is the slave of the master. Aristotle worries about cases where this does not appear to hold – for instance, 'wing' of bird – and argues that 'bird' is not the proper correlate but 'that which has wings' (6b37–7a5). The proper description is one that will complete the schema '____ *R* wing' in a way that any creature having wings will fall under the description.[59] Again Aristotle's position makes sense on a picture of language where predicate terms including relatives denote features of objects in the world. Here, too, the issue of ontological dependence raises its troublesome head. Since the winged creatures are substances, why say, as Aristotle does, that primary substances are never relatives (8a15–18) and that relatives are ontologically posterior to substance? It is tempting to attribute the following position to him: with respect to surface grammar 'that which has wings' appears to be a substance sortal, but in fact it names an attribute (being winged) that the substance possesses in virtue of a relation it stands in to something else (a wing). As a general account of relatives, this had better not be correct, however, for if it is, Aristotle is in trouble. The relevant relation is not between the property of being a master and the property of being a slave, for instance; it is between two human beings, one of whom is the master of the other who is his slave. Again, the nature of the *pragma* that makes the attribution of a relational term true provides the answer. 'Socrates is a father' is true just in case 'Socrates' denotes a person who stands in a particular relation to another person. As Aristotle puts it,

> What is relative then is that which is just what it is said of another or in some other way in relation to something else. (6b7–8; cf. 8a38–b3)

With respect to 'father', the *pragma* '⟨name of male parent⟩ *R* child' is irreducible; but with respect to a true substance sortal, the *pragma* consists simply in an individual falling under the sortal. 'Socrates is a man' is true just in case 'Socrates' denotes a human being. The referent of the relative term 'father' is a complex state of affairs consisting of a primary substance standing in a particular relation to another primary substance and, for this reason, the relative cannot simply be identified with either the primary substance or the relation. Not only substances but also items falling under the other categories stand in various relations. Knowledge is another example given by Aristotle of a relative (6b2–6). The first stage of the analysis is the same; knowledge denotes the complex state, 'mental disposition *R* something knowable'; however, a mental disposition is open to further analysis, 'a certain state *R* bearer of the disposition'.

Aristotle's conception of relatives is such that it seems to commit him to proposition-like states of affairs that are irreducible and such objects would appear inconsistent with the anti-Platonism of the *Categories*. The schema, __ *R* __, is irreducible as a description of a relative, and it determines the collection of objects to which the relative term applies. Its ontological correlate, however, is a complex object consisting in the case of

59 '*R*' stands for relation in this schema and those that follow.

'father' in a primary substance and a primary relational attribute, standing in the relation of being a male parent to another individual. This attribute is not an abstract object; it is a feature of Socrates. Aristotle's analysis of a relative term, 'father', which refers to a concrete particular, assimilates the item that the term signifies, a complex object consisting of a primary substance and a relational attribute, to an attribute. In a similar vein, Aristotle suggests that the double listing of states and conditions under quality and under relatives is not problematic, because the individual (i.e., primary) quality is not a relative but the general (i.e., secondary) state or condition is said in relation to something else (11a20–37). This remark as well as Aristotle's frequent use of the locution 'relatives are spoken of . . .' indicate that Aristotle's primary focus is on secondary relatives that are said of other things. In the case of relatives, moreover, what is present in but not said of the object is, from another perspective, not primary, because the satisfaction of the schema that allows one to use a relative term correctly of an individual substance or characteristic is always dependent upon the existence of other more basic objects.

Several recent commentators have concluded that Aristotle is committed to shadow objects, sometimes called kooky objects, such as the pale ⟨one⟩, that belong to a populous ontology, which includes nonsubstantial individuals as well as concrete particulars. Kooky objects resemble substances in that they are proper subjects in which properties inhere; they are unlike substances in that they coincide with substances. The kooky object, the pale one, which is the proper subject of Socrates' pallor and coincides with Socrates, serves as the referent for the definite description 'the pale ⟨one⟩' when used of Socrates. Interpretation (b) extends this line of reasoning to all items that are present in a subject but not said of a subject. Kooky objects have been defended on the grounds that they are required to explain Aristotle's treatment of accidental unities in the *Topics, De Sophisticis Elenchis* and the *Metaphysics* and more recently on the grounds that kooky objects are needed to explain Aristotle's handling of the category of relatives.[60] It would be premature to evaluate the evidence cited from the *Metaphysics* and other later works for this position. Insofar as the *Categories* is concerned, however, if the discussion of the types of predicates is read in light of the distinctions Aristotle draws in *Categories* 2, then one need not have recourse to kooky objects to find referents for terms naming relatives, qualities, or any other category. *Categories* 2 yields two types of basic entities, primary substances, the ultimate subjects, and the things that are present in them but not said

60 Matthews (1982) argues for kooky objects primarily on the basis of *S.E.* 179. White (1971, pp. 177–97) argues that in *Met.* V 6 Aristotle fails to distinguish between one and many place uses of 'one' and consequently rejects Leibniz's Law for accidental unities. See also Spellman (1995, chap. 2).

of them (the basic attributes): proper names or demonstratives ('this' 'that') may be used to pick out these items; however, more general terms, i.e. terms having broader extensions, also name these entities. The context of use determines their referents. For instance, when the sentence, 'This man is pale' is asserted about Socrates, 'this man' refers to Socrates, a primary substance, and 'pale' refers to his pallor, a primary quality. The case of relatives is somewhat more complicated. Since Socrates is rational and bipedal, it is tempting to think that these characteristics also belong to the relative denoted by 'father' in the sentence 'Socrates is a father'. Not so, says Aristotle; the relative is arrived at by stripping away all the characteristics that are accidental to the relation, leaving only a subject standing in a particular relation.

> When everything is stripped away that is accidental to a master, for instance, being two footed, being receptive to knowledge, being a man, and the only thing left is being a master, a slave will always be said in relation to that. (7a35–39)

The relative appears to be a bare particular having the relational property in question. If so, then the relative is a kooky object on at least one account of this notion. However, by appealing to the difference between the relative that is present in and not said of a subject and the one that is both, Aristotle could distinguish between the complex characteristic present in Meno, namely, Meno *R* his slaveboy, and the relative 'master', which is present in any particular having the relational property of being a slave owner. The relative is best construed as '_____ having the relational property *R**', not because its referent is a kooky quasi substance different from the individual having the property *R**, but because this paraphrase secures the generality of a predicate naming a relative, which is a complex, albeit genuine, feature of the individual.

Aristotle is still not completely off the hook, however, because the distinction between primary and secondary attributes and its extension to cover relatives generates primary attributes that seem to coincide with individual substances. In order to include relatives, the notion of attribute has been stretched by Aristotle to include a primary substance standing in various relations to other primary substances. Although his analysis of relatives falls short of generating peculiar subjects, it does result in a conception of attributes that is at once richer and more complex than most. The advantages of assimilating relatives to attributes are several – at least from Aristotle's perspective. Doing so maintains the distinction between basic subjects and their attributes, and it grounds all true predicates in an ontology of realities, real subjects and their real attributes.[61] There are, moreover, distinct types of attributes, corresponding to each of the

61 Cf. Moravcsik's (1967, pp. 125–45) statement that "the categories jointly must contain all the universals and particulars that Aristotle would acknowledge as existing."

categories except substance. Aristotle, for the most part, attempts to show that at least at the level of inherence, every attribute falls under one and only one category. Considering the suggestion that many qualities are actually relatives, Aristotle argues that

> in nearly all such cases the genera are said in relation to something, but none of the particulars is; for knowledge as a genus is called just what it is of something else, for knowledge is of something else, but none of the particulars is called just what it is of something else, for instance, grammatical knowledge is not called grammar of something else, nor musical knowledge called musical knowledge of something else. . . . Therefore the particulars are not relatives. But we are said to be such and such through the particulars, for we have these. We are called knowers because we have one of the particular kinds of knowledge. (11a23–34)

Even though Aristotle stops short of asserting that this is always the case, his determination to defend the general thesis that a specific characteristic or entity falls under only one category provides further evidence that the categories classify referring expressions. Their referents are primary substances and primary attributes.

In sum, interpretation (a) does not posit any entities other than those named by Aristotle, namely, primary substances and attributes and the terms that refer to them and secondary substances and attributes and their definitions, and interpretation (a) has proved to be, in spite of initial appearances, consistent with Aristotle's treatment of the troublesome category of relatives. Thus interpretation (a) seems to carry the day. At the basic ontological level, there are only ordinary, concrete particulars (primary substances) and primary attributes; at the next level, there are natural kinds (secondary substances) and general attributes. Since a speaker must use a proper name, a demonstrative, or a definite description to refer uniquely to an ontologically basic particular or attribute, common predicates (detached from a particular context) refer to anything satisfying the definition of the term (*logos kata tounoma*). The definition specifies the nature of the secondary substance or attribute. This conception of predicates is consistent with, and presumably motivated by, the theory of meaning stated in *De Interpretatione* 1, which posits a correspondence between meanings and things in the world. The primary referents of universal terms (primary substances and primary attributes) engender concepts that are the meanings of the terms. Because primary substances and attributes instantiate secondary substances and attributes, the meaning of a universal term specifies the nature of the secondary substance or attribute.

Further evidence that Aristotle has the same two-tiered view of predicates belonging to the other categories and their ontological correlates as he has of substance sortals and their ontological correlates is found in *Topics* I 9.

For each of such predicates, if it is said of itself or the genus is said of it, indicates an essence [*ti esti*]. When it is asserted of something else, it does not signify essence, but a quantity or quality or one of the other predicates. (103b36–39)

In *Topics* I 9 and throughout the *Categories,* Aristotle is concerned to establish that the basic types of linguistic expression correspond to the basic categories of reality. Complete thoughts expressed in sentences are the primary vehicles of meaning, but these consist of smaller units of meaning, significant words and phrases. These units are significant just because the extralinguistic world shares a similar structure. Aristotelian categories are categories both of beings and of linguistic items. In addition, the distinction between substance and property in the world is reflected in the distinction between subject and predicate in a sentence. In both instances, the existence of a single unified entity, a concrete particular or a complete thought or assertion, is consistent with the analysis into the more basic ontological categories of substance and property (quality, quantity, and so forth) or the more basic linguistic categories of subject and predicate, because the relation between substance and property or subject and predicate is such that a single item results from their combination. By distinguishing between types of components, Aristotle is able to offer an explication and maintain the primacy of the individual and the complete thought corresponding to a *pragma.*[62]

5 Sentences

Aristotle analyzes meaning in terms of the relation between a word (a linguistic sign), a language user, and the world; the relation is such that it is possible for the language user to combine the word with other words to make an assertion and such that it is possible for the word to be a constituent of a true assertion. Consequently, in the *De Interpretatione* the description of language is immediately followed by a classification of the components of simple sentences and that by a classification of types of assertoric sentences.

In *De Interpretatione* 1–3, the study of uncombined terms is redefined as the study of names and verbs.

A name [ὄνομα] is then a sound significant by convention, which has no reference to time, and of which no part is significant [σημαντικόν] apart from the rest. . . . The limitation 'by convention' [κατὰ συνθήκην] was introduced because nothing is by nature a name but only when it becomes a symbol; since inarticulate sounds, such as those which animals make, indicate something, yet none of these is a name. (16a19–29)

62 The tension between primary individuals, either ontological or linguistic, and analysis and hence intelligibility is developed not only in the *Cratylus* by Plato but also in the *Parmenides* and perhaps most brilliantly in the last section of the *Theaetetus* (201D–210A).

Here, being significant by nature is contrasted with being significant by convention; Aristotle wants to make it absolutely clear that language is a cultural artifact. A particular sound that is a name has significance for a speaker/hearer because she is a member of a linguistic community. Being a symbol is a necessary condition for being significant by convention. Symbol (σύμβολον) is the term Aristotle uses at 16a3 to explain the relation between the spoken word and the associated mental state. The internal state is an internalized meaning of a word used by a community of speakers. While stating a general definition of 'name', Aristotle uses the occasion to make the relation between the internal correlate of a word and the common meaning of the word for speakers of a public language clear.

In fleshing out the claim that no part of a name is significant, Aristotle uses a proper name, Kallippos (Noble-steed) as an illustration (16a21; cf. *Poetics* 1457a13). This is but one instance of many in which Aristotle seems to draw no distinction between proper names and common nouns. Admittedly, this is a weakness of his semantics; notwithstanding, the failure to draw this distinction is consistent with the theory of meaning stated at 16a3–8, because a proper name denotes its bearer by an internal state just as a common name does. The ability of two language users to communicate with each other using a proper name depends upon their each having a notion correlated with the sound of the proper name that fixes the referent of the name as the same individual.

Next, Aristotle defines the other basic component of a sentence:

> A verb [ῥῆμα] is that which, in addition, signifies time. No part of it has an independent meaning, and it is a sign [σημεῖον] of something said of something else. (16b6–7)

Names and verbs are the basic units of meaning. Unlike Hermogenes' account in the *Cratylus*, Aristotle's theory of meaning will not be handily disposed of by including the elements (syllables and letters) of significant sentential parts (names and verbs) under the range of application of the theory. Names and verbs combine to form significant expressions made of parts (16b26–27; *Poetics* 1457a23–27). The parts, because significant in themselves, determine the significance of the sentence; the meanings of the parts, however, are not independent of the context of usage. The sentence and the linguistic context in which the sentence is embedded in effect select the appropriate meanings for the significant parts of the sentence. Whether the expression has a truth value and what its truth conditions are are also relevant to the determination of the meanings of its parts. Aristotle points out that every sentence is significant; that not every sentence makes an assertion; and that only those sentences that do have truth values (17a1–4). Simple sentences are formed by combining a single subject and a single predicate. Simple sentences may be combined by conjunction or disjunction to form complex sentences. Not surprisingly, the simple and complex sentences that interest Aristotle in the *De Interpretatione* are those that make assertions.

There are two types of simple assertions, namely, affirmations and negations. An affirmation asserts that a particular predicate holds of the subject; and a negation, that a particular predicate does not hold of the subject. Pairs of affirmations and correlative negations are classified as either contradictories or contraries. Not every statement consisting of a single term for the subject and a single term for the predicate is a simple assertion or negation. The assertion is simple just in case each term stands for a single thing in fact (*De Int.* 18a13–26, 20b12–22).

If one name is given to two things which do not make up one thing, there is not a single affirmation. For example, were one to give the name 'cloak' to horse and man; 'a cloak is white' would not be a single affirmation. For to say this is no different from saying 'a horse and a man is white' and this is no different from saying 'a horse is white and a man is white'. (18a18–23)

As mentioned above, the reference of a term determines its meaning, according to Aristotle. 'Cloak' in this example has two distinct meanings, because it includes under its extension two distinctly different species, and thus a superficially single, affirmative sentence turns out upon analysis to be a compound sentence. The character of a sentence is a function of how its components stand in relation to the objects they represent. In a simple affirmation, for instance, the object named by the subject term is understood to have the property named by the predicate term; in a simple negation, the subject is understood to lack the property named by the predicate term.

6 Ontological Presuppositions

Despite differences in emphasis, the *Categories* and *De Interpretatione* taken together present an analysis of meaning and syntax that underscores the correspondence between language and reality. The types of basic linguistic units correspond to basic ontological units. In the *Categories,* having introduced the distinction between being a subject (ὑποκειμένον) or being something said of or present in a subject, Aristotle goes on to identify subjects in the primary sense with substance (οὐσία) and to assert their ontological primacy.

So that all the other things are either said of the primary substances as subjects or in them as subjects. If the primary substances did not exist, then it would be impossible for any of the other things to exist. (2b4–6)

The ontological primacy of subjects in reality is reflected in language. In a logically impeccable sentence, the subject term denotes a real subject. Predicate terms refer to the characteristics of real subjects. The importance Aristotle assigns to substances (property bearers) in relation to properties is reflected in his conception of the basic truth functional unit as an assertion in which a predicate ascribing a characteristic is said of a subject. Conversely, the fact that there are well-formed, true sentences where the subject term names an item falling under a nonsubstance category (e.g., 'blue is a color') probably influenced Aristotle's treatment of the categories other than substances. They, too, are categories of *onta* (things that are) and are analyzed in terms of the same distinction between primary and secondary ontological levels.

Although the notion of what counts as a primary substance changes, when the distinction between matter and form becomes fundamental to Aristotle's ontology, the notion of natural subjects and predicates remains a constant feature, as we shall discover.[63] By the time he writes the central books of the *Metaphysics,* the notion of what counts as a primary substance has been transformed. From the *Physics* on, Aristotle leans heavily upon the distinction between matter and form in his analyses of change and substance. The relation of form to matter is described as one of predication, as is the relation of property to property bearer.

> By matter I mean that which in itself is neither a particular thing nor a quantity nor assigned to any other of the categories by which being is defined. For there is something of which each of these is predicated [κατηγορεῖται] whose being is different from that of each of the predicates (for the others are predicated of substance, while substance is predicated of matter). (*Met.* 1029a20–24)

Here, too, as in *Categories* 2, there are four types of basic objects, consisting of two types of subject and two types of predicates. These are matter as ultimate subject and substance as proper subject, and substance as predicate and all other predicates. Matter now seems to fulfill the requirements of a subject that is neither present in nor said of a something else, but it lacks specificity and hence is not a primary subject (1029a7–26). Form as the source of the distinctive features of a compound of matter and form is said of a subject (matter) but is not present in a subject. Form and matter together constitute concrete substances, the primary substance of the *Categories.* Items falling under the nonsubstance categories retain the same relation to substances that they had in the *Categories.*

> So too there are many senses in which a thing is said to be, but all refer to one starting-point; some things are said to be because they are substances, others because they are affections of substance, others because they are a means towards substance, or destructions or privations or qualities of substance, or productive or generative of substance, or of things which are said in relation to substance, or

63 In what follows I touch briefly on topics to be explored in greater detail in Chapters 5 and 6.

negations of one of these things or of substance itself. (1003b6–10; cf. 1028a13–15)

In *Categories* 4, Aristotle decides that uncombined terms signify either substance, quantity, quality, relation, place, time, position, state, action, or affection (1b25–2a3). Referring to the *Categories* in *Metaphysics* VII 1, Aristotle finds that being in one sense is "what a thing is or a this; and in another sense it means a quality or quantity or one of the other things that are predicated as these are" (1028a11–13). The division between subjects and predicates is secured at the level of ontology and reflected in language. Simple expressions map unto the world according to the kinds of things that exist there. All simple predicates have a niche under one or another category. In the *De Interpretatione* where assertoric sentences, because they are the bearers of truth, occupy center stage, distinctions are drawn and claims made that presuppose the correspondence between terms and things that are (*onta*). To explain when two predicates that are singly true of a subject can be combined into a single predicate that is true of that subject (21a15–17), Aristotle appeals to the difference between essential and accidental predicates, thus invoking a distinction that is made on extralinguistic grounds. Notwithstanding, in the *De Interpretatione* ontological questions are assigned to another area of inquiry.[64]

Moreover, the conceptual map embedded in language will be an aid in recognizing relations obtaining among ontological categories. On the linguistic map, 'substance', 'living thing', 'animal', and 'horse' form a nested series of concepts in which each successor term is a universal with a narrower scope that falls under all the preceding terms. The ontological order in the *Categories* where the most basic object would be the concrete (individual) horse, nevertheless manifests the same structure. Reflection on the linguistic scheme will produce the recognition that if 'dog' falls under the same series of wider universals as 'horse', then 'dog' and 'horse' are two species of the same genus. Indeed with an important proviso, the relation between language and the world warrants an even stronger inference.[65] The mental state that makes a linguistic sign significant is individuated by its content; the intentional object is a likeness of an extralinguistic object according to *De Interpretatione* 16a3–8. Because of the relational character of likeness, the linguistic sign is linked through its meaning to the external world. This is true even in the case of general terms that do not apply to any actual existents. The mythical kind-term 'goatstag' (τραγέλαφος) is significant (16a16–17); the conception of such a creature is derived from the meanings of the terms com-

64 See, e.g., 17a13–15: why two-footed land animal is one thing and not many belongs to a different inquiry.

65 The proviso insists upon the extramental origin of concepts.

bined in its name, goat (τράγος) and stag (ἔλαφος). These terms satisfy the likeness constraint and so in a derivative sense does τραγέλαφος. Moreover, this term will also satisfy the truth constraint, because the term can be a component of a true assertion, for instance, 'A goatstag is a mythical creature'. Let us put aside such examples and turn to the basic categories of language and thought. The distinction between subject and predicate is a fundamental feature of many natural languages. Suppose that 'S' is the linguistic category 'subject' and that 'S' is a fundamental linguistic category, then to show that S (the ontological correlate of 'S') is a basic ontological category, given the assumption that the basic categories of thought correspond to those of reality, it is sufficient to establish that humans carve the world up into S's and not-S's. To find out whether we do or not, Aristotle turns to the conceptual scheme embedded in language in the *Categories,* the *Metaphysics,* and elsewhere.

It is one thing to move freely between the categories of language and those of reality, and it is another to adduce nonlinguistic evidence in support of dividing the world up in this manner. In the *Categories* and *De Interpretatione,* Aristotle does the first but not the second. Consequently, it might seem better to construe his statements about *onta* and *pragmata* as claims about the ontological presuppositions of a natural language, and indeed there is nothing that prevents us from reading these texts in this way. The advantages of this approach are several and obvious – claims about language are empirical and Aristotle's analysis of language seems to warrant many of his conclusions narrowly construed. The drawback is that the circumspect metaphysics that could make use of such findings is not Aristotle's. In the *Metaphysics,* he clearly wants to make claims about what is *simpliciter,* not about what is presupposed by a particular language, and he invokes the analysis of being found in the *Categories* in support of the ontology he offers.[66] Similarly, the account of the acquisition of first principles in *Posterior Analytics* II 19 tacitly depends upon the objectivity of the relation between internal states (the *pathemata*) and natural kinds (the *pragmata*).[67] Nevertheless, Aristotle may have arrived at this ontology largely as the result of reflecting on the nature of language and then, with his usual optimism about human epistemic capabilities, he may have concluded that the ontological presuppositions of a natural language adequate to the task of describing the world, as we experience it, could be made the basis for metaphysical generalizations that go beyond the justification provided by linguistic analysis.

66 *Metaphysics* VII 1 introduces the discussion of substance with a list of the many senses in which a thing may be said to be that recalls *Categories* 4.

67 Aristotle is not a nominalist; natural kinds are not primarily mental constructs but features of the world and hence *pragmata.* Cf. *De Int.* 17a38: "Some things [τῶν πραγμάτων] are universal, others individual."

Need we conclude that Aristotle's tendency to generalize the results of his inquiry into language to epistemological and metaphysical contexts shows that he fails to recognize that investigating the foundations of language and investigating the foundations of knowledge and ontology are distinct enterprises? To do so seems unfair. Aristotle differentiates between the topics covered in the *Categories* and the *De Interpretatione* and those covered in the *Metaphysics*. He regularly distinguishes between words and sentences and extralinguistic states of affairs and, more generally, between semantic questions and epistemological and ontological ones. Moreover, he makes these distinctions without any of the established conventions for formal languages and other markers that have made the perspicuous treatment of such topics much easier for later generations of philosophers. Insofar as Aristotle's handling of ontological questions is problematic, the source of his difficulty seems to be his unflagging common-sensical optimism about what humans are capable of knowing.

Aristotle envisages a language and a logic where subjects, simple objects having referents in the extralinguistic world, combine with predicates attributing one sort of characteristic or another to them to form sentences having truth values and expressing complete thoughts.[68] Not all words said in combination make assertions, but those sentences that do either correctly state what is the case or fail to do so and hence are either true or false (cf. 19a33–4). A distinction between composite and incomposite objects of thought is drawn in *Metaphysics* IX 10 and *De Anima* III 6. Incomposite objects seem to be primitive subjects; composite objects are combinations of ideas described in nearly the same terms as sentences made up of subjects and verbs. The picture of language and thought encapsulated in the sketch at *De Interpretatione* 16a3–8 is developed from a number of different perspectives in later as well as earlier works. The theory of the syllogism found in the *Prior Analytics* takes terms, not propositions, as the basic unit through which inferences are drawn. The analysis of the kinds of existents in the *Categories* and elsewhere makes substances and their properties the basic ontological units rather than states of affairs or events. The realist epistemology of the *Posterior Analytics* requires basic objects that are immediately apprehended and not mediated through mental manipulations. Aristotle's multifaceted approach forces the interpreter to adopt a similarly multifaceted strategy for explicating his views.

68 Cf. *De Int.* 17a22–24: "A simple statement [ἀπόφανσις] is a spoken sentence, with meaning [φωνὴ σημαντική], about whether something holds of a subject or not, [in the present, past, or future] according to the divisions of time."

7 Preview

The epistemic, ontological, and psychological foundations of Aristotle's philosophy of language will be explored in the chapters that follow. If all the pieces fall into place, as Aristotle believes they do, then among other things, he has met the challenge to the philosophy of language that the *Cratylus* presents. In the *Cratylus,* as we have seen, Plato scrutinizes two accounts of meaning – one a form of naturalism, the other, of conventionalism. According to the first, words are natural signs of objects; according to the second, they are conventional signs. Naturalism is shown to be required if one is to give an adequate account of truth; conventionalism, however, is shown to provide a more satisfactory account of the way in which the words of a natural language acquire, maintain, and change their meanings.[69]

In the *De Interpretatione,* Aristotle chooses to negotiate a compromise between the two rejected alternatives. The relation between written and spoken words is conventional, as is the relation between spoken words and the mental states that are the vehicles of meaning; different languages correlate different sounds with the same intentional content and the same sound with different contents. However, the relation between the mental state and the object it represents is natural – the same for all humans – and is secured by resemblance. Plato's objections to a naturalistic approach where meaning is a function of resemblance are avoided by blocking the argument from sounds to ontology. If Aristotle is right and two speakers, each using a different natural language, express the same mental state when they use different sounds for the watery stuff that comes down from the sky, and this is generally the case, then the ontological commitments of any two natural languages would either be the same or be consistent – should one (less-developed) language lack a category that the other possessed. Plato's objections to a thoroughgoing conventionalism turn on the claim that an adequate account of truth presupposes a single, coherent ontology, whereas stipulated meanings support numerous different and potentially incompatible ontologies. Aristotle's compromise, however, is not open to these objections.

The description of form found in the central books of the *Metaphysics* provides a further buttress for the ontological side of Aristotle's story. Form makes the thing of which it is the form what it is. A piece of marble, for instance, is a statue of Athena, just in case the form of Athena (in this instance, a distinctive shape) is realized in that bit of marble. A flesh-and-blood creature is a human being just in case the form of human being (in

69 Using nearly the same terms as Aristotle in *De Interpretatione* 1, Epicurus speaks to this difficulty and suggests that originally the sounds uttered by the members of different tribes stood in a natural relation to the *phantasmata* and only later were words adopted on the basis of convention (*D.L.* X 75).

this instance, a distinctive functional organization) is realized in that chunk of flesh and blood. In the case of the statue, the form existed first in the sculptor's conception and then in the marble; in the case of the human being, the form existed first in human beings and subsequently as the biologist's conception of human essence. In both cases, however, the form is such that it can be realized in a physical object and in human thought. If Aristotle succeeds in developing this position, then with respect to essences, the claim that the meaning of a term bears a natural, nonarbitrary relation to the objects the term refers to will be secured.

Aristotle's picture of language is spare and elegant; it is, in addition, designed to support a realist epistemology. If to know is to grasp what is the case, then if basic linguistic categories correspond to basic ontological categories, the apprehension of the latter will be expressible in a natural language.[70] When, in the *De Interpretatione,* Aristotle wants to call attention to what is asserted rather than to the terms used to make the assertion, he appeals to the psychic state symbolized by the words (24b2–6). Meanings are grounded in the world because the mental states, which are the vehicles for meanings, resemble extramental objects. With meanings firmly anchored in the world, language can serve as the means for expressing truths.

In *Posterior Analytics* II 19, Aristotle sketches a picture of the relation between the human mind and the world where the mind is able to grasp the basic categories of reality.[71] Looking at Callias, the perceiver sees a man, and this enables her to grasp the concept 'man'. Bringing this passage to bear on the *De Interpretatione*'s account of meaning yields the following picture: existing in the world, the mind apprehends its structures – the types of natural objects and the modes in which entities exist as basic subjects or their characteristics. The impact of the world on us through our senses and intellect produces the concepts that provide the foundations of knowledge and language, for empirically produced concepts not only are the basis of science, they also serve as the intentional content of the internal states that words symbolize. When one acquires a natural language, one acquires a classification scheme that is embodied in these internal states and expresses their contents. The concepts of natural language are roughly isomorphic with the things that are; scientific concepts are isomorphic with the things that are. Since these objects have stability, senses of words are stable and, for general terms, reference is fixed by sense, so that human beings equipped with a language are able to refer to and describe real objects.

70 Plato takes a similar epistemic line; see, e.g., *Sophist* 263. Cf. *Cratylus* 385b; Parmenides, *On Truth*.

71 Irwin (1988) makes a strong case for attributing metaphysical realism and foundationalism to Aristotle in the *Analytics*.

2

Truth and Necessary Truth

No sooner has Aristotle summarized his theory of meaning in the *De Interpretatione* than he turns to the topic of sentences. Sentences are the basic linguistic item to which truth values can be assigned, and they are made up of linguistic units that have meaning. To avoid the problems of the *Cratylus,* Aristotle draws a sharp distinction between the basic units of meaning and the basic truth-functional entities.[1] He also acknowledges that language has functions other than assertion. That said, sentences have truth values in virtue of what is expressed by the sentence, and this is a function of the meaning of the parts of a sentence. A sentential part has a meaning just in case it is a conventional sign for a thought, the content of which is determined by its relation to an object that is external to the thought. Combining terms to make an assertion yields a statement that expresses a nexus of external features. Whether the assertion is true or not depends upon whether this nexus obtains in fact. Certain peculiarities of Aristotle's discussion of truth – more accurately described as a discussion of falsity – fall into place when one recognizes that Aristotle's starting point is a conception of truth-functional entities that are compounds. These compounds are constructed from meaningful (but not independently truth-functional) linguistic units. Similarly, certain peculiarities of his conception of necessity fall into place when it is recognized that for Aristotle the force of the necessity predicate is to indicate that the nexus of features always obtains.

Not only does Aristotle's theory of meaning motivate his analyses of truth and necessity, his analyses of truth and necessity also have important consequences for the interpretation of his theory of meaning. If, for instance, Aristotle subscribes to a correspondence theory of truth, the

1 In the *Cratylus,* Socrates argues that the name is a tool (ὄργανον) for teaching and discrimination (*Crat.* 387d–388c). Aristotle, by contrast, denies that a single term or even every sentence is a tool: "Every sentence is significant, not as a tool [ὄργανον] but as has been said by convention. Not every sentence is an assertion, but only those to which truth and falsity belong" (16b33–17a2).

pragma of which the *pathema* is a likeness would be an extralinguistic object (as we hypothesized in Chapter 1). If he subscribes to a coherence theory of truth, the *pragma* would be internal to the conceptual system.[2]

Early in the *De Interpretatione,* Aristotle makes the subject of his investigation truth-bearing sentences, as distinguished from other meaningful strings of words (16b33–17a7), and not so many pages later, he raises the problem of future-tensed, contingent statements and necessity in *De Interpretatione* 9. Shortly thereafter, he attempts (not altogether successfully) to work out the entailment relations obtaining between pairs of modal statements. Ever since Aristotle's pioneering work, analyses of truth and necessary truth have figured importantly in philosophical logic. In the technical and specialized context of modern philosophy, these notions have been partially separated from their ancient roots in questions about knowledge and reality. Aristotle, however, puts forth the summary theory of meaning in *De Interpretatione* 1 as the first step in articulating an account of truth-bearing sentences and necessarily true sentences. The meaning of a sentence in the *De Interpretatione* is a function of the relation between the sentence and the state of affairs expressed by the sentence, because the significance of a linguistic expression depends upon reference to an external object. The difference between a true and a false sentence is whether the state of affairs expressed by the sentence actually obtains. This picture of meaning and truth suggests that Aristotle accepts a correspondence theory of truth and an externalist conception of necessity, according to which a sentence is necessarily true, if it is always true.[3] The topic to be investigated in this chapter is whether these expectations are met. Does Aristotle subscribe to a correspondence theory of truth? Does he have an externalist conception of necessity?

Because meaning is a function of reference in the *De Interpretatione,* the relevance of truth conditions to meaning is evident, and one might expect Aristotle promptly to define truth. This expectation is not met by Aristotle, who tends to view truth as an unproblematic notion. Neither the *Categories* nor the *De Interpretatione* explicitly defines truth, although the notion figures importantly in arguments found in these works, where Aristotle's treatment of truth and necessity is in the course of laying the groundwork for his syllogistic theory. We must look to the *Posterior Analytics* and *Metaphysics* for his analysis of these concepts. The analysis he offers, I shall argue, is one that emphasizes the correspondence between sentences and external objects. As in the case of predication and meaning, Aristotle raises questions about truth and necessity as properties of statements and answers them in terms of the characteristics of the correspon-

2 The difference between taking the *pragma* to be an extralinguistic object or merely an ontological presupposition of a particular language was discussed in Chapter 1, section 6.

3 As formulated, this definition of necessity does not have a modern counterpart, but it is, as we shall discover in this chapter, the one that best captures Aristotle's conception.

ding states of affairs (*pragmata*). By itself, this practice does not settle the matter in favor of a correspondence theory of truth, because Aristotle might have construed *pragmata* in these contexts as propositions or mental constructs. In order to clarify Aristotle's semantic theory, I shall look, in this chapter, first at Aristotle's handling of the notion of truth in a variety of contexts and then at his analysis of the concept of necessary truth.

1 Truth and Assertions

One conception of truth that figures in Aristotle's writings is closely related to the notion of truth found in Plato's later writings. Investigating the nature of true statements in the *Sophist,* Plato gives the following characterization: a true statement is one that states about its subject the things that are as they are (263b).[4]

At *Categories* 4b8–9, Aristotle says:

For it is by the facts of the case, by their being or not being so [τὸ πρᾶγμα εἶναι ἤ μή εἶναι] that a statement is called true or false.

In *Metaphysics* IV 7, Aristotle gives a similar account:

To say of what is that it is not, or of what is not that it is, is false, and to say of what is that it is, and of what is not that it is not, is true. (1011b26–27)

According to this conception of truth, the proper object of the truth predicate is an assertoric sentence, which may be either a thought or an utterance.

Just as there are in the mind thoughts which do not involve truth or falsity, and also those which must be one or the other, so it is in speech. For truth and falsity imply combination and separation. (*De Int.* 16a9–11)[5]

. . . For falsity and truth are not in things [πράγμασιν] . . . but in thought [διανοίᾳ]. (*Met.* VI 4, 1027b25–27)

Aristotle's emphasis on thoughts as the bearers of truth is a direct consequence of his theory of meaning; utterances mean what they mean, because their constituent terms signify thoughts. The thoughts that are the ultimate bearers of truth in the *De Interpretatione* have much in common with propositions in the modern sense; they differ, however, in being tensed. For this reason, commentators are in general agreement that statement-making sentences, not propositions, are the items to which the truth predicate applies in Aristotle's logic.[6]

4 Cf. *De Int.* 19a33–34: "Since true statements correspond with facts [πράγματα], it is evident that when things are such that with respect to contraries whichever chance allows is possible, the corresponding affirmation and denial have the same character."
5 Cf. *Cat.* 2a7–10; and *Met.* 1027b18–28, 1051b1–17.
6 See W. Kneale and M. Kneale (1962, pp. 45–54); Ackrill (1963, p. 114 and *passim*).

Unlike in the *Categories* and *De Interpretatione,* one finds in the *Metaphysics* not only the conception of truth as a property of sentences, but also a variety of other apparently disparate conceptions of truth, or at least disparate motivations for treating the topic. The broad conception of truth as historically accumulated knowledge is often in evidence, as is the closely related notion of the identity of truth and being. *Metaphysics* II emphasizes that truth is attainable by human beings.[7]

The investigation of the truth is in one way hard, in another easy. A sign of this is the fact that no one is able to attain the truth adequately, while, on the other hand, we do not all fail, but every one says something true about the nature of things and while individually we contribute little or nothing to the truth, by the union of all a considerable amount comes to be. (*Met.* II 1, 993a30–b4)

Beginning with the assumption that human minds are able to get it right by having thoughts that correspond to extramental realities, Aristotle is more interested in analyzing the anomalous cases of fallibility than in defining the obvious. In the metaphysical lexicon (*Metaphysics* V), Aristotle defines falsity but not truth (V 29) and considers a definition of being (V 7) that identifies it with truth.[8] The construal of being as truth is taken up again in *Metaphysics* VI and IX. Yet another conception of truth seems to be in play in *Metaphysics* IX 10, where Aristotle describes a kind of truth that is an infallible grasp of indivisible essences.

In short, Aristotle has many things to say about truth but leaves the notion of truth undefined. Faced with this array of remarks, an interpreter might despair of finding a core conception of truth here at all. This would be a mistake, I believe, for Aristotle's various remarks on the topic of truth give expression to a coherent and interesting, underlying conception of truth. A first step toward elucidating this conception of truth is to ask what type of theory of truth is implicit in what Aristotle says about truth in each instance and then to consider whether the same theory of truth is found in all these texts.

2 Correspondence Theory of Truth

What makes a thought or a statement true? If the sentence states what is the case, Aristotle says, it is true. This formula is open to different interpretations. Aristotle's favorite term for the state of affairs expressed by a true assertion is *pragma,* however, and this term has a decidedly realist ring. Adopting a realist interpretation of *pragma* and applying Aristotle's definition of truth to the sample sentence, 'Socrates is bald', we get the following analysis: if Socrates exists and is in fact bald, then the sentence

7 Cf. *Politics* 1264a1–5.

8 *Met.* 1024b27–28: "A false statement is the statement of what is not insofar as the statement is false."

'Socrates is bald' is true. To generalize: truth is a function of the correspondence between thoughts or the words that express them and things, and the objects to which expressions refer exist independently of the way in which humans conceptualize and describe them. Truth as the coherence of ideas yields a very different picture of signification and reference. On a coherence theory, truth is determined in relation to a particular linguistic and conceptual framework. Meanings, instead of presupposing reference to external objects, would be likenesses of concepts; that is, the *pragmata* at issue would be propositions. These differences notwithstanding, Aristotle appears to subscribe to a coherentist test for truth in certain spheres while maintaining a correspondence theory of truth. Evidence for truth as correspondence is found in the *Organon* and in many places in the *Metaphysics;* evidence for the appeal to coherence in assessing truth is found in *Metaphysics* IV.

There is broad support for the conception of truth as correspondence in Aristotle's writings. Perhaps the most straightforward statement of this position is found in *Metaphysics* IX 10:

> ⟨Truth and falsity⟩ depend on the side of objects [τῶν πραγμάτων] on their being combined or separated, so that the one who thinks the separated to be separated and the combined to be combined has the truth, while the one whose thought is contrary to that of the objects is in error. . . . It is not because we think truly that you are pale, that you are pale, but because you are pale we who say this have the truth. (1051b2–9)[9]

Here Aristotle not only gives a perspicuous summary of the correspondence theory of truth but also the reason why he is deeply committed to it. It makes truth a function of human thought getting it right about states of affairs that exist independently and provide the standard for evaluating beliefs.

Aristotle's commitment to the conception of truth as correspondence is also voiced at *Categories* 14b18–23:

> And while the true statement [λόγος] is in no way the cause of the object's existence, the object [τὸ πρᾶγμα] does seem in a way the cause of the statement's being true; it is because the object exists or does not that the statement is said to be true or false.

In the vexing discussion of future contingents in *De Interpretatione* 9 (to be discussed in section 4), Aristotle is troubled by what he takes to be a problem for a proponent of a correspondence theory of truth. In this discussion, the notion of truth as correspondence is cashed out as the view that the truth of an assertion depends upon the assertion's corresponding to an independently existing, ontologically prior state of affairs. Aristotle worries that if a sentence about a future event – for instance, a naval

9 Cf. *Cat.* 14b14–23.

battle – is true at the moment it is spoken or thought, then the occurrence of the event will be necessitated from that moment on. Despite great differences of opinion among interpreters of *De Interpretatione* 9 about the details of Aristotle's presentation and analysis of this difficulty, there is general agreement that the problem Aristotle raises is based on the worry that the Principle of Bivalence applied to singular statements about the future will entail determinism.[10] Irrespective of Aristotle's wisdom or lack thereof in framing the question in this way, the only context in which the question could arise is one in which a correspondence theory of truth is presupposed.

Had Aristotle defined truth in the philosophical lexicon, *Metaphysics* V, he would have made our task easier, but he chooses instead to define falsity. Aristotle is optimistic about human capacities for language, perception, and understanding, and thus the belief that fails to correspond to reality is the anomaly requiring explanation, not the one that is true. Since the goal of rational activity is to achieve truth, the analysis of falsity also serves as a diagnosis of where an inquiry might go astray. The account of falsity found in *Metaphysics* V 29 is strangely complex. Instead of defining falsity in terms of a statement's failure to assert what really is the case, Aristotle discusses first the falsity of the thing (*pragma*) and then the falsity of the formula (*logos*). The first type seems to describe certain states of affairs that do not or cannot obtain (1024b16–21). Aristotle gives two examples, namely, the fact that 'commensurate with a side' cannot combine with 'the diagonal of a square' and the fact that when you are not sitting, 'you' and 'sitting' do not combine. The notion of a false *pragma* is hard to interpret. Aristotle's first example suggests that the *pragma* is a proposition, not the external referent of the false statement, because ex hypothesi the false *pragma* does not exist in actuality. It is possible, however, to interpret Aristotle's description of the false *pragma* as a hypothetical claim about what the *pragma* would be were the corresponding statement true; so interpreted, the falsity of the *pragma* consists in the demonstrable impossibility or nonexistence of the *pragma*. Aristotle then extends this notion of falsity to cover things that are but give rise to false impressions, for instance, dreams (1025a5). We are now back on familiar ground, for here the *pragma* is construed by Aristotle as a cause external to the mental state, as in the case of meaning. The second type of falsity, where falsity attaches to a formula (*logos*), seems to represent a more restricted version of the familiar notion that a false statement predicates something of a subject that does not belong to it. Aristotle's one example is the false *logos* that results from attaching the definition of circle

10 The body of ancient and modern commentary on this chapter is extensive. For a sample of recent treatments, see Anscombe (1956); Frede (1970); Hintikka (1973, chap. 8; 1977); Kneale and Kneale (1962, pp. 45–54); McCall (1966); Sorabji (1980); Waterlow (1982b).

to the term 'triangle' (1024b28). This prompts Aristotle to discuss *logoi.* He points out that in one sense every object has only its own proper *logos* (i.e., the statement of its essence) and in another sense it has many (i.e., other true descriptions of what it happens to be). Aristotle's examples are the statement of what it is to be Socrates and the description of Socrates as musical (1024b31). In short, the *logos* that may be false is an expression that states what a thing is, either strictly speaking or coincidentally.

The odd thing about this chapter is that there is no discussion of garden-variety false statements.[11] The explanation lies in the picture of meaning found in the *Categories* and *De Interpretatione.* With respect to meaning, the two crucial elements are the external *pragma* and the *logos,* the content of the thought accompanying the spoken sound. It is not surprising then to find Aristotle analyzing the notion of falsity in terms of these two items. This is why he talks about states of affairs and definitions when we might expect him to speak of statements that fail to correspond to actual states of affairs. When the proper referent of the term and the proper object of the *logos* are the same, the *logos* tells us what the object it is predicated of is (e.g., Socrates is a man); when they are different, the *logos* describes a feature of the subject (e.g., Socrates is pale). The *logos* of man is truly predicated of Socrates, as is the predicate 'man', whereas the *logos* of pale is falsely predicated of Socrates even if the predicate 'pale' applies to him. The *logos* of pale fails to attach to anything in the false sentence 'Socrates is pallor' because 'Socrates' denotes the man not the color of his skin. The false *logos,* Aristotle says, is without qualification (ἁπλῶς) the *logos* of nothing (1024b31–2).

A complex model of correspondence is at work here. Instead of a simple failure of correspondence between assertion and state of affairs, the relation between the two is mediated by the meanings and referents of terms. Falsity attaches both to states of affairs and to the failure of meaning to transfer to the subject of a definition. It is as if the two components of the putative relation between a *logos* and a *pragma* individually fail, and in either case the relation does not hold. This is another manifestation of the tension between Aristotle's desire to make words and phrases the ultimate bearers of meaning and to make statements (certain concatenations of words and phrases) the ultimate bearers of truth, while making both meaning and truth dependent upon the relation between linguistic expressions and the world.[12] In *Metaphysics* V 29, he analyzes falsity in terms of the components of the sentence and the components of the extralinguistic correlate of the sentence. This analysis is consistent with the *Categories'* correlation of types of predicates with types of existents. In *De Interpretatione* 3, however, Aristotle hesitates to make the reference of

11 See, e.g., Kirwan's (1971) notes on this chapter.
12 See Chapter 1, section 3.

a term in a sentence a function of its meaning in isolation, because he recognizes that truth attaches to the sentence. The eccentricity of *Metaphysics* V 29's account of falsity signals Aristotle's recognition of this tension within his semantics and his desire to lessen it by diagnosing the failure of a sentence to be true in terms of the relation between its constituent terms or the relation between the objects signified by the terms. The tension arises precisely because of Aristotle's commitment to truth as correspondence.

At this point the case for correspondence is strong, and so the only remaining issue is whether Aristotle is also committed to a coherence theory of truth. Let us turn then to *Metaphysics* IV, where a coherence theory of truth appears to be implied by the strategy he adopts for defending the Law of Noncontradiction. Aristotle rightly recognizes that a formal proof of a fundamental logical law would be a *petitio principii.* His strategy is twofold – to argue that every type of rational discourse presupposes the Law of Noncontradiction (LNC) (1005b22–34) and then to take on all opponents of the law in a series of dialectical proofs (1006a13–1009a5).[13] The opponent of the principle is charged with making the case against it. Aristotle argues that there is no winning strategy available to the opponent of the LNC, for without presupposing the LNC, the opponent can make no assertion whatsoever in defense of his position. What seems to be at issue is the coherence of the opponent's beliefs. Similarly, by showing that the LNC is a principle that is common to all the sciences, Aristotle has shown that rational inquirers value coherence and consistency.

If the LNC is defended by an appeal to coherence, is this not evidence that Aristotle accepts a coherence theory of truth for metaphysically basic principles? Perhaps. The reductio arguments of IV 3 turn on the requirements of meaning. No argument, indeed no speech act, can perform its intended function unless the LNC is accepted by both speaker and listener. Nor will Aristotle allow the challenger to win by saying nothing, for an opponent adopting that strategy would no longer be acting like a human being and would be no better than a vegetable (1006a11–15). Since discourse of any sort including thinking presupposes the LNC, the very possibility of having beliefs depends upon the tacit acceptance of this principle. In order to make any assertion including the denial of the LNC, it is necessary to assign the phonetic signs used to express the assertion specific and rigid meanings. This is what turns out to be impossible if the LNC is rejected. The assignment of a particular sign to a meaning is conventional (16a27–29); it is a function of the conceptual framework instantiated in a given language. Notice, however, that the conceptual framework construed as the deep structure common

13 The role of dialectic in Aristotelian science will be discussed in Chapter 5, section 4.

to all adequate natural languages might have (and according to *De Interpretatione* 1 does have) an objective, extramental origin.

In order to buttress his defense of the LNC, Aristotle goes on to develop arguments against subjectivism and relativism in the fifth and sixth chapters. These doctrines are incompatible with the belief that truth in the case of assertions and beliefs depends on the correspondence between thoughts and the world. Aristotle frames the attack on the competing theories in terms of the correspondence theory of truth. The test, he says, for those who claim that all appearances and beliefs are true is whether the reality (τὰ ὄντα) is such as their theories suggest (1009a14–15). Protagorean relativism summed up in the slogan "man is the measure of all things, of the things that are, that they are, and of the things that are not, that they are not" was held to be self-refuting according to a venerable ancient tradition originating with Plato. Protagorean relativism thus understood runs afoul of the LNC, for it licenses the conjunction of *P* that one person believes to be true with not-*P* believed by another. By rejecting the LNC, the Protagorean could neutralize the charge that relativism is self-refuting. By the time Aristotle takes up Protagorean relativism in *Metaphysics* IV, however, a flat-footed rejection of the LNC, he believes, has been shown to be impossible. Nevertheless, he is concerned to defeat theories of truth that undermine (or appear to undermine) the alleged universality of the LNC; and the basis of his concern is not simply the LNC but the desire to shore up the position that truth has an objective basis. Aristotle hopes to accomplish this by showing the implausibility of the rival theories.

Protagoras's assertion that all beliefs and appearances are true has considerable potential to challenge the most basic presuppositions of Aristotle's semantics. Even though Aristotle initially claims that this position entails that everything must be at once true and false (1009a8–36), he also recognizes that a circumspect statement of Protagorean relativism need not commit the relativist to the denial of the LNC. If the doctrine that every appearance is true is cashed out as the claim that "the appearance is true not in itself, but for him to whom it appears, and at the time when it appears, and in the way and manner in which it appears" (1011a20–24, Tredennick trans.), then a subjective relativism would be consistent with the LNC – unless human psychology were such that a person could simultaneously and coherently affirm and deny the same proposition. That the latter is not psychologically possible, Aristotle believes, has already been established. Moreover, even if it appears true to some individual that the LNC is false, if a distinction is allowed between a first-order, relativized truth predicate and metalevel, logical truth, the principle could still be affirmed.[14] At the metalevel, Callias's belief that

14 Cf. Burnyeat (1976, pp. 172–95). Burnyeat distinguishes between a first-order rela-

the LNC is false, while true for him, is consistent with Socrates' belief that the LNC is true, and hence at the metalevel the LNC has not been called into question.

Still, Aristotle resists the generalization of circumspect relativism to the claim that a first-order belief is true just in case someone holds that belief and it is true for that person (and not for others who dispute it). Aristotle's reasons are several: namely, relativism is implausible, it introduces an anomalous relation, and it would collapse the distinction between subject and object of thinking. Relativism is implausible, because it entails that past events existed and future ones will exist only if thought about. This result is, of course, implausible from a realist perspective, but to derive Aristotle's conclusion one must presuppose a correspondence theory of truth as well as a Protagorean one, such that if the sentence 'It rained yesterday' is true, this sentence must appear to someone to be true and thus (assuming correspondence) it rained yesterday. In addition, the Protagorean theory is incompatible with the analysis of relatives in the *Categories*.[15] In a two-place relation, *x* is double *y*, for example, the substitution of a term for *x* will determine the term to be substituted for *y*, for instance, 8 is double 4 but not double 2 or 16. Generalized relativism, by contrast, posits a relation between the thinking subject and the object of thought such that a single subject stands in that relation to an indefinite number of objects, whereas a proper relative, according to Aristotle, has only one correlate (1011b7–12).

A further consequence of relativism, Aristotle believes, is that the human ceases to be a thinking subject and becomes instead an object of thought (1011b9–11). This objection is probably best interpreted in light of the anti-Protagorean arguments found in the *Theaetetus* (152a–183c). There Plato introduces the so-called Secret Doctrine about perception – one consequence of which is the generation of twins, a perceiving subject and a perceived object for every perception; for instance, a perception of white is to be explained by the production of a seeing eye and whiteness.[16] If the only reality the object possesses lies in its being perceived, then the only reality the subject possesses lies in its perceiving. Both subject and object are reduced to collections of ephemeral states. Under these conditions, Aristotle believes, the self or 'I' would only exist as a mental construct. In addition, knowledge and meaningful discourse, Plato argues, would be ruled out by a Heraclitean flux of constantly changing perceptual states and objects. One way to avoid the phenomenalistic reduction of the subject would be to posit prior and independ-

tivized truth predicate and a nonrelativized truth predicate and concludes that Protagorean relativism is self-refuting. I agree that the distinction is needed but believe that relativism need not run afoul the LNC.

15 *Categories* 7.

16 I discuss this passage at greater length in Modrak (1981, pp. 35–54).

ently existing subjects and objects, whose causal interaction produces the phenomena of perception and the fluid features thus apprehended. This move, however, is not open to the philosopher asserting the generalized version of relativism. An alternative open to the relativist that Aristotle does not explore would be to grant the reduction of subjects to mental states and objects to perceptible properties and then argue for the truth of relativism. Aristotle does not attempt to establish that fixed subjects are required to make sense of relativism, and hence he fails to show that truth cannot be defined by a relativist in relation to beliefs and perceptions. What he hopes to have shown is that relativism flies in the face of common sense.

Instead of decisive counterarguments, Aristotle offers a series of elliptically stated objections to relativism. These objections are designed to demonstrate that an opponent cannot successfully attack the universality of the Law of Noncontradiction on the basis of Protagorean relativism and to show that realism is a more commonsensical doctrine than relativism. Relativism provides a reason for preferring a coherence theory of truth to a correspondence theory, but a realist lacks this motivation. Thus Aristotle sees no reason to adopt a generalized version of the coherence theory of truth implied by his initial approach to the defense of the LNC, and he continues to appeal to correspondence in discussions of truth in *Metaphysics* IV and elsewhere.

3 Truth and Simples

Many thoughts represent complex states of affairs where two or more notions are combined, for instance, the thought that Socrates is sitting. But if Aristotle is right, some thoughts express simple natures or notions, for instance, the essence of an infima species. Here, the thought may be, and typically is, expressed in a string of words, but the nature it reveals is single and unified.[17]

> There is a definition [ὁρισμός] not where a formula [λόγος] is identical in meaning to a word . . . but where there is a formula of something primary [πρώτου]; and primary things are those which do not imply the predication of one element of another. (*Met.* VII 4, 1030a6–11)[18]

This raises a problem for Aristotle's account of truth. Restricting the notion of truth to statements or complex judgments has the result that the components of true statements are not themselves true. Toward the end of the *Theaetetus,* Plato presents "Socrates' dream," which hypothesizes knowable complexes made up of undefined simples.[19]

17 Cf. *De Int.* 20b12–19; *Met.* VII 12, 1037b8–14.

18 The query about definition raised in this text will be discussed in Chapter 5, section 2.

19 Plato, *Theaetetus* 201E–210B.

But in fact there is no formula [λόγος] in which any of the primary things [τῶν πρώτων] can be expressed; it can only be named, for a name is all there is that belongs to it. But when we come to things composed of these elements, then, just as these things are complex, so the names are combined to make a formula, a formula being precisely a combination of names. (*Theaetetus* 202b1–5; trans. follows Cornford)

In the dream, the simples or perceptibles are immediately given and are not amenable to definition; these in combinations constitute accounts (*logoi*) that are knowable because definable in terms of their constituents. The correct interpretation of Socrates' dream is a vexed topic. According to some commentators, the dream is about the justification (or lack thereof) of the basic objects of mathematics;[20] other philosophers, including Aristotle (I believe), have understood Plato's dilemma as applying much more broadly to any foundationalist account of knowledge.[21] The definition of truth found in the *Categories* and *De Interpretatione* limits the application of this notion to complex objects, namely, assertions that either combine or separate two or more simple ideas. The simples are neither true nor false. The picture is very similar to the one subjected to criticism in the *Theaetetus*. In the *Posterior Analytics,* Aristotle grants Plato that the basic premises of a science must be known in a different way than the complex judgments derived from them. The attempt to justify the basic objects in the same way as demonstrable propositions will produce either an infinite regress of premises or circular justification, neither of which will meet the requirements for knowledge. Aristotle also believes that the basic premises must be true, necessary, and immediate. If immediate, the first premises cannot be reached by conjoining two (or more) discrete notions, but this seems to leave Aristotle without an answer to the *Theaetetus* challenge because the basic premises would seem to be true simples.[22]

Aristotle's response is to show that the apprehension of basic objects is possible, because not all understanding is discursive knowledge (ἐπιστήμη).[23] Corresponding to the different types of knowledge (γνῶσις) are different types of thoughts. Taking note of the difference between simple and complex objects of intellection, Aristotle recognizes a similar difference between their modes of apprehension, namely, be-

20 Morrow (1970, pp. 309–33), for instance, emphasizes the relevance to mathematics of Socrates' dream, but he believes the theoretical model presented there applies to other disciplines as well.

21 The issues raised for foundationalism will be discussed in Chapters 4–6.

22 In Chapter 5, I shall argue that Aristotle does have an answer to this challenge in the *Metaphysics*. Insofar as the present discussion is concerned, it is sufficient to note that the distinction between basic objects and composites does raise the question whether to define truth for the basic objects as well as the composites.

23 Plato, on the other hand, makes the elements unknowable (ἄγνωστα) and their combinations knowable (γνωστάς) (*Tht.* 202b).

tween simple apprehension and discursive reason. In the *Metaphysics* at 1051b21–27 and in the *De Anima* at 430a26-b6, he distinguishes between propositional truths recognized through discursive reasoning and indivisible intelligibles that are simply grasped.[24] Both passages distinguish between simple and complex intelligibles and consequently distinguish between two types of intellection. Apart from insisting on simplicity, Aristotle does not say much in these passages about what sort of object would be indivisible. If we look elsewhere in the corpus for examples of indivisible intelligibles, the *infima species* seems to be the most likely candidate. The definition that expresses the essence of an *infima species* does not involve predication (1030a7–17); it is a unified and simple object.[25] The apprehension of a simple essence would be the intellection of an indivisible object. Since truth is ultimately a property of thoughts, the distinction between indivisible and composite thoughts engenders a notion of a different type of truth in *Metaphysics* IX. Typically, when Aristotle talks about the truth of a thought, he has in mind thoughts asserting that something is the case; the thought that *x* is *y* is true just in case *x* is *y*. The constitutive notions (*x*, *y*) are said to be neither true nor false. This leaves Aristotle confronted by the problem raised by Socrates' dream. His response is to posit a special type of truth that applies to indivisible thoughts that cannot be analyzed into component notions.

> Neither truth nor falsity will be still present in the same way as in the previous cases. . . . contact [θιγγάνειν] and assertion [φάναι] are truth (for assertion [φάςις] is not the same as affirmation [κατάφασις]) and ignorance is non-contact. For it is not possible to be in error regarding the question what a thing is, except incidentally; and in the same way it is not possible to be in error regarding non-composite substances. (1051b21–28; Ross trans.)

For an indivisible thought to be true seems to mean no more than that it is an object of consciousness. The difference between assertion and affirmation is explained in *De Interpretatione* 4:

> A sentence is a spoken sound with meaning some part of which is significant in separation – as an assertion, not as an affirmation. (16b27–28; trans. follows Ackrill)

The notion of falsity in the sense appropriate to a mistaken judgment has no application to thoughts about indivisible essences precisely because these thoughts are simple. While a person might fail to grasp a particular indivisible object, she could not be mistaken about it, only ignorant

24 *Met.* 1051b21–27 emphasizes the immediacy of the apprehension of the simple objects; *De An.* 430a26–b6, the role of *nous* in combining the components of a composite judgment. Both texts affirm that truth and falsity strictly speaking apply only to composite judgments.

25 Berti (1978) points out that all Aristotle's examples in *De An.* III 6 are separated essences of material objects and argues that what is at issue is being indivisible in potentiality.

of it.[26] Aristotle appears to be committed to two notions of truth, namely, truth in the familiar sense where the truth predicate applies to statements in speech and their counterparts in thought and a second sense of truth appropriate to the apprehension of an indivisible object of thought. The statement that fails to be true is false, while the attempted intellection of an indivisible that fails is ignorance. Aristotle seems to be ambivalent about calling the correct apprehension of a simple essence 'true'; he avoids that description in the *De Anima* and apparently rejects it at *Metaphysics* 1027b27–28.[27] Despite vacillation about terminology, Aristotle elsewhere reaffirms his bottom line in *Metaphysics* IX 10 that knowledge requires both complex thoughts and incomposite ones and that the knower must get both right. What a true judgment about a composite and a successful apprehension of a simple have in common is that both fall under a broad notion of truth according to which a thought is true just in case it is an accurate representation of what is the case in reality. As Aristotle states this principle, the true corresponds to what is and the false to what is not (1051b33).

Because being true is synonymous with correctly representing what is and because the uncombined terms have meaning and represent objects, Aristotle sometimes uses 'true' to describe cognitions that are not assertoric but intellectual or perceptual graspings of what is. He unblushingly talks about two kinds of truth corresponding to the different modes of thinking in IX 10. This is reminiscent of *Metaphysics* V 29, where (as we have seen) Aristotle analyzes false statements in terms of 'false' components, and he includes among false things, pictures and dream-images that produce an impression that something is the case that is not (1024b17–26). Aristotle also seems to believe that many simple mental representations, both intellectual and sensual ones, have, at least implicitly, a propositional structure.[28] This may explain why he is willing to describe simple apprehensions as true or false. As a consequence of the meanings of the linguistic terms used to express a thought, the structure of the thought mirrors the external state of affairs that is the measure of the truth of the thought. Aristotle's notion of truth is not so much fuzzy as it is broad – broad enough to include simple objects and yet at the same time accommodate the standard of use of 'true'. For Aristotle, as for us,

26 This is Aristotle's version of Plato's revision of Parmenides' edict whereby apprehending what is as having characteristics that are not is possible, apprehending what is not simpliciter is not possible (*Soph.* 258e).

27 It is possible, although somewhat of a stretch, to interpret Aristotle's comment at 1027b27–28 as ruling out thought (*dianoia*) about incomposites and leaving open the possibility that truth and falsity might reside in something other than *dianoia* in this instance.

28 This aspect of Aristotle's thought will be explored in more detail in Chapters 3, 5, 7, and 8.

'true' and 'false' in their standard use apply to assertions in thought and speech.

4 Necessity

Another predicate of statements that plays an important role in Aristotle's logic is that of necessity. Like truth, Aristotle construes necessity (also possibility) as a predicate that belongs to a statement in virtue of the character of the corresponding state of affairs. Statements are constructed out of subjects and predicates. Whether a given statement is true or necessary depends upon whether its elements correspond to an actual combination of the objects they refer to, in which case the statement is true, and whether the combined elements of the statement represent an actual combination that always obtains, in which case the statement is always true and asserts a necessary connection between its subject and predicate.[29] Today necessity is often understood in terms of analyticity. A necessarily true sentence is a sentence that is true in virtue of its logical form (for instance, 'A is A') or in virtue of the meanings of the terms employed (for instance, 'A bachelor is an unmarried man'). Sentences with empirical content may be true but never necessarily true. Such an account of necessity might be called an internalist one, because to determine whether a sentence is necessary in this sense, one need not appeal to anything external to the meaning of the sentence. The account of 'belonging necessarily' that Aristotle develops in *Posterior Analytics* I 4 arguably makes necessity a matter of definition. This suggests that in certain contexts he may have embraced an internalist conception of necessity, which would be unfortunate. An internalist conception of necessity would be inconsistent with the theory of meaning, according to which, meaning cannot be understood in terms of the content of the mental state alone, because the content is determined in relation to an external object. In this and the following section, we shall examine Aristotle's various accounts of necessity to determine whether he has a coherent account of necessity that is consistent with his theories of meaning and truth.

Necessity, broadly defined, is central to Aristotle's conception of knowledge. From the *Organon* to the biological treatises, in order to ensure the timeless character of science, Aristotle requires the sentences providing the foundation of a science to express necessary truths.[30] Since the same sentence about a contingent state of affairs may on one occasion be true and on another false, were contingent statements made the basis of a science, its claim to truth would be precarious at best. Aristotle finds that scenario totally inconsistent with his conception of science

29 In section 5, the ways in which Aristotle modifies his core notion of necessity will be discussed.

30 *Pst. Anal.* 88b30–34; *N.E.* 1139b22–24; 1140b31–33; *Part. An.* 642a3–13.

(*episteme*).[31] He envisages empirical sciences having basic premises that are necessarily true and have empirical content. The question then is: does Aristotle have a single and coherent concept of necessity? If so, what are its contours?

Looking for a definition of apodeictic necessity, one finds it, not in the discussion of modality in the *De Interpretatione* and *Prior Analytics,* but in the *Posterior Analytics.* The topic is demonstrative knowledge in the *Posterior Analytics,* and there the focus shifts from the syntactic to the semantic features of sentences. Since these features depend upon the connection between the sentence and what is asserted by the sentence, 'necessary' applies to the relation between the predicate and the subject; a predicate is necessary if what it predicates of the subject always belongs to the subject. According to *Posterior Analytics* I 4–6, demonstration is an inference from necessary premises and the notion of necessity is explicated by defining a class of predicates that inhere necessarily in their subjects. To define necessity, Aristotle appeals to the notions of 'essential attribute' and 'commensurate universal'.

> I call 'commensurately universal' [καθόλου] an attribute which belongs to every instance of its subject, both essentially and as such. It is clear that all commensurate universals inhere necessarily in their subjects. (73b27–29; Mure trans.)

Belonging in every instance and essentially turn out to be the salient features of the definition of commensurate universal, for Aristotle goes on to say that belonging as such is the same as belonging essentially (73b28–32). What Aristotle means by 'belonging in every instance' is pretty straightforward; an attribute belongs in every instance if it belongs to any arbitrarily selected instance of the subject. This condition is met under the broader notion of universal (καθόλου) found in many other places in Aristotle's writings; the second condition, belonging in itself, restricts the present definition in a way that makes it applicable to the type of predication under discussion, namely, belonging of necessity. This is a narrower notion of universal (καθόλου) than found elsewhere in the Aristotelian corpus. To mark this difference, καθόλου in this context has traditionally been translated as 'commensurate universal' – a practice to be followed here.

Aristotle's explanation of belonging essentially (per se) and as such is more perplexing.[32] In I 4, Aristotle offers four separate explications of per se predications at (1) 73a35–38, (2) 73a38–b4, (3) 73b5–10, and (4) 73b10–16. The first two passages define per se predication in terms of a definitional nexus between the subject and the predicate of a demon-

31 For the same reason, Aristotle argues against the claim of spontaneity and chance to be proper causes in *Physics* II 4–6.

32 See Barnes's (1994) commentary on I 4; Ferejohn (1991, chaps. 3–5); and McKirahan (1992, chap. 7).

strative premise. An attribute belongs per se (καθ' αὑτό) if it is so related to the subject that either the subject cannot be defined without mentioning the attribute or the attribute cannot be defined without mentioning the subject (73a34–b5). The relation between 'line' and 'triangle' illustrates the first type of per se predication and that between 'curved' and 'line' the second. Aristotle's intent seems clear enough in these cases, namely, to make the connection between subject and predicate in a sentence, where the predicate is said of the subject essentially, a matter of definition. This conception of per se predication is all of a piece with Aristotle's oft-repeated claim that the definiens of a concept is one, even though the verbalization of the definiens typically consists of several terms. Aristotle pictures the practice of scientific definition as the act of unpacking a single concept and in the course of this predicating one term of another.[33] At the end of the chapter, when Aristotle sums up his position at 73b17–20, it is in the language of the first two definitions: "What is said to belong per se in the sense of belonging in the predicates or of being belonged in, holds both because of itself and from necessity" (b17–18). In short, the definition of being necessary as a relation between an attribute and its subject that is secured by a definitional nexus is Aristotle's preferred definition in I 4.

Does this make the first two types of per se predication canonical and the other two passages irrelevant to understanding Aristotle's notion of necessity? On this point, there is considerable disagreement among recent commentators. In keeping with a long tradition of commentary, Jonathan Barnes asserts that only the first two types of "in itself" predication "are directly relevant to the characterization of demonstrative propositions."[34] Michael Ferejohn adds that the second type of per se predication is needed, because it gives Aristotle a way to handle the relation between a genus and its differentiae – a tool that Ferejohn believes Aristotle lacks in the *Categories*.[35] Neither Ferejohn nor Richard McKirahan, however, would limit per se predication to the first two descriptions given in I 4. McKirahan argues that the account of a third type of per se predication makes an important contribution to the theory of demonstration by describing a kind of per se predication that the subjects within a subject genus satisfy.[36] Ferejohn, noting that the first two types of per se predication would include only analytic premises, argues that Aristotle recognizes this limitation and to avoid it offers the fourth explication of per se.[37]

33 This line on the character of Aristotelian scientific definitions will be developed and modified in Chapters 3–5.

34 Barnes (1994, p.112).

35 Ferejohn, (1991, chap. 5). The second type of per se predications can also serve as conclusions of demonstrations, which the first type cannot.

36 McKirahan (1992, chap. 7). See also Wedin (1973); Barnes (1994, pp. 114–16); Graham (1975); Granger (1981).

37 Ferejohn (1991), chap. 6.

Turning then to the third and fourth cases of per se predication: at 73b5–10, Aristotle draws a distinction between per accidens and per se predication. Aristotle concludes this section with the remark that "things which are not said of a subject I call per se, and those which are said of a subject I call per accidens" (73b8–10). The fourth explication (73b10–16) defines the per se relation in terms of causal connection. Aristotle gives this example:

But if because of itself, then in itself – e.g., if an animal dies while being sacrificed, on account of the sacrifice, since it died because of being sacrificed, and it was not incidental that it died while being sacrificed. (73b13–16)

This example is noteworthy, because, at a minimum, it reminds us that Aristotle is committed to a picture of language and demonstrative science that construes the properties of statements, being true and being necessarily true, as having extralinguistic correlates. A demonstrative science may display "causal" relations that are a function of the definitions of its basic concepts, but causal relations are not thereby reduced to mere analytic truths. If the fourth type of per se predication is granted the same status as the first two, then statements expressing empirical relations that are not matters of definition would be admitted as demonstrative premises and conclusions in I 4.

Ferejohn argues correctly (I believe) that the fourth type of per se predications can serve as demonstrative premises and conclusions, and they include contingent premises (empirical truths).[38] Consequently, the fourth account of per se predication in I 4 enables Aristotle to include empirical premises, not just analytic ones, under the purview of demonstrative science.[39] This extension would have several advantages. It would, for instance, explain why in the *Posterior Analytics* Aristotle draws many of his examples from the empirical sciences.[40]

Aristotle develops the notion of per se predication in order to define a concept of necessity that will fit demonstrative premises of all the sciences. Entailment by true premises is not sufficient to ensure that a demonstrative conclusion has the requisite necessity; the premises must also be necessary.

Again, demonstration is a necessary thing because the conclusion cannot be otherwise, if it has been demonstrated without qualification; and the causes of this

38 McKirahan (1992, p. 95) believes that the fourth type of per se predication concerns causal sequences of events and not predication; as does Barnes (1994, p. 117).

39 Ferejohn (1991, chap. 6).

40 For a clear statement of the issues raised by Aristotle's choice of examples in the *Posterior Analytics,* see Barnes (1969; reprinted in 1975). Other commentators have argued that the empirical premises accepted by Aristotle can be reduced to premises asserting relations between species and their essential attributes; the latter relations are arguably definitional. See Joachim (1922, pp. xxvi–xxviii); Mansion (1976, 1981); but see also Sorabji's (1980) critique of Mansion.

necessity are the first premises, since the propositions from which the syllogism proceeds cannot be otherwise. (*Met.* V 1015b6–9)

Premises that are instances of the first or second type of per se predication defined at 73a34–b5 would be analytic in the modern sense, but more importantly, for Aristotle, they would display the actual, unchanging character of the object described. The two terms making up the premise would pick out two features of the object that are invariantly found together in the context specified by the premise. This type of necessity ultimately resides, not in the formal structure of a definition, nor in the terms making up the premise, but in the things that these terms denote. If the things are so related as to constitute a single nature of an enduring kind, the relation is necessary. In short, Aristotle refuses to concede that necessity, even when it is a matter of definition, is inconsistent with the sentences to which it pertains having empirical content.[41] Necessity thus construed strikes Aristotle as central to a satisfactory explanation, because it is rooted in the nature of the things that the explanation is about. Necessity thus construed is also consistent with Aristotle's making meaning dependent upon reference to external realities.

The distinction between de dicto necessity (Nec [Every *A* is *B*]) and de re necessity (Every *A* is Nec *B*), originally drawn by Medieval logicians, has frequently found its way into discussions of Aristotle's modal logic and conception of necessity.[42] Is the necessity that Aristotle requires of the premises and conclusions of demonstrative science necessity de dicto or necessity de re, or some hybrid of the two? Recent commentators have also not agreed about the correct answer to this question.[43] Necessity de dicto – construed in the usual way as an expression of intrinsic necessity – would not satisfy Aristotle's objectives in the *Posterior Analytics,* because a universal statement about a fictitious kind, for instance, goatstags, would (if based on the nominal definition of the object) be necessary de dicto. The difference between the definitions that can serve as demonstrative premises and nominal definitions is that the former, but not the latter, are instantiated by actual existents (90b30; 93b29–37). Still, arguably, the account of necessity in I 4 is about de dicto necessity. Aristotle introduces the topic of per se predication with the claim that demonstration must be "deduction from what is necessary" (73a24). His objective then is to define a notion of necessity for demonstrative premises having the form, Nec (Every *A* is *B*). His favored notion of per se predication, namely, the first two types of per se predication defined at

41 Cf. the well-known argument of Kripke (1972, pp. 253–355) that some necessary truths are known a posteriori.

42 For the history of this distinction, see Kneale, 1962.

43 Mansion (1976) argues for de dicto necessity on the basis of *Posterior Analytics* I 4. Sorabji (1981, pp. 205–44) argues that at least some of Aristotle's definitional truths are necessary de re.

73a34–b5, makes the necessity of a premise in a demonstrative argument a function of the definitions of its terms (cf. 74b5–11). Necessity thus defined is de dicto. On the other hand, Aristotle's fourth account of per se predication is clearly a claim about an individual possessing one characteristic, dying, because it possesses another, having had its throat slit (73b13). The universal statement, Nec (Every animal having its throat slit dies), derives its necessity not from an intrinsic relation between the two predicates, but from an external, invariant causal sequence. The justification for asserting the universal modal sentence is provided by de re sentences about particulars, having the form, Animal *A*'s throat was slit and necessarily it died. Aristotle's conception of per se predication then is not easily classified as either de dicto or de re necessity.[44] For Aristotle, the reality expressed by a necessarily true statement is more fundamental than its logical form; if the (external) state of affairs expressed by the statement obtains of necessity, then the statement is necessary. The difference between the first and second types of per se predication and the fourth is evidence that Aristotle's starting point is whatever obtains necessarily, irrespective of whether the relation can be expressed in an intrinsically necessary sentence.

It is a commonplace that Aristotle's modal logic suffers from his tendency to conflate de dicto and de re modality.[45] It has been suggested that this is a result of his lacking a perspicuous way to formalize these sentences and his being hampered by the limitations of a term logic, in contrast to a propositional logic.[46] While no doubt these factors contribute to Aristotle's difficulties, there is another, and I believe, more compelling reason that Aristotle vacillates between the two formulations. Treating necessity as a predicate modifying the whole sentence is supported by Aristotle's logical theory – even if some of his examples fail – and supported by his analysis of modal statements in *De Interpretatione* 12–13. His theories of meaning and truth, however, lead him to believe that truth is a property of certain concatenations of concepts, and that extralinguistic states of affairs are the ultimate determinants of truth and modality. Because the basic truth-functional entity, the assertoric statement, is not the basic unit of meaning, the term or more properly the concept, there arises a tension between the two perspectives. From one perspective, the simple, assertoric statement is a unitary proposition. From the other, the statement is a composite, the meaning of which is determined by its component concepts. Meaning is determined by reference to extralinguistic objects, and thus what is asserted by a sentence is also determined by ref-

44 In other contexts, de re necessity often takes precedence in Aristotle's thinking. See Smith (1989, pp.126–7).

45 The pair of sentences 'N (every *A* is *B*)' and 'Every *A* is *N* (*B*)' illustrate the difference between a de dicto and a de re modal assertion.

46 See, e.g., Kneale and Kneale (1962, p. 40).

erence to extralinguistic objects. The evaluation of the truth and/or necessary truth of a statement will be – on this picture – a decision about whether a particular concatenation actually obtains sometimes or always. According to the *Categories,* the things that are are substances and their attributes; in the *De Interpretatione,* meaning is determined by reference to actual existents and truth by the correspondence between sentences and extralinguistic states. Thus if a statement expresses a necessary truth, it does so in virtue of the real relation between the entities that the subject and the predicate represent. The crucial relation, from this perspective, is the one between an ontological subject and something that is necessarily predicated of it.[47] As a consequence of his theory of meaning, Aristotle sometimes speaks as if the necessity predicate applies only to the predicate and not to the whole sentence, because whether the predicate always attaches to the subject in fact is what is at issue for him.

In *De Interpretatione* 9, Aristotle raises a metaphysical puzzle – the interpretation of which is vexed. On one plausible reading, the question Aristotle sets out to answer is: Does accepting the Principle of Bivalence for future contingent statements necessitate the occurrence of events? This principle has the consequence that of a pair of contradictory statements, one is true and the other false. Suppose the principle is applied to a pair of contradictory statements about a contingent state of affairs, for instance, a future naval battle. If today the sentence 'There will be a naval battle tomorrow' is either true or false, it appears that deliberations about whether to engage the enemy tomorrow are pointless, because, either the sentence is true, in which case the sea battle will occur of necessity, or the sentence is false and of necessity there will be no sea battle. Aristotle offers a solution to this problem:

> So, since true statements correspond with facts [πράγματα] it is evident that when things are such that with respect to contraries whichever chance allows is possible, the corresponding affirmation and denial have the same character. This happens with things that are not always so or are not always not so. With these it is necessary for one or the other of the contradictories to be true or false – not indeed, this one or that one, but as chance has it; or for one to be true rather than the other, yet not already true or false. (19a32–39)

Many proposals have been made as to how to interpret this solution.[48] I do not propose to decide this issue here but rather to sketch two plausible and popular lines of interpretation in order to determine what can be learned about Aristotle's general conception of necessity from *De In-*

47 Cf. the comment made by Smith (1989, p. 127) that "Aristotle tends to regard possibilities strictly so called as matters of the inherence of properties in subjects."

48 From ancient to modern times, commentators have quarreled about the interpretations of Aristotle's position; see, for instance, Ackrill (1963, pp. 132–42); Anscomb (1956); Frede (1970); Hintikka (1973, 1977); Kneale and Kneale (1962, pp. 45–54); McCall (1966); Sorabji (1980, chap. 5); and Waterlow (1982b).

terpretatione 9. According to the historically most popular interpretation (1), in the case of future contingents, Aristotle rejects the valid inference from the Law of the Excluded Middle (*P* v ~*P*) to the Principle of Bivalence (every statement is true or false).[49] On another reading (2), Aristotle accepts the inference mentioned in (1); what he rejects is not the Principle of Bivalence as such but the implication that this principle necessitates the occurrence of a future event, namely, 'necessarily *P* v necessarily ~*P*'.[50] If the first is his position, then his solution is completely wrongheaded.[51] In order to maintain (2), Aristotle must differentiate between simple and conditional necessity. Or, on a variant of (2) proposed by Sarah Waterlow, Aristotle accepts bivalence where the two values are true and not true rather than true and false.[52]

Aristotle recognizes the difference between absolute and relative necessity in other contexts, and he standardly uses 'necessity' (ἀνάγκη) and its cognates in the *Analytics* to indicate entailment.

> One might show by an exposition of the terms that the conclusion is not necessary simply, although it is necessary in relation to the premises. (*An. Pr.* I 10, 30b32–33)

This offers some support for interpretation (2), as does Aristotle's elaboration of his position in *De Interpretatione* 9.

> What is, necessarily is, when it is; and what is not, necessarily is not, when it is not. But it is not necessary that everything that is, is; nor that everything that is not, is not. For to say that everything that is, is of necessity, when it is, is not the same as saying unconditionally that it is of necessity. (19a23–26)

Neither passage provides decisive support, however, for the second interpretation.

The question of whether Aristotle accepts the Principle of Bivalence (interpretation 2) or rejects it (interpretation 1) is perhaps not as significant for our purposes as understanding why Aristotle frets about this problem at all. Besides assuming the truth of a statement about a future occurrence, several additional assumptions are needed to support robust determinism: the necessity of logical truths, a correspondence theory of truth, and tensed assertions as the objects of inference. Aristotle seems to be committed to all three. Logical relations between pairs of sentences are determined by the syntactic features of the sentences; as a result, no matter what the substitution instances are, the logical relations between

49 For a helpful discussion of the history of this strategy and an argument that it is no more open to objection than any other more recent strategy, see Sorabji (1980, pp. 91–6).

50 Cf. Anscombe (1956).

51 The only coherent strategy that would allow Aristotle to reject the Principle of Bivalence would be the rejection of a two-valued logic. For further discussion of these issues, see McCall (1966); and Prior (1953, pp. 317–26).

52 Waterlow (1982b, pp. 106–7).

the sentences will hold and hence be necessary. Because Aristotle also accepts a correspondence theory of truth, he is troubled by the apparent deterministic consequences of applying the Principle of Bivalence to future-tense, singular sentences. His response is either to restrict (or modify) the universality of the Principle of Bivalence or to deny the necessity of the relation between a sentence's being true and the asserted state of affairs actually obtaining (cf. 19a33–35). The latter relation is the basis for Aristotle's claim that the past and the present are necessary (19a23–24). Interpretation (1) maintains the universality of the connection between truth and necessary occurrence and (2) maintains the universality of logical truths but qualifies the implications of correspondence in the case of a true future singular statement, where the occurrence of the future event is not simply necessary.

The alternative strategy proposed by Waterlow provides a way to construe Aristotle's position that maximizes its internal coherence. According to Waterlow, in a number of different works Aristotle develops a single, consistent conception of possibility, which she labels RT-possibility, where possibility is temporalized and relative to the actual. Applying this notion of possibility to the analysis to *De Interpretatione* 9, she concludes that the problem that concerns Aristotle is the issue of opposed truth values in the case of future-tensed pairs of antithetical statements when these pairs represent contingencies.[53] For these pairs, one is not true and the other false, because were truth in this instance construed as truth-as-opposed-to-falsity, the truth of *P* would entail the falsity of not-*P* (106). If so, then '*P*' had to be true (i.e., not-*P* was false in relation to all times), and contingency is eliminated (i.e., the conditions for R-T possibility cannot be met). For pairs of singular, future-tensed antithetical statements referring to the same particular event, one is true and the other not true. Construing the two relevant truth values as true and not true instead of true and false would allow Aristotle to retain the Principle of Bivalence for future-tensed contingent statements, Waterlow argues. Even if one is unwilling to attribute a distinction between pairs of truth values to Aristotle, the insight that drives Waterlow's analysis of R-T possibility, namely, that modality is relative to actuality for Aristotle, should be embraced. This conclusion fits Aristotle's conception of per se predication and explains his worry about contingency in *De Interpretatione* 9, on any plausible interpretation of his solution.

5 Hypothetical Necessity

In *Posterior Analytics* I 4, the definition of necessity is such that the premises of many empirical sciences would seem to be excluded from the

53 Waterlow (1982b, chap. 5).

purview of demonstrative science.[54] As Barnes, Ferejohn, and others have argued, this would be highly problematic, because many of the examples cited in the *Posterior Analytics* are drawn from the physical sciences.[55] Aristotle seems to have several strategies for dealing with this difficulty. The two strategies he leans on most heavily in the natural sciences are (a) weakening the criteria for simple necessity and (b) admitting principles that hold for the most part as objects of knowledge. Both of these strategies will be explored in this section in order to determine the range of application of the concept of necessity in Aristotelian sciences and in order to complete our investigation of Aristotle's analysis of the modal predicate, necessary, and the consequences of that analysis for the interpretation of his theory of meaning. The extension of necessity to cover hypothetical necessity provides striking evidence for an externalist conception of necessity. The necessity predicate for Aristotle is the linguistic marker of a real relation between extralinguistic objects; the N-predicate simply indicates that what is asserted obtains always or – here Aristotle hesitates – for the most part. Thus construed, the concept of necessity is applicable to a wide range of cases. Aristotle has little motivation to limit the applicability of this concept to analytic relations, and he does not limit it in his scientific treatises.

In *Posterior Analytics* I 4, an attribute belongs necessarily, if and only if it belongs to every instance of its subject per se and as such (73b27–29). Above we concluded that the account of per se predication was, contrary to initial appearances, compatible with allowing necessarily true sentences to have empirical content. Nevertheless, the paradigm cases of per se predication were analytic truths. Evidence that Aristotle not only allows for the possibility of empirical content but is also concerned to develop a conception of necessity that fits the premises of the empirical sciences cannot be found in the *Posterior Analytics*.[56] It can be found in the definitions of universality and necessity that Aristotle gives in later treatments of scientific methodology.

Aristotle does not contrast simple necessity with other sorts of necessity in *Posterior Analytics* I 4, but it is likely that, had he done so, he would have identified simple necessity with the type of necessity possessed by per se predications in the first two senses of per se. In other contexts, Aris-

54 Here, as above, I am taking Aristotle's canonical notion of necessity to be defined in accordance with the first or second sense of per se predication, i.e., in terms of a definitional nexus between the terms of a demonstrative premise. Allowing demonstrative premises to be necessary in the fourth sense of *per se* predication is one way to resolve this problem. See Ferejohn (1991, chap. 6).

55 See Barnes (1969, pp. 133–7); Ferejohn (1991, chap. 5); Mignucci (1981, pp. 173–203).

56 The fourth type of per se predication in I 4 may be Aristotle's attempt to extend his treatment of necessity to empirical propositions. It is, however, at best a short-lived effort, already abandoned in the summary at the end of the chapter. See note 47.

totle weakens the condition on simple necessity to true in every instance, and, as a result, he tends to equate simple necessity with eternal truth.[57] In the *Nicomachean Ethics*, for instance, Aristotle remarks:

Therefore, the object of scientific knowledge is of necessity. Therefore it is eternal; for things that are unqualifiedly of necessity are all eternal; and things that are eternal are ungenerated and imperishable. (*N.E.* VI 3, 1139b22–24)

Of the natural sciences, this conception of necessity fits cosmology best. The *De Generatione et Corruptione* distinguishes between absolutely necessary cyclical changes and others.[58] The indestructible heavenly bodies whose motions describe spheres circling the earth for all eternity pose no challenge to the investigator seeking to frame a cosmological theory in accordance with the *Analytics'* conception of science. Moreover, even the less stable elements of the sublunar world are defined by certain essential attributes – for instance, fire is hot and dry – which explain the behavior of the elements in forming other compounds and their roles as agents of change (see 642a35–b3).[59]

Merely extending the conception of simple necessity to other natural sciences would be problematic, and in *Physics* II 9 Aristotle recognizes another type of necessity.

For why is a saw such as it is? To effect so-and-so and for the sake of so-and-so. This – that for the sake of which – then cannot be realized unless the saw is made of iron. It is, therefore, necessary for it to be of iron, if it will be a saw and perform its function. What is necessary then is necessary on a hypothesis; it is not necessary as a result. Necessity is in the matter, while 'that for the sake of which' is in the definition. (200a10–13)

Hypothetical necessity, according to Aristotle, applies to the case of artifacts and other objects coming into existence for an end, including natural objects. If there is to be a saw, the form of saw must be realized in an appropriate material. Equipped with only soft materials, an artisan no matter how capable cannot produce a saw. Similarly in nature, a lung requires a material that readily expands (669a14–b2). The possession of iron is not sufficient to generate a saw, but under the assumption that iron is the only suitable material, its possession is a necessary condition. Since

57 Cf. Hintikka (1973, pp. 136ff.). See also Waterlow (1982a), according to which all modal notions employed by Aristotle are temporalized and relative to the actual; on this analysis, Aristotle is in no position to make a distinction between simple necessity and eternal truth.

58 Cf. *Met.* 1026b27.

59 Much has been written on the question of whether hypothetical necessity applies to material necessity, and if it does not, whether this means that teleological explanations are ultimately reducible to material ones. See, e.g., Charlton (1970); Balme, (1972); Gotthelf (1976); Cooper (1985). Irrespective of the position one takes on this question, Aristotle's remarks about necessity due to the matter suffice to establish that any case of material necessity will satisfy the constraints of the *Posterior Analytics'* definition of necessity.

a hypothetically necessary, antecedent condition may obtain without the realization of the object in question, the fact that the object comes into existence is contingent. This, however, does not undermine the necessity of a hypothetically necessary proposition, for instance, (*S*) if a saw exists, it must be made of iron. If Aristotle's claim that iron is the only material that has the requisite properties is true (200a12), then (*S*) will be true in every instance and universal in application. Suppose, however, that there are other materials available and that a functional saw exists that is not made of iron. In this case, Aristotle might argue that a reformulated version of (*S*) would obtain. Under a sufficiently broad description, being made of such and such material will be universally true of saws. While a saw need not be made out of iron, if there is another equally hard substance available, it must be made of a hard substance that takes a sharp edge; strictly speaking, the hypothetically necessary relation holds between the material under the most general description applicable and the object.[60] It might still turn out that the material belongs to saws, because saws fall under a broader classification such as instruments for cutting, in which case the hypothetically necessary proposition would still not be primary although it would be universal (cf. 74a3–4). The solution to this difficulty would again be a reformulation of (*S*).

Does the consequent of (*S*) predicate an essential property of its subject? Aristotle entertains the suggestion.

> Perhaps the necessary is also in the definition. For if one defines the function of sawing as being a certain kind of dividing, then this cannot be unless the saw has teeth of a certain kind: and these cannot be unless it is of iron. (200b4–7)

If the material is part of the definition, then the hypothetically necessary attribute will be essential.[61] Since in the *Metaphysics*, however, Aristotle argues against making matter part of the definition of the essence, here he may have in mind a different claim, namely, that the type of material is fully determined by the material requirements for the realization of the function specified in the definition.[62] This is more problematic in light of the *Analytics'* conception of an essential attribute; for all that, Aristotle might believe that a slight modification of the definition of per se in I 4 would allow him to include, under the definition of necessary inherence, not only the attributes directly mentioned in the definition but also the ones that are direct consequences of it. The predication of an attribute of this sort would be true in every instance, albeit as a necessary, not a sufficient, condition. Aristotle is motivated to modify rather than reject the

60 At *Parts of Animals* I 1, 642a9–13, Aristotle envisages a series of premises to cover a similar case: the first posits a hard material and the second, either bronze or iron.

61 This will be true both of the abstract specification of ax that the artisan uses in making an ax and of the particular ax.

62 Cf. *Met.* 1036b27–29, 1037a22–24.

Analytics' position that the principles of a science are necessary, because he has an externalist conception of necessity. Necessity may be determined by the structure of the statement expressing a necessary relation, as in the case of the first two types of per se predication. However, at a deeper level, necessity is always determined by real relations in the external world. If what a necessary statement is about is necessary, the statement is necessary. This construal of necessity is, in part, a consequence of the *De Interpretatione* theory of meaning.

Because Aristotle believes that the universal generalizations of a biological science express real relations, he wants to articulate a concept of necessity that can be applied to them. Not surprisingly, he adopts the same strategy used for the material sciences and invokes hypothetical necessity. In *Parts of Animals* I 1, Aristotle introduces the topic of hypothetical necessity in terms familiar from the *Physics* and *De Generatione et Corruptione:*

> For necessity holds unqualifiedly of eternal phenomena; and hypothetical necessity holds of everything that is generated by nature as in everything that is produced by art, for instance, a house or something else. For if a house or other such product is to be realized, it is necessary that such and such material shall exist; and it is necessary that first this and then that shall be produced . . . until the end and that for the sake of which is reached. (639b24–31)

Hypothetical necessity is Aristotle's device for including the material cause in the case of coming to be under his concept of necessity. Hypothetical necessity thus understood maintains the priority of the formal cause in relation to the material cause, as does Aristotle's insistence upon functional definitions of organic bodies. A hand is not a hand unless it can perform the usual work of a hand (640b36–41a6).[63]

When Aristotle illustrates the method of explanation to be used in *Parts of Animals* I 1, he cites the case of respiration of which, although the whole process occurs for the sake of something, any arbitrarily selected stage will follow from the antecedent stages and material conditions by necessity (642a32–35). This illustration suggests that explanations of specific biological processes will often exhibit the regularity required by the stripped down version of simple necessity, where true in every instance is the salient feature.

A quite modest revision of the requirements for necessity in the *Physics* stretches that notion to include hypothetical necessity. In the *Parts of Animals,* however, Aristotle mentions three cases of hypothetical necessity, and two of these appear problematic.

63 A similar claim about universal generalization and natural science in general is made by Joachim (1922, pp. xxvii–xxviii), who argues that Aristotle believes that true sentences asserting that something happens for the most part can be eliminated by the substitution of appropriate unqualified universals.

Hence we should if possible say that since this is what it is to be a man, therefore he has these things; for he cannot be without these parts. If not this, then as near as possible to it, and we should either say altogether that it cannot be otherwise, or that it is at least good thus. (640a33–37)

How significant is the fact that here Aristotle broadens the concept of hypothetical necessity? The first type listed corresponds to the *Physics*' notion of hypothetical necessity. The context in which an essential attribute is predicated of a species determines whether the universal claim is hypothetically necessary or simply necessary. If the essential attribute is predicated in a context where a developmental process is at issue, then the universal statement is hypothetically necessary. If the universal statement takes the form of a universal generalization about the essential properties of a biological species, it meets the weaker criterion for simple necessity. The second type of necessity is arguably an unexceptional extension of the first. The saw's being made out of a hard material follows from its essence, but if the saw did not have other features derived from its made being made of iron, for instance, weight, it would not exist at all.

The third case seems to overturn the *Physics*' attempt to explicate hypothetical necessity in terms of the definition of the object that comes to be.[64] The definition of οἶκος (house) poses broad constraints on the materials that one can use to build a house and the steps that must be taken in order to produce from those materials a structure that will protect humans and chattel from the forces of nature.[65] Although it might be better to use a certain type of timber because it will last longer than any other type of timber, the definition will be satisfied by structures built with other types of timber. Hence the decision to use especially durable timber rests on extradefinitional considerations – perhaps the desire to build a structure that will endure for centuries.

For this reason, and because the context in *Parts of Animals* I 1 is somewhat ambiguous, we might wonder whether Aristotle intended to include the case of being better under hypothetical necessity. Perhaps, he merely intended to extend the concept of explanation to include, in addition to hypothetically necessary comings-to-be, also natural comings-to-be and changes that occur because it is better thus.[66] Elsewhere in the biologi-

64 This feature may explain why Aristotle does not always assimilate the case of the better to that of the necessary. In *De Gen. An.* I 4, he contrasts things happening through necessity (διὰ τὸ ἀναγκαῖον) to those happening on account of its being better thus (διὰ τὸ βέλτιον). However, since many explanations in biology appeal to what is better, here Aristotle includes it under hypothetical necessity.

65 Cf. *Metaphysics* VIII 2, 1043a15–18: those who define a house as stones, bricks, and timbers are speaking of the potential house, for these are the matter; but those who propose 'a receptacle to shelter chattels and living beings', or something of the sort, speak of the actuality.

66 I am indebted to J. Lennox for this suggestion.

cal corpus, Aristotle seems to contrast something's happening by necessity with its happening because it is better. For example, at *De Generatione Animalium* 738a33–b4, Aristotle asserts that the formation of the residue that provides the material for generation occurs necessarily in the female's body, because her system is too cold to ferment nourishment and blood and produce sperm; for the sake of the better, however, nature diverts the residue to the uterus and uses it for reproduction (cf. 717a15–17). This passage and others like it would decide the issue in favor of exclusion, except that Aristotle seems to be contrasting simple material necessity with what comes about because it is better, thus leaving the question of whether the latter is a case of hypothetical necessity unsettled.

Aristotle spells out the notion of final cause in the case of natural changes by appeal, not merely to some end or other but by appeal to what is better. The notion of a final cause in nature is defined in terms of 'better thus' (198b7) or 'the good' (983a32).[67] A sequence of events that is necessitated by the end of a process is hypothetically necessary; if that sequence is governed by nature, it will also be for the sake of the good. This leaves Aristotle with no motivation to distinguish between biological explanations in terms of final causes that invoke what is better thus and other explanations in terms of final causes that appeal to hypothetical necessity. Interpreting the definition of a natural species in accordance with his teleology has the consequence that in cases where there are several possible developmental sequences, the most optimal one will be realized.[68] Where the definition of an organ might be realized in a number of different structures, it will be realized in the structure that is best for the species in question.[69] In *De Generatione Animalium* II 6, Aristotle says that because nature does nothing in vain, it is necessary that the separation of the eyelids occur at the same time that the animal acquires the ability to move them (744a37–b1). Since the naturalist must appeal to the final cause to explain such phenomena and since hypothetical necessity is introduced in the *Physics* in order to specify the sense in which changes explained teleologically are necessary, Aristotle extends the notion of hypothetical necessity in *Parts of Animals* I 1 to cover explanations in terms of what is better thus.

Having abandoned the requirement that the attribute belong essentially to the subject, Aristotle substitutes a weaker relation between the

67 Cf. *Part. An.* 639b20–22, 645a22–27.

68 Any developmental sequence that would produce an organ capable of performing the function that is essential to the organ is a possible developmental sequence, only one of which is actualized in a given species.

69 Because the function of an organ defines it, Aristotle recognizes that very different physical structures can serve as the function and hence be the same organ in different species; e.g., the ability to smell is realized in quite different bodily parts in marine and land animals (cf. *De An.* 421b9–23).

subject and its hypothetically necessary attributes, such that hypothetical necessity is mediated through a strong teleological principle of natural development.[70] The biologist, like the cosmologist and the mathematician, investigates necessary relations. Paradigmatic features of species will inhere in any arbitrarily selected member of the species, unless the individual is maimed, and thus the true in every instance condition is maintained. In many instances, moreover, a hypothetically necessary attribute will also be essential to the species in question. By expanding the notion of necessity to include the third case of 'better thus', Aristotle is in a good position to claim that any sentence describing a characteristic feature of a species will express a necessary relation. Having recognized that not all the characteristics that the biologist investigates are essential attributes, Aristotle broadens the criteria for necessity rather than rejecting that notion as inapplicable in biology.

Aristotle's ubiquitous appeal to necessity, whenever the first premises of a science are at issue, is easily documented. Eliciting from these texts a consistent account of necessity has proved difficult. The notion of necessity that has emerged seems to have both an intensional component and an extensional one. In *Posterior Analytics* I 4, the favored definition of necessary predication makes necessity a consequence of definition. Demonstrative premises would be necessarily true, because true by analysis; their truth could be determined solely by appeal to the meanings of their constituent parts. However, even in *Posterior Analytics* I 4, a nonanalytic sense of necessity is introduced with the mention of a causally determined necessity. In other works, moreover, the weakening of the condition on belonging necessarily to belonging in every instance allows the laws of empirical cosmology to be viewed as just as necessary as the axioms of geometry. Hypothetically necessary, universal sentences also satisfy the true in every instance criterion. In the case of biological principles, this is even true of universal explanations that appeal to the better thus criterion.[71]

Is the concept of necessity that Aristotle develops in a number of contexts consistent with his theory of meaning? That was the question we set out to answer. Aristotle's practice of modifying the notion of necessity to fit the science at hand complicated our task. At this point, it should be clear that Aristotle does not draw a sharp distinction between an analytically necessary statement and necessity as a consequence of the external state of affairs that makes the statement necessarily true. In many con-

70 Furley (1985); and Sedley (1991). Both apply a strong teleological principle to all physical explanations in Aristotle, but this is too broad a construal; the principle is needed only in the case of certain explanations in biology.

71 This is not true in the case of artifacts because one need not build the best house possible to have built a house. Nature in Aristotle's view does in effect always select the better end.

texts, Aristotle explicitly subscribes to an externalist conception of necessity, on which the latter would explain the former. Aristotle might have offered a simple, syntactic account of hypothetical necessity as a necessary conditional sentence of the form, Nec [if *P*, then *Q*]. When he first introduces hypothetical necessity in *Physics* II 9, he comes fairly close to defining it in this way. However, he quickly shifts to talking about the material cause of an object, construed as a necessary condition for the existence of the object, as being necessary in relation to the object. A real relation, material constitution, or a stage in an actual developmental sequence, the existence of eyelids, for instance, is hypothetically necessary for the object so constituted or the functional capacity thus acquired. His theory of meaning makes meaning ultimately dependent upon the relation between specific mental states of language users and the external world, and thus (happily for Aristotle) the answer to our question is that his account of necessity is of the right sort for his semantics.

6 Language and Science

The theory of meaning summarized at *De Interpretatione* 1, 16a3–8, asserts that the significance of a term is determined by the object (*pragma*) to which the term refers.[72] The most likely interpretation of this claim construes the object referred to as an extralinguistic existent. If this interpretation (defended in Chapter 1 here) is correct, one would expect Aristotle to have a correspondence theory of truth and to give an externalist account of necessity. In this chapter, we have found that these expectations are met. A further consequence of Aristotle's conception of truth and necessity is the conception of the basic principles/premises of a science as expressions of necessary truths. This conception is evident in the definition of necessary premises in *Posterior Analytics* I 4, and it motivates Aristotle's application of the concept of necessity to the premises of the empirical sciences elsewhere. The next step in our investigation is to discover whether Aristotle's theory of meaning is also supported by the account of definition in the *Posterior Analytics* and by the account of theoretical science found in later writings.

In the *Categories* and the *De Interpretatione,* Aristotle's account of meaning and truth presupposes the mind's ability to get it right about the basic categories of reality and to express this knowledge in words. If these presuppositions prove to be justified, the strength of his position is apparent, for his account of meaning and truth is otherwise thorough and persuasive. The challenge Aristotle still faces is to resolve the tension be-

72 Strictly speaking, the significance of a term is due to its being a sign of a mental state. The mental state has the character it has, however, because it is a likeness of an external object, pace Kretzmann (1974, pp. 4–5).

tween his conception of science as a system of propositions expressing invariant essences and relations and his conception of language as empirically based and socially conditioned. One strategy open to Aristotle is to show that his theory fits the practices of mathematicians, scientists, and philosophers. By situating the explanation of the truth and necessity required by a science of its first premises in the world of physical objects, Aristotle strengthens the case for the applicability of his theory of meaning to the language of science. The next two chapters will look at Aristotle's attempt to establish that the paradigms of knowledge accepted in the theoretical sciences are consistent with his conception of meaning and truth.

3

Language of Science

That a spoken sound is significant is a function of its having an internal correlate in the mind. In semantic contexts, Aristotle identifies the mental state with a *logos* treated as a meaning or a specification of meaning in a definition. This condition on meaningful sounds is augmented by the requirement that true sentences must also correspond to extralinguistic states of affairs. A true sentence is reducible to an internalized *logos*, its meaning, since the sounds and/or graphic representations of it are signs of the mental state. Thus the correlation between the internal content and the external object specified by the theory of meaning becomes a threat to the existence of knowledge – or at least to our having any confidence that any particular sentence or body of assertions, such as those making up a demonstrative science, are true. Aristotle seeks to defuse this threat by in effect contextualizing the two relevant aspects of meaning, the *pathema* as a *logos* that is expressible in a natural language and the *pathema* as a likeness to an extralinguistic object. The context in which these are considered in the *Posterior Analytics* is the theory of demonstrative science, specifically, the theory of definition and the account of the origin of universals. The basic sentences or premises of a demonstrative science are true ex hypothesi. A demonstrative science is a deductive science, moreover, and this means that definitions of basic objects will be included among the primary premises. In the *Posterior Analytics,* Aristotle investigates the nature of scientific definition at length.

Because Aristotle's semantic theory is such that the basic concepts of a science will be, from one perspective, objects existing in the mind and, from another, objects existing in the world, to explain the acquisition of basic scientific concepts poses a fundamental challenge. Whether Aristotle ultimately meets this challenge remains to be seen. In view of the importance of the topic, it should come as no surprise that Aristotle takes several stabs at describing the way in which universals, the building blocks of language and knowledge, are acquired by human beings – in *Physics* I 1, *Posterior Analytics* II 19, and *Metaphysics* I 1–2. In *Physics* I 1, the acquisition of concepts is assimilated to the task of defining the basic terms of a science, as it is (for the most part) in *Posterior Analytics* II, and this approach will be examined in the next section. In *Posterior Analytics* II 19 (to be discussed in sections 2 and 3), Aristotle explains the acquisition of the basic concepts of a demonstrative science almost entirely from the perspective of the knowing mind, and in *Metaphysics* I 1–2, we find a similar emphasis. The connection between the external object and its internal concept is explained in part in *De Anima* III 8 (to be discussed in section 4), where Aristotle makes the perception of the external object the vehicle for the intelligible features of the object.

1 Definition and the Method of Division

The *Physics* opens with a discussion of the acquisition of general terms and first principles. Beginning with the statement that the things that are mixed together (συγκεχυμένα) are better known and clearer to us in contrast to the elements (στοιχεῖα) and principles (ἀρχαί) that are better known in themselves (184a21–23), Aristotle continues:

> Much the same thing happens in the relation of the name to the formula [λὸγον]. A name, e.g., circle, means vaguely a sort of whole; its definition [ὁρισμός] analyzes this into particular features. A child also at first calls all men 'father', and all women 'mother', but later distinguishes each of them. (184b10–14)

The picture is one of a group of one sort or another that is apprehended and labeled (circles, men, women) and then the constitutive concepts or parts are differentiated. To recognize circles is to be able to distinguish between circular shapes and other shapes. To recognize a circular shape, one need not possess the definition of circle. The latter is arrived at by analysis. According to Euclid, a circle is "a plane figure contained by one line such that all the straight lines lying on it from one point among those lying within the figure are equal one to another" (*Elem.* I, Defs.).[1] This definition, unlike the inchoate notion of circle, has distinguishable parts, which are, because articulated, individuated. Despite the obvious dissimilarities between the component concepts of a definition and concrete individuals, the infant's ultimate ability to distinguish between its mother and father and other persons of the same sex also involves analysis and individuation. The infant discerns that, besides having many features in common with other men, its father has certain distinctive features. This enables the infant to use πατρήρ correctly.

Aristotle mentions definition at the beginning not only of the *Physics* but also in many other treatises on specific topics in natural science and

1 Cf. *Post. Anal.* 92b20–22 for an abbreviated version of this definition. Even though Euclid's codification of geometry dates to the third century, many of the definitions and proofs found there are much earlier in origin.

philosophy. Definition is discussed at length in the *Posterior Analytics* because definition is an important component of demonstrative science. In the *Posterior Analytics,* the discussion centers on the examination of the Platonic theory of division. In *Physics* I 1, Aristotle uses διαίρειν (to divide) to describe the process that yields elements and first principles (a23), and then he immediately mentions definition. For Aristotle, the question of how to articulate a concept in a definition becomes the question of whether the method of division is the appropriate method to employ to articulate a concept.[2] Plato's method of division is the background theory against which Aristotle develops his account of definition.

The object of the method of division as employed by Plato (and indeed by Aristotle) is to produce precisely articulated analyses of concepts.[3] As described by Plato in the *Sophist* and elsewhere, division involves two processes. First, similar particulars are collected and grouped together under the most comprehensive term that seems to apply to them, for example, sophists under sophistry and types of sophistry under art.[4] Second, the comprehensive term is divided into two or three, slightly less general universals that fall immediately under it, and then the universal that the particulars seem to fall under is selected, and another cut is made in the same manner. This process continues until the narrowest universal that the particulars fall under is reached. The first sample division in the *Sophist* produces a definition of the art of angling:

> One half of all art was acquisitive – half of the acquisitive art was conquest or taking by force, half of this was hunting, and half of hunting was hunting animals; half of this was hunting water animals; of this again, the under half was fishing; half of fishing was striking; a part of striking was fishing with a barb, and half of this again, being the kind which strikes with a hook and draws the first from below upward, is the art which we have been seeking. (221a–c; Cornford trans.)

At this point, division has produced a precisely defined concept that fits the particulars. The initial, predefinitional understanding of angling was of a sort of fishing, a kind of whole; after the application of the method of division, angling is understood in terms of the genus and particular differentiae that define it. This fits Aristotle's description of definition at 184b13.[5]

2 Definition by division is discussed at length in *Posterior Analytics* II 13, *Metaphysics* VII 12,and *Parts of Animals* I 2–3.

3 Balme (1987, pp. 69–89) points to Plato's use of hunting metaphors in the characterization of division in the *Sophist* as evidence that, like Aristotle, who uses the same metaphor, Plato takes it as his primary objective to define not classify objects (p. 70).

4 *Sophist* 218e–232a; *Statesman* 258b–267c; *Philebus* 16c–17a.

5 The further examination of Aristotle's handling of division in the *Posterior Analytics* in this chapter and in the *Metaphysics* and *Parts of Animals* in Chapter 5 will establish that Aristotle adapts Plato's method to meet the needs of a demonstrative science. Cf. Balme (1987, pp. 71–80), who cites three innovations made by Aristotle in the Platonic method

Whereas a definition of angling is easily produced in the *Sophist,* the attempt to define the sophist's art initially generates six different definitions and finally, after the resolution of certain metaphysical puzzles about negation and not-being, a seventh and truly adequate definition. On the one hand, the six attempts at division of the concept 'art' in order to produce a definition of 'sophist' dramatize the Eleatic stranger's claim that the sophist is a slippery fellow, who is hard to catch, but presumably Plato is also using them to demonstrate how division should proceed.[6] The first issue to settle is whether the items collected at the outset and subsumed under the definition are individual sophists or particular types of sophistry; the assumption, however, that individuals are the initial objects of collection that are then subsumed under the basic concepts to be defined makes the most sense of Plato's procedure.[7]

The first five divisions produce what at first blush appear to be five perfectly adequate definitions of five different types of sophist; the sixth division, about which the Eleatic Stranger and Theaetetus express reservations, affords a description of activities that might fall under the term 'sophistry' in common parlance. The hypothesis that the initial divisions are guided by fixing attention on one or more actual persons falling under the extension of the term 'sophist' as used in ordinary language gives us a handle on why the first six definitions are generated and also why the seventh and last definition is deemed superior to its predecessors. The Stranger initiates a search for the sophist and then as the result of employing six different strategies for dividing 'art' and the subordinate universals produces six different definitions of the term 'sophist' – each of which seems to fit certain actual sophists. The second and third definitions differ only in that according to the second, the sophist travels from city to city as a merchant of ideas, and according to the third, the sophist stays in one city as a retailer of ideas. The third and fourth definitions dif-

of division, and Ferejohn (1991, pp. 19–31), who argues that the function of division for Aristotle is to establish that demonstrative premises are primary and immediate.

6 In the initial presentation of the six definitions of 'sophist', the specification of the divisions is sometimes elliptical and different terms sometimes appear in the summary of the definition than were used in the original division. For instance, at 223c hunting is contrasted with exchange, yet the division taken over from the earlier definition of angling divides acquisitive arts into those employing conquest and exchange and those employing conquest into combat and hunting. At the beginning of the first definition, hunting is simply divided into the hunting of land and water animals (221e) as it had been in the case of angling, but in the summary of the first definition, hunting is implicitly divided into animal hunting and some other unnamed category and animal hunting divides into the hunting of land and water animals (223b). Even the number of definitions that the division has yielded eludes Theaetetus, who, summing up the results, confuses the fourth and fifth definitions at 225e as he recognizes at 231d. These differences make the task of diagramming the method of division more difficult; the illustration to follow stays as close to the text as possible.

7 Plato does not seem to distinguish between class inclusion and class membership. See Moravscik (1973).

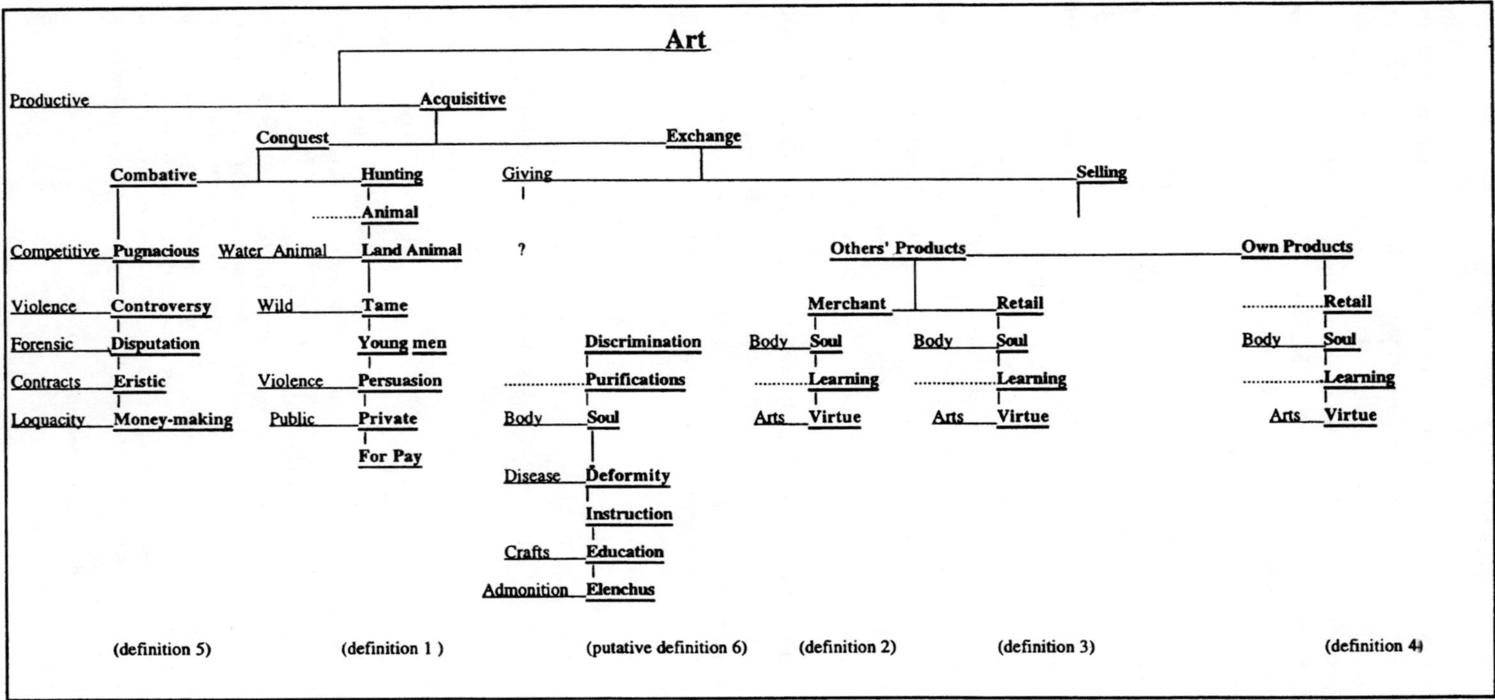

Illustration of the initial attempt to define 'sophist', which yields six different definitions (*Sophist* 221c–232a). Bold-faced type indicates concepts that figure in at least one definition. The two concepts resulting from a division of a broader concept are connected by a horizontal line. The final steps of each definition are in the same column.

fer only in that according to the third, the sophist retails the goods of another, and according to the fourth, the sophist retails his own work. Included among these definitions is a description (definition 6) that no doubt Plato would accept as a specification of Socrates' art: "a purifier of the soul from conceits that block the way to understanding" (232e). The inclusion of this definition is evidence that the initial divisions represent an attempt to classify usages of the term as applied to individuals; since many of Plato's contemporaries considered Socrates a sophist, he would have been included in the initial collection of sophists.[8] The Eleatic Stranger sets all these definitions aside, however, on the grounds that they fail to capture the single nature shared by all sophists. At a deeper level, the defect revealed by the plethora of definitions is not that these definitions fail to delineate a concept that fits some persons called sophists, nor that taken jointly they fail to have exactly the same extension as σοφιστής (sophist) in ordinary language, but rather that these definitions are too closely tied to the extension of the term to articulate the common core concept that is at issue here.[9]

Now does it strike you that when one who is known by the name of a single art appears to be master of many, there is something wrong with this appearance? If one has that impression of any art, plainly it is because one cannot see clearly that feature of it in which all these forms of skill converge, and so one calls their possessor by many names instead of one. (232a; Cornford trans.)

A perspicuous rendering of the core concept will enable the philosopher to differentiate between correct and incorrect applications of the term.

In short, there are several stages of collection and subsequent division. First, the individuals falling under the extension of the concept as popularly used are collected under a generic concept and the subsequent divisions produce a group of narrowly circumscribed concepts that disjunctively hold of all the individuals in the first collection. Then these concepts are collected for a renewed attack on the problem.[10] The final definition articulates the core notion shared by all the particular concepts that (correctly) fall under the definiendum: "the art of contradic-

8 Had Socrates been sharply distinguished from the sophists in the popular imagination, Aristophanes' caricature of Socrates in the *Clouds* would not have succeeded. Cf. Dover (1971, pp. 50–77), who argues that Socrates was well known in Athens in 424/23 and that Aristophanes, while aware of the differences between Socrates and the sophists, did not attach any importance to these differences. "But in order to understand the *Clouds* we must make an imaginative effort to adopt an entirely different position, the position of someone to whom all philosophical and scientific speculation, all disinterested intellectual curiosity, is boring and silly. To such a person distinctions which are of fundamental importance to the intellectual appear insignificant, incomprehensible, and often imperceptible" (p. 71).

9 Cf. Aristotle who also rejects possibility of genuine definition (ὁρισμός) by conjunction (92b30–32, 1030b7–13; cf. 93b35–38).

10 Cf. Aristotle's description of collection and division at *Post. Anal.* II 13, 97b16–26.

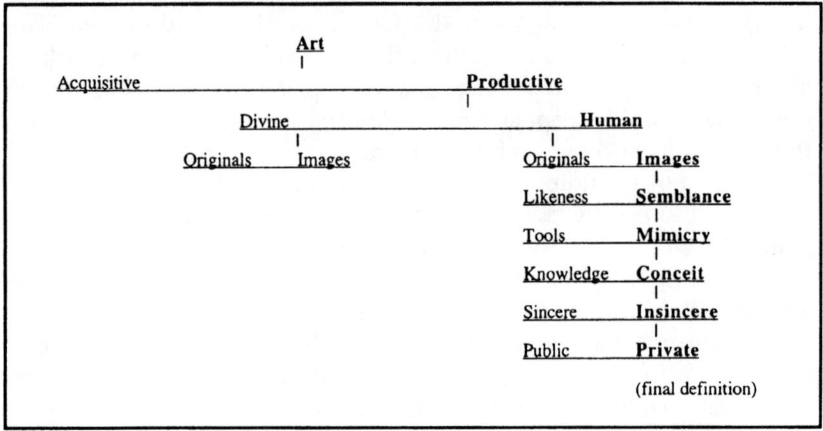

Illustration of final and authoritative definition of 'sophist' by division (*Sophist* 264e–268d).

tion making, descended from an insincere kind of conceited mimicry of the semblance-making breed, derived from image making, distinguished as a portion, not divine but human, of production" (268c–d). The final definition achieves this objective by determining a concept that applies to five of the particular concepts and excludes the purifier of souls. This concept would apply to all and only the types of activity that Plato believes to be genuine instances of sophistry. Because at this stage the inquiry is guided by intensional rather than extensional considerations, the definition is normative and need not hold of all the individuals falling under the extension of the term as ordinarily used. If this picture of Platonic division is right, then the analogy drawn between definition and the correct use of a name in the *Physics* can be understood as drawing attention to another case where a group of particulars are made intelligible by articulating the features that are shared and those that are distinctive. The term 'sophist' is applied to a large number of individuals without distinguishing between them. The initial definitions produced by division make their differences explicit while the final definition, the one that captures "the genuine sophist," reveals the distinctive features of all forms of sophistry properly delimited and excludes the purifier of souls who employs *elenchus* and might mistakenly be called a sophist. All the definitions by division canvassed in the *Sophist* distinguish within the whole group of persons denoted by 'sophist' in ordinary discourse the particular concept(s) (τὰ καθ' ἕκαστα) that are applicable to each case. Here we might compare the linguistic behavior of the child in the *Physics* who applies the terms 'mother' and 'father' too widely. Insofar as a term is applied without reference to its proper definition, it is applied to an indefinite number of individuals, one of whom may fall under its proper extension and several of whom do not. Its extension is restricted to a definite group by the definition.

Plato's description of division in the *Sophist* has proven a useful tool for interpreting Aristotle's brief remarks about definition in *Physics* I 1. In addition, the first five definitions of sophist jointly are coextensive with the final definition, and the final definition differs from these formulations in specifying the essential features of a sophist. The difference corresponds to the distinction Aristotle draws between nominal and essential definitions, between the lexical definitions of natural language and the technical definitions required for science. This difference also brings to the foreground one of the challenges Aristotle faces – how to accommodate the normative function of scientific definition in contrast to linguistic definition. The first six definitions of 'sophist' are "Aristotelian" in being based upon the assumption that the meaning of the term 'sophist' is determined by its extension. Definition by extension is easily handled on the *De Interpretatione* theory of meaning. The final, intensional definition of 'sophist' is more problematic, and yet not only Plato's normative definitions but also Aristotle's definitions of essence refine and correct the definitions that capture ordinary linguistic meanings.

Definition is discussed at length in *Posterior Analytics* II, as is division as a method for establishing definitions. In the *Posterior Analytics,* Aristotle investigates whether essential nature can be demonstrated, whether demonstration and definition are the same thing, whether there is more than one type of definition, and whether substance can be defined through division. In II 3, Aristotle begins by citing a number of reasons why definitions of essence are not demonstrations of essence. No sooner has he concluded that "there is no identical object of which it is possible to possess both a definition and a demonstration" (91a8–10), than he reconsiders the matter.

> Is deduction – i.e., demonstration – of what a thing is possible or, as our recent argument assumed, is it not possible? (II 4, 91a13–14)

Aristotle believes that a statement of the essential nature of an entity is required for demonstrative knowledge of the entity. Such statements are definitions. More generally, a demonstrative premise expresses an essential connection, in virtue of which the premise is necessarily true.[11] This makes the question of the epistemic warrant of a definition of essence a pressing matter for Aristotle. He considers whether division is a form of proof that yields definitions. He grants that the method of division may yield definitions; however, he rejects division's claim to be a type of inference (91b12–27; *Pr. Anal.* 46a32–7). The definition is arrived at

11 See Chapter 2, section 4.

through division by making a number of assumptions in the course of the division; using the Platonic method of division to show that a human is a mortal animal, the definer assumes that humans are animals and consequently begs the question (46b7–12). The truth of the formula that results from the application of the method of division is not guaranteed by the procedure. Nor can division ensure that the predicates constitute a genuine unity, which is a requirement for real definition (92a29–33). Following this line of argument to its apparent conclusion, Aristotle arrives at an impasse.

It appears then from these considerations that neither definition and syllogism nor their objects are the same, and further that definition neither demonstrates nor proves anything, and that essence is not known either by definition or by demonstration. (II 7, 92b35–39)

Upon the reexamination of these issues in II 8–12, Aristotle concludes that the essential nature of a thing that has a cause other than itself is known through demonstration, although it is not demonstrated, and that the essential nature of a thing that has no cause other than itself is expressed in immediate (indemonstrable), primary premises. Some of the initial *aporias* about definition were the result of not differentiating between types of definition.

Therefore one type of definition [ὁρισμός] is an indemonstrable account [λόγος] of the essence, another is a deduction of an essence, differing in aspect from a demonstration; a third type is the conclusion of a demonstration of essence. (II 10, 94a11–14; cf. 75b30–32)

Although a demonstrative science may include all three types of definitions, the first type is the most important, for only definitions of this type will be included among the basic premises of a science.

In II 10, Aristotle also resolves another puzzle about definition raised in II 7; this puzzle challenges the assumption that there is a difference between a definition that merely explicates the meaning of a word (a nominal definition) and a definition that reveals an essence (92b27–35).[12] Intuitively, there seems to be some difference between the two, and in II 7, having argued that definitions of essences are not proofs, Aristotle worries about how to specify the difference between them and mere specifications of linguistic meaning.

If, therefore, the definer proves either what a thing is or what the name signifies, then if it has nothing at all to do with what a thing is, a definition [ὁρισμός] will be a formula [λόγος] signifying the same as a name. But that is absurd. (92b26–28; cf. 92b5–8, b31–32)

12 Not only does the distinction between nominal and real definitions play a central role in the account of definition in *Posterior Analytics* II 7–10, it also plays a central role in the discussion of substance in *Metaphysics* VII; for the latter, see the discussion in Part II, Chapter 5.

The definition (*logos*) of the name covers a variety of cases. Definitions of this sort may hold of nonexistent objects such as goatstags (92b7–8). They may also be wholes, the unity of which is secured by conjunction, for instance, the lines of the *Iliad* (92b32, 93b35–37), or by disjunctive wholes, for instance, the different characteristics labeled μεγαλοψυχία (pride) (97b13–25). Differences among the items classified as accounts to be distinguished from definitions of essence have prompted some commentators to maintain that not all these cases are types of nominal definition. Some have argued that only existing objects can have nominal definitions, and others have argued that the nominal definition should be distinguished from a mere definition of a name.[13] If the difference between linguistic definitions and scientific ones is Aristotle's primary concern, however, he would be better served by a notion of nominal definition that covers all the items he discusses, since they correspond to recognizable types of linguistic definition.

The distinction between nominal and real definitions is, nevertheless, somewhat surprising in the context of a theory of meaning that has made meaning a function of reference to extralinguistic objects. A simple one-to-one correlation holding between linguistic concepts and types of existents would result in all linguistic definitions being partial or complete real definitions. For good reason, Aristotle explicitly rejects this naive picture in the *Posterior Analytics.* Even though linguistic meaning depends upon some relation between the mental content and its referent, the mental content expressible as the linguistic meaning may be confused or may lack specificity.

Both nominal and real definitions are expressible in language. Any significant expression, irrespective of whether its referent actually exists, will have a nominal definition. Unlike the nominal definition, a proper definition is an account of the cause of the thing's existence, and it is a statement of the essential nature of the thing (93b29–94a10).[14] Ex hypothesi, a definition of essence must be satisfied by actually existing entities, which possess the essence in question. Aristotle looks for some intrinsic characteristic of the definition of essence that would differentiate it from a nominal definition. One indication of the difference between the two, he finds, is that the nominal definition possesses only an artificial unity, while the real definition is one essentially (93b35–37). Because the definitions of basic objects must be unified in a nonarbitrary manner, Aristotle is prompted to revisit the method of division in II 13.

Despite his earlier reservations about division, Aristotle resuscitates the method of division in II 13, not as a form of demonstration, but as a

13 The former position is taken by Bolton (1976); the latter, by Demos and Devereux (1988, pp. 133–54).

14 Aristotle claims that knowing the cause of a thing's existence is the same as knowing what it is (93a3–4).

method of definition. A definition arrived at by division does not prove that the definition it yields is satisfied by any actual existent; consequently, the role Aristotle envisages for division is that of clarifying and systematizing the definitions of a science, not producing them out of whole cloth.[15]

> To establish a definition by division, one should aim for three things – grasping that which is predicated in what the thing is, ordering these as first or second, and establishing that these are all there are. (97a24–27)

The method of division is useful in distinguishing the differentiae of a genus, and it ensures that no differentia has been omitted (96b25–97a6).

> But it makes a difference which attributes are predicated first and following, e.g., whether we say animal-tame-biped, or biped-animal-tame. For if every definable thing consists of two elements and animal-tame forms a unity, and again out of this the differentia man is, then what we assume has necessarily been reached by division. (96b30–35)

Since, at each stage, the differentia cited is predicable of all the preceding terms, but not of the succeeding terms, division produces an ordering of the differentiae that displays the unity of the definiens. This is the role Aristotle assigns the method of division in a demonstrative science; this is a more restricted function than Plato envisaged for division, and construing the goal of division as a device for establishing the unity of the definition results in Aristotle's emphasizing successive differentiation.[16]

Aristotle envisages a process of collecting cases that fall under the same term, for example, 'pride', and then of searching for the common character (97b16–26).[17] There need not always be a common character; in which case, the attempt at definition by division reveals that despite a common term more than one concept is involved. Division begins with an assumed genus and an assumed *infima species* and then attempts to articulate the *differentiae* of the genus in a way that yields the *infima species* in question. If the method is employed systematically, it will alert the would-be definer to problematic initial assumptions. No amount of attention to procedural details will make division absolutely foolproof, and

15 J. Lennox (1987, pp. 90–119) defends a role for division in the preexplanatory stage of Aristotelian science. Cf. Ferejohn (1991, p. 29).

16 Cf. Balme (1987, pp. 73–4), which argues that the requirement for successive differentiation in the *Posterior Analytics* is an Aristotelian modification of Platonic division that is itself modified in *Parts of Animals* I 2–3. Because I agree with Balme that the latter text's treatment of division has more to do with metaphysics than logic, I shall address it in Chapter 5.

17 The method of division described by Aristotle at 97b16–26 seems to be the same method as the one labeled dialectic and offered as the method of philosophy by Plato in the *Sophist* at 253d. Division as a method for displaying the unity of a definition to be employed in a demonstration must meet the additional requirement of successive differentiation.

thus Aristotle does not retract the charge that division establishes a definition based on initial assumptions that are simply accepted.[18] Like demonstration, definition by division will secure its results in relation to its initial starting points.

2 The Foundations

Aristotle pays surprisingly little attention to the question of the ultimate origins of basic concepts. The distinction between real and nominal definitions in this context is a distinction between concepts that represent things precisely as they are and concepts that refer to external objects but lack the characteristics required of scientific definitions.[19] As we have seen, neither the method of division nor the requirements of meaning guarantee that a putative definition of essence expresses a real nature. The challenge facing Aristotle is to give an account of the apprehension of the basic concepts expressed in real definitions. Many, perhaps all, of the basic premises of a demonstrative science are definitions of basic objects. While Aristotle has recommended a method for producing the right sort of definition, that method, like demonstration, is based on the presupposition that unmediated knowledge of basic objects is possible. In the last chapter of the *Posterior Analytics,* Aristotle finally addresses this question.[20] He construes it as a question about the acquisition of basic universals by the human mind. As described, the process seems to be one that yields both the universal concepts required by natural language and the exact concepts required for demonstrative knowledge. The basic universals that are the building blocks of language, art, and science are acquired through the knower's encountering the *pragmata* of the physical world. The encounter with the world is essential; fully developed universal concepts, Aristotle argues, are not innate (99b26–32). The external world manifests a particular structure and the human mind possesses an innate capacity to apprehend this structure on the basis of perception and memory.[21] An individual acquires language through perception and memory. He or she learns to

18 Even though an unsuccessful attempt at division may lead the definer to modify the initial assumptions, whenever a definition is successfully generated, its derivation depends upon a set of initial assumptions that are not discharged in the course of the division.

19 Cf. Demos and Devereux (1988, p. 146): "However, grasping a nominal definition does entail 'knowledge of existence' in the sense of the ability to discern genuine instances when confronted with them."

20 The literature on *Posterior Analytics* II 19 is extensive. Important among the recent contributions are Barnes (1994); Lesher (1973, pp. 44–68); Kahn (1981); Kosman (1973); and Modrak (1987a, chap. 7).

21 From here on out I shall use 'mind' to mean 'human mind'. This is not the place to consider the nature of divine mind. I have discussed the latter in Modrak (1987b; 1989; and 1991, 755–74).

associate the sound ἄνθρωπος (*anthropos*) with the content of the idea acquired through perceiving human beings.

Four times, and each time quite cryptically, Aristotle tells a story about the mind's ability to retain the contents of perceptions and group memories together on the basis of similarity and finally to generalize from particular cases to natural kinds and other universals. The final attempt is made at 100a15-b3:

> What we have just said but not said clearly, let us say again: when one of the undifferentiated things takes a stand, the first universal is in the mind [ψυχῇ] for although one perceives the particular, perception is of the universal, e.g., of man but not of Callias the man. Again a stand is taken in these, until the undivided, that is, the universal stands, e.g., such and such an animal stands until animal stands, and in this in the same way. (100a15-b3)

It is striking that here, as in *De Interpretatione* 1, the universal is viewed as a mental content standing in a particular relation to an external object. The character of the mental state is determined by the object. The process begins with the perception of objects in the world. These objects present themselves as concrete individuals and simultaneously as exemplifications of universals. The characteristics of an individual (e.g., Callias) are determined by the kind of thing the individual is. Callias cannot have four legs; if he is not maimed, he must have hands rather than paws. Such human characteristics differentiate him from all nonhuman objects, including other animals, and they are much more important and immediately present to sense than the features of his hands that differentiate him from other humans. Thus Aristotle claims that the perception is not properly speaking of Callias the man, but of man; that is, it is of (an exemplification of) the universal human being. This universal is a natural kind. To apprehend it is to grasp a feature of the world. The object not only exemplifies a particular species, it also exemplifies the other universals that the species falls under; Callias is not only a human but also an animal and also a living being.

In the *Categories,* species such as man are said to be more properly substance than genera such as animal, and in *Metaphysics* VII, Aristotle argues that the species form is substance but denies that the genus is (1038b30–33). The distinction between the substance type and other kinds the individual falls under is also in evidence in II 19. Aristotle portrays the mind's apprehension of the broader universals, such and such animal and animal, not as the immediate consequence of the perception of the individual but rather as a consequence of the recognition that the individual exemplifies a lower-level universal. Just as the characteristics of Callias are largely determined by his being human, the characteristics of the natural kind, human being, are largely determined by its falling under the broader universal, such and such animal (e.g., tame pedestrian), and that in turn by falling under animal.

It is noteworthy that this description, like its three predecessors in II 19, is centered on a series of cognitions and cognitive processes. The few references to the mind (soul) in this context emphasize its passivity, its role as the seat of the cognitive processes. It is striking that here, as in *De Interpretatione* 1, the universal is viewed as a mental content standing in a particular relation to an external object. The character of the mental state is determined by the object. Aristotle insists upon the agency of the external object of perception in the *De Anima.* In II 19, we are told that the soul is capable of undergoing a process that issues in knowledge of universals. In the *Metaphysics,* when describing rudimentary generalizations, Aristotle talks about many memories producing the faculty (*dunamis*) of experience (980b29). By sketching the details of the cognitive process in a way that makes the apprehension of a universal the result of successive manifestations of an external object as an object of cognition, Aristotle hopes to eliminate any peculiarly mental characteristics of the objects of knowledge and thereby eliminate the need to posit any source other than the external world for our concepts.

A very similar description of the acquisition of universals is found in *Metaphysics* I 1, with the difference that the topic is approached from a sketch of the historical advance of knowledge. Just as the individual moves from the particulars of sense perception to the universals of knowledge, collectively humans have moved from the immediate concerns of survival, initially met through ad hoc solutions based on perception and experience, to the arts based on generalization that enabled effective problem solving and ultimately generated leisure time. With leisure, people were able to achieve the abstract level of understanding characteristic of mathematics, philosophy, and the other theoretical sciences. This account supplements the one in the *Posterior Analytics* by appealing to a historical process and by developing in far greater detail both the characterization of experience, which provides the bridge between the particulars of perception and the universals of art and science, and the characterization of philosophy, which stands at the pinnacle of science and is its paradigmatic exemplar.

> Now art arises when from many notions gained by experience one universal judgment about similar cases is produced. For to have a judgment that this helped Callias when he was ill of this disease, and similarly in the case of Socrates and in many individual cases, is a matter of experience; but to judge that it has helped all such persons, marked off in one class, when they were ill of this disease, e.g., phlegmatic or bilious people when burning with fever – this is a matter of art. (981a5–12)

As described here, experience consists in many notions (ἐννοημάτων). The external world through sense perception acts on the mind, producing not only perceptions and memories, but also particular conceptualizations of the observed phenomena. The experienced person is in a position to articulate these observations in sentences describing the effects of the medication on this patient and that one. Experience comes into play when past and present observations are grouped together and common features are recognized and generalizations based on these features are made. Aristotle remarks that experience can be as useful in a particular instance as art (981a13-b9); whether Socrates is given the appropriate medicine on the basis of experience or on the basis of the art of medicine will make no difference to his recovery.[22] By grouping together appropriate memories, the experienced person is able to make use of generalizations and to bring past observations to bear on the present situation. Insofar as this person employs generalizations, experience can be said to produce homespun universals, and Aristotle's description of experience in the *Posterior Analytics* suggests as much.[23] What experience does not yield are universals in the technical sense of the *Posterior Analytics*' definition of universal, and Aristotle often marks the divide between experience and art by employing the contrast between particular and universal in the strict sense.[24] The scope of the universals of art and science should be such that the universal is predicable of all and only those objects that exemplify the universal characteristic at issue, and this is equally true for the universal principles of art and science, where one universal description is predicated universally of another. The difference in scope and character between the rudimentary universals of experience and the universals of art and science parallels the difference between linguistic meanings and scientific definitions.

The dynamic aspect of the relation between the sensible particular and the universal is also more fully developed in *Metaphysics* I. In contrast to *Posterior Analytics* 100a16–18, where the role of the universal in perception is stressed, *Metaphysics* I stresses the importance of the individual to the exercise of an art.

> For the physician does not cure man, except in an incidental way, but Callias or Socrates or some other named in this way, who happens to be a man. (981a18–20)

The art of medicine consists in knowledge of the universal regularities governing human health. These universals are culled from the experience of treating ill human beings. But unless the medical practitioner is able to apply the appropriate universal to an actual case of illness in an individual, the practitioner will fail to exercise the art. Even though the theoretical sciences do not bring universals to bear on particulars in the way that the arts must, the continuity of the process from perceptual experience to art to science ensures that putative knowledge here too would

22 See *N. E.* 1141b16–21, *Met.* 981a13–24.

23 At *Posterior Analytics* II 19, 100a6–9, Aristotle glosses experience as the whole universal now stabilized in the soul, from which art and science come.

24 See, e.g., *Met.* 981a15–20.

be evaluated in terms of how well the universal fits observation. For instance, a putative geometrical relation that, when applied by the architect or the navigator, led to failure would undoubtedly prompt the geometer to reconsider.[25] Unlike experience, according to *Metaphysics* I, art and science provide an understanding of causes. Through experience, a person recognizes that such and such is so but not why it is so.[26] In this respect, too, experience is more akin to perception than science (cf. 981b10–11). Knowledge that something is the case precedes knowledge of its cause (89b29–31). Aristotle envisages a progressive development where there are no quantum jumps between cognitive stages but rather smooth transitions from one stage to another as understanding deepens. First, someone notices that a particular medication benefits an ill Socrates; in time she grasps that this type of medication alleviates the suffering of other individuals having similar symptoms; subsequently recognizing the regularity governing the medication's effectiveness, she understands why it is beneficial.

Both in *Posterior Analytics* II 19 and in *Metaphysics* I 1, the cognitive movement is from particulars to universals. A different cognitive process seems to be involved in the articulation of concepts described in *Physics* I 1.

> What is to us plain and obvious at first is rather disordered mixtures [τὰ συγκεχυμένα], and later the elements and principles of which become known to us by analysis. Hence we must advance from the universal to particulars; for a whole is better known through sense perception, and a universal is a kind of whole; for the universal comprehends many things within it, like parts. (184a21–26)

On closer examination, this passage turns out to be about the movement from particulars apprehended in a mix of related items to precisely defined universal concepts. According to the story told in the *Posterior Analytics,* memory collects and groups together similar perceptual contents. It is the source of the mixture mentioned in the *Physics.* Memory groups together round shapes or adults of the same sex. Since the grounds for forming these groups are perceptual and not yet fully articulated, the particulars are mixed together and mistakes of the sort the infant makes are common. In time the mind begins to make the rudimentary discriminations characteristic of experience. The young child, who is able to identify its own parents correctly and to recognize that other children may have different parents, may not be able to articulate the grounds for these discriminations. This child would fit Aristotle's description of the person having experience without knowledge. An older child who has a precise

25 Typically, however, Aristotle stresses the priority of abstract knowledge to the practical art employing it. See, e.g., *Metaphysics* I 1 and *Politics* 1282a7–12.

26 Cf. *Post. Anal.* I 13, which also ranks knowing why (τὸ διότι) over knowing that (τὸ ὅτι); cf. *N.E.* VI 7.

concept of mother knows the relevant universal.[27] A mature biologist possesses the type of *episteme* under which the concepts of female and male parents are subsumed.

In *Posterior Analytics* II 19, Aristotle speaks of a rout stopped in battle and the resumption of positions. This metaphor also suggests a conglomerate of individuals where the distinctions between different types and roles of warriors has been lost. When the rout ends with the army reassembling and standing its ground, there is an ordered arrangement of men that displays the functional differences among individuals as well as their functional equivalence.[28] The former aspect is emphasized in *Physics* I 1 and the latter in *Posterior Analytics* II 19. Putting the two texts together produces a coherent story about the acquisition of the precise definitions of science. This story, moreover, can accommodate the jumble of objects presented in sense experience. Initially presented in a way that seems to defy definition, the contents of perceptions display a structure that once recognized provides the basis for definition and knowledge.

The spotlight is on the relation between particular and universal and the relation between the corresponding faculties, perception and knowledge, in all three texts, *Posterior Analytics* II 19, *Metaphysics* I 1, and *Physics* I 1. All three address the topic of the knowledge of first principles. The first does so within an abstract epistemological framework, the second with an eye to characterizing the most abstract, theoretical science, first philosophy, and the third with an eye to characterizing the least abstract, theoretical science, natural science.[29] That Aristotle begins both the discussion of the objects of metaphysics and the objects of physics by probing the intimate connection between the objects of perception and the objects of knowledge and exploring the dual character of both shows how much importance he attaches to this relation. The extralinguistic world of objects is immediately accessible to the human cognizer through perception; an exercise of perception is the realization of features of the world as features of consciousness.[30] Both language and knowledge depend on the apprehension of universals. To avoid the bifurcation of the world into the world of objects and the world as configured in human languages and described by human sciences, Aristotle elaborates an account of the characteristics of extramental objects such that the universals of language and science are expressions of these characteristics. In *Posterior*

27 The knowledge of universals required to understand a particular sentence in a natural language would fall short of *techne* or *episteme* (forms of knowledge in Aristotle's technical sense) because these are constituted by understanding the relations obtaining among an interrelated group of universals.

28 Cf. *Politics* 1261a23–27.

29 Aristotle divides the theoretical sciences into three types: first philosophy (*sophia*), the most abstract, mathematics and natural science, the most concrete (*Met.* I 2, *Met.* VI 1, *E.N.* VI 8). All the theoretical sciences are more abstract than and superior to the arts.

30 See Modrak (1987a, chaps. 5 and 6).

Analytics II 19, Aristotle concentrates on the apprehension of the objects that are articulated in the first principles of a demonstrative science. The account he gives where natural kinds determine universal concepts and principles provides further evidence that meanings are individuated by relations to external objects as required by his theory of meaning.

3 Basic Concepts and First Principles

In the preceding section, Aristotle's discussion of *archai* in *Posterior Analytics* II 19 was read as a description of the acquisition of the first principles of art and science. This interpretation is not without detractors. For centuries, commentators have puzzled about and quarreled over Aristotle's intentions in II 19. Is Aristotle describing the process by which concepts are acquired or a process by which the basic premises of a demonstrative science are acquired? While the latter is his stated objective, his examples ('human', 'animal') suggest the former. Elsewhere I have argued that this dilemma is false because the distinction between basic premise and basic concept is alien to Aristotle's thinking.[31] Why this is so should become clearer as we examine Aristotle's notion of a basic concept. A second area of disagreement among commentators is the relation between Aristotle's four descriptions of the cognitive process labeled *epagoge,* by which the mind acquires basic concepts or principles, and his assertion that *nous* is the faculty by which the basic concepts or principles are known. Let us consider this question first and having settled it return to the issue of the characteristics of basic concepts.

Let us turn to Aristotle's four attempts to describe the acquisition of basic concepts (99b32–100b5).[32] Although all four descriptions concern a process that begins in perception and terminates in the apprehension of universals, they differ from each other in interesting ways. The first two

31 Modrak (1987a, chap. 7; and 1981, pp. 63–83). Kahn (1981) correctly sums up Aristotle's view when he says that for Aristotle there is no dichotomy between a conceptual and a propositional view of principles.

32 A preliminary comment about terminology: in order to minimize the assumptions built into my account, I shall use 'basic concept' for Aristotle's basic objects (concepts or principles) and 'universal' to translate his terms, τὸ καθόλου or τὰ καθολου. Aristotle uses a plethora of terms to describe the object of investigation in II 19. He initiates the inquiry as one concerning *archai,* principles (99b17); in the description of the cognitive process yielding the objects of art and science, he uses a variety of terms, namely, *katholou,* universal (100a6, 100a16, 100b2, 100b5); *arche,* principle (100a8); *prota,* primitives (100b4); and *protai archai,* primary principles (99b21). He also describes this object as a one over many (100a7), which is undifferentiated (100a16) and undivided (100b2). Finally, *nous* is said to grasp *archai,* principles (100b9, b12). No harm will be done by stipulating that 'basic concept' includes Aristotle's 'primitives', 'primary principles', and 'principles', nor will this practice prejudice the case in favor of my interpretation. Even if one wishes to argue that Aristotle distinguishes between basic concepts and basic premises in II 19, the argument cannot be based on his use of *prota, protai archai,* and *archai.*

descriptions characterize the process in terms of the shifts from one cognitive state to another, namely, from perception to memory, to experience, to art and science. The last two descriptions of the process are more informative because they trace the evolution of the object of the original cognition (perception) to the object of the final cognition (*episteme*), from the perception of an individual human being, Callias, to the scientific understanding of the universal human being. Aristotle concludes:

Indeed it is clear that we must recognize the primitives [τά πρῶτα] by induction; for even perception introduces the universal [τὸ καθόλου] in this way. (100b3–5)

Epagoge (ἐπαγωγή) is standardly translated as 'induction', but we should not lose sight of the fact that '*epagoge*' is Aristotle's term for the process described in II 19, and this process is a far cry from the modern identification of induction with empirical generalization from as large a sample as possible to a general conclusion.[33] Throughout the *Analytics, epagoge* is associated with the apprehension of the indemonstrable basic premises of demonstration, as is *nous.* The same account is given by Aristotle in the *Nicomachean Ethics.*

Induction [*epagoge*] is then the starting-point, even of the universal, while syllogism proceeds from universals. Therefore there are starting-points from which syllogism proceeds, which are not reached by syllogism; it is therefore by induction that they are reached. Scientific knowledge is then a state of capacity to demonstrate. (*N.E.* VI 3, 1139b28–32)

In II 19, the universals, human, such and such animal, and animal are grasped by *epagoge.*

What does Aristotle believe the mind has grasped when it acquires the universal concept, *anthropos?* There are a number of possibilities: (a) The person is able to sort objects into *anthropoi* and non-*anthropoi;* (b) the person is now in a position to use the word '*anthropos*' correctly in conversation; (c) the person has grasped the concept of *anthropos* required for knowing what a human being is. The difference between these cases is considerable. Very young children, who are not yet language users, are capable of the type of sorting involved in case (a). To have a functional definition of the sort required for ordinary communication (case b) is a far cry from having the precise concept needed by the scientist (case c). Both the precision and the complexity of the notion grasped by the mind increase from (a) to (c). The unanalyzed perceptual simples of Socrates' dream in the *Theaetetus* might suffice for the prelinguistic sorting involved in (a).[34] In *Physics* I 1, Aristotle describes a stage where the speaker, a

33 The identification of induction with empirical generalization is well known today, but there are also more fine-tuned theories of induction that may be closer to what Aristotle has in mind.

34 See *Theaetetus* 201e–210b; Socrates' dream is discussed in Chapter 2, section 3, and Chapter 5.

young child, uses a term in an eccentric manner, 'mother' for all women, followed by a stage where the speaker, still a young child, uses the term correctly (case b). There is no evidence that Aristotle thinks the child has acquired the precise notion needed by the scientist (case c).[35] The child has a nominal definition; the scientist, a real definition.

Cases (a) and (b) may, for Aristotle, be necessary stages preceding the acquisition of the basic concepts of art and science. Socratic *elenchus* and Platonic division also envisage such a stage. At this stage, the speaker has a nominal definition and a term. Whether the speaker is mistaken or ignorant of the concept will depend upon the character of the concept. If it is a derived concept, then the speaker having only a nominal definition is mistaken; if it is a basic concept, the speaker is ignorant.[36] By contrast, the basic concepts of art and science are not apprehended by means of nominal definitions, nor are they apprehended by the mind as inexplicable simple terms.[37] To have a basic concept '*C*' is to be able to sort objects into C's and not-C's, and the outcome of the sorting corresponds to a real difference between the objects. To have acquired the concept 'human' or even 'mother' is to recognize (at least some) of the essential features of the object in question. There is no difference between knowing the concept '*C*' and knowing what a C is. To know what a C is is to grasp the real definition of C.[38]

The *Posterior Analytics, Metaphysics,* and *Physics* discussions of first principles call attention to the parallels between the cognitive processes that issue in the understanding required for nonscientific thinking about an *infima species* and the ones that produce the definition of the *infimae species* required for demonstrative science. Natural languages, according to Aristotle, provide a good first approximation to the correct grid for understanding the world. The names of substances in a natural language typically correspond to existing kinds of substances. The definition (*logos*) that a native speaker uses to determine the correct application of a substance sortal provides a first approximation to the technical definition of the substance. This *logos* includes some of the salient features of the kind (for example, being tame, two-legged, and rational, for '*anthropos*'). This understanding of the term is made more systematic, when by division the *differentiae* and the genus are distinguished and properly ordered. Under analytic scrutiny, it may turn out that a single term refers

35 At first sight, Aristotle's choice of 'mother' and 'father' as examples in a preliminary discussion of definitions in natural science may seem bizarre, but for the author of *De Generatione Animalium* the scientific analogues of these concepts would have been obvious.

36 See also the discussion of indivisible concepts in Chapter 2, section 3, and Chapter 6, section 3.

37 Cf. Bolton's (1987, pp. 156–66) study of the way that the technical account of *sperma* in *Generation of Animals* is initiated by the specification of what we call *sperma.*

38 The ontological implications of Aristotle's conception of real definition will be explored in Chapter 5.

to more than one *infima species* or that the ordinary definition lacks one or more of the distinctive *differentiae.* In the favored cases, this process yields real definitions of basic objects. The basic premises of a demonstrative science are definitions of basic objects expressed in universal, affirmative statements.[39] The comparison between the two stages of division illustrated in the *Sophist* and the two types of definition (linguistic and scientific) that interest Aristotle is obvious, as is the importance for Aristotle of providing a bridge between the two.

If the ability to know basic premises develops over time, then there is room for false starts. This seems to fly in the face of Aristotle's claims about their immediacy and necessity. The question then becomes how best to interpret the role of *epagoge* in securing scientific definitions. There are several possibilities: (a) *epagoge* supplemented on occasion by division yields putative first premises, but a different cognitive power, *nous,* has immediate insight into them and recognizes those that are necessarily true or (b) *epagoge* supplemented on occasion by division yields putative first premises that in the favored cases are necessarily true. If (a) is the case, then the possession of an adequate scientific language would require some form of cognition besides receptivity to basic concepts determined by the external world. Despite the popularity of (a) and other interpretations sharing the same conception of *nous* as (a), I prefer (b). It is more consistent with the conception of the two types of reasoning, deduction and *epagoge,* and the two types of premises, demonstrable ones and indemonstrable ones, that shapes the account of demonstrative knowledge. The first principles of a deductive system must be such that they cannot be deduced within the system, Aristotle argues at the outset of the *Posterior Analytics.* The term ἄμεσος (immediate) literally means 'without a middle.' Aristotle uses it to mark a premise that cannot be deduced through a middle term from other premises in a way that satisfies the requirements of demonstration. This use of ἄμεσος does not have the epistemic connotation of being self-evident that the use of 'immediate' by later philosophers to characterize first principles does have.

Posterior Analytics II 19 begins with two questions about first premises: How do they become known and what is the disposition for knowing them? In the case of demonstrable premises, the same two questions have two different answers: the first is answered with demonstration and the second with *episteme.* In II 19, the first question is answered with *epagoge* and the second with *nous.* The relation between demonstration and *episteme* is the relation between the method a demonstrative science employs to establish its findings and the science as a unified body of knowledge about a particular subject matter. Given this understanding of demonstrative science, it is not surprising that Aristotle conceives the relation

39 *Post. Anal.* 90b3–4, 24–27.

between the method for establishing the indemonstrable first principles of a demonstrative science (*epagoge*) and the knowledge of them (*nous*) along the same lines as the relation between demonstration and *episteme.*[40] This picture is consistent with what Aristotle has said up to this point in the *Analytics* about *epagoge* and *nous* and about the starting points of demonstration.[41] Because the knowledge of the basic premises is ultimately derived from experience of the world, both *epagoge* and *nous* are associated with the apprehension of particulars as well as universals.[42] In II 19, Aristotle asserts that just as demonstration is not the starting point of demonstration, neither is *episteme* the starting point of *episteme,* and thus he concludes that *nous* is the starting point of *episteme* (100b5–17). This conclusion is based on the theses that only two belief states, *episteme* and *nous,* are always true, and that *nous* is more accurate (ἀκριβέστερον) than *episteme.*

There will be no scientific knowledge [ἐπιστήμη] of the first principles [ἀρχῶν] and since except mind [νοῦν] nothing can be truer than scientific knowledge, it will be mind that apprehends the first principles. (100b10–14)

It should be noted that nowhere in this argument does Aristotle make any attempt to discredit the role of *epagoge* in the acquisition of first principles by a mind. What is said is fully consistent with *nous*'s being the outcome of successful instances of inductive reasoning; it is also compatible with *nous*'s playing a role in *epagoge.*[43] Finally, there is no mention of self-evident propositions, nor is *nous* described as a form of immediate awareness of first principles that is self-certifying.

Nous is said to be more accurate and truer than *episteme* at 100b5–12, however, and this has been thought to rule out interpretation (b). A hard notion on any account, 'truer than' makes sense only if it is a function of the character of the object of the belief and not a function of the correspondence between the belief and an external state.[44] On this construal, a belief that is more intelligible, because its object is more basic, would be truer than less intelligible beliefs. The simpler and more universal the object of belief is, the more intelligible it is, according to Aristotle (87a31–37; *Met.* 982a25–27). The notion of greater accuracy has a similar sense in Aristotle's writings where simpler and more general principles, such as the axioms of arithmetic, are said to be more accurate than more specific principles, such as the axioms of geometry. Similar considerations motivate the remark that the first principles are better known

40 There is considerable evidence that Aristotle thinks that deductive and inductive reasoning exhaust the possibilities for forms of reasoning that produce knowledge (*Pr. Anal.* 68b13–14, *Post. Anal.* 81a38–b9, *N.E.* 1139b25–34).

41 *Pr. Anal.* 67a21–26; *Post. Anal.* 72b20–30, 81a38–b9, 84b37–85a1, 88b30.

42 *Post. Anal.* 78a34–35, 88a5–8; *N.E.* 1143b2–6.

43 See Kosman (1973); Lesher (1973); Modrak (1981).

44 See the discussion of 'truer' in Chapter 2, section 1.

(γνωριμώτεραι) than are the derived principles. Their being better known is a consequence of their being prior to other principles. In sum, Aristotle does not use 'truer than' or 'more accurate than' or 'better known than' to mean self-evident or infallible. Under the influence of the much later Cartesian tradition, philosophers have too quickly found in Aristotle notions that are alien to his epistemology.

The greatest challenge to interpretation (b) is its apparent failure to provide a philosophically satisfying epistemology. Demonstrative science promises to produce understanding on the hypothesis that its conclusions follow necessarily from first premises that are true, universal, and necessary; the premises are indemonstrable and known through *epagoge* and *nous*. According to (b), there is nothing about *epagoge* that guarantees that every empirical generalization is true, let alone commensurately universal and necessary. Even if one grants that a knower employing *epagoge* can arrive at universals having all of these characteristics, the knower will not be justified in believing that a first principle has the right epistemic character. A particularly succinct statement of this difficulty is found in Irwin:

> The product [*nous*], however, cannot depend for its warrant on the induction that has produced it; for such warrant would not explain how a proposition grasped by *nous* could be naturally prior to the demonstrated propositions derived from it. (135)[45]

The reasoner, as Irwin sees it, grasps certain propositions on the basis of deduction and others on the basis of induction. The knower must be justified in accepting certain propositions, however acquired, as first principles that are naturally prior to any other principles. This ability depends upon the noninferential awareness of the principles as immediately true; it is in this way that *nous* certifies the truth of the propositions it grasps. Read in this way, Irwin contends, Aristotle's account of scientific knowledge succeeds where it would otherwise fail (136).

Granted, natural priority is an Aristotelian requirement for first principles. It is less clear, however, what follows from this fact. An internalist defense of priority where all that is at issue is the relationship between the cognitive activity of the mind and the propositions it grasps would require a self-warranting form of intuition. An externalist defense of the sort, I believe, Aristotle presupposes throughout, makes the natural priority of certain propositions a function of the causal priority of certain objects and relations falling within the domain of a particular science. Proximity to the earth explains why certain heavenly bodies do not twinkle and not conversely, Aristotle says, even though being proximate to the earth and not twinkling are coextensive properties of heavenly bodies

45 Irwin (1988).

(78a28–78b2). This is how Aristotle would have scientists distinguish between first principles and other true, universal propositions belonging to the same domain. But, the critic might charge, this only pushes the problem to another level for now an immediate grasp of causal priority seems to be presupposed. Causal priority is a brute fact grasped by *epagoge*, and so we have come full circle to the question of whether what is grasped by *epagoge* can be immediate. A proposition is immediate if and only if it is not derivable through a proper middle term (72b18–22). The cognitive priority of first principles reflects the natural priority of causes; first principles are immediate in Aristotle's sense, even though the recognition of causal priority is through *epagoge*.

There is an important difference between believing that (a) if proposition *P* is grasped by *nous*, proposition *P* is true, necessary, universal, and immediate and believing that (b) *nous* is a special kind of awareness that certifies that proposition *P* is true and necessary. While the final lines of II 19 (100b5–17) are compatible with either (a) or (b), what Aristotle says in the preceding lines of II 19 as well as his conception of the relation between the world and object of thought argues strongly in favor of attributing (a) to him. On the other hand, if (b) were Aristotle's position, the knower would know that the proposition was true, necessary, universal, and immediate, and thus the knower would have no reason to doubt that proposition *P* was a first principle. If (a) is Aristotle's position, then a putative knower might doubt that proposition *P* is a first principle, even if it is. In *Metaphysics* I, Aristotle appeals to the interpersonal character of the acquisition of true beliefs to explain the accumulation of knowledge – individually we often make mistakes; in groups, we often hit upon the truth (993a30-b4).[46] If a consensus develops among the experts in a particular field that proposition *P*, which falls within the domain of their subject, is true, necessary, universal, and immediate, there is good reason to believe that proposition *P* is a first principle. The explanatory power of a demonstrative science as a whole provides the justification for believing that its first premises have the requisite character. Aristotle believes that the world is intelligible and that the relation between the real intelligible structures of the world and the mind is such that these structures act on the mind through the senses and cause it to apprehend them; as Aristotle says, "the mind [ψυχή] is so constituted as to be capable of being so affected" (100a14). As to having good reason for accepting the premises of a demonstrative science, the sciences themselves provide a pragmatic justification for the acceptance of their first principles. There are obvious (at least to Aristotle) examples of demonstrative science. His analysis of demonstrative science has established the requirement that there must be nondemonstrative knowledge of first premises having the character-

46 See Chapter 2, section 1.

istics he has outlined in the *Analytics*. *Nous* just is nondemonstrative knowledge of this sort. The apprehension of a definition of essence is *nous* and it is the consequence of *epagoge*. *Epagoge* begins with the perception of concrete objects. The perception of concrete objects is also the starting point of the process that engenders the concepts articulated in linguistic definitions. The shared cognitive basis ensures that the real concepts articulated in scientific definitions are more adequate (because simpler, more comprehensive, and more accurate) representations of the same objects as linguistic universals.

Interpretation (a) has yielded a coherent story about the relation between the cognitive grasp of meanings and the apprehension of scientific definitions. Interpretation (a) has many detractors, however, who believe that it is indefensible as an epistemological position. Interpretation (a) does not result in Cartesian certainty. Fortunately, a number of modern epistemologists have challenged the Cartesian conception of knowledge.[47] Some philosophers, most notably W. V. O. Quine, have questioned any attempt to draw a sharp distinction between noninferential, theory-neutral, observation sentences and inferential and theory-dependent sentences; without this distinction, it is not possible to show that a natural science is a deduction from sensory evidence.[48] The project of rational reconstruction should be abandoned as the goal of epistemology, and epistemology should be viewed, they argue, as a branch of psychology. In view of the variety and popularity of anti-Cartesian approaches to the foundations of science, Aristotle's position may prove to be more adequate if interpreted in light of (a), for which there is better textual evidence, than if interpreted in light of (b). In the absence of countervailing evidence, there is good reason to believe that the propositions accepted as first principles by the experts in a field (together with the propositions derivable from them) are really the first principles of that branch of knowledge. Despite the appeal to a consensus of the relevant experts, coherence in this case, for Aristotle, is evidence of objective truth.[49]

4 Defense of Empiricism

While untroubled by Cartesian worries, Aristotle is keenly aware of a rationalist alternative to his epistemology and theory of meaning. The *Posterior Analytics* begins with a reference to the Learner's Paradox of the

47 The epistemic demand for absolute certainty has been challenged on a number of fronts in recent literature, even by foundationalists. See inter alia Alston (1993) and Goldman (1979, 1986).

48 Quine (1969). For a defense of the observation/inference distinction, see Fodor (1984, pp. 23–43).

49 See Chapter 2, section 2.

Meno and Plato's answer that learning is recollection is rejected in II 19.[50] The Learner's Paradox – namely, that a person cannot learn either what he or she does not know or what he or she does know – seems to have the result that all knowledge must be derived from prior knowledge. Aristotle accepts this conclusion for demonstration but rejects it for the inductive process resulting in knowledge of first principles.[51] In II 19, he describes the latter in hopes of showing that his solution to the paradox is, all things considered, more satisfactory than Plato's. The paradox can be generalized to cover the acquisition of the mundane universals of a natural language, and Aristotle's solution has a linguistic counterpart.

On several crucial issues, Aristotle is in full agreement with Plato: knowledge is possible and it is the apprehension of universals that are not subject to the anomalies of concrete individuals; moreover, the deep structure of language is natural and mirrors reality. Aristotle agrees with Plato that only insofar as the buzzing confusion of the Heraclitean world of sense experience is structured by universals is it intelligible. The fact that the structure exists in the world of ordinary experience is crucial from Aristotle's perspective, and this is what differentiates his position from Plato's.[52] Plato locates the ultimate source of the innate structures that order our perceptions in an ideal reality that we recollect. Recollected concepts are projected by our minds on confusing, transitory sensory contents. For Aristotle, projection is not involved here, but what is involved instead is the cognitive act of eliciting structures that are found in the world from perceptions displaying these structures.

> Now it is strange if we possess ⟨first principles⟩ from birth; for it means that we possess apprehensions more accurate than demonstration and fail to notice them. (*Post. Anal.* 99b28–29)

Aristotle argues instead for attributing a cognitive capacity to human beings that develops out of a capacity we have from birth, the capacity for sense perception.[53] His argument stresses the continuity of our perceptions with the derivations we ultimately embrace. *Posterior Analytics* II 19 describes the evolution of the universal from the perception of a concrete

50 *Epagoge* is also mentioned in this context in the *Prior Analytics* at 67a21–23.

51 Induction used as a method of pedagogy does depend on the teacher's having prior knowledge of the outcome (71a1–10).

52 Kornblith (1993) defends a conclusion that is similar to Aristotle's: "Our conceptual and inferential tendencies jointly conspire, at least roughly, to carve nature at its joints and project the features of a kind which are essential to it. This preestablished harmony between the causal structure of the world and the conceptual and inferential structure of our minds produces reliable inductive inference."

53 Cf. recent epistemologists who argue that the mechanisms governing belief formation are the product of human evolution and thus because veridical beliefs would be on the whole more adaptive than nonveridical ones, our belief producing mechanisms must be reliable. See, e.g., Quine (1969, pp. 126–7); and Dennett (1981); for a criticism of this approach, see Stich (1990, chap. 3).

exemplification of the universal and thus lays to rest at least one reason for doubting that perception is the source of universals. Aristotle hopes to persuade us of the wisdom of his approach by displaying the continuity between the perception of a concrete particular and the scientific descriptions applying to the particular. At first blush, the particular as an object of perception seems to act directly on our minds whereas the conceptualization of it as falling under this or that linguistic or scientific universal seems to depend more on the mind than the object. By stressing the emergence of the universal from the encounter with the particular in *Posterior Analytics* II 19, *Metaphysics* I 1, and *Physics* I 1, Aristotle assimilates the apprehension of universal principles to the perceptual grasp of sensible particulars.

Aristotle is confident that all human knowledge can be derived from objects presented through sense perception. All objects of thought are ways of conceiving perceptible objects, as Aristotle explains in *De Anima* III 8.

> Since there is no actual thing separate in existence, so it seems, apart from sensible magnitudes, the objects of thought are in the sensible forms, both the abstract objects and all the states and affections of sensible things. (*De Anima* 432a3–6)

Another part of Aristotle's confidence in his brand of empiricism is stated at *De Anima* 431b1: "Actual knowledge is identical with its object." This thesis is an expression of Aristotle's conception of cognitive faculties – perceiving, thinking, knowing, all are activities that simply are the realization in consciousness of features of objects having a mind-independent existence.[54] The objects of perceiving and thinking are such that the act of apprehending them is fully determined by the object. In both cases, the cognitive activity is the realization of characteristics of the object. There is nothing left over on this picture, which is the activity as distinguished from its object. Just as under optimal conditions, the eyes add nothing to the colors seen, under optimal conditions, the mind adds nothing to the universals apprehended. Indeed, it is this feature of cognitive acts that prompts Aristotle to model the activity of a purely actual, divine substance on human thought.[55] There is, to be sure, a difference between a universal structure existing in the world and that structure as apprehended by a mind. The apprehension is dependent upon the mind whose act of apprehension it is; the universal structure in the world exists independently of the mind. The latter presupposition, critical to Aristotle's semantics and epistemology, fits uneasily with the nominalistic strand in his thinking in the *Categories* but serves him well in the *Posterior Analytics*.[56]

54 This will be discussed in greater detail in Chapters 7 and 8; see also Modrak (1987a).

55 Modrak (1991, pp. 755–74).

56 This tension is not resolved in the *Organon* but will be in the central books of the *Metaphysics*. See Part II in this volume.

If the mind is conceived as an inert, blank tablet, then it is very hard to give a satisfactory account of the abstract objects, universal concepts, and propositions that are constitutive of knowledge in its several forms. If, on the other hand, the intellect is assigned too large a role, then either realism must be abandoned in favor of some type of subjectivism or a world of ideal objects must be posited. Aristotle is determined to stay clear of the pitfalls of either alternative, and so he argues repeatedly and at some length in the *Metaphysics* against the most formidable of their ancient proponents, Protagoras and Plato, respectively.[57] Aristotle's brilliant solution is to posit not an inert mind but a continuously active one and then to limit its activity to the realization of its objects.[58] Just as a catalyst enables a chemical reaction to occur but is not a component of its outcome, human cognitive activity enables the perceptible and intelligible features of things to be realized without containing extraneous material supplied by the mind.

Aristotle, like Plato, is a realist about the objects of knowledge. Does Aristotle provide a better defense of epistemological realism than Plato? Perhaps. The ontology presupposed by Aristotle's account is simpler than Plato's; here there are only physical objects and their properties, including human beings with the capacity for perception, language, and intellection. Notwithstanding, Aristotle must posit the objective reality of the structures apprehended by the mind, just as Plato must ultimately posit the reality of ideal objects. Were we able to take a god's eye perspective, we would be able to determine whether the human mind imposes universals and order on chaotic sense data or whether the physical world displays order and general features, which are evident in sense experience and apprehended by the mind. Aristotle must adopt the second-best strategy, but the only one available to a mere mortal, namely, analyzing cognition and language in order to support the view that an object as cognized is the same object as an extramental existent. The strength of his position will depend upon how successful he is in this effort.

5 Common Notions and Science

Aristotle's theory of meaning posits universal concepts that are shared by all speakers. The concepts are the same because the things of which they are likenesses are the same. Different languages employ different linguistic signs for the same concept and to refer to the same object. The

57 To mention only some of the more developed criticisms of Protagoras or Plato in the *Metaphysics: Metaphysics* IV 5–6 is an extended argument against Protagorean relativism; *Metaphysics* I 9, VII 13–15, and XIII 4–7 are devoted to the critique of Platonic Ideas.

58 Although modern epistemology does not afford an example of precisely this strategy, Kornblith (1993) inter alia argues that human inferential processes are peculiarly suited to making correct inferences with respect to natural kinds.

summary statement of the theory of meaning in *De Interpretatione* I 1 leaves unexplained how concepts arise in the mind that are likenesses of external objects. The next step, the step taken in the epistemological discussions surveyed in this chapter, is to develop an account that makes the external objects the causes of the concepts. The vocal sounds that speakers of different languages use for "horse" are quite different, but a horse is a horse whatever it is called. All members of the species *Equus caballus* share the same characteristics. For this reason, there will also be general cross-cultural agreement about the observable features of horses, even if certain features are under contention, for instance, whether horses are sacred to the gods. The agreement is due, Aristotle believes, to the fact that the species exists independently of us and causes us to have certain perceptions. Because of the nature of our minds, these perceptions cause us to form the common concept that is the meaning of the various vocal signs used by human beings to name the species. Although horses are often given proper names, unlike the common noun, these names play a relatively minor role in the dissemination of information about horses, and Aristotle's analysis of meaning fits common nouns better than proper names, the function of which seems adequately explained by the relation between the linguistic sign, the proper name, and the individual called by that name.[59]

The ability to communicate understanding is central to Aristotle's conception of knowledge. From the *Posterior Analytics* to the *Nicomachean Ethics,* Aristotle uses the activity of teaching as a model in order to establish the criteria of rationality. Because the transmission of knowledge from teacher to student must be achieved through either deductive or inductive arguments to secure conviction, Aristotle concludes that there are only two types of reasoning (*N.E.* 1139b25–29; cf. *Pr. Anal.* 68b13–37). The ability to teach belongs to the person having knowledge as distinguished from know-how (*Met.* 981b7–10, 982a12–19). The more intelligible the objects of a science are, the more easily they are communicated to others by the person who possesses the science. The transmission of information from teacher to student depends upon the existence of a common vocabulary containing terms, the reference of which, though not fully grasped by the student, is accessible to both student and teacher. Aristotle envisages a process where at first the student mouths the words of the teacher without understanding (*N.E.* 1147a21–22) and in the favored cases ultimately uses the same terms as the teacher with understanding. Aristotle's answer to the Learner's Paradox is as much about the acquisition of a language appropriate to discourse in a specific science, for instance, geometry or biology, as it is about the intellectual grasp of the first premises of a specific science.

59 See discussion of this point in Chapter 1, section 5.

The first principles of a demonstrative science are expressed in sentences, the meaning of which must be such that the correspondence of the sentence to an external state of affairs is ensured. *Posterior Analytics* II 19 is Aristotle's attempt to tell a story about the cognitive object, the mind, and the world that establishes the possibility of such correspondence. Not only does Aristotle seek to respond to this challenge in the *Posterior Analytics,* but he also returns to the topic when he lays the foundations for the treatment of natural science in the *Physics* and of first philosophy in the *Metaphysics.* Significantly, the examples he uses in the *Physics* and *Posterior Analytics* ('mother', 'father', 'human') are concepts that figure in ordinary discourse as well as in scientific discourse. Aristotle's choice of examples may be motivated by his desire to tie the universals of science to ordinary experience. These examples also call attention to the continuity of ordinary language with the language of art and science. Art and science employ universals that, Aristotle argues, are refinements of ordinary concepts. The same phenomena make natural languages possible as make art and science possible. An independently existing, physical world acts on the sense organs of human beings, causing them to have certain perceptions, and because the human mind has certain capacities, it is able to elicit from perceptions of concrete particulars universal structures found in the world. This process yields common concepts that function as meanings for the vocal sounds employed by a community of speakers. Refined common concepts serve as the basis for the specialized languages employed by the practitioners of the various arts and sciences. The language of science evolves from natural language, and the capacity for forming the general concepts required for meaningful discourse of all sorts, from ordinary language to scientific discourse, evolves out of the perceptual capacities of human beings.

A passage from *Prior Analytics* I sums up Aristotle's conception of the way in which science develops out of ordinary experience:

> Hence it is the business of experience [ἐμπειρίας] to give the principles which belong to each subject. I mean, for example, that it is for astronomical experience to supply the principles of astronomical science; for once the appearances were adequately apprehended, the demonstrations of astronomy were thus discovered. Similarly with any other art or science. (*Pr. Anal.* I 30, 46a17–22)

The world acts on human beings in a way that leads to natural language concepts of specific phenomena and produces specific groupings of these concepts as, for instance, astronomical ones. Such groupings provide investigators of the phenomenon in question with a definite subject to investigate (cf. 46a10–17). These investigations result in the refinement of the concepts of astronomical experience and the comprehension of the concepts required for astronomical demonstrations.

In the next chapter, we will look at Aristotle's analysis of the three types of theoretical science, namely, mathematics, natural science, and metaphysics, to see whether he succeeds in establishing that the basic concepts of these sciences reflect the character of an objective reality, because they are elicited from experience by the human mind.[60] The test of Aristotle's account of first principles in *Posterior Analytics* II 19 and his semantics as applied to scientific contexts is whether he is able to develop a satisfactory account of the first principles of mathematics, natural science, and metaphysics.

60 Cf. Modrak (1989, pp. 121–39).

4

Three Types of Science

How a mind grasps universals is addressed all too quickly in *Posterior Analytics* II 19. The challenge facing Aristotle is to fill out this quick account in a way that makes the acquisition of universals intelligible. This would be a challenge under any conditions; however, the importance of meeting this challenge is enormous for Aristotle, whose logic and theory of demonstrative science recognize only inferences through universals. The theory of meaning in the *De Interpretatione* does not identify significant sounds with universal terms; however, universal terms are much more common in ordinary discourse than are proper names for individuals, and Aristotle's claim that the mental state is the same for all humans who share a concept supports the identification of meanings with universals. Finally, and perhaps most significantly, knowledge requires universals. On this point, Aristotle (as we have seen) is in complete agreement with Plato. He differs in making experience the basis for the knowledge of universals. *Posterior Analytics* II 19 sketches the process involved, making no distinction between the universals required for ordinary discourse and those required for science, or between the universals required for one type of science or another. Elsewhere, Aristotle recognizes three types of theoretical science (mathematics, physical science, and metaphysics). These differ as their objects differ with respect to primacy, universality, and intelligibility. *Posterior Analytics* II 19 would lead us to expect that universals having the epistemic characteristics required by a particular science would be grasped through the inductive process (*epagoge*). Conversely, if this is not the case, the claim to generality of the *Posterior Analytics* account of first principles would be undermined. This, in turn, would leave in doubt the account of definition developed above.

The story told in the *Posterior Analytics* about the origin of universals as objects of knowledge will prove persuasive only if a plausible case can be made that the universals constitutive of the three types of theoretical science originate in the objects of perception. To see exactly how the objects of science are derived from empirical investigations, we should examine Aristotle's descriptions of the three theoretical sciences. A good place to begin is his characterization of the three in *Nicomachean Ethics* VI 8.

> One might ask why a boy can become a mathematician, but not a philosopher or a physicist. Is it because the objects of mathematics are abstractions while the first principles of these other subjects come from experience, and young men have no conviction about the latter but merely say the words, while the essence of former is not obscure? (N.E. VI 8, 1142a16–19)

In this passage, the division of science into three basic types is not Aristotle's motive so much as is his desire to differentiate between mathematics and the other theoretical sciences. To this end, he invokes a distinction between objects apprehended through abstraction (δι'ἀφαιρέσεως) and those derived from experience (ἐξ ἐμπειρίας); corresponding to this difference is a difference in the characteristics required of the knower. By considering these differences, we may be able to get clearer on the role of *epagoge* as the means for acquiring universals in each of the three theoretical sciences. The universals grasped in each science and expressed in its basic premises differ with respect to separability from physical objects and mutability. The universals that are the objects of physics are not separable and they accommodate the mutability of physical objects. These characteristics are consistent with such universals being exemplified in physical objects. Because they are fully exemplified in concrete objects, these universals seem likely to fit the description of secondary substance and properties in the *Categories* and the semantics of the *De Interpretatione*. The objects of mathematics are separable by abstraction; abstract universals of this sort seem harder to reconcile with Aristotle's semantics and epistemology. The objects of first philosophy appear to be even more problematic, because here the claim to separability is asserted without qualification. Can a plausible case be made that in spite of these obstacles the universal concepts of all three theoretical sciences are grasped by *epagoge?* Can a case be made that the meaning of the terms employed by these sciences is a function of reference to external objects?

These questions are important within the context of Aristotle's epistemology and within the context of his semantics. From one perspective, scientific definitions assign meanings to the terms for the basic objects of the science. From another, however, they are expressions of knowledge and first principles. From yet another perspective, they furnish paradigms of the relation between a term and its referent. Reference determines meaning and in the epistemically favored case the meaning expresses the nature of the external object. This is what a scientific definition does: it states a meaning that is a real nature. Brevity notwithstanding, the genetic account of *Posterior Analytics* II 19 makes the impact of the world on the senses and the mind responsible for the emergence of meanings expressible in scientific definitions. If Aristotle frames the account of the acquisition of the basic concepts of the three types of theoretical science in accordance with the genetic account, then he gives us yet one more reason to interpret the theory of meaning in *De Interpretatione* 1 as identifying the object (*pragma*) that determines meaning with the external referent of the word.

In order to better understand Aristotle's conception of universals and his confidence that universals are derived from experience, I propose to consider the process by which, according to Aristotle, the universals falling under each of the three theoretical domains – namely, mathematics, natural science, and first philosophy – are acquired. In section 4 of this chapter, dialectic, a method that Aristotle finds useful for the clarification of concepts, especially in the *Metaphysics*, will be investigated as a possible alternative to the empirical method of apprehending universals described in *Posterior Analytics* II 19.

1 Basic Concepts of Mathematics

As the *Nicomachean Ethics* description makes clear, the method by which the truths of mathematics are known is distinctive. Notwithstanding, in the *Posterior Analytics*, mathematics is one type of demonstrative science, among others. Because the premises of a demonstrative science are indemonstrable, they must be assumed within the context of demonstration. The examples Aristotle cites to illustrate this claim are drawn from arithmetic and geometry.

> I call first principles in each kind those which it is not possible to prove to be. Now both what the primitives and what the things dependent on them signify is assumed; but that they are must be assumed for the first principles and proved for the rest – e.g., what a unit or what straight and triangle signify must be assumed, and that the unit and magnitude are; but that the others are must be proved. (*Post. Anal.* I 10, 76a31–36)

Offered as a description of the starting points of demonstration, this passage is striking in its use of exclusively mathematical examples. These are chosen by Aristotle because here the case is clear: the definitions of the basic objects are stated and the existence of the basic objects posited prior to the construction of proofs. Demonstration treats these definitions as assumptions. Like the basic concepts of the other demonstrative sciences, the first principles of arithmetic and geometry must be known in order for these disciplines to be forms of knowledge. Since abstraction is mentioned as part of Aristotle's standard description of mathematical objects, it is reasonable to suppose that mathematical objects are grasped through a process of abstraction. The natures of these objects are specified in the definitions that serve as the starting points for arithmetic and geometry. Are the meanings of mathematical terms as conventional as is the association of a particular sound with a particular meaning? If so, Aristotle's theory of meaning would not apply to mathematical terms and definitions, unless the notion of a *pragma* is extended to include abstract objects. As we have discovered, Aristotle goes to considerable lengths to avoid admitting into his ontology objects that lack concrete exemplifications, and thus the implications of positing abstract *pragmata* for his semantics extend beyond the narrow domain of philosophy of mathematics.

Were abstraction to turn out to be a mode of *epagoge* as described in *Posterior Analytics* II 19, Aristotle might be able to avoid positing independently existing abstract objects. Were abstraction to turn out to be a distinctive mode of knowing first principles, Aristotle would have a harder time avoiding this step. There are several indications that the process of grasping the basic objects of mathematics through abstraction is a special case falling under the inductive process described in II 19. In the *Posterior Analytics,* many of the examples of demonstrative science are drawn from arithmetic and geometry, and thus to give an account of the apprehension of the first principles of demonstrative science that did not apply to mathematics would be very peculiar. Surely Aristotle would have mentioned their exclusion had he intended to exempt them.[1] On the contrary, Aristotle argues that the only way a student of mathematics can acquire the relevant universals is through *epagoge* (81b2–6). Moreover, to exempt abstract objects would have vitiated his claim to offer an alternative epistemology to that of the Platonists. When Aristotle looks at the origins of mathematical knowledge in *Metaphysics* XIII and elsewhere, he argues for the derivation of mathematical concepts from ordinary concepts and objects. Even though thinking about mathematical objects is a distinctive way of conceptualizing certain properties, it remains, nevertheless, just another way of thinking about physical objects. When we think about man qua man, we think about an indivisible object, and when we think about man qua body, we think about a solid (*Met.* 1078a23–26). Any one of a virtually unlimited number of objects may be thought about in a way that generates geometrical or arithmetical objects. Moreover, since a characteristic of this sort can serve as the basis for further inferences, thinking about a single arbitrarily selected physical object may give rise to a whole system of interrelated concepts.

1 Barnes (1969, p. 129) points out that the ratio of mathematical examples to other examples is higher in the first book of the *Posterior Analytics.* Nevertheless, I believe that had Aristotle intended to exclude the mathematical sciences from consideration in II 19 he would have done so explicitly.

The arithmetician posits one indivisible thing and then considers whether some attribute belongs to man qua indivisible (1078a24–25).

Mathematical objects are prior to physical objects in one sense; they are prior in definition (*logos*) (1077b1–14). Aristotle assimilates this type of priority to the priority of any attribute to the compound of that attribute and a substance; for instance, pale is prior to pale man. The definition of pale is a component of the definition of pale man. The analogy seems to break down, however, upon reflection. Pale man is an accidental unity; a sunburnt Socrates is still a man. Socrates, like any other three-dimensional object, cannot cease to be three-dimensional without ceasing to be Socrates. Yet, as Aristotle points out in *Metaphysics* VII 3, if we strip away all the features of Socrates that make him a human and leave only three-dimensionality, the essence of Socrates, the source of his thisness, will have been lost (1029a12–16). This is Aristotle's reason for claiming that the definitional priority of mathematical characteristics should not be confused with ontological priority. There is, in addition, an apparent tension between Aristotle's account of the acquisition of the first principles of mathematics by abstraction from conceptualizations of physical objects and the claim that mathematical definitions are prior to the definitions of physical objects. Pressed on this score, Aristotle would no doubt respond by reminding us that the order of discovery (what is clearer to us) is opposite to the order of intelligibility. We arrive at definitions of the basic objects of mathematics by reflection on physical objects; the definitions we give of mathematical objects are conceptually prior to physical objects because they are components of the accounts of the natures of physical objects.

Aristotle sometimes speaks as if abstract geometrical characteristics were properties of physical bodies on a par with hardness or temperature and other such properties, but setting out his considered view he is more careful.[2] In *Physics* II 2, Aristotle begins with the claim that physical bodies contain surfaces, volumes, lengths, and points, but he goes on to assert that the mathematician does not consider these features as [ᾗ] the limits of a physical body (193b23–33). In *Metaphysics* XIII 3, he is even more explicit: mathematical objects exist neither in separation from

2 Lear (1982, pp. 161–2) urges us to take these passages at face value. On his reading of Aristotle, "physical bodies do actually contain the surfaces, lengths, and points that are the subject matter of mathematics" (p. 163). On my reading, they only contain these objects potentially. The latter allows us to accommodate all of Aristotle's remarks, both those suggesting distinct mathematical objects and those insisting on the empirical basis of mathematics. It also allows for a uniform treatment by Aristotle of all mathematical objects, whereas on Lear's reading the basic objects are properties of physical objects while the more complex are mental constructions (p. 180). Moreover, since Lear is hard pressed to find physical objects that actually embody geometrical properties, it turns out that the geometer typically deals with mental constructions.

physical objects nor in physical objects, but in another way (1077b15–17; cf. 1078a3–5). To secure the claim that mathematical objects do not exist in a full-bodied sense apart from physical objects, Aristotle offers an analysis of abstraction that explains dependency without thereby reducing mathematical properties to physical properties.

Aristotle shies away from claiming that perfect exemplifications of mathematical properties exist as physical characteristics, and so he denies that mathematical properties exist in physical objects.[3] Aristotle's reluctance on this score may be due to the influence of Plato, who argues persuasively in the *Phaedo* that the conception of absolute equality cannot be identified with the equality exhibited by two physical objects (74a–e). But, the rationalist might object, if typically mathematical objects are imperfectly exemplified in physical objects, how can a thinker move from the uneven straight edge of a physical object to the geometer's straight line without introducing a Platonic geometrical object of the sort argued against in *Metaphysics* XIII? Thus challenged, Aristotle would probably invoke the conceptual priority of a positive characteristic to its privation and argue that the physical edge, even though itself not perfectly straight, is straight (not crooked), and for this reason it can serve as the basis for the geometer's thought.[4] The physical characteristic is potentially perfectly straight in the same way that a child is potentially a mathematician; in both cases, a further evolution is required in order to realize the potentiality, yet characteristics that the child or the physical object actually have ground the possible (future) existence of a particular mathematician or the possible conceptualization of the straight qua straight.

Aristotle contrasts existing materially with existing in actuality (ἐντελεχέᾳ) and asserts that mathematical objects exist materially (ὑλικῶς; 1078a31).[5] Just as the bricks that are potentially a house must be worked

3 One puzzling passage, *De An.* 403a12–14, seems to identify geometrical and physical properties, for Aristotle says there that the straight qua straight touches the bronze sphere at a point but only because it is not separate (χωρισθέν). To make this passage consistent with Aristotle's other descriptions of mathematical objects, we have to treat it as an ellipsis. Filled out his point is the following: a physical object with a straight edge can touch a bronze sphere at a (nongeometric) point, a spatially extended region on the surface of the sphere; a straight line (the straight qua straight) can touch a (geometric) sphere at a dimensionless point. The first case provides the ontological underpinning for the second, because the mathematical objects, line, sphere, point, are modes of conceptualizing the physical characteristics. Interpreted in this way, the mathematical example fits the larger context where Aristotle is arguing against a reductionist account of psychological properties while maintaining their ontological dependence upon the body. It is also worth noticing that Euclid (and presumably earlier geometers) uses very similar language to define the notion of a tangent to a circle and to construct proofs employing that notion (*Elements*, III Def. 2, III 18 and 19).

4 Cf. 411a5–7. By means of that which is straight we discern both straight and crooked; for the carpenter's rule is the test of both, but what is crooked does not enable us to distinguish either itself or the straight.

5 Both W. Ross (comm., *Aristotle* Metaphysics) and H. Tredennick (trans., *Aristotle* Metaphysics) correctly construe (ὑλικῶς) as potentially. See also 1051a21–32.

up by the builder into a house, the straight as a physical characteristic must be worked up by the geometer into the concept of a line. In this case, the work is intellectual and Aristotle attempts to capture its character with the qua [ᾗ] locution. By thinking about the straight physical object insofar as it is straight, the mathematician realizes a potentiality in thought that is not realized concretely.[6] As Aristotle puts it, "Obviously, the potentially existing ⟨geometrical constructions⟩ are discovered by being brought to actuality; the reason is that the thinking is an actuality" (1051a29–32). The analogy with material potentiality, if taken too literally, will be problematic, because it lends itself to a mentalistic account of mathematical objects where the mathematician imposes mathematical forms on perceptible qualities. It is more helpful to think in terms of a series of potentialities; the physical characteristic has the potentiality to become an object of perception and thought; the physical characteristic qua object of thought is the cognition of the imperfectly straight; this cognition has the potentiality to become the cognition of the straight qua straight (the perfectly straight); and that cognition has the potentiality to become the basis for further geometrical operations involving the line.[7] While these nested potentialities can only be realized in relation to certain kinds of thinking, they are genuine potentialities, and the objects they are realized in are not mere projections of the mathematician's mind.[8] It must be admitted, however, that certain questions about mathematical discourse remain to be answered. The mathematician's definition of straight is not a likeness, except in a very attenuated sense, of a property exemplified by a physical object. Nor does the linguistic definition of straight seem to be a mere likeness of an imperfectly straight object.

The unique ontological status of mathematical objects also challenges Aristotle's theory of truth as correspondence. The definitions of the basic objects of arithmetic and geometry are first principles; what makes them true? A quick and easy way to defuse this issue would be to point out that these definitions are stipulated at the outset by the mathematician; that is, they are true by fiat. Aristotle would be no happier with that answer than Plato was.[9] An alternative would be to stress the internal co-

6 Aristotle denies that the rejection of a concrete infinite will undermine mathematics where the concept of the infinite can be understood in terms of certain operations such as extending a finite straight line as far as the mathematician wishes (*Phys.* 207b27–34; cf. 203b22–25).

7 Cf. 1078a23–25. Moreover, nested potentialities are very much a part of Aristotle's concept of matter; cf. 1049a18–27.

8 According to *Met.* IX 7, something possesses a *dunamis* to be acted upon or to act when nothing else besides the appropriate agent or patient is needed for the realization of the *dunamis*. This means that if thought about in the right way (i.e., if the mathematician's *dunamis* to act on the object is realized), the potentiality of the straight to become the geometer's line will be realized.

9 Cf. Plato, *Republic* VI, 511a: "This then is the class that I described as intelligible; it is true,

herence of geometry as a whole and offer this as evidence for the truth of its first principles. A final strategy, and the one Aristotle adopts, is to provide the basis for an attenuated notion of truth as correspondence to the external world. In its standard application, the correspondence theory requires that the state of affairs asserted by the sentence actually hold. Abstract objects are not real without qualification, and so literally construed correspondence would require that mathematical properties be fully instantiated by physical objects – a position Aristotle rejects. Straight lines do not correspond to perfectly straight edges in the world; a straight line is, however, a conceptualization of a property existing in the world. Such conceptualizations are likenesses of the external characteristics, and this explains why we are able to use mathematical terms such as straight to refer to the features of the world. That said, the ultimate constraints on the basic objects of mathematics are provided by abstract objects, the natures of which are specified in technical definitions.

In sum, the basic concepts of mathematics are arrived at in a way that is unique and at the same time is rooted in the physical world. Both of these characteristics are captured by Aristotle's use of such expressions as δι'ἀφαιρέσεως, ἐξ ἀφαιρέσεως, and ἐν ἐφαιρέσει.[10] By appealing to the notion of ἀφαιρέσις (taking away), Aristotle reminds us that the way the mind arrives at abstract objects is by stripping away the characteristics of concrete objects. By contrasting the objects grasped through abstraction (δι'ἀφαιρέσεως) to those grasped through experience (ἐξ ἐμπειρίας), Aristotle calls attention to the differences between the way the mind grasps the basic objects of mathematics and those of the other sciences. Like the latter, the former can be included under the cognitive process described in *Posterior Analytics* II 19, because abstraction begins with the perception of ordinary objects and terminates in the apprehension of the basic objects of the mathematical sciences. According to the *Posterior Analytics,* the arithmetician must posit the existence of the unit and define it; *Metaphysics* XIII 3 details how the concept of the unit is arrived at from the concept of man. In *Posterior Analytics* II 19, Aristotle describes how the mind arrives at the concept of man. The crucial difference in methodology between the abstract and other theoretical sciences resides in the mathematician's manipulation of an object that has been abstracted from its physical base. The mathematician does not check (and often cannot check) his or her findings against the observable world of objects; thus experience is only marginally useful. This difference would also complicate the account of mathematical terms as significant sounds. Because the object the term refers to is derived through abstraction from concrete ob-

but with the reservation first that the soul is compelled to employ assumptions in the investigation of it, not proceeding to a first principle because of its inability to extricate itself from and rise above its assumptions."

10 *Post. Anal.* 81b3, *De An.* 403b15, 429b18, 431b12, 432a5; *Met.* 1061a29, *N. E.* 1142a18.

jects, there is a causal link between the meaning of the term and the world. Because the arithmetical unit is actualized as an object of thought, the term 'unit' employed by the mathematician refers to an abstract object. Reference to abstract objects forces a different reading of the theory of meaning, because an abstract object is not, according to Aristotle, a fully independent object. While external to the particular utterance of a mathematical sentence about the abstract object, the object is, nonetheless, dependent upon the way humans conceptualize the world. To avoid weakening the notion of an external *pragma* to include concepts in the standard case (that of meaning for natural languages), Aristotle could offer a modified theory of meaning for mathematics, just as he offers a modified ontology to assimilate mathematics under his epistemology.[11]

2 Natural Science

Natural science differs from mathematics in a number of respects – in subject matter, in types of explanatory principles, and in methodology. In all three respects, natural science easily fits Aristotle's capsule description ἐξ ἐμπειρίας (through experience). Natural science deals with the functions and affections of material bodies (*De An.* 403b12–13), and it studies physical bodies qua subjects of change and motion. Not only are the characteristics studied by the natural sciences inseparable in fact from physical bodies, but they also cannot be described in separation from the notion of body.[12] As a result, an adequate description of a concrete object within the context of a physical theory is always more complex than a mathematical representation of that object, and the construction of the physical theory is much more closely tied to observation. This is an advantage with respect to semantics. The terms of natural science, like those of ordinary language, refer to features of the external world. The challenge for Aristotle will be to explain the difference between common sense generalizations and natural language descriptions of the world and the natural sciences.

In the *Physics*, Aristotle provides a broad overview of the structure of natural science, its methodology, its distinctive features, and its core subject matter. Reintroducing the topic of his investigation in *Physics* II 1, Aristotle says that it is nature (φύσις), the existence of which is obvious, and that to attempt a proof of its existence would be absurd (193a3).

11 This is a topic that Aristotle does not specifically address. There is good reason, however, to suppose that he believed his treatment of language could be extended to technical languages.

12 The objects of natural science are, however, separable in account (κατὰ τὸν λόγον) from other characteristics of bodies (*Physics* 193b4–6, 194b12–14); the objects of mathematics are separable in thought (τῇ νοήσει; 193b32–34).

Nature [φύσις] is a source or cause of change and remaining unchanged in that to which it belongs primarily and in itself, and not incidentally. (192b21–23)

With these words, Aristotle isolates what he takes to be the essential features of nature. Φύσις (nature) is the umbrella term φύσις which all the objects, attributes, and relations studied by the natural scientist fall. Widely used in ordinary language and in earlier Greek philosophy, the term φύσις has a long history. Aristotle aims to give a perspicuous analysis of the concept as it figures in the construction of theories about natural objects, from theories about the four basic elements to ones about the human soul, from theories about the movement of the celestial spheres to ones about the movement of animals. The analysis proceeds from the identification of change as the core concept and then an exploration of the latter concept. The course of this investigation determines the structure of the remainder of the *Physics*.

The preliminary analysis of change in *Physics* I 7 finds its elements to be the subject that undergoes the change and the form that is gained in the change.

Everything comes to be from both subject [ὑποκειμένου] and form [μορφῆς]. For in a way 'musical man' is composed of 'man' and 'musical'; you can analyze it into the definitions of 'man' and 'musical'. It is clear then that what comes to be will come to be from these elements. (190b20–23)

This analysis is the outcome when the logical and ontological conception of basic subjects and their attributes found in the *Categories* (and discussed in Chapter 1 here) is applied to the problem of change. What the *Physics* adds to the earlier picture is the requirement that whenever an account of change is given, it should mention an enduring substratum that has lost or gained a characteristic. This has several consequences. No longer seen as an unanalyzed simple, the concrete particular is construed as a complex consisting of an underlying matter and a form – not until the *Metaphysics* does Aristotle fully develop all the implications of this conception for ontology.[13] Since in the *Physics* the distinction between substratum and form is applied to any case where a characteristic is lost or gained, a form need not be the substance of the particular but simply any one of its characteristics. Even when the notion of form is taken broadly, Aristotle withholds judgment in *Physics* I about whether the form or the substratum is substance (191a19–20). The distinction between form and substratum in the *Physics* is relative to the explanatory context. In some contexts, the concrete particular is the subject of the change, in others, the material of which the particular is made counts as the subject (cf. 190b23–29).

13 The notion of form found in the central books of the *Metaphysics*, and its importance to Aristotle's account of definition will be explored in Chapters 5 and 6.

The role experience plays in the acquisition of a natural science seems pretty straightforward. In order to construct a science of bodies in motion or bodies undergoing other types of change, we must observe the natural phenomenon in question and propound a theory that fits our observations (cf. *Pr. Anal.* 46a18–24). Since natural science aims to articulate the physical principles that explain observable phenomena, the actual behaviors of actual bodies serve as constraints on theory. It is more difficult for an astronomer to formulate a theory of actual celestial motions than to develop an abstract and idealized model of solids in circular motion. The latter, although simpler and more elegant, will fail to capture the actual motion of actual bodies. More factors will have to be kept in mind and integrated into the physical account, making it more cumbersome and imprecise. The notion of a geometrical solid is a much simpler notion than that of a moving body, even though both objects are three-dimensional. Even if we envisage geometrical solids in motion, we cannot merely project the mathematical theory on the physical world, because it will not address the mechanical questions that the physical theory must answer.[14] Understanding why a particular physical theory is true necessarily includes the recognition that its basic principles correctly represent the phenomena to be explained.[15]

Aristotle's general account of natural science in the *Physics* and his account of specific sciences in other treatises are shaped by the epistemology developed in the *Posterior Analytics*.[16] Notwithstanding, physical science also poses certain problems for the model of demonstrative science. The major difficulty is the tension between the conception of science as consisting in timeless universals and the mutability of natural objects. Unlike the objects studied by the mathematician, which, because they are considered in abstraction, are not subject to change (1026a13–15), physical objects are subject to change – in the sublunar realm, to generation and corruption, alteration, and locomotion; and in the celestial realm, to locomotion. Aristotle's answer, as we discovered in Chapter 2, is to make the proper objects of the natural sciences natural kinds and their essential attributes. Regularly recurring events (e.g., the phases of the moon) are amenable to explanations in terms of universal relations. Unique

14 Cf. *De Caelo* 299a2–16: "But this last theory which composes every body of planes is, as the most superficial observation shows, in many respects in plain contradiction with mathematics . . . the impossible consequences which result from this view in the mathematical sphere will reproduce themselves when it is applied to physical bodies, but there will be difficulties in physics which are not present in mathematics; for mathematics deals with an abstract and physics with a more concrete object [διὰ τὸ τὰ μὲν ἐξ ἀφαιρέσεως λέγεσθαι τὰ μαθηματικά τὰ δὲ φυσικά ἐκ προσθέσεως]."

15 This requirement has a parallel in the case of ethics; there, too, Aristotle insists that the young due to lack of experience cannot master the subject (*N.E.* 1095a2–4).

16 That Aristotle's biological theory is framed in accordance with the epistemology of the *Posterior Analytics* has been argued in a number of recent papers. See, e.g., Bolton (1987); Gotthelf (1987, 1991); and Lennox (1987).

events are not, and thus in *Physics* II Aristotle admits chance as a fact, but not an explanation.

First then we observe that some things always come to pass in the same way, and others for the most part. . . . But since there is a class of events besides these – events which all say are by chance – it is clear that there is such a thing as chance and spontaneity. (196b10–16; cf. *Post. Anal.* 87b19–25)

Both chance and spontaneity are incidental causes. Unlike a proper cause, an incidental cause does not stand in a necessary relation to its effect. The flute player is an incidental cause of the house she builds, because it is not in virtue of her musical skill that she is able to construct a dwelling. Having differentiated between types of causes and types of ontological subjects and predicates, Aristotle is able to limit explanation in natural science to immutable universals, while acknowledging the mutability of the individuals falling under the universals. The universal, because present in the individual, is present to the mind from its encounter with the individual through perception and enables the mind to form concepts and use linguistic universals. The universal principles of natural science express real relations in the world. The existence of these relations makes the world intelligible. Languages, both natural and technical, are the vehicles for expressing our understanding of these extramental structures. Both natural and technical languages also afford insight into how that understanding is possible, because language exhibits a parallel structure. This is the case Aristotle wants to make; he does not have all the tools he needs until he explores the nature of real definition in *Metaphysics* VII. That said, the case for symmetry between the structure of the external world and our theories about the world is supported by the theory of meaning of the *De Interpretatione,* the genetic account of *Posterior Analytics* II 19, and Aristotle's conception of the basic objects of mathematics and natural science.

3 Basic Concepts of Metaphysics

The challenge facing Aristotle at the beginning of this chapter was to show that the first principles of the sciences recognized by him were such that they might be derived from experience of sensible reality in accordance with the genetic account of *Posterior Analytics* II 19. The hardest case is yet to be addressed – that of first philosophy (*sophia*). In addition, in no other work outside the *Organon* is Aristotle as concerned with issues surrounding meaning and definition as in the *Metaphysics.* In the description of the diverse yet single subject matter of first philosophy, Aristotle appeals to linguistic considerations both to show that all the nonsubstance categories presuppose that of substance and to include the study of universal relations such as identity and contrariety.

Sophia, according to Aristotle, "is both scientific knowledge [ἐπιστήμη] and intuitive reason [νοῦς] about the objects that are the most precious by nature" (1141b3). Aristotle's most detailed description of *sophia* is found in *Metaphysics* I 2. There, its objects are said to be the most universal (μάλιστα καθόλου), and furthest from the senses, the most knowable (μάλιστα ἐπιστητά), and first principles and causes including the good (the cause for the sake of which). Of all forms of knowledge, σοφία alone exists wholly for its own sake (982b28). It is also the most divine (θειοτάτη) and precious (τιμιωτάτη) form of knowledge (983a5). According to the middle books of the *Metaphysics* (IV–IX), σοφία investigates being qua being.

Aristotle's justification for treating being qua being as a proper subject genus is found in *Metaphysics* IV 2:

> For not only in the case of things which are predicated of one [τῶν καθ' ἓν λεγομένων] does the investigation belong to one science, but also in the case of things which are predicated in relation to one nature [τῶν πρὸς μίαν λεγομένων φύσιν]. (1003b12–14)

Aristotle frames the question about the unity of the subject matter of metaphysics as a question about things under a description (τῶν λεγομένων). Metaphysics takes as its starting point the conceptual framework implicit in natural language and science. The goal is to uncover the presuppositions of that framework. What makes being qua being a unified subject genus is that beings are said in relation to a single nature; on further investigation, that nature turns out to be substance. Turning to the question of which topics fall within the province of this science, Aristotle comes up with a long list.

> It is clear then that to study being *qua* being [τὰ ὄντα . . . ᾗ ὄντα] also belongs to one science. And everywhere science deals chiefly with that which is primary, and on which the others depend, and on account of which they get their names. If, then, this is substance, it will be of substances that the philosopher must grasp the principles and the causes. (1003b17–19; Ross trans.)

In addition to the principles and causes of substance, metaphysics will investigate certain basic concepts such as sameness and difference, unity and plurality, part and whole.

> For if not the philosopher, who is it who will inquire whether Socrates and Socrates seated are the same thing, or whether one thing has one contrary, or what contrariety is, or how many meanings it has [ποσαχῶς λέγεται]? And similarly with all other such questions. (1004b1–4)

Aristotle includes relational terms here on the grounds of their universality. This same feature, however, makes the association of a particular meaning with a relational term puzzling – as Plato pointed out in a variety of contexts and Aristotle echoes in the query about the number of meanings they have. On the *Categories* picture of relations, the relation is predicated on the basis of the exemplification of a complex property.[17] This still leaves, after all, the acquisition of such concepts and the understanding of the terms associated with them surrounded in mystery. *Metaphysics* IV 3 expands the list of topics to be addressed still further to include basic logical truths for the reason that "these truths hold good for everything that is, and not for some special genus apart from others" (1005a22–24). In the course of the *Metaphysics,* these topics are duly investigated. The study of being qua being is interpreted as the study of fundamental logical laws in *Metaphysics* IV, as the study of primary being in *Metaphysics* VI and XII, and the study of substance in general in *Metaphysics* VII–IX.[18]

Aristotle defines metaphysics as a science investigating conceptual issues from the foundations of science to the foundations of logic and language – as is clear from the last three passages cited. Aristotle must juggle seemingly conflicting positions in order to maintain his definition of metaphysics and simultaneously support the thesis that the basic concepts of σοφία are empirically based and acquired through *epagoge.* If they are not, then he will be unable to include terms referring to these concepts under his theory of meaning. The situatedness of metaphysics in the conceptual framework of language and science challenges the semantics of the *De Interpretatione,* for it raises the possibility that the truth of metaphysical claims will depend on coherence not correspondence. This in turn would suggest that, contrary to the theory of *De Interpretatione* 1, it is not necessary to consider the relation between descriptions of the world and the world to have knowledge about conceptual issues. Yet when criticizing the Platonic theory of forms Aristotle argues that *sophia* is primarily concerned with the causes of appearances (φανερῶν; 992a25).[19]

Aristotle, it seems, introduces the label, being qua being, to provide a rubric under which to pursue any wholly foundational inquiry that deals with laws, concepts, or beings that lie beyond the scope of the specialized sciences. Despite Aristotle's arguments to the contrary, the unity of first philosophy is questionable, but his arguing for its unity and insisting upon a single genus, being qua being, as the subject matter attests to the hold of the *Analytics'* conception of science on him.[20] Aristotle recognizes that even were humans to accomplish the task of completing every special science, there would still be some questions of interest to a philoso-

17 See Chapter 1, section 4.

18 While dating the different books of the *Metaphysics* is a somewhat tricky business, it is generally agreed that the central books belong to Aristotle's middle period and book XII to his early period.

19 Aristotle recognizes that the characteristics mentioned above seem to support different notions of σοφία (cf. 995b12, 996b9–14).

20 The *Posterior Analytics'* conception of a subject genus is reaffirmed in *Metaphysics* IV – "of every genus that is one, there is one perception and one science" (1003b19–20).

pher that would remain unanswered. Unwilling to abandon the requirement that a science have a unified and cohesive subject matter, Aristotle construes all such questions as different queries about the same subject, being qua being, and hence as appropriate to one science.[21] The theme that provides internal unity to what otherwise appears a diverse list of topics, grouped under a single heading, is the study of the semantic foundations of an epistemically adequate natural language. An investigation of this sort would appropriately look not only at the ontological presuppositions of the language (What are its basic objects? Are objects falling under all of its fundamental categories equally basic? etc.) but also at its logical presuppositions and conceptual adequacy (What are the basic logical principles required for making assertions? What is the correct understanding of universals such as sameness and contrariety required for conceptualizing the world of experience as an object of knowledge?) The search for basic objects yields the analysis of substance, and the search for logical principles yields the Law of Noncontradiction and the Law of the Excluded Middle. The analysis of basic concepts (sameness, difference, contrariety, unity, plurality, etc.) leads to the specification of the different senses in which the terms for such concepts are employed and an insistence upon disambiguating their use in contexts demanding precision.

The greatest threat to the claim that all knowledge including *sophia* is derived from experience is found not in *Metaphysics* IV's characterization of being qua being; it is found in Aristotle's capsule description of the distinctive characteristics of the objects of metaphysics. In order to distinguish between *sophia* and the other types of theoretical science, Aristotle attaches primary importance to two characteristics of its objects, separability and immutability (403b16, 1026a7–22, 1060a12). The objects of *sophia* include being qua being, substance in general, and divine substance in particular.[22] To contemplate such objects qua separable might mean to reflect on them without regard to the subjects that instantiate them (cf. 1078a17). This would not, however, distinguish philosophy from mathematics – if the issue is separability from physical instantiations. On the other hand, one might think that the issue is one of separability from any subject whatsoever and that the objects of *sophia* are pure universals comprehended apart from their instantiations.[23] But this interpretation runs afoul of Aristotle's criticisms of Platonic ontologies

21 Owen (1960, 1965) emphasized the unifying function of the doctrine of focal meaning. Even if we grant that the predicate 'being predicated in relation to substance' defines a group of objects as the objects of metaphysics, we might still doubt that its subject matter constitutes a single genus.

22 In the *Metaphysics,* being qua being is the subject genus throughout; however, in the central books, Aristotle construes the study of being qua being as the study of substance and in XII as the study of divine substance.

23 Indeed, this would be compatible with one of the criteria mentioned above, namely, μάλιστα καθόλου.

and would be incompatible with the account of first principles in *Posterior Analytics* II 19. Fortunately, another interpretation is available. When Aristotle says that the objects of natural science are subject to change, he means that the subjects it investigates are subject to change (not that the principles constituting a particular science are subject to change); analogously, the description of the objects of *sophia* as separable would mean that the subjects *sophia* investigates are capable of separate existence in the sense that a concrete substance is χωριστὸν ἁπλῶς (1042a31).

To be separable in this sense is to exist as an ultimate subject of properties. "Nothing else besides substance is separable [χωριστόν] for everything else is said of a substance as substratum" (185a31–2; cf. 1060b2, 1077b3–5). For this reason, the objects of σοφία, unlike the objects of mathematics and physical science, are separable in themselves.[24] The search for a substance that is eternal and immutable leads in *Metaphysics* XII 6–9 to the divine mind, whose thought is a thinking of thinking (νόησις νοήσεως νοήσις). To study intelligible objects qua separable as distinguished from studying them in separation from other properties of their concrete instantiations is simply to study that aspect that accounts for separability in the more mundane sense of accounting for separate existence. This feature is identified with substance, and this in turn with actuality, thus engendering the analysis of divine substance in terms of the pure actuality of a certain kind of thinking.

In fact there are two notions of separability at work in Aristotle's various descriptions of theoretical science.[25] 'Separable' may mean 'conceptually distinct' (χωριστόν κατὰ λόγον, χωριστὸν λόγῳ, χωριστὸν τῇ νοήσει).[26] In this sense, the physical sciences treat their objects as separable: "There are many statements about things only qua movable, separate [χωρίς] from the nature of each of these things and their attributes" (1077b24–5). In *De Anima* I l, Aristotle describes all the objects of theoretical science as separable. Their different objects are cognized as separable: (1) qua functions and affections of bodies; (2) not qua affections of bodies but derived from abstraction; or (3) qua separable (403b10–16). The first is the province of the natural scientist; the second, of the mathematician; and the third, of the philosopher. There is a second sense of separability, however, paraphrased by expressions such as 'qua separable' (ᾗ χωριστά; ᾗ κεχωρισμένα) or separable in itself

24 At 1060a10–13, Aristotle says that we should investigate whether there is anything separable in itself and belonging to none of the sensibles. As it turns out, all the objects of σοφία satisfy the first condition and divine substance the second.

25 Cf. Bonitz, *Index Aristotelicus* 860a11 and 27.

26 A distinction is drawn between conceptual separation and simple or physical distinctness in numerous works (*Phys.* 193b4, b34, 194b12–14; *De Gen. et Corr.* 320b24; *De An.* 413b14, b29, 427a3, 429a11, 431b12–17, 432a20; *Met.* 1016b2, 1017b25, 1042b29–31, 1078a22).

(χωριστὸν καθ'αὑτό), where 'separable' typically means 'ontologically distinct', that is, capable of separate existence.[27] "For those things are prior in substance which when separated from other things surpass them in the power of independent existence" (1077b2–3). Divine substance wholly satisfies the second separability criterion, whereas other substances (because they share in potentiality with respect to change of one sort or another) meet it less adequately.[28]

At first glance, it seems peculiar that the acquisition of *sophia* should resemble natural science in being ἐξ ἐμπειρίας instead of being ἐξ ἀφαιρέσεως. Mathematical concepts are potentially in the world and are actualized in the act of thinking them. There need not be any perfectly straight edges in the physical world in order for the geometer to conceive a straight line on the basis of an actually existing (imperfectly) straight edge.[29] By contrast, the descriptions of physical science are checked by reference to the world; a failure of correspondence is a reason to abandon the description. Can Aristotle tell a similar story about the objects of metaphysics? The explanation must lie in the character of its objects. Since perceptible objects are the vehicles for all intelligible objects (*De An.* 432a3–6), the objects of metaphysics must differ from other intelligibles with respect to the relation between the object of thought and its perceptible counterparts.

Insofar as metaphysics is the study of substance in general or being abstractly conceived, it is easier to make out the connection with experience. But why does Aristotle include divine substance among the intelligibles that are derived from experience? His answer is found in *Metaphysics* VI 1: "The primary science deals with separable and immutable things . . . for these are the causes with respect to appearances [τοῖς φανεροῖς] of things divine" (1026a18). The account of divine substance given in *Metaphysics* XII is argued for on the basis of observable phenomena, the movement of the heavenly bodies, and an analysis of motion that makes the very possibility of eternal motion depend on a perpetually moving body and an unmoved mover. The analysis of the last notion produces the characterization of divine substance. In short, the procedure employed here is the same as the procedure employed in physical science; the difference is that the philosopher ultimately posits a sub-

27 One might wish that Aristotle would systematically distinguish between χωριστά and κεχωρισμένα, but the corpus fails to support a distinction of this sort. Nor is ᾗ χωριστά used exclusively for the objects of metaphysics; e.g., at 1026a10 it is used to describe mathematical objects.

28 Cf. Frede (1987, chap. 6), who argues that divine substance is paradigmatic as substance.

29 Cf. Sextus Empiricus, *Adversus Mathematicos* 3. 57–58: "Aristotle affirms that the length without breadth the geometers talk of is not inconceivable but can come into our minds without any difficulty . . . we perceive the length of a wall, he says, without thinking simultaneously of its breadth."

stance that lacks motion and magnitude and hence cannot be an object of natural science (1078a13–14; cf. 198a27–29).

The objects of *sophia* are ex hypothesi the most intelligible, the most exact, and the most universal. It is a striking feature of Aristotle's conception of metaphysics that he believes that objects having these characteristics can be grasped by the mind ἐξ ἐμπειρίας. The theory of meaning sketched in *De Interpretatione* I makes meanings a function of the impact of the world on human minds. The implication of Aristotle's conception of metaphysics is that neither universality nor intelligibility pose a threat to the theory of meaning, since the meanings of terms for the most intelligible and universal objects will be accessible through experience. The strict definitions of the objects of *sophia* (because derived through *epagoge*) can be viewed as refinements of linguistic definitions. The latter are the result of the encounter between creatures having certain cognitive and linguistic capacities and the world.

Our discussion of the three types of theoretical science has shown that Aristotle can make a persuasive case for his claim that all concepts are grasped on the basis of experience. Some concepts (those of physics and metaphysics) are acquired directly by induction from observables; others (those of arithmetic and geometry) are acquired by abstracting from universals derived from observables. This provides an answer to the epistemological question about the origin of universals; it does not provide a full answer to the semantic question about the ontological status of concepts. This question arises in connection with all universals but seems especially difficult in the case of concepts that are ex hypothesi either separable through abstraction (mathematical concepts) or simply separable (metaphysical concepts). Whether Aristotle has an answer remains to be determined. Before turning to his ontology in search of his answer, we should consider what contribution dialectic makes to the acquisition of concepts.

4 *Endoxa* and Dialectic

Posterior Analytics II 19 describes a process by which the human mind grasps universals. This description has proven consistent with the account Aristotle gives of the apprehension of the first principles of mathematics, natural science, and metaphysics. Notwithstanding, several features of Aristotle's practice as a scientist and a philosopher, which are yet to be discussed, pose a challenge for the present interpretation. These are (a) Aristotle's practice of reviewing earlier theories and common opinions (*endoxa*) at the outset of inquiries and (b) his use of dialectical arguments. Aristotle devotes much of the first book of the *Physics* to the critical discussion of his predecessors' views, and the remainder of the work is peppered with commentary on earlier accounts. The survey of *en-*

doxa plays an equally important role in the *Metaphysics*. The survey of *endoxa* seems more theory laden than does the progression from perceptions of physical objects to universals described in *Posterior Analytics* II 19. To the extent that the first principles of a demonstrative science are derived from an examination of *endoxa,* determinations of truth would be internal to the theories themselves. This would challenge the semantics of the *De Interpretatione,* where words refer to and (in some instances) are predicated of external objects. More crucially, according to Aristotle's theory of meaning, the relation between the mental *pathema* and its external object is natural and universal; to the extent that Aristotle's handling of *endoxa* or his use of dialectical argument establishes the epistemic priority of coherence as a test of truth, then to that extent the naturalness and universality of the deep structure of language are called into question. It is quite conceivable that radically different linguistic structures could support coherent conceptual schemes that were themselves incommensurate.

The dialectical arguments of *Metaphysics* IV may, as some have argued, establish dialectic as a method of science. If so, then the question becomes: Can dialectic, like abstraction, be subsumed under the inductive process of *Posterior Analytics* II 19? Whether the obstacles posed by Aristotle's use of *endoxa* and dialectic to the extension of the II 19 account will stand up to further scrutiny remains to be seen. If dialectic, like abstraction, turns out to be a type of *epagoge,* then dialectic poses no special threat to the theory of meaning. Or, if dialectic turns out not to be a method for arriving at first principles, it poses no threat.

Endoxa and *dialectic* are also of interest, because they are relevant to the analysis of meaning. Aristotle often and quite appropriately turns to the *endoxa* to determine what a word means. *Endoxa* would seem to be the primary source for linguistic definitions. Dialectic as a method for clarifying conceptual relations would seem an invaluable tool for drawing verbal distinctions. These considerations buttress the intuition that Aristotle needs to integrate his use of *endoxa* and dialectical method into his epistemology in a way that does not undermine his theory of meaning. Too little dependence on these methods will threaten his ability to account for the significance of natural language terms; too much dependence on them will threaten his claims about the universality and verisimilitude of the deep structure of language.

Metaphysics I provides some insight into how Aristotle sees the relation between the derivation of universals from sense experience and the survey of the *endoxa,* which is a persistent feature of his approach to the theoretical, as well as the applied, sciences. As described in I 1, perceptions of the world yield concepts of ordinary objects (the concepts of experience), and these in turn yield the concepts employed in the arts, and finally the concepts of the theoretical sciences emerge. The concepts of pure mathematics and natural science are grasped before the more difficult concepts of philosophy. As noticed in Chapter 3, Aristotle envisages the history of human intellectual achievement as a continuous process of refinement and correction. Mistakes were undoubtedly made on the way to acquiring the first principles of such mundane arts as that of house building. Humans did not learn how to build structures that would withstand the ravages of time and weather overnight, and they certainly did not arrive at the basic concepts of the theoretical sciences overnight.

As a result, when all such inventions were already established, the sciences which do not aim at giving pleasure or at the necessities of life were discovered, and first in the places where people had leisure. (981b20–22)

Envisaging a continuous evolution of universals from simple concepts to complex propositions, Aristotle would naturally assume that his job as both a philosopher of science and a natural scientist would require him to be actively engaged in the effort to achieve greater precision and clarity about the relevant universals. By presenting and testing the received theories in the discipline, Aristotle is doing precisely this. Because he believes that knowledge in all areas is cumulative, Aristotle is deeply committed to the examination of earlier theories. Because he believes truth is reached through a winnowing process, not by a direct and immediate grasp of self-evident universals, he subjects his predecessors' views to harsh criticism. In point of fact, Aristotle often seems too intent upon eliminating rival theories and too eager to subsume earlier positions under his own, and no doubt the outcome of these tendencies sometimes is the distortion of an earlier view.[30] But it is also clear that the way Aristotle handles earlier theories is motivated by his conception of the acquisition of the universals of art and science. Whenever Aristotle believes that a predecessor – even one he is highly critical of – has gotten it right, he will acknowledge this, as when he comments that the truth itself has forced Empedocles to say that "the ratio (*logos*) is the essence and real nature of things" (*Part. An.* 642a18–20). In *Physics* I, Aristotle elicits the correct account of the structures underlying change from a critical examination of his predecessors' accounts of change. What is required for a change to occur is the existence of an underlying substratum and a pair of contraries, one of which inheres in the substratum prior to the change and the other, after the change. This analysis, according to Aristotle, simultaneously reveals what is right about the earlier view that nothing can come into existence or go out of existence and where the earlier view went astray (191a23-b27).[31] These examples are typical of Aristotle's use

30 As is widely acknowledged, Cherniss (1935) made a persuasive case for Aristotle's distortion of pre-Socratic theories.

31 Offering his own doctrine as a corrected version of past insights is a standard modus operandi for Aristotle. See, e.g., *Met.* I 3–4, *Phys.* I 4–8.

of the *endoxa* as a heuristic device, that is, as a way to clarify the nature of an inquiry and to yield the nominal definitions with which an inquiry begins. Were this the only use of *endoxa,* it would be unproblematic. Aristotle sometimes uses the *endoxa,* however, to support claims to know. A case in point is his argument that an adequate explanation will answer four questions about the phenomenon.

The doctrine of the four causes is stated in *Physics* II 3 and II 7, and the final cause (in addition to the material, efficient, and formal causes recognized by earlier philosophers) is made a requirement for adequate explanation of natural phenomena.[32] Aristotle offers relatively little defense of this doctrine in the *Physics;* we must look to *Metaphysics* I to find a defense of the fundamental character of the four causes. The claim that they constitute the exhaustive list of types of genuine explanations is justified by a detailed survey of received theories in *Metaphysics* I 3–10. This raises the question whether (in the end) a normative principle of natural science, namely, the requirement that an adequate explanation address the four causes, is justified solely on the basis of *endoxa* and thus by appeal to a coherence theory of truth.[33] As a descriptive account of the foundations of science, the doctrine of the four causes is on firm ground. The topic is scientific explanation, and the data would be the structure of actual sciences. The claim to truth of the doctrine would be justified by an appeal to the correspondence between scientific practice and the proffered philosophical analysis. Aristotle also makes normative claims on this basis, however; these are all the types of explanation worthy of investigation, and every science should address them. Here, there is a larger problem, because not all the sciences attach the same weight to the four types of explanation delineated by Aristotle – as he recognizes.

Addressing the final cause is central to the task of framing a theory about a natural phenomenon, but of no importance as a distinct requirement for the mathematician. This is especially clear in the case of biology. It would be quite difficult, certainly misguided, Aristotle believes, to offer an explanation of the changes an acorn undergoes in the course of sprouting without reference to the oak tree and a developmental sequence from acorn to tree.[34] In *Parts of Animals* I 1, Aristotle remarks,

32 The doctrine of the four causes is not asserted in its canonical form in the *Posterior Analytics,* although two passages suggest it. At *Post. Anal.* II 1, 89b23–25, Aristotle mentions the following four questions: (1) whether the connection of an attribute with a thing is a fact, (2) what is the reason of the connection, (3) whether a thing exists, and (4) what is the nature of the thing. (4) τί ἐστιν? is the only question that appears in the same form on the list of questions in *Physics* II 7. In *Post. Anal.* II 11, 94a20–23, four causes are listed: (1) the definable form, (2) an antecedent that necessitates a consequent, (3) the efficient cause, and (4) the final cause.

33 Cf. Chapter 2, section 2.

34 The importance of a particular type of teleological explanation in biology has been defended recently by Mayr (1974, 1982), who distinguishes between teleonomic activities

"No abstraction can be the subject of natural science, since nature acts in every case for the sake of something" (641b11–13). A complete explanation in natural science will include an explanation in terms of a final cause. In only one context does Aristotle make any effort to find a role for a final cause in mathematics. At the conclusion of *Metaphysics* XIII 3, presumably to meet a sophistic objection, he urges a distinction between the good as the end of conduct (τὸ ἀγαθόν) and the beautiful (τὸ καλόν).[35] Mathematics displays the order, symmetry, and definiteness that are constitutive of beauty. The beautiful in mathematics, however, unlike the good in natural science, is a consequence of the rigor and simplicity of the arguments themselves.[36] This somewhat ad hoc extension of the final cause to mathematics reveals the tension between the descriptive and the normative functions of the four causes in Aristotle's philosophy of science.

Aristotle thinks that, on the one hand, the justification of the explanatory role of the four causes is largely a matter of showing that previous philosophers recognized all but the final cause and that, on the other hand, these explanatory principles classify explanations that articulate real causal relations. He makes no attempt to justify the normative role of his theory. The explanation is no doubt to be found in two primitive assumptions: (a) the mind is such that it can grasp universals (*Posterior Analytics* II 19), and (b) collectively, humans arrive at the truth (*Metaphysics* II 2). The first assumption (a) interpreted in light of the theory of meaning yields a conception of any genuine science as an interrelated body of propositions that express real natures and relations. The second assumption (b) interpreted in light of a correspondence theory of truth yields the result that the classification of the types of explanation characteristic of the sciences provides a classification of the basic types of real relations. These assumptions provide a justification for Aristotle (if not for us) for viewing scientific and philosophical theories as expressions of real relations and, conversely, real relations as discoverable from an analysis of scientific theories. In addition, the belief that universals in the mind arise from real causes with which they are formally identical explains,

that play an important role in biological explanations and cosmic teleology, which "modern science rejects without reservation" (1982, p. 50). Cf. Wimsatt (1972).

35 *Met.* 1078a33-b5. The sophistic objection that mathematics takes no account of the good is raised at 996a29–36. Since, however, the good is typically identified with the final cause by Aristotle (e.g., 982b10), this resolution amounts to the claim that for mathematics there is no final cause outside of the form of the reasoning.

36 When describing the four causes in *Physics* II 7, Aristotle mentions mathematics only in connection with the formal cause (198a16–18). The list of four causes in *Posterior Analytics* II 11, however, mentions 'an antecedent which necessitates a consequent' instead of the material cause; in the *Physics*, Aristotle says that the premises of an argument are the matter for its conclusion (195a18) but subsequently limits the material cause to things that come into being (198a20–21).

within limits, the reliability of generally accepted opinions (*endoxa*). Because they are generally reliable, *endoxa* are appropriate starting points for inquiry in disciplines where the objective is knowledge.

The survey of *endoxa* in the *Physics* and elsewhere is modeled on the method Aristotle describes in *Topics* I 11 under the rubric of "dialectical problems," where the goal is the examination of a disputed point. Aristotle gives instructions for setting up a dialectical problem: if one is a philosopher, the object should be to obtain the truth by examining a thesis put forth by philosophers that is not widely accepted by ordinary people. One of the sample questions suggested by Aristotle is Is the universe eternal or not? He argues for the former in the *De Caelo* and the eternality of motion in the *Physics.* More generally, Aristotle systematically employs the techniques of dialectic in presenting and examining the relevant *endoxa* in his works. What is more controversial is whether Aristotle embraces a third mode of argument that is neither deductive nor inductive as a way to establish truths, not just to clarify theses and sharpen lines of analysis.

The method used to establish basic logical laws or common axioms in *Metaphysics* IV has been cited as evidence that Aristotle has changed his mind about the role of dialectic in science. In the *Posterior Analytics,* Aristotle mentions dialectic and another nameless, hypothetical science whose domain includes the common axioms in their full generality (77a26–32), but turning to the knowledge of first principles, he describes an inductive method of eliciting the universal from observable particulars (88a2–5; 100a3–5).[37] By contrast, in *Metaphysics* IV 3–4, the Law of Noncontradiction is defended on the basis of its role in argument and speech.[38] There are two stages in this defense. Initially, Aristotle claims that the LNC is a principle that must be understood in order to understand anything else (1005b15–31). Then he takes on those who claim to believe the contradictory of this principle. In a thought experiment, the hypothetical critic of the LNC is put to the test. Every line of defense that the opponent tries is shown to presuppose the principle that his argument seeks to overturn. The second stage has been the locus of the argument that dialectic is accorded a new importance by Aristotle in the *Metaphysics.*[39] If the elenctic arguments of IV 4 are a form of dialectic and

37 While in *Posterior Analytics* I 11 Aristotle stops short of identifying the science that investigates common axioms with dialectic, he does mention dialectic and points out that it has no single subject genus.

38 I shall use the abbreviation LNC throughout this section. It should be noted that PNC is another standard abbreviation for the Law of Noncontradiction and that PNC will be used in a direct quotation from another author.

39 As originally argued by Owen (1960), Aristotle assigns dialectic the role of establishing the first principles of metaphysics. Irwin developed this line of interpretation in terms of a special kind of dialectic (strong dialectic) that is capable of establishing truths (*Aristotle's First Principles*).

secure the truth of the LNC, then Aristotle has adopted a conception of scientific method that is inconsistent with his semantics, for reasons discussed in Chapter 2. If, however, the point of the elenctic arguments is to refute the opponent of the LNC on his own turf, then the appeal to coherence rather than correspondence is internal to the refutation and unproblematic for Aristotelian semantics.

In Socratic elenchus, a thesis is put forth by the interlocutor, who is shown in the course of Socrates' cross-examination to be committed to a position that contradicts the original thesis.[40] At 1006a29–b34, Aristotle invites the opponent to assert some proposition that is inconsistent with the LNC, for instance, 'This is a man and is not a man'. Aristotle argues that this sentence is significant only if 'This is a man' is significant; for this to be the case, 'man' must be taken in a specific sense (M_1). The point is not that 'man' must have only one meaning; it is rather that understanding a sentence in which 'man' occurs is a function of taking 'man' in a specific sense. Moreover, 'man' in sense M_1 cannot signify the same thing as 'not-man' in sense M_1. On behalf of the opponent of the LNC, we might object: suppose M_1 just is the concept of an entity that is and is not a man; then both 'man' and 'not-man' could have the same meaning. If Aristotle's only reason for ignoring this possibility is the LNC, then he has not shown that his opponent must presuppose the LNC. If, however, the ultimate bearers of meaning are simple concepts, as Aristotle believes for independent reasons, then the significance of a complex concept of the sort required for 'man-and-not-man' will be a function of the meaning of each of its constituents.[41] If either of its constituents is vacuous, the complex will no longer have a distinct meaning; if both are vacuous, the complex will no longer be significant. If both have distinct meanings, 'man' will not signify the same thing as 'not-man' and Aristotle is vindicated. From this, it follows that 'to be a man' (in sense M_1) cannot signify the same thing as 'not to be a man' (in sense M_1). Up to this point, Aristotle has argued on the basis of what is required for meaning. As the final move against the LNC's challenger, he concludes that a particular object cannot be both a man and not a man in fact, although it might be so in name – in an artificially constructed language. (To be such and such in fact, Aristotle assumes, is to have a character that corresponds to a distinct meaning.) This conclusion contradicts the critic's original

40 As presented in Plato's early dialogues, the object of the elenchus is a thesis put forward by Socrates' interlocutor, which is shown to be inconsistent with another position accepted by the interlocutor. In the *Meno,* for example, Meno makes several attempts to define 'virtue' at 71e, 73d, and 77b. Each definition is rejected in turn after it is found to be incompatible with some other position Meno accepts. In the *Charmides,* the definitions of 'temperance' offered by Charmides at 159b, 160e, and 161b meet the same fate.

41 See Chapter 1, sections 2, 3, and 5, and Chapter 5, below.

thesis. Aristotle gives a number of similar arguments (negative demonstrations) in IV 4 for the LNC.

Whether or not negative demonstration is a form of dialectic is an open question.[42] A dialectical argument, according to the *Topics,* employs as premises opinions that the majority of people accept or opinions accepted by one's opponent. While majority opinion favors the Law of Noncontradiction, the argument against the hypothetical opponent fits the second description. *Topics* I envisages a broad role for dialectic; it is said to be useful to the philosophic sciences (101a28) and to be a tool for investigating first principles irrespective of methodology (101b3–4). In the *Metaphysics,* Aristotle associates the development of dialectic (διαλεκτική) with Plato and describes dialectic as a method that enables the dialectician to examine basic concepts such as the same and the different on the basis of *endoxa* without knowing their essences; he also contrasts dialectic with philosophy (987b32, 995b23, 1004b17–27, 1078b25). Nevertheless, Owen argues that dialectic is accorded the status of a method of science in *Metaphysics* IV and not earlier because not until *Metaphysics* IV does Aristotle acknowledge the possibility of a science of common axioms.[43] Irwin distinguishes between strong dialectic, namely, the use of dialectical procedures applied to a restricted set of common beliefs, and ordinary dialectic.[44] According to him, Aristotle employs strong dialectic in *Metaphysics* IV 4 not in order to demonstrate the LNC but to give us a reason to believe the LNC is true.[45] The elenctic arguments, Irwin reasons, show that the opponent of the LNC is committed to a conception of a subject of properties that presupposes the LNC.

> O ⟨the opponent of PNC⟩ and Aristotle agree that scientific study presupposes a subject with properties, but O denies that it presupposes a subject satisfying PNC. To show that O is wrong, Aristotle seeks to show that O has no object of study left if O refuses to presuppose PNC. (Irwin, p. 181)

Having asserted that the LNC is the most certain of principles, Aristotle then establishes that having a belief of any sort presupposes the LNC. In contrast to Irwin, Alan Code argues that the metaphysician's job is not to prove first principles, to establish their truth, but "to prove things about the common axioms" (p. 354).[46] The elenctic arguments of IV 4, ac-

42 According to Owen, Aristotle's conception of dialectic changed. Common axioms are recognized through dialectic in the *Organon,* but not before *Metaphysics* IV is dialectic accorded the status of a method of science (1960, 175–6).

43 See, however, Berti (1996), who argues that from the *Topics* on, Aristotle envisages a role in science for dialectic.

44 Irwin (1988, chap. 9). Irwin construes Aristotle's distinction between the method of philosophy and dialectical method as the distinction between strong dialectic and ordinary dialectic.

45 Against Irwin, Code (1986b, pp. 341–8) argues that Aristotle does not demonstrate the PNC, but he does demonstrate that the PNC is the most certain principle of all.

46 Code (1986b, pp. 354–7).

cording to Code, are intended to establish the priority of the LNC, not its truth, and for that reason Aristotle thinks he is entitled to assume its truth throughout. The point is to show why anyone who accepts the LNC must accept it as true and required for significant thought.

At the end of IV 3, Aristotle argues for the LNC's being the most certain principle of all.

> For a principle which every one must have who understands anything that is, is not a hypothesis; and that which every one must know who knows anything, one who comes to a special study must also have. It is clear then that such a principle is the most certain of all; which principle this is, let us say next. For the same attribute at the same time to belong and not belong to the same subject and in the same respect is impossible. (1005b15–20)

The strategy of this argument, whatever its shortcomings, challenges the thesis that the elenctic arguments of IV 4 are intended to establish the truth of the LNC. Aristotle appears to assert the universality of the Law of Noncontradiction on the basis of its ubiquity in IV 3; every special science presupposes the LNC. In this case, I believe, the special sciences play the role of 'observables,' and universal principles accepted by all in application to their specific subject matters would be elicited in the manner described in *Posterior Analytics* II 19. Irwin's objection to this line of argument is that the *Analytics* makes the knowledge of first principles depend on immediate intuition of these principles (*nous*) and that no such appeal to *nous* is made here. If, on the other hand, the interpretation of *Posterior Analytics* II 19 offered in Chapter 3 is correct and *nous* is simply the settled dispositional knowledge of principles arrived at inductively, then *Metaphysics* IV 3, by mentioning the LNC's experiential basis – namely, what one must know to know anything – is making reference to the way the LNC is known. That said, it must be admitted that the 'empirical' defense of the LNC is based on a generalization about human epistemic capacities. Unless human cognitive capacities are situated in the world, this defense will fall short of establishing a mind-independent basis for the LNC. The task of determining how much support Aristotle's theory of cognition provides for his epistemological realism will be deferred until Chapters 7 and 8.

The elenctic arguments in IV 4, I believe, are introduced to persuade any self-proclaimed disbelievers by refuting them and, as noted in Chapter 2, these arguments are backed up by further arguments in IV 5–6 against relativism in its various guises.[47] Dialectical arguments are needed

47 Here I disagree with Code (1986b). Despite the inclusion of technical theses in some of the elenctic arguments of IV 4, Aristotle's target is surely a proponent of a competing philosophical account of reasoning and reality, as it is in the following chapters of *Metaphysics* IV. Aristotle introduces the elenctic arguments by mentioning that there are people, including some of the physical philosophers (τῶν περὶ φύσεως), who believe it is possible to reject the LNC (1005b35–1006a3).

in IV 4 because certain philosophers, namely, Heraclitus and Protagoras, had challenged the universality of this principle.[48] These philosophers are not going to be persuaded by evidence showing that all the special sciences presuppose the LNC; after all, their target is not simply the LNC but the special sciences' claim to providing privileged access to knowledge. For them, a 'proof' of the LNC that is internal to their mode of philosophizing is necessary. In order to put forth their alternative theories, they must make use of assertion. Aristotle's arguments against them are designed to show that even the simplest assertion presupposes the truth of the LNC.

In the arguments against the opponent of the LNC, the debt to Socratic elenchus is obvious. It does not end there, however, for fundamental to Aristotle's critique of the *endoxa* is that same 'Socratic' confidence that truth will out, if a thesis is developed and then scrutinized for internal contradictions or consequences that fly in the face of observation or common sense. Aristotle credits Socrates with seeking the essence in things, for recognizing the importance of inductive arguments, and for emphasizing universal definitions (1078b27–31). For Aristotle, the survey of the earlier views and the use of dialectical problems are heuristic devices to be used to focus an inquiry that hopes to get beyond puzzles to positive results. Experience issues in concepts that are adequate for language. Lexical concepts are expressed in nominal definitions. In order to move beyond mere lexical concepts to real definitions of essence, the scientist employs the survey of *endoxa* and dialectical arguments to arrive at a consistent set of definitions, but the scientist cannot justify the claim to know on the basis of these methods. Whether a putative definition of essence expresses a real nature is a function of the correspondence between the concept expressed in the definition and an external object.

Thus interpreted, the use of dialectic in *Metaphysics* IV, like the critique of *endoxa,* complements the induction of universals from perceptions of particulars. Aristotle envisages a process of winnowing and clarifying views that precedes the recognition of the first principles proper to a particular science. The *endoxa* are a source of universals, some of which might possess the requisite features to serve as basic objects of a theoretical science or as well-grounded universals to be used as the basis for further generalization. To decide whether they are promising candidates in either capacity, Aristotle employs dialectic and the critique of the *endoxa* – and he would no doubt urge other philosopher/scientists to do the same. Both methods allow investigators to build on previous work in the

48 Cf. Aristotle's description of his strategy at *Met.* 1009a20: "Those who argue for the sake of argument can be cured only by refuting the argument as expressed in speech and words." Cf. 1063b7–16.

field while avoiding the mistakes of their predecessors. There is here neither a slavish respect for earlier teachings nor a wholesale rejection of them as worthless, and this approach is just what we would expect from the author of *Posterior Analytics* II 19 and *Metaphysics* I 1.

The survey of *endoxa*, the arguments in support of the doctrine of the four causes, and the Laws of Noncontradiction and the Excluded Middle all share the feature of taking the products of human reasoning as their starting points. For this reason, they seemed to challenge Aristotle's claim that experience is the origin of all universals. On closer examination, however, Aristotle's treatment of these topics supports the picture of parallel structures – real causal structures in the world and human cognitive capacities that are uniquely suited to apprehending real relations and objects – that we found in *Posterior Analytics* II 19 and *De Interpretatione* 1. How lexical items, words, linguistic definitions, and sentences hook up with the world of concrete objects and real relations is partly explained by the theory of meaning: written and spoken words are arbitrary signs of concepts that are likenesses of the objects, relations, and states of affairs expressed by lexical items. The objects encountered in experience are particulars, and thus the formation of a concept that is the concept of a particular is easy to understand. In order for universal concepts to be likenesses, the external object must in some sense also manifest universal characteristics. This much is clear from *Posterior Analytics* II 19 and Aristotle's analysis of the three forms of theoretical science; however, Aristotle has not yet offered an ontology that makes this phenomenon fully intelligible.

5 Essences and the Basic Concepts of Science

That speakers possess concepts corresponding to basic ontological categories is implied by Aristotle's description of language in the *De Interpretatione.* Evidence for the existence of such concepts is provided by the theoretical sciences. Moreover, Aristotle's conception of the three types of science is, it seems, consistent with the account of *epagoge* in *Posterior Analytics* II 19. As if to emphasize this point, Aristotle uses the same natural kind to illustrate how concepts are acquired simpliciter and how concepts appropriate to the theoretical sciences are acquired. In *Posterior Analytics* II 19, the concept of animal is derived from that of human. In *Metaphysics* XIII 3, the concept of a unit is derived from that of human. In *Physics* I 7, the concept of an underlying subject is derived from that of a human becoming musical. As these examples show, what the mind does with a given conceptualization of a concrete particular is in large measure a consequence of the interests of the thinker. None of the broader universals are such that the only cognitive access to them is through the concept of a human being. Notwithstanding, Aristotle's use of the concept 'human' in a variety of different contexts attests to his determination to show how even quite abstract concepts are derivable from the concept of a particular natural kind that is obvious to us from our earliest perceptions.

On the one hand, Aristotle's descriptions of the acquisition of the basic concepts of the theoretical sciences support his contention that these concepts originate in the world. A concrete particular, Socrates, for instance, thought about in terms of its essence yields the concept of the natural kind, human; Socrates thought about as an instantiation of an indivisible essence yields the concept of a unit; Socrates thought about as an instantiation of a changing object yields the concept of a persisting substratum. The connection between the basic objects of the sciences and the physical world is maintained. On the other hand, the versatility of the human mind suggested a quite different picture to the Platonists, who contrasted the characteristics of universals to those of particulars. Concrete particulars were for them but poor reflections of separately existing essences. In order to link all universals to concrete particulars, Aristotle emphasizes the importance of the first-level concepts, the essences of concrete individuals, and their characteristics. From the *Categories* and the *De Interpretatione* on, the first-level concepts are both likenesses of the particular and expressions of the universal; the first-level concept of this particular human is simultaneously the expression of the concept human that is predicable of other humans. These anchor all the other concepts to the world that they represent under various conceptual schemes (e.g., that of physical science). This leaves Aristotle with an ontology of concrete objects and essences and the need to secure the relation between the two. This is the task he undertakes in the central books of the *Metaphysics*.

PART II

Definition and Essence

5

Definition and Ontology

The most basic existents in the *Categories* are particular substances and particular attributes. Meaning in the *De Interpretatione* is a function of reference to existents. Definitions of the basic objects of a demonstrative science must express real natures, according to the *Posterior Analytics*. Equally as much as science, language depends upon the apprehension of universals. Linguistic and scientific definitions articulate universal concepts. There is an apparent tension between the role of universals in Aristotle's epistemology and semantics and the *Categories* doctrine that universals are secondary and dependent upon human classificatory schemes. This is one problem Aristotle faces in the *Metaphysics*.

Another problem facing Aristotle is how to explain the relation between the meanings of the terms of natural language and the meanings of terms in scientific discourse (often the same linguistic sign has both uses.) Science requires meanings that correspond precisely to reality. Natural language requires words (at least designative ones) that refer to real existents. There can be no doubt that Aristotle distinguishes between the two cases. The nominal definition of a natural language term may express a concept that has no exemplifications, for instance, 'goatstag', or it may embody an imperfect understanding of the real existent, for instance, 'human.' What, then, is the difference between a meaning expressed in a linguistic definition and a meaning expressed in a definition of essence? This concern motivates the discussion of definition and essence in *Metaphysics* VII.

From the *Physics* to the *De Caelo* to *De Partibus animalium,* Aristotle develops a methodology to produce first principles having the universality and necessity required by the *Analytics* model of science. Science in all its varied forms consists in the knowledge of universals, and these are ultimately derived from perceptions of the physical world. Aristotle never wavers in his determination to show that the behavior of the changing objects of experience can only be explained by appeal to unchanging patterns exhibited by these same objects. By the time he writes the central books of the *Metaphysics*, Aristotle has narrowed the problem of accounting for first principles down to establishing the basis for the shared assumptions of the sciences. A natural or mathematical science is restricted to a specialized subject matter. There must then be a distinct discipline, Aristotle argues, that investigates shared principles and assumptions; this discipline is philosophy, the third type of theoretical science (cf. 982a5–b3, 1003b19–1004b17). The focal point of philosophical investigation in *Metaphysics* IV is the study of the elements of the conceptual scheme common to all the sciences and ordinary discourse, namely, logical laws and basic categories, and in *Metaphysics* VII–IX the emphasis is on the character of the most basic objects. Basic objects must be definable, and their definitions cannot merely be stipulated. These definitions must be such that they express a nature that is simple (to block a regress of definitions) and such that they are intelligible. To tell a story that meets both these desiderata is not easy, and Aristotle tackles his task from several different angles in the central books of the *Metaphysics*.

The conflict between positing simple, basic objects grasped somehow, perhaps through perception, and the requirements of science is vividly portrayed in the *Theaetetus*. Socrates has a dream that knowledge consists in the apprehension of indefinable simples and accounts (*logoi*) that are combinations of the simples. This position is untenable, Plato's Socrates argues, because it will lead either to an infinite regress of accounts or to unknowable basic units (*atoma*).[1] In the *Analytics* and elsewhere, Aristotle argues against an infinite regress of reasons and argues for indemonstrable first principles.[2] Suppose a science consists in basic objects that are somehow apprehended in a way external to the science and that these objects are then combined in various ways to form accounts (or arguments). The basic objects, if simple, will be unintelligible; there will be no account (*logos*) possible of them. If they are unintelligible, Plato argues, then how can they function as components of the *logoi* expressing knowledge? The basic definitions of Aristotelian science are vulnerable on this score, because the basic objects of a science must be simple to block a regress of first principles and they must be definable.[3] Aristotle's account of definition in the *Metaphysics* is designed to satisfy these requirements in a way that is consistent with realism about the external world.

The ontological commitments of Aristotle's theory of meaning and of his conception of science are clear, and they motivate the analysis found in the central books of the *Metaphysics*. In these books, the alternative on-

1 The implications of this argument for Aristotle's account of truth were explored in Chapter 2, section 3.

2 At *Metaphysics* 994b20–23, Aristotle says that an infinite regress of definitions would destroy science.

3 Cf. *Metaphysics* VII, 13, 1039a15–21.

tology afforded by the Platonic theory of Ideas is subjected to rigorous criticism and seems never to be far from Aristotle's thought. Unless the existence of ideal objects is granted, Plato argues, no satisfactory account of knowledge or language can be given.[4] Determined to falsify this claim, Aristotle argues for the intelligibility of the physical world.

The skeptical puzzles raised in the *Theaetetus* challenge both Aristotle's account of meaning and his account of first principles. Plato's Socrates appeals to a Heraclitean conception of a constantly changing physical world to refute the position that knowledge is perception and to argue further that in a Heraclitean world meaningful speech will be impossible.[5] Although Aristotle's study of existing sciences casts considerable light on what is wrong with this picture, he has not yet located the element of stability in the world of changing objects that grounds meaning and truth. Aristotle's answer to Socrates' dream is found in the *Metaphysics.* The elements of his solution are the concepts of indivisible essences, real definitions, and immanent forms. This chapter explores Aristotle's conception of real definition and essence. The following chapter centers on his conception of form as the functional organization of a concrete individual and as an essence of a species.

1 Requirements of Speech and Knowledge

The Heraclitean of the *Theaetetus* posits a sensible realm that is constantly changing.[6] No word has a stable meaning, moreover, because there are no stable objects to fix its meaning. Suppose 'white' means just that characteristic of objects that is picked out when one points to a white surface and further that, before the word 'white' can be uttered, the surface changes color and that this is also true for all other surfaces and color terms. 'White' would be meaningless as a color term under these conditions, since there would be equally good reasons to call the same surface 'black' or 'red'. Now one might grant this about the names of colors, while arguing that all these terms were synonymous and meant 'color,' a property of surfaces to cause sensations of red, black, and so on. But this move, Plato would argue, is not open to the Heraclitean, for it presupposes the existence of at least one, identifiable, enduring object having surfaces the colors of which are constantly changing. Were the objector to eliminate talk about objects and surfaces and maintain that the qual-

4 *Crat.* 439a–440e; *Rep.* 475e–480a, 507b–511e. See also Chapter 1 in this volume.

5 The *Cratylus* also discusses meaning against the backdrop of a Heraclitean worldview. There, however, Plato's Socrates supposes that words can capture the nature of changing objects and then argues that the fact that the meaning of terms change over time would rule out the possibility of grasping real natures in words. See Chapter 1 in this volume.

6 In what follows, I plan to develop the Heraclitean position described by Plato in the *Theaetetus* (152d–183c). Whether this is what the historical Heraclitus had in mind is a topic for a different inquiry than the present one.

ity color is continuously exemplified throughout the changes, Plato would respond that the Heraclitean cannot adopt this solution, because it would mean that qualities escape the flux. The existence of enduring objects or properties of any sort is ruled out on the Heraclitean theory. If the empirical referents of words determine their meanings, then the Heraclitean flux renders all sounds meaningless. Plato's solution as reported by Aristotle is to posit ideal objects:

> ⟨Plato assumed⟩ that there can be no general definition of sensible things which are always changing. Things of this other sort he called 'Ideas' and held that all sensible things are named after them and in virtue of their relation to them; for the things which have the same name as the Forms exist by participation in them. (*Met.* 987b6–10)

On this picture, language becomes a device for imposing structure on what would otherwise be a confusing swirl of impressions. The reference of words to objects in the perceptible world is mediated through the stable, ideal objects that furnish the meaning of the terms used to describe the physical world. In sharp contrast to the concrete particulars named after them, Platonic Ideas are unchanging, not subject to generation or decay, are just what they are independent of context, and are not dependent upon the perspective of the knower.[7] These characteristics make the Ideas uniquely suitable to secure the meanings of the words referring to them and to serve as the objects of knowledge.

While rejecting Platonic Ideas, Aristotle accepts many of the epistemic requirements defended by Plato, namely, that objects of knowledge must be unchanging universals, substances, and essences, and that definitions expressing the essences of basic objects secure the foundations of knowledge. Natural languages also depend upon the existence of objects having many of the characteristics of Platonic Ideas.

> Were one to say that the word has an infinite number of meanings, it is clear that discussion [λόγος] would be impossible; for not to have one meaning is not to have any meaning at all, and if words have no meaning, reasoning with each other, and in truth with oneself, has been destroyed. (*Met.* 1006b6–9)

These requirements notwithstanding, Aristotle believes that Plato's ideal objects are an ontological complication that can be avoided by a proper analysis of the ontological underpinnings of science and language. The rejection of Platonic Ideas means that, unlike Plato, Aristotle cannot explain the significance of a linguistic term by appeal to an a priori intension that determines the range of application of the term to concrete objects. On the Platonic account, meanings are determined by Ideas, not by concrete referents of words, and hence the vicissitudes of physical objects pose no threat to the stability of meanings. The challenge facing Aristo-

7 *Rep.* 475e–480a.

tle is to find features of concrete referents that are such that meanings determined by reference to physical objects can be stable.

The plausibility of Plato's anti-Heraclitean argument in the *Theaetetus* turns on whether the fact of change in the world of sense experience rules out every kind of persistence. Aristotle rejects this crucial inference. As soon as the possibility of characters that endure for more than an instant is granted, then the potential exists for there to be at least some stable empirical concepts. Colors and other perceptible properties are obvious candidates. They are apprehended directly through the senses, and sense experience appears to be required for learning these concepts. The congenitally blind person, for example, lacks color concepts.[8] Recognizing that it is not necessary that any particular individual be unchangingly white for λευκόν to be significant, Aristotle posits a persistent property of physical surfaces, namely, acting on transparent media in a way that transmits the ratio of light to dark that causes a perception of white.[9] This empirical property determines the meaning of white (λευκόν).[10] The importance of sensory qualities and terms naming them to science is marginal, and so the strategy just outlined has limited application. Aristotle must develop a principled account of the foundations of science and language that explains meaning and reference without appealing to ideal transcendent objects.[11]

Lexical items occurring in the statement of a scientific definition have meaning if they successfully refer to stable external objects. Articulating the character of these referents is at the heart of the ontological investigation undertaken in the central books of the *Metaphysics*. Aristotle describes his project in terms that reveal the close connection in his thinking between the theory of meaning and the study of being as being. In *Metaphysics* IV 2, VII 1, and VII 3, Aristotle appeals to the notion of predication to establish that τὸ ὂν ᾗ ὂν (being as being) is a proper subject of study and that οὐσία (substance) is primary being. In these chapters, there seems to be the same equivocation in Aristotle's handling of predication as in the *Categories*.[12] Here, too, the philosophical inquiry into

8 *Physics* 193a7–9 allows the congenitally blind person to have the terms for colors without having the appropriate concepts (νοεῖν δὲ μηδέν).

9 Aristotle draws the first distinction necessary for making this case in *Categories* 5, where he argues that only substances remain numerically the same while admitting opposites: "For in no other case could one bring forward anything, numerically one, which is able to receive contraries. For example, a color which is numerically one and the same will not be black and white" (4a10–17, Ackrill trans.).

10 *De Anima* II 7, *De Sensu* 3; see also Modrak (1987a, chap. 3).

11 The role of perceptible properties is less limited in natural science for Aristotle than for us. According to him, the basic physical qualities are tactile (hot, dry, wet, cold), and natural kinds cannot be explained without reference to their material properties; this leaves only the sciences of abstract objects, namely, arithmetic and geometry, where the role of perceptible properties appears negligible.

12 Aristotle's description of these categories in the *Metaphysics* is the same in broad outline

what is real begins with the categories of ordinary language and thought. Here, too, the discussion seems to hover between predication in a linguistic context and a primitive relation between kinds of entities. In *Metaphysics* IV 2, having pointed out that a single nature is indicated not only by the univocal use of a predicate (*kath' hen* predication) but also by the use of a predicate in relation to the same subject (*pros hen* predication), Aristotle argues that *to on* (being) is predicated *pros hen* even though it is predicated in many senses.

For not only in the case of things which are predicated of one does the investigation belong to one science, but also in the case of things which are predicated in relation to one nature; for even these in a sense are predicated of one. It is clear then that it is the work of one science also to study being *qua* being. (*Met.* 1003b12–16)

On the one hand, Aristotle develops the notion of *pros hen* predication in order to maintain that the proper objects of study are existing things of various sorts, not an abstract idea of Being, and at the same time to make room for the study of being as being.[13] The last is important, because first philosophy, metaphysics, will not be a science, unless it has a single, unified subject. Aristotle employs the notion of *pros hen* predication in order to argue that being as being is such a subject.

On the other hand, however, the appeal to *pros hen* predication is a device for using linguistic analysis to establish the ontological priority of substance that was asserted but not adequately established in the *Categories*.[14] Whatever is said to be is said to be either a substance or to stand in one relation or another to substance. This finding is reaffirmed in *Metaphysics* VII, where it becomes the basis for claiming that *ousia* is primary being because it is prior in definition, knowledge, and time (1028a32).

At first blush, the ordinary notion of predication appears to figure in these discussions. Aristotle explains that *to on* is predicated in many senses, because sometimes it signifies an essence and a this, sometimes, a quality or a quantity, or one of the other categories. Signification here is reference-based meaning; that is, of the things called existents, some happen to be substances, some qualities, some quantities, and so on. Aristotle appears to be verging on the recognition of later logicians that, as

as in the *Categories,* but this is not true of the detailed analysis of the categories in these works. The account of substance is far more nuanced in the *Metaphysics.* In both works, the list of basic categories is the same, and the independence, both conceptual and ontological, of substance in relation to the other categories is defended. In the *Categories,* however, concrete individuals are the primary substances; in the *Metaphysics,* concrete substances are not primary substances because they are compounds of form and matter.

13 In the *Posterior Analytics,* Aristotle denies that τὸ ὄν is a genus (92b12). He does not retract that claim in the *Metaphysics;* rather, he argues that τὸ ὄν ᾗ ὄν is a proper object of study and describes it as a πρὸς ἕν predicate.

14 See discussion in Chapter 1, section 6.

Quine put it, "to be is to be the value of a bound variable." Aristotle goes on to argue, however, that all ascriptions of being are instances of *pros hen* predication because the core notion is that of substance (*ousia*). The grounds for this move seem to be primarily ontological rather than linguistic. When one points to an item in the world and asks, "What is that?" the standard answer falls under the category of substance. When the relation between substance and other existents such as qualities or quantities is analyzed, one finds that all other existents belong to substances as properties, as spatial or temporal locations, or as relations. Consequently, Aristotle concludes in *Metaphysics* VII 1 that the primary signification of *to on* is the essence or substance of the existent and that anything other than substance is said to exist in relation to substance.

In *Metaphysics* VII 3, Aristotle continues to frame the ontological inquiry in linguistic terms by examining uses of 'substance' (οὐσία).

'Substance' is said, if not in many senses, still at least in four: for both the essence and the universal and the genus are thought to be the substance of each thing, and fourth of these the substratum. (1028b33–36)[15]

Here, as in the case of scientific definition, Aristotle seems to be intent upon rendering a term found in ordinary discourse more precise in order to make the term more useful to the scientist (in this case the metaphysician).[16] *Ousia* in ordinary discourse surely did not have as its primary meanings, essence, universal, genus, and substratum.[17] The first three are drawn from philosophical discussions, especially those in Plato's Academy. The fourth, namely, the composite that serves as the substratum of properties, is an Aristotelian innovation. It is the philosopher's job (Aristotle believes) to tease out the ontological implications of ordinary language in order to better understand reference and meaning and in order to express philosophical insights perspicuously. Aristotle makes the analysis of the modes of predicating being the starting point of the study of substance, and this indicates how determined he is to situate what will prove to be a quite abstract metaphysical investigation in the conceptual framework shared by all speakers of Greek and by extension the framework belonging to any adequate actual language. Meaning is determined by reference. The referents of linguistic items are external (nonlinguistic) objects. In light of his conception of meaning, it should

15 Although Aristotle employs the same strategy in the case of *ousia*, namely, pointing out that *ousia* is said in more than one sense, he also implicitly contrasts its use to that of *to on*, which is said in many senses.

16 First philosophy is one type of theoretical science and natural science another; in both cases, it is appropriate to talk about the scientist (the expert employing a form of theoretical science).

17 Elsewhere, Aristotle acknowledges that some things are substances by common agreement, whereas others (including essence and substratum) are deemed substances on the basis of argument (*Met.* 1042a6–16).

not surprise us that Aristotle treats the investigation of what is as, inter alia, an investigation into the implications of language.

Aristotle uses the phrase (*to legomenon kath' hauto*) to describe the proper object of definition throughout *Metaphysics* VII. The phrase as used in the *Metaphysics* is open to several interpretations. There are several points of contact between this notion and that of per se (*kath' hauto*) predication as defined in *Posterior Analytics* I 4, but also some differences.[18] In the philosophical lexicon, Aristotle says that the expression *kath' hauto* is used in many ways and he goes on to list five senses:

(1) the essences of each thing, e.g., Callias is Callias *kath' hauton* . . . (2) whatever is present in the 'what,' e.g., Callias is an animal *kath' hauton* . . . (3) whatever attribute a thing receives in itself directly or in one of its parts, e.g., a surface is white *kath' heauten* . . . (4) that which has no cause other than itself . . . man is man *kath' hauton* . . . (5) whatever attributes belong to a thing alone qua alone. (*Met.* 1022a25–36)

Of these meanings, the first and the fourth seem the most relevant to the use of the phrase *to legomenon kath' hauto* in *Metaphysics* VII. If the first meaning is taken, the proper translation would be 'that which is said in virtue of itself' and the function of the phrase would be to distinguish essential predication from other types of predication. The second meaning is a corollary of the first that extends the notion to cover the conceptual parts of a definition of essence. If the fourth meaning is taken, the translation would be 'that which is said ⟨to exist⟩ separately' and the function of the phrase would be to distinguish a class of predicates that name independent existents. In VII 4, Aristotle initiates the linguistic (λογικῶς) discussion of definition by appealing to the identity between the essence of each thing and what it is said to be in itself (1029b14). The basis for this move would seem to be the first meaning of *kath hauto,* because a definition of *X*, according to Aristotle, is the statement (*logos*) of the essence of *X* (1031a12).[19] In other contexts, translators tend to prefer the fourth sense, and the phrase is often glossed "self-subsistent thing."[20] Perhaps, both senses are intended, for essence and existence are very closely connected in Aristotle's philosophy.

Linguistic intuitions shape not only Aristotle's analysis of substance as essence in *Metaphysics* VII but also his treatment of substance as substratum. Aristotle identifies three kinds of subjects in VII 3:

Further the substratum [τὸ ὑποκείμενον] is that of which everything else is predicated, while it is itself not predicated of anything else. Hence we must first determine its character; for the substratum is thought above all to be substance. And

18 See discussion of per se predication in Chapter 2, section 4.

19 The linguistic analysis of substance, found in VII 4–6, will be examined in detail in section 2 of this chapter.

20 See, for instance, Ross translation of *Met.* 1032a5.

in one sense matter is said to be of such a sort, in another, shape, and in a third, the compound of these. (*Met.* 1028b36–1029a3)

The identification of matter with the subject of change in the *Physics* would seem to make the matter of concrete particulars the ultimate subject (cf. 190b23–27).[21] After pointing out that if form is prior to matter, it will also be prior to the composite of matter and form, Aristotle develops the case against the strong prima facie claim that matter has to be primary substance, because matter is the ultimate subject. Matter is reached by applying the method of the *Categories* for determining the underlying subject, namely, stripping away in thought the features that are predicated of the object to produce a bare bones conception of the subject. There the method yielded a conception of primary substance that was neither in a subject (ἐν ὑποκειμένῳ) nor said of a subject (καθ' ὑποκειμένου) (1a20–1b6). This description was satisfied by the concrete substantial individual. The same method has a different outcome in *Metaphysics* VII 3, where the distinction between matter and form is made. The result is that neither the form nor the composite of matter and form would be primary substance, but rather the primary subject would be the stuff of which the form is predicated to constitute the composite.

Consequently the ultimate substratum is in itself neither a particular thing nor a quantity nor anything else; nor is it then the negations of these, for negations also will belong to it only incidentally. (*Met.* 1029a24–26)

This line of reasoning, if pursued, would, as Aristotle points out, result in the identification of substance with matter, and so he introduces additional criteria for substancehood.[22] Substance is a 'this' and precisely what a thing is. As a distinguishing feature of substance, being determinative is more important than underlying other characteristics, and the characteristics of substance are not those of matter in the sense of the most basic, underlying subject. The most basic, underlying subject is wholly indeterminate; it is the subject of which substance, form, is predicated. Being a substratum of properties, in contrast to being a substratum for form, is retained as an identifying characteristic of substance, and being the substratum for form becomes the defining characteristic of matter (1029a23).

The notion of substratum figures importantly in the account of substance in the *Metaphysics*, and its determination is by a method that straddles the line between ontology and linguistic analysis. As in the *Categories*, the discussion of substance as substratum in VII 3 is couched in linguistic terms – subject, predication, and negation – and, as in the *Categories*,

21 Similar considerations did lead the Stoics to identify body with the real.

22 Aristotle's conception of matter is more nuanced than this argument, which identifies matter with the ultimate (and hence wholly characterless) subject, would suggest. See discussion in Chapter 6, sections 2 and 3.

the ontological position Aristotle defends is consistent with the linguistic intuition that some terms are proper subject terms and others, predicates.[23] Because determinate subjects are assigned pride of place in the theory of substance, accounting for reference in the case of substance sortals will be relatively unproblematic. Further analysis in *Metaphysics* VII establishes that primary substance is just what it is in itself; it is not subject to generation, decay, or alteration.[24] In short, primary substance in the central books of the *Metaphysics* has all the characteristics of Plato's Ideas that make them useful to the epistemologist and philosopher of language. In VII 5, Aristotle concludes that substance in the strictest sense is essence, and definition in the strictest sense is the *logos* of the essence (1030a6–1031a14).

2 Definition and Essence

Definitions expressing real natures are fundamental to Aristotelian science (as we have seen). A definition answers the 'What is ___?' (τί ἐστι) question, and so does the statement of the essence of the type of entity in question. To articulate the essence of a basic object is the goal of scientific definition. Aristotle sometimes refers to the real definition using the phrase, the account (λόγος) of the '*ti esti*', and in the *Metaphysics* he frequently describes the object of definition as the essence (τὸ τί ἦν εἶναι).[25] These notions have application to entities falling under all the categories; however, most fundamentally, they indicate substance (1030a17–b12). This is because the *ti esti* question is asked about subjects and the primitive subjects are substances. "What is that?" when asked by a speaker pointing to Socrates will typically prompt the response 'a human being' (a substance sortal), even though the speaker might go on to explain that the context of the question had been misconstrued and that the right answer was 'a husband' (a relative).[26] Extralinguistic referents, basic objects existing in the world, are required for meaning on Aristotle's theory. The identification of the definition of essence with the substance of the physical object is one part of Aristotle's strategy for explicating the relation between a linguistic item, a word or its mental correlate, and the extralinguistic referent. To explicate the relation between essence, definition, and substance is Aristotle's primary objective in *Metaphysics* VII.

When Aristotle first approaches the topic of essence in VII 4, he describes his remarks as linguistic (λογικῶς) and then immediately justifies this approach by pointing out that the essence of each thing just is what

23 *Met.* 1028b36–37; 1029a7–9, a21–26.
24 See 1037a33-b4, 1033b17–19, 1032a5–6.
25 The second formulation is found at *Met.* 1017b22, 1031a12, 1042a17.
26 See Chapter 1, section 4.

the thing is said to be in itself (*kath' hauto*).[27] Aristotle goes on to argue that the essence of a thing excludes all extraneous (nonessential) characteristics, including certain types of *kath' hauta* attributes.[28] The essence of the surface, for instance, does not include whiteness (1029b16–22).[29] The statement of the essence is a synonymous paraphrase that captures the nature of the definiendum without circularity or redundancy. If 'surface' is mentioned in the definiens of surface, then the definition is unsatisfactory. These requirements ensure that a definition in the technical sense will meet the criteria laid down for the premises of a demonstration in the *Posterior Analytics,* for a sentence is necessarily true only if what is predicated of the subject belongs to it *kath' hauto.*[30]

Mere synonymy, however, is not enough, according to Aristotle:

> Therefore there is an essence only of those things whose formula [λόγος] is a definition [ὁρισμός]. And there is a definition [ὁρισμος] not where a formula [λόγος] is identical in meaning to a word . . . but where there is a formula of something primary [πρώτου]; and primary things are those which do not imply the predication of one element of another. (*Met.* VII 4, 1030a6–11)[31]

Definition in the strict sense then is not merely a statement of the necessary and sufficient conditions for the application of a term. In addition, the object of the definition must be primary and simple (below I shall refer to this as the unity condition). This conception of definition leads Aristotle to conclude that only substances have essences and definitions chiefly, primarily, and simply (1031a13).[32] The *Categories* analysis of quality, quantity, and the other types of predicates is the basis for this conclusion, because these predicates must be defined in relation to items falling under the category of substance.

This, in a nutshell, is the argument of *Metaphysics* VII 4–6, but how persuasive is it? We may be reluctant to grant Aristotle's conclusions that a compound term, for instance, 'pale man', has no definition strictly speak-

27 After citing other works in support of taking λογικῶς to indicate plausibility, rather than truth in other contexts, Ross (correctly I believe) suggests that λογικός in this context may mean ἀκριβής (Aristotle's *Metaphysics,* II, comm., 1924, p. 168). More recently, commentators have favored the translation 'logical' and have stressed the dialectical character of the discussion that employs puzzles. See, e.g., Ferejohn (1994).

28 It should not be forgotten that Plato frequently uses the phrase '*auto kath' hauto*' to describe Forms. See, e.g., *Sym.* 211b, *Parm.* 129a, d.

29 The passage is difficult, and it has been interpreted a variety of ways. I agree with Gill (1989) that Aristotle's conclusion is clear, if not the argument.

30 Aristotle's conception of strict definition is all of a piece with his making definitional dependence the salient feature of per se predication when he summarizes that notion at 73b6–21. See the discussion of *Posterior Analytics* I 4 in Chapter 2, section 4, in this volume.

31 The characterization of definition found in this text will be discussed further in Chapter 6, sections 2 and 3.

32 That definition in the strict sense is the *logos* expressing the essence and hence pertains primarily to substance is asserted in a number of other contexts in the *Metaphysics.* See, e.g., V 8,1017b22; VII 7,1032b14.

ing, or that a single term (for instance, 'snubness') whose referent is compound (concavity in a nose) is similarly indefinable. There are two distinct issues here. First, there is a serious question about the plausibility of Aristotle's conclusions, if they are taken to be claims about dictionary definitions of ordinary language terms. Second, although the question of plausibility is less pressing, if his goal is taken to be determining the parameters of technical definition appropriate to the sciences and/or abstract ontology, there is still a question about whether his account of definition is too restrictive. Aristotle points out that a single term need not correspond to a simple concept; he makes this point with an arbitrary example. Let 'cloak' mean 'pale man'.[33] The definiens will, Aristotle argues, contain two conceptually independent components (1029b14–1030a7). Suppose this were not the case; then the term 'cloak' (pale man) would have a single referent, a man or a pale thing. Neither is satisfactory, for not all humans are pale, nor are all pale things human. If we seek to remedy this problem by building into the concept of pale a reference to man or conversely, we will produce a redundant definiens, for which the original problem arises. Whether we grant Aristotle that this argument shows that 'cloak' (pale man) is indefinable will depend upon whether we agree with Aristotle that a definiens should be conceptually simple and unified. Suppose we refuse to accept this and assert that 'cloak' is an appropriate object for definition, then it will be difficult to explain the intuition that there is something right about analyzing the concept 'pale man' into the more basic components, man and pale.[34] Such an analysis, moreover, would fit ordinary linguistic practice. This suggests that Aristotle is right at least to this extent – that unlike the definition of a simple concept, the definition of a compound concept is derivable from more basic definitions.

If one grants that concepts should be analyzed into their elemental components, which in turn are defined, one will then be left either with a regress that destroys all meaning, Aristotle believes, or one will arrive at basic concepts that are not amenable to further analysis. To avoid the consequence that the most basic concepts will be unanalyzable and indefinable and hence unintelligible, Aristotle envisages basic concepts that are both simple and definable. In order to guard against a regress of primary premises, Aristotle stipulates that the definiens of a basic concept must constitute a unit; the statement of a definiens may consist of more than one term, but the elements of the definiens are not predicated of each other. The definiens expressing the essence that is the substance of a concrete particular has the requisite character, Aristotle believes, because the

33 Ἱμάτιον is one of Aristotle's favorite examples. He often uses it as an arbitrary assigned name having a compound meaning. See, for instance, *De Int.* 18a18–20, and *Met.* 1045a25–28.

34 Aristotle discusses this possibility in *Metaphysics* VII 6.

conceptual priority of substance ensures that the definition will not consist of several independent concepts, which would ex hypothesi be more basic than the defined concept. Other categories of existents, for instance, qualities or quantities, are conceptually dependent on that of substance; in order to define the quality 'pale', one must mention surfaces and, in order to define the latter notion, one must mention extended bodies. Because the unity condition on definition is not met, at the end of VII 5 Aristotle hedges in answer to the question of whether nonsubstantial simple existents have definitions in the strict sense. The suggestion is made but not explored that they have proper definitions, albeit ones that are not primary and simple. Why Aristotle believes that the inclusion of a relation to substance in a definition of a quality or quantity makes the definiens less unified than the inclusion of the genus in the case of substance is not explained in *Metaphysics* VII 4–6. Part of the explanation probably lies with the taxonomic conception of definition (inherited from Plato) that is much in evidence in the *Categories* and *Topics*, even though the fit between the taxonomic model and definitions of essence is imperfect at best. Another part of the explanation lies with Aristotle's ontological commitments. Were absolutely basic definitions possible for items in the nonsubstance categories, then the essential definition of a substance would consist in items that have simple and basic definitions, just as the definition of an item in a nonsubstance category contains an independent element that has a simple definition. Not only would this generate a deductive circle of basic premises of the sort that Aristotle rejects in *Posterior Analytics* I 3, it would also challenge substance's claim to ontological priority.

Another and a more easily answered question is whether Aristotle's handling of notions such as 'pale man' commits him to the existence of referents for terms that are not reducible to substances and their properties. There is little evidence that it does. He asserts that 'pale man' and 'being a pale man' are not the same, and he defends this claim on the grounds that being a man and being a pale man are not the same. Minimally, this would require that both 'man' and 'pale man' be meaningful expressions that would enable us to distinguish between the use of 'pale man' as a referring expression and the expression of the essence of the thing referred to. Aristotle would, most likely, appeal to the priority of substance and the unity condition on definition to ground the distinction between being a man and being a pale man. 'Pale man' contains one term (man) that has a definition (*horismos*) in the strict sense and another (pale) that has a definition in a secondary sense; taken together these two definitions give us a *logos* of 'pale man'; this *logos* is not a *horismos* but is perfectly adequate to the task of explicating the meaning of the phrase. Arguably, the expression 'pale man' refers to any individual human who happens to be pale. The essence of the individual, who is a pale man, is not given by the *logos* of 'pale man'. In light of Aristotle's conception of the relation between meaning and reference, it is clear that, however we construe the referent of 'pale man', it cannot be a simple, nonsubstantial individual, for if it were, 'pale man' would have a simple definiens. One tack to take is to insist that in the sentence 'Socrates is a pale man', 'pale man' refers to Socrates. An alternative – proposed by Lynne Spellman as a strategy for dealing with puzzles about Aristotle's notion of referential opacity – is to distinguish between Socrates and Socrates-qua-pale-man. Socrates and Socrates-qua-pale-man are numerically the same but not identical.[35] On her reading, the referent of 'pale man' is not Socrates but a specimen of the kind, pale man. Were one to follow Spellman here, one would still be left with a complex notion, that of being a specimen of a kind, that would not generate a simple definiens.

In *Metaphysics* VII 5, Aristotle is concerned about another case, which, unlike the arbitrary example of 'cloak', is a word in common parlance and one that immediately suggests to the reader of the *Physics* and the *Metaphysics* Aristotle's notion of enmattered form.[36] The term is 'snub' (σιμόν); to define snub, it is necessary to mention both its form (concavity) and its matter (nose), and thus its definition appears to be compound and not unified. By using 'snub' as an example of a problematic term, one that can only be defined by adding a determinant that threatens to engender an infinite regress (1030b28–37), Aristotle makes it clear that he considers the various difficulties raised by compound concepts for the theory of real definition to be important. These are not idle linguistic puzzles but ones that bear directly on his analysis of substance, which in turn has ramifications for his theory of scientific definition and his theory of meaning. Not surprisingly, in light of his conception of definable items, Aristotle subsequently identifies essence, the preeminent object of definition, with substance without matter (1032b14).

Aristotle's interest in compound concepts, such as 'pale man', is motivated by his theory of meaning and his conception of science. Words refer to physical objects, and all more abstract ontologies such as that of geometry are ways of conceiving physical objects. Physical objects are not simples; they have a variety of characteristics; Socrates is not only a man but also a pale thing. Physical objects are the substrata for change. The analysis of change proposed in the *Physics* treats every object undergoing a change as complex, consisting of a persisting substratum and a characteristic to be lost and replaced by its opposite. Factors taken account of in a correct causal explanation are real, Aristotle believes, and the terms of the explanation must successfully refer to these features of the world. The issue under consideration in *Metaphysics* VII 4, namely, the defin-

35 Spellman (1995, chap. 2).
36 See, for instance, *Metaphysics* 1037a30–32, *Physics* 194a2–15; cf. 186b22.

ability of terms for complex objects, raises an important ontological issue, which will have far-reaching consequences for Aristotle's theory of meaning and his conception of scientific definition. The question is: How should the referent of a conceptually complex notion be construed?

Aristotle's initial discussion of alteration in the *Physics* raises the same question. In *Physics* I 7 in the analysis of the factors involved in a change, the example is that of a man becoming musical. The initial state may be described by two simple terms or one complex one, namely 'unmusical' and 'man' or 'unmusical man', and similarly, the resultant state, by the simple terms, 'musical' and 'man' or by the complex expression 'musical man'. Aristotle uses the terms, τὸ ἄμουσον (the unmusical) and τὸ μουσικόν (the musical) for the simple descriptions of the characteristic that is lost or gained. Were Aristotle using 'the musical' and 'the unmusical' in the standard way, the expression would indicate the attribute in question, in this case, musicality or the lack thereof.[37] That he is using them in this way seems likely, since he also uses nouns to characterize the factor that is lost or gained in a change (190b15, b28). This factor is a particular attribute instantiated by the individual undergoing the change. Recent commentators have resisted the present line of interpretation and made the simple factors, the man and that which is unmusical and that which is musical.[38] One reason for adopting the latter approach is to explain Aristotle's claim that the unmusical ceases to exist when the man becomes musical. If 'the unmusical' is an expression for an abstract noun indicating the lack of musicality, Aristotle would apparently be claiming that the universal characteristic ceased to exist when lost by a single individual (cf. *Met.* 1017b33–35). Various proposals have been made as to how to construe 'the unmusical' if not as an abstract noun.[39]

The solution, I believe, is to be found in the *Categories'* distinction between attributes that are present in and not said of a subject and those that are said of a subject.[40] The unmusical that is destroyed in the process of the man's becoming musical is the former.[41] The attribute that is present in and said of a subject is the usual meaning of the substantive expression τὸ ἄμουσον. More precisely, the linguistic universal, lack of musicality, is predicated of many individuals; it is not specific to a particular individual undergoing a change in musicality. According to the *Categories*, it is because the attribute is present in a particular man that the lack of

37 In Greek, the use of the neuter article with an adjective usually serves to produce a substantive.

38 See Charlton (1970, pp. 70–5), for a clear statement of the issues and an argument for treating these as concrete expressions, and Spellman (1995, chap. 2). Cf. White (1972–3, pp. 57–85).

39 See note 38.

40 See Chapter 1, especially section 4.

41 A further advantage of the interpretation is that it fits Aristotle's view that change, strictly speaking, is between a pair of contraries (224b27).

musicality is said of him. On this picture, it is easier to understand why Aristotle sometimes uses the adjective substantively, sometimes the abstract noun, and in one place (*Phys.* 190a7) the masculine form of the adjective, for the simple factor that is gained in the change. It is also easier to understand why, when Aristotle defines accidental sameness in *Metaphysics* V 9, he uses τὸ μουσικόν as a definite description that denotes the person in which the attribute of musicality inheres.[42] If in a particular context the term τὸ μουσικόν refers to the attribute of musicality that is present in but not said of a particular individual, then to use the same term to refer to the individual would fall within the boundaries of acceptable linguistic practice. Standardly, according to Aristotle, to say that a man is unmusical is to assert that a particular attribute inheres in him and simultaneously to predicate the universal of him. Aristotle's conception of an attribute accommodates a distinction between an attribute as instantiated and the same attribute in its full generality that is more nuanced than the linguistic conception of an attribute, whether expressed by an adjective used substantively or a common noun.

Up to this point, we have allowed Aristotle to treat the lack of an attribute in *Physics* I as an attribute, but arguably his view has an untoward consequence. It would seem to result in every particular's having an infinite number of attributes – all of its positive attributes and, in addition, the lack of every other attribute that is (or could be) exemplified in the world. Besides being unmusical, Callias is not the sum of two and three or a loud sound. For Aristotle, this is simply the wrong way to construe the privation that is one terminus of a change a particular undergoes.[43] If Callias is the sort of being that can become musical, then Callias possesses a potentiality for gaining this characteristic prior to the change. This potentiality is an actual characteristic belonging to Callias; its possession is a necessary condition for the change to being musical. Treating a lack of musicality as one of Callias's attributes is not based merely upon the fact that the set of positive attributes belonging to Callias does not include musicality. What Aristotle is intent upon establishing in *Physics* I 7 is that the change the man undergoes from being unmusical to being musical can be reduced to a pair of simple factors, namely, an underlying substratum, the man, and a characteristic that is replaced by its opposite. The ontological analysis that reduces the musical man to a substratum/substance and a property lends support to the linguistic analysis of *Metaphysics* VII 4 that reduces the term for pale man to the simple terms 'pale' and 'man' and denies that the compound notion is a proper object for definition. The compound term refers to any concrete individual

42 This passage is discussed in greater detail in Chapter 6, section 4.

43 See *Metaphysics* 1046a31–34, where Aristotle defines two senses of privation – the second of which is relevant here.

satisfying the *logos* of 'pale human'; it may also be used in a definite description to pick out a particular pale human, for instance, the pale man in the corner. In either case, the individual referents of the phrase turn out under ontological scrutiny to be compound, each consisting of a substantial individual and an instantiated property.

The analysis that Aristotle offers of essence and definition in *Metaphysics* VII 4–6 reaffirms a number of theses about language and ontology found in the *Categories*. Central to both works are the following: (a) linguistic categories of simple, significant terms have ontological correlates; (b) the ontological relation of inherence has a linguistic analogue in predication; (c) substance is primary both ontologically and conceptually. *Metaphysics* VII agrees with the *Posterior Analytics* about the need for definitions of basic objects, that is, definitions that meet the unity condition. The ultimate building blocks of knowledge are basic objects and their definitions. An infinite regress of premises or definitions of basic objects would totally undermine the claim to know, as would a regress of differentiae within a definition. In *Posterior Analytics* I 22, Aristotle argues that the elements of a proper definition must be finite in number (82b37–83a1). In an indemonstrable, basic premise, there is no distinction between subject and predicate (*Post. Anal.* 84b33–85a1). Knowledge rests ultimately on the definitions of the indivisible species (*ta atoma*) (*Met.* 994b16–23), because such definitions have the required character.

The definition of essence is the linchpin in Aristotle's conception of the relation between the extramental world of objects and that world as conceptualized by human language and science. Lexical items, spoken and written words, are conventional signs of things in the world. What allows these arbitrarily assigned signs to function as tools for understanding is the associated concept expressed in the definition. As an explanation of a real nature, the definition connects the linguistic sign to the object in a way that grounds the intelligibility of the object. This is why Aristotle begins the inquiry into substance in *Metaphysics* VII by setting out the requirements for strict definition. It is also the reason why he returns to the problem of the unity of the definiens in Chapter 12. The *Theaetetus* puzzle about simple objects suggests a picture of language where the basic, indivisible objects are labeled (have arbitrarily assigned names), but these elemental names are of no help in explicating the natures of the basic objects. Aristotle's answer is to posit names that have definitions that are such that the definition does not threaten the simplicity of the basic object. The definition of essence does not, Aristotle argues, involve the predication of ever more basic concepts to constitute the definition. It is unified and hence does not generate a regress.

In the case that is the most important from the epistemic point of view, the object of definition is indivisible (*atomon*), and this feature must be reflected in the definition. The unity of definition is discussed at length in VII 12, and, as in the *Analytics,* the discussion focuses on definitions produced by division.[44] The main difference between the two discussions is the heightened concern with the unity of the definiens in the *Metaphysics.*[45]

Now let us treat first of definition [ὁρισμός] in so far as we have not treated of it in the *Analytics;* for the problem stated in them is relevant for our discussions concerning substance. I mean this problem: why then is that, the formula of which is a definition, a single thing, as for instance, in the case of man, 'two-footed animal' for let this be the formula of man? Why then, is this one, and not many, viz. 'animal' and 'two-footed'? (1037b8–14)

One easy way to defend unity is dismissed at the outset, namely, to claim that since the differentiae mentioned in the definition belong to the same subject they constitute a unity. Aristotle points out that because this is true of all the characteristics of a subject, a list of characteristics need not produce a unified definiens; the attempt, for example, to produce a definition of 'pale man' fails to produce a unified definiens (1037b14–18). Aristotle recognizes that he needs some principled way to make out the difference between a putative definition of 'pale human' and a real definition of 'human' that mentions several differentiae, including 'two-footed' and 'featherless'. The test Aristotle proposes is that only genuine differentiae of the preceding differentia be used, for instance, 'two-footed' is a genuine differentia of 'footed' but 'featherless' is not. The difficulty with this test is that it seems to leave Aristotle in the unfortunate position of choosing between a too narrow final differentia, two-footed, or a list of differentiae of a genus, two-footed and featherless, that are not differentiae of each other. It seems unlikely that a single differentia, such as two-footed, would be adequate as a definiens expressing the essence of a species of an organism as complex as a human being. Yet a list of final differentiae that are not conceptually linked would be equally problematic. In this case, the sole source of unity appears to be the genus, but then the formula 'two-footed, featherless animal' would fare no better than the formula 'pale human'.

Aristotle often emphasizes the dependence of division on a prior conception.

⟨The definer asks⟩ 'Is man animal or inanimate?' and then assumes – he has not inferred – that man is animal. Next, animal is either terrestrial or aquatic: he assumes that man is terrestrial. Moreover, that man is the complete formula, terrestrial-animal, does not follow necessarily from the premises: but he also assumes

44 Aristotle's interest in the method of division is well established elsewhere. His discussion of division in VII 12 provides support for the view that VII 12 is authentic. See also Aristotle's discussion of division in *Parts of Animals* I 2–3.

45 The account of division in the *Posterior Analytics* and the implicit reference to division in *Physics* I 1 were discussed in Chapter 3, section 1.

this. It makes no difference whether he does this with many differentiae or few. (*Post. Anal.* 91b17–23)[46]

On the assumption that the differentiae being ordered by a division are genuine differentiae of a genus that corresponds to a natural kind, Aristotle's concern with the right order of the differentiae and his concern that the final differentia contain the other differentiae can be seen as a way of making division a method for displaying and comprehending the unity of the substance.[47] His example, two-footed animal, is much too easy a test case, if the goal is to formulate definitions of essence that apply to actual existents. A far greater challenge is posed by Aristotle's scientific account of human nature. In order to decide whether the method of division will be up to the task, let us consider Aristotle's definition of an entity he describes as "substance in the sense of actuality," namely, the soul. Various suggestions are made about the nature of the soul in *Metaphysics* VII 10: either it is the animal or the living thing, or it is something different (1036a17–26). One must look elsewhere to find Aristotle's final position.

In the *De Anima,* in answer to the question 'What is a soul?' Aristotle envisages a nested series of psychological capacities such that the higher ones contain the lower ones; the perceptual powers, for instance, contain the nutritive powers. The soul, the substance of the living being, is always one soul whether it consists in a few nutritive capacities or in the whole array of nutritive, locomotive, affective, and cognitive capacities of a human being. The integration of the psychic capacities making up a particular type of soul is secured by nesting capacities rather than compounding them. As this example makes clear, the unity of the final differentia is one where conceptual unity is postulated, not one where the differentiae contained in the final differentia are such that the unity of the final differentia could be deduced from the subsumed differentiae (cf. *Post. Anal.* 92a28–33).[48] Because the psychic capacities are nested, Aristotle can treat the rational soul as analogous to the final differentia of a division in that the presence of rationality implies the presence of all of the lower psychic capacities and the final differentia implies the other differentiae from which it was derived by division. However, the method recommended in *Metaphysics* VII 12 that ensures that 'two-footed' results from the division of footed cannot be used to derive rational capacities

46 Cf. the detailed critique of division as a method for defining natural species in *De Partibus Animalium* I 2–3.

47 See *Post. Analytics* 96b30–97a4; *Metaphysics* 1038a8–33.

48 If the unity of the final differentia is granted, then the unity of the definition made up of the final differentia and the genus can be defended on the grounds that the relation between the final differentia and the genus is that of actuality to potentiality (cf. *Physics* 200b7–8; *Met.* 1045a34). On another interpretation, the subsumed differentiae define the genus. These issues will be addressed in Chapter 6, sections 2 and 3.

from perceptual ones, or the latter from nutritive ones. Aristotle is left without a formal test for the cohesiveness of a definiens.[49]

There might, nevertheless, be a material test for the unity of a definition: the definiens is the *logos* of a proper essence. A proper essence is identical to the substance of which it is the essence, and the formula of a proper essence would be one because the substance is one. Substance in this context cannot be identified with the concrete individual but instead is identified with an indivisible object. The object must be indivisible, not just undivided, for any attribute of a subject will not be divided from the subject as a matter of fact; the white dog, for as long as the dog is white, is a single undivided whole, but it is not an indivisible object, for the dog might very well survive a change in fur color. Rover will not survive a change from being a dog; the concrete substance and its essence are indivisible. Since Rover is subject to death and decay, however, this type of indivisibility is of less interest to Aristotle than the indivisibility of the species dog with its essence. The *logos* of the essence is the form of the indivisible species and the abstract counterpart of the enmattered *logos*/form that is constitutive of the individual substance. The intrinsic unity of the substance ensures that the real definiens is unified (1037b24–27, cf. 1045a12–14). The picture of basic objects that are indivisible but amenable to definition is Aristotle's answer to the challenge posed by Plato in the *Theaetetus* to a foundationalism based on simple unanalyzable objects. Aristotelian basic substances are simple but intelligible because definable in terms of the differentiae of the proper genus. Because the definiens is both unified and analyzable, it provides a basis for knowledge. Such definitions are intelligible because analytic, and yet they do not lead either to a regress (because the indivisible species is not a compound consisting of other more basic entities) or a circle (because the indivisible species is not defined in terms of anything else).

Aristotle is still not off the hook, however, because he seems to be guilty of circular reasoning, if he argues for the unity of the definition from the indivisible character of the species. Starting from the role of essence in proper definition, Aristotle argues that a primary substance is identical to its essence (1032a5–6). A proper definition is one where the definiens states just what the concept is. The attempt to define 'pale man', by contrast, reveals two conceptually independent concepts. The effort to unify the definition by, for example, building a reference to man into the definition of pale leads to a redundant definition when it is combined with the definition of man in the definition of 'pale man'. This leads to the

49 This finding is all the more striking because, in the case of soul, the object of the definition is a primary substance and essence. The problem is only exacerbated when the definition of a generalized compound substance such as human is at issue.

conclusion that essence is the proper object of definition. The requirements of definition allow us to discriminate between objects having essences in a primary sense and those accidental compounds that have essences only derivatively.

Perhaps Aristotle has a way out of this circle. Definitions clarify conceptual relations. At least in some instances, conceptual unity is the sort of thing that can be determined without appeal to anything beyond the concepts themselves; perhaps, contrary to what was said above, this is always true of the definiens of a proper definition. Definition by division would then be a method for eliminating concepts having only superficial unity and for displaying the indivisibility of concepts which are truly indivisible. Essence is the paradigm object of definition and the object of a proper definition must be a unified concept; consequently, an accidental unity will not have an essence strictly speaking.[50] Accidental unities (for example, pale man) coincide with concrete substances (for example, Socrates), and thus Aristotle concludes that essence is one with the substance only in the case of indivisible species (1032a4–6, 1037b2–7).[51] Were there an internal means for picking out proper definitions and hence genuine essences, Aristotle would have an answer to the charge of circular reasoning. Despite the appeal that having an analytic mechanism for determining the unity of a definiens holds for Aristotle, he does not, in the end, opt for making the definition the final arbiter of whether a putative essence is indivisible. This is explained in part, I believe, by his reservations about the method of division, especially its dependence upon assumptions that cannot be justified on the basis of division; and this may be just as well, because Aristotle does not succeed in formulating criteria for establishing the unity of the differentiae making up a definition. In the *Analytics,* Aristotle wraps up his critique of the method of division with an optimistic assessment of its usefulness: although it is not a method of proof, the method of division can be used to ensure that differentiae are not left out of a definition and to display the proper order of the differentiae.[52] *Metaphysics* VII 12 ends on a more tentative note with Aristotle wondering what the basis for distinguishing between prior and posterior terms is and suggesting that the account given there has been preliminary (1038a33–35). At the end of the day, a definition is one because it expresses the essence of a substance that is one. That there are such substances and that the mind is able to recognize them are treated as primitive assumptions by Aristotle.

50 Cf. *Top.* 103b16–19: "An accident is not one of the terms in the definition."

51 In Chapter 6, we shall revisit the vexed topic of whether the composite substance is definable. See also Gill (1989); Ferejohn (1994).

52 See Chapter 3, section 1.

3 Real Definition and Ordinary Definition

According to the analysis of definition in VII 4–6, the objects under investigation are things that are said in virtue of themselves (*kath' hauta*), namely essences. This approach to definition is easily understood in light of the account of definition in the *Analytics*. The first principles of demonstrative science must express *kath' hauta* relations (73b16–18).[53] The definitions of basic objects envisaged in the *Posterior Analytics* meet this requirement, because the definition is simply the articulation of the concept. The definition provides an analysis without introducing extraneous elements that would undermine the unity and simplicity of the concept. Aristotle remarks in *Metaphysics* IV 4 that the essence of each thing is what is said of it in virtue of itself, and thus in VII 6 he concludes that the essence is the proper object of definition. Essences are expressed in definitions stated in words. Essences are identical to the species of which they are said and are the same in one way as the individuals that exemplify them (1032a4–11). Predication is an ontological relation that has a linguistic correlate in *Metaphysics* VII, as in the *Categories*. Narrowing the discussion to essences has several consequences. It eliminates compound concepts as appropriate objects of definition (as we saw in the preceding section), and, more problematically, it results in an account of definition that seems to have limited usefulness for either an epistemologist or a philosopher of language.

Strictly speaking, a definition is the *logos* of the essence and its constituents are the differentiae and most properly the final differentia of a genus.[54] Definition applies most properly to substances that are indivisible and identical to their essences. Ordinary language, however, depends upon there being a *logos* corresponding to every meaningful term. The nature of these definitions should be investigated by the philosopher of language. Aristotle seems to dismiss such definitions in the *Metaphysics*, where he equates them with mere synonymous strings of words. As Aristotle says with disdain, anything can have a definition in this sense (1030a6–11). Has Aristotle given us in spite of himself an account of definition that is of little help in understanding meaning? Since a natural language is an important tool for categorizing and comprehending experience, a conceptual divide between the definitions of ordinary language and genuine definitions would be problematic – all the more since knowledge is based on experience. Moreover, as a philosopher, Aristotle often argues from features of ordinary language, and this practice presupposes continuity between ordinary and technical definitions.[55]

53 See Chapter 2, section 4.

54 *Met.* 1017b22, 1030a6–10, 1037b24–27, 1038a18–21, 1042a17–18.

55 Aristotle frequently appeals to what is evident in a relevant definition in support of substantive conclusions. See e.g., *Physics* 236b24, 244a7. See also Chapter 3, section 6, in this volume.

Aristotle may think about the relation between the two types of definition in this way: linguistic definitions state sufficient conditions for the application of natural language terms to extralingustic objects, properties, and events. The meaning correlated with a particular sound is a consequence of the impact of an external reality on the human mind, and the majority of the significant words of a natural language will be tools for understanding the world. They will, however, often be very crude tools, because the distinctions that Aristotle is at pains to draw in the *Posterior Analytics* and the *Metaphysics* between simple and compound objects, between definitions expressing necessary truths and ones correlating terms with ordinary senses, are not drawn in natural language. The metaphysician's task is to refine these tools by setting out the requirements that a definition of essence must meet.

Synonymy is required of all definitions, but it appears to be the sole requirement for linguistic definitions (definitions of terms occurring in a natural language). If a string of words signifies the same thing as the definiendum, it counts as a definition. As a shared feature, synonymy might, nevertheless, serve as a basis for moving from an ordinary definition to a proper definition of an infima species. Suppose there is a linguistic definition of 'human'; it will be synonymous with 'human', it will signify the same thing (*pragma*) as 'human'.[56] Reflecting on the nature of the *pragma* (the human being) might lead to a revision of the definition; the revised definition might serve in turn to increase the understanding of the nature of humans, and so on, until by a series of approximations the real definition was apprehended. The vast majority of the words of a language, however, do not denote indivisible species and thus will never have real definitions of the sort recommended in *Metaphysics* VII. If no terms except those naming infimae species were of interest in science, then nothing else would need to be said about the role of ordinary definitions. The actual situation for Aristotelian science is quite different. In addition to the genera of infimae species, predicates falling under the other nine categories are also important. The basic properties of matter, for example, are qualitative, namely, hot and cold, wet and dry.[57] Change, the central genus for physical science, would be classified as a kind of action or reaction.[58] This probably explains why in VII, despite

56 Cf. *De Interpretatione* 16a6–8: "But what these [spoken sounds] are in the first place signs of – affections in the soul – are the same for all; and what these affections are likenesses of – actual things (*pragmata*) – are also the same."

57 The analysis of the sublunar material into four basic constituents (fire, air, water, and earth) and their essences into two basic pairs of opposites is found in *De Generatione et Corruptione* II 1–8. In *De Anima* III, Aristotle uses this analysis to defend the claim that there is no sixth sense because the five senses are adequate to the task of perceiving a physical world that is so constituted.

58 *Categories* 14 lists six basic types of change. These are differentiated by the category in which the change occurs, namely, substance (generation and corruption), quantity (in-

his preoccupation with substance, Aristotle claims that definition and essence belong primarily to substance but to the other categories secondarily (1030a28–32). Up to a point, Aristotle can justify this conclusion by appeal to the *Categories*. Items falling under the nine nonsubstance categories are simple. A proper definition of a simple object possesses conceptual unity. The difficulty Aristotle faces squarely in *Metaphysics* VII arises from his insistence upon the ontological priority of substance. Simple objects in the other nine categories can neither exist without substance nor be specified without reference to substance. The dependence on substance compromises the simplicity of these objects and the concepts corresponding to them, and thus Aristotle struggles to find an account of scientific definition that will fit all of the concepts that are absolutely basic in Aristotelian science.

On the one hand, the definitions employed in any science worthy of the name must be proper definitions; that is, they must express essences of basic objects. They cannot be merely synonymous expressions, nor even merely the statement of necessary and sufficient conditions for the application of a term. On the other hand, Aristotle clearly believes that linguistic definitions of the relevant concept, as well as earlier attempts at stating a scientific definition, provide clues to the discovery of the proper definition. In order to define the notions that are central to a particular inquiry, Aristotle begins with the received definitions and then refines the preliminary definitions in order to capture the essence of the subject at hand – as is clear from even the most cursory survey of his writings. Definitions in different domains are linked by the assumption that they are about the same objects. Aristotle looks for groups of approximate definitions of the same object that will, if properly massaged, yield up the definition of essence. The relation between the proper definition and its antecedents lies outside the purview of the *Metaphysics* account of definition. If Aristotle's epistemic practice has a justification, it is to be found in his theory of meaning.

The epistemic requirements for a scientific definition are more rigorous than those for a linguistic definition. Nevertheless, even linguistic definitions are universals applying to an open-ended number of particular cases. The end of speech is communication; the very possibility of communication depends upon the hearer's response to an utterance connecting him or her to the *pragma* signified by the speaker's words. A stable relation between the sound and a *pragma* that both the speaker and the hearer associate with the sound is required. Although other explanations might be given, Aristotle posits a relation between language users and enduring, public objects that secures the meanings of common nouns and verbs and enables one speaker to communicate with another.

crease and decrease), quality (alteration). The process of change is not itself a substance or quality, etc. (5b3–4).

He likes this explanation, because it is straightforward and commonsensical. Why do you understand me when I use 'cat'? We each associate that sound with a species of animal that exists in reality and that we perceive through our senses. The scientific and linguistic definitions of 'cat' are about the same object; they connote the same natural kind; the kind is exemplified by its members and hence the definitions apply to many of the same individuals. (Unlike the scientific definition, the linguistic definition might apply to individuals that are not members of the natural kind.)

Is there some method for evaluating the popular definition and determining whether it is a real definition or not? The method of division might be used to show that instead of one unique and unified definiens, there were several equally plausible ones from the standpoint of natural language.[59] The definition might be subjected to various dialectical tests to determine whether it applied to all and only instances of the concept to be defined. These methods pinpoint weaknesses and eliminate definitions; they do not show that a candidate satisfying all their requirements is a real definition. In *Physics* IV 7, for example, considering the question whether a void exists or not, Aristotle begins by saying that we ought first to determine what 'void' means. The accepted definition, namely, 'place in which there is nothing', is then analyzed in terms of Aristotle's technical definition of place, from which it follows that the void does not exist. This example illustrates the way Aristotle believes common usage can provide a handle on understanding a concept; by interpreting the linguistic definition in terms of previously defined theoretical notions, Aristotle is able to transform the linguistic definition into the technically correct one. The appeal to theory in this case also reveals, however, the limitations of the method. At some point, the investigator must appeal to indemonstrable definitions of basic objects.

> The preexistent knowledge required is of two kinds. In some cases the fact must be assumed, in others the meaning of the term must be understood, and sometimes both assumptions are essential. (*Post. Anal.* 71a11–13)

Indemonstrable definitions are formulae capturing the essences of enduring objects, species types, and their properties.

In several places in *Metaphysics* VII, Aristotle remarks on a difference between the essence or substance and the universal name of the species.

> But 'man' and 'horse' and terms which are thus applied to individuals [τὰ οὕτως ἐπί τῶν καθ' ἕκαστα], but universally, are not substance but a whole composed of this particular formula [λόγου] and this particular matter treated as universal; and regarding the individual, Socrates is already composed of ultimate matter and similarly in all other cases. (*Met.* 1035b27–31; trans. follows Ross; cf. 1037a7)

59 This use of division is illustrated by Plato in the *Sophist* when the popular concept is shown to include six distinct notions. See the discussion in Chapter 3, section 1, in this volume.

The universal terms 'man' and 'horse' predicate both the substance (the form) and the material substrate of the concrete individual. The predicate 'man' is a generalization of a composite of matter and form; it is the composite taken universally. Ross's translation of the phrase (τὰ οὕτως ἐπί τῶν καθ' ἕκαστα) as "terms thus applied to individuals" is, I believe, truer to Aristotle's words than more recent translations that take the phrase to denote universal composites, for instance, "the entities thus related to particulars."[60] The terms in question do signify, and thus do predicate, universal composites of the particulars. These composites are distinct from the substance as form or *logos,* which strictly speaking is predicated only of matter, not of the individual substance (1049a34–36; cf. 1038b4–6). A species name such as 'man' or 'horse' refers to the species construed as a universal composite of form and matter, and thus a genuine species name appears to have a technical definition as well as a linguistic meaning. The technical definition of the universal composite of matter and form would lack the unity of a definition of essence, but it might well serve as a bridge between the linguistic meaning and the definition of essence. The universals of ordinary language are based on experience and refer to concrete particulars; they express generalizations of the common character of the particulars. The common character includes both material and formal features. The linguistic definition often includes accidental as well as essential features. The scientist attempts to separate the essential, formal features from the others. The goal is to arrive at a definition that articulates the formula (*logos*) of the essence of the particulars of experience. The *logos* of the essence is the articulation of the form without matter. Thus construed, the relation between the linguistic definition and the scientific definition of a species mirrors the relation between the perception of the man Callias and the apprehension of the universal man as described in *Posterior Analytics* II 19. The individual is a composite of form and material; the form (essence) of the individual determines its character. The essence determines the concept expressed in the scientific definition; the composite of form and matter determines the concept expressed in the linguistic definition.

4 *Theaetetus* Puzzles Revisited

This chapter began with several of the *aporiai* of the *Theaetetus.* In closing let us revisit those *aporiai.* A theory of meaning that relies on physical objects to serve as the referents of words and secure the meanings of terms will be undermined, Plato argues, by the instability of these objects, which

60 The latter translation is Gill's (1989, p. 122). Other recent commentators adopting a similar reading are Charles (1994, p. 78) and Irwin (1990, pp. 249 and 571, n. 5), which takes 1035b27–31 to be about the formal compound, i.e., about Aristotle's universal forms.

are continually changing. Aristotle's response is to study being as being and examine the notions of definition, essence, and substance in the effort to construct an ontological alternative to Platonic Ideas. Not only are stable objects required for meaningful discourse and knowledge, but the basic objects should also be simple so that conceptual analyses will ultimately terminate. Simple primitives combine to form compound concepts. The difficulty with this appealing ontological and epistemological picture, according to Plato, is that the primitives cannot be both simple and intelligible. If the primitives are amenable to definition (i.e., have a *logos*), then they are not truly simple. If they are indefinable, then the compound objects will be as well. Aristotle attempts to avoid both horns of this dilemma by giving an account of definition that allows a definiens to provide an analysis without undermining the unity of its object. To this end, he limits definition in the strict sense to *to kath' hauto legomenon* (that which is said in virtue of itself). In addition, he argues for the conceptual and ontological unity of the definiens. Although expressed in a string of words, a definiens of a simple object does not involve predication of one part of another. Aristotle considers various strategies for defending this claim, for example, making the relation between the differentiae and the genus in a definiens analogous to the relation between form and matter, or using the method of division to display the unity of the definiens. In the end, Aristotle is unwilling to depend on these strategies alone. The unity of the definiens is a function of the unity of the object to which the definition applies. A primary substance is simple, and thus its definition will be similarly unitary.

There is still a missing piece in the argument for the unity of the defining formula. Aristotle formulates the problem of the parts of the formula in *Metaphysics* VII 10 and in the following two chapters grapples with this problem without fully resolving it.

> Since a definition is a formula, and every formula has parts, and as the formula is to the thing [πρᾶγμα], so is the part of the formula to the part of the thing, the question already arises whether the formula of the parts must be in the formula of the whole or not. (1034b20–23)

The answer Aristotle needs to give is that the parts of the proper definition are peculiar in that they are the analysans of the concept defined and yet they are not ontologically prior to the definition. Insofar as the definition is the articulation of a single nature grasped through perception and induction, Aristotle would seem to be justified in claiming that the terms of the definition are themselves definable only in the context of the definition. In this sense, the parts of the definition are not only ontologically but also epistemologically dependent upon the definition. This would avoid the regress of definitions that Plato envisages in the *Theaetetus,* if the elements are themselves knowable. In VII 11, however,

Aristotle does not give this answer and the chapter ends on an aporetic note.

> And in the case of definitions, how the elements in the formula are parts of the definition, and why the definition is one formula (for the thing is clearly one, but in virtue of what is it one thing, since it has parts?); this must be considered later. (1037a17–21)

The concern arises in part because the elements of the formula are not merely terms but are also the things predicated by those terms, and thus a definiens consisting of several terms seems to presuppose distinct ontological elements. Aristotle does ultimately resolve this difficulty about the parts of the definition, I believe, but to discover his solution, we must look at his account of essence and form.

6
Logos as Substance

The ontological requirements of language and knowledge, as Aristotle understands them, are such that enduring characteristics of mutable and transient individuals are needed. This prompts Aristotle to identify forms, in contrast to concrete particulars, with primary substance in the central books of the *Metaphysics* and to develop an account of the relation between form and matter that is informed at every stage by a concern with linguistic definition and a conception of essence as the exemplary object of knowledge. A crucial concept in this effort to knit together several objectives is λόγος (*logos*). The term *logos* is used by Aristotle in many contexts and for many things, from strings of symbols to forms, from speech to definition. In *Metaphysics* VII, Aristotle exploits the ambiguity of *logos* to display the common feature of a thought and its referent in the world. The *logos* actualized in matter is a composite substance, and the same *logos* realized in thought is a meaning. This is a puzzling doctrine but also by this point in our inquiry a familiar one. Not only does Aristotle assign *logos* both an ontological role and a linguistic one, he also uses *horismos* (definition in the strict sense) and *pathema* (vehicle of meaning) to indicate linguistic items and ontological ones. The real definition is a feature of the world, not just a specification of a meaning; the *pathema* is both a state of mind and its content (a meaning).

At every stage, the description of ontology is guided by the requirement of rational accessibility. Not only must the ontology be intelligible from a theoretical perspective, it must be accessible at the pre-theoretical level of perception and ordinary language. These tenets are developed and defended in the central books of the *Metaphysics*. At the heart of Aristotle's picture of the relation between language and the world is the thesis that essences have physical realizations and that the very same essences are cognitively accessible as meanings and objects of thought. The present chapter continues the examination of this thesis begun in Chapter 5, by probing Aristotle's claim that the enmattered form is the very same *logos* that is asserted in the definition of the essence of the individual composite substance. We shall look at both sides of this identity claim by attending to Aristotle's analysis of definition and his analysis of composite substance. The identity claim has several important consequences. The requirement that a definition in the strictest sense express an essence of an infima species is one of the consequences for definition, as is the requirement that the definition be a genuinely simple concept; the requirement that the form determine the character of the composite is one of the consequences for ontology, as is the requirement that the form be one with that of which it is the substance.

1 The Same *Logos*

In the discussion of division as a method for displaying the unity of the definiens in *Metaphysics* VII 12, Aristotle reaffirms his commitment to the thesis that the definition is one because the substance is one. In the preceding chapter, the recognition that definitions have parts prompted Aristotle to assert that, nevertheless, the definition is one, if the thing (*pragma*) is one (1037a17–19). In neither chapter does Aristotle claim to have a solution to puzzles about the unity of definition; he only claims to be certain that there must be a solution. There are several sources of these puzzles for Aristotle. Having identified form with essence and the object of definition, and having construed definition as the articulation of essence, Aristotle is confronted in the case of enmattered forms with questions about the inclusion of descriptions of the matter in the definition. He argues that matter is a part of the concrete individual, but not part of its form and hence not a part of its definition.

> But only the parts of the form are parts of the formula [λόγου] and the formula is of the universal; for being a circle is the same as the circle, and being a soul the same as the soul. But of the composite, e.g., this circle, i.e., one of the individual circles, whether perceptible or intelligible (I mean by intelligible circles the mathematical, and by perceptible circles those of bronze and of wood) – of these there is no definition, but they are recognized by thought or by perception; and when they pass from this realization it is not clear whether they exist or not; but they are always stated and recognized by means of the universal formula. (1035b34–1036a8)

Although matter is easily discounted as a proper part of the form and definition in VII 10, Aristotle grants in VII 11 that there remains a problem about the proper parts of the definition, and in VII 12 he acknowledges that the method of division is limited in its capacity to establish the unity of the definition.

Returning to the challenge posed by concrete individuals, on the one hand, and Platonic Ideas, on the other hand, to his theory of definition in VII 15, Aristotle asserts that there are two kinds of substance, concrete substances that are enmattered *logoi* and *logoi* simply (1039b20–22). By making the *logos* (formula) that is asserted by the definiens the very same form as the *logos* that is realized in matter, Aristotle hopes to secure the unity of the definition and the intelligibility of the substance.[1] Setting aside the many puzzles Aristotle's notion of *logos* raises for the moment, let us sketch his position. At a minimum, he deserves credit for having offered an ingenious theory that allows him to construe the extramental reality in a way that yields an ontology that is fully intelligible and expressible in a suitably sophisticated language.

The proper definition (*horismos*) is the *logos* of the essence (1017b11, 1031a12). Since individuals are not definable (1036a5), the identification of the substantial individual with the enmattered *logos* eliminates the claim of both the concrete individual and the Platonic Idea, construed as an individual, to be an object of definition or of knowledge. The analysis of the concrete individual into formula (*logos*) and indefinable matter separates an intelligible universal element from the source of individuation (matter). The materially realized form is the substance of the concrete individual. Aristotle emphasizes the sameness of form by choosing *logos* as the term for both. The premise that the *logos* grasped in thought is the same as the form of the concrete substance provides the missing link in the *Analytics* account of definition and induction.[2] The physical realizations of certain structures determine the nature of mind-independent reality. The structures having physical realizations are also, as it happens, cognitively accessible (100a14). Because the mind is such that it is affected by the external *logos* presented in perception, the *logos* that is grasped at the end of the inductive process is, in the favored cases, the essence of the substance in question.

To summarize: a particular structure, a *logos*, is instantiated as a substantial individual, is a constituent of a composite universal, and is the essence constituting the proper definition of the substance in question. The *logos* is such that when realized in matter it yields a concrete substantial individual. The same structure realized in a generalized notion of matter constitutes a composite universal. The same structure is the essence of the substantial individual and is expressed in the definition of essence. Because the *logos* (form) is the same in the substantial individual as in the composite universal, the (composite) natural kind, that serves as the meaning of the name of the natural kind under which the individual falls, the linguistic meaning is a function of reference to concrete substances. Because the same structure is constitutive of the definition of essence, the definition of essence expresses a real nature existing in the world. Because the *logos* is the same in the composite universal as in the definition of essence, the linguistic meaning represents a first ap-

1 Cf. *De Anima* 403a25–b9.
2 See Chapter 3, especially section 3.

proximation to the nature that is precisely expressed in the scientific definition. Still, much work remains to be done by Aristotle to explicate the notion of a substantial form as an enmattered *logos* that has the very same structure as the *logos* expressed in a definition of essence. To evaluate his success (or lack thereof), we must look at his account of substantial form and his account of the relation between form and matter in the concrete individual in *Metaphysics* VII–IX.

The form (*logos*) as a cognitive content is a meaning. Speakers of different natural languages will use different sounds to express the *logos*, but the *logos* will be the same – at least for all speakers who have gotten the essence right. As Aristotle says in the *De Interpretatione*, the *pragma* that the internal state represents will be the same for all knowers (16a5–8). The absolutely unrestricted character of knowledge is nicely maintained on this picture, where every prospective knower potentially stands in the same relation to the *pragma* as the actual knowers, all of whom comprehend the same *logos*, irrespective of the languages they use.[3] The *logos* is one because the *pragma* is one (1037a17–19).

A critic might object, nevertheless, that all this talk about sameness of *logos* creates an illusion of intelligibility where none is present. The claim is: the *logos* of elephant that exists in the biologist's thought is the same as the *logos* of a huge lumbering creature – but what does this statement mean? Does it mean that there is a miniature elephant lumbering about in the biologist's mind? Aristotle's favorite illustrations of his notion of form as embodied are products of human art. The shipbuilder has a plan for a ship, and once that plan is executed, the result can be evaluated in terms of how well or how poorly the physical structure realizes the antecedent plan. Here, it makes perfect sense to talk of the ship being the same as the plan or different from it.[4] Similarly, the physician has a conception of a healthy body that he attempts to realize in the patient's body; the physician might, for instance, try to achieve a proper balance of the humors.[5] If the treatment succeeds, a new order is realized in the bodily parts, namely, balanced humors. Health, the physician's objective, consists in realizing in the body of the patient the configuration of bodily parts that the physician has in mind. It should come as no surprise that Aristotle's two favorite examples of the form as an object of thought and as the organization realized in matter are drawn from house building and medicine.[6] In both cases, it is relatively easy to see how the same struc-

3 Cf. Plato, *Cratylus* 389d.

4 Cf. *De Partibus Animalium* 640a16–18: "Because the form of the house is such and such, that is, the house is such and such, it comes to be in this way. For the process of generation is for the sake of the house not the house for the sake of the process."

5 See Hippocrates, *On the Nature of Man* 4–5; *On Diseases* IV 32–33. The importance of maintaining the proper balance and order of bodily organs and fluids is well attested to in Greek medicine. Cf. *Physics* 246b5.

6 In the *Metaphysics*, these two examples are used repeatedly. See, e.g., 1013b23, b32,

tural plan could exist in the mind and in a concrete manifestation. House building is a particularly clear model of a plan realized in a complex structure; medicine, while less clear on that score, has the advantage of revealing the role of structural principles in the functioning of a complex living body.

It is important for Aristotle's account of knowledge and meaning that embodied structural principles determine the character of the particulars of experience. This explains his attention to the details of the relation between form and the composite of form and matter in *Metaphysics* VII–IX.

2 Form and Matter

On the question of ontological primacy, *Categories* 5 comes down squarely in favor of the concrete substance. A more complex ontology, however, is evident not only in the *Metaphysics* but also in the *Analytics* and in the treatment of language and logic in the *Categories* and *De Interpretatione.*[7] There is an apparent tension between the ontology of real universals and the claim that what is ultimately real are the concrete particulars of ordinary sense experience.[8] A corresponding tension plagues the relation between perception and knowledge. In *Metaphysics* VII–IX, Aristotle attempts to develop and defend an ontology of form and matter that will resolve these tensions. Matter is the substratum in which form is realized. Matter does not exist unenformed but, in and of itself, matter is without characteristics; it is "potentially what the form is actually."[9] Concrete substances having the same form are different individuals, because the form is realized in different matter. Socrates' form is the same as the form grasped by the person who knows what a human being is. The (real) definition of human being articulates the essence of human being and this essence makes Socrates the substance he is. He is, however, a concrete substance, not a universal, and this is explained by his compound nature, namely, the form of human being realized in a particular body. The big picture is pretty clear; but matters get much more complicated when we look at the details. What is the relation between the form of the individual, which is shared by other members of the same species, and the

1019a16, 1027a2, 1032b13, 1046a27, 1070b33. Cf. *De Partibus Animalium* 639b18–20, 640a5–8.

7 Universals are taken to be epistemically and semantically prior to particulars in all these works. Because concrete particulars exemplify universals, the apprehension of particulars by the mind provides the basis for meaning and knowledge.

8 Not all recent commentators agree that the composite is downgraded from primary substance in the *Metaphysics;* for a particularly clear argument that it is not, see Gill (1989).

9 Even the most basic material elements are composed of matter enformed by the two basic pairs of contraries: the hot and the cold, and the wet and the dry (*De Gen. et Corr.* II 1–5).

species (the natural kind)? If definitions of species names contain generalized descriptions of matter, as Aristotle asserts (1035b27–31, cf. 1037a6–7), and the definition of essence is the object of science, in what sense are these two definitions about the same object in the world? Or, to put this question in a different way, Aristotle has good reason for asserting that the same *logos* is expressed concretely as a substantial individual and abstractly as a cognitively accessible essence that is captured fully by the proper definition and partially as a meaning of a natural language term. The *logos* thus conceived, however, seems to threaten both the unity of the individual consisting of form and matter and the uniqueness of the individual. Does Aristotle give an account of the unity and uniqueness of the substantial individual that is compatible with the conception of that individual as an enmattered *logos*?

The approach to these issues Aristotle adopts in *Metaphysics* VII 4–6, 10–16 emphasizes the abstract character of definition as the expression of an indivisible and universal essence. At first blush, the discussion of generation and questions about the destructibility of the essences of generated individuals in VII 7–9 seems out of place.[10] Notwithstanding, from a broader perspective, Aristotle's concern with questions about sensible substance, including the role of form in the generation of a sensible substance, makes perfect sense.[11] As Aristotle points out in VII 11, the nature of sensible substance is relevant to the discussion of definition.

> For it is for the sake of this that we are also trying to determine the nature of perceptible substances, since in a way the inquiry about perceptible substances is the work of physics, i.e., of second philosophy; for the physicist must come to know not only about the matter, but also about the substance according to the formula, and even more than about the other. (1037a13–17)

First philosophy is the study of the foundations of the other theoretical sciences, as indicated here by Aristotle's gloss of 'physics' as 'second philosophy'. Concrete individuals are crucially important to Aristotle's account of the apprehension of universals in the *Posterior Analytics* and to his theory of meaning. The individual is primary in the order of perception and the basis for the knowledge of universals – universals that concrete particulars exemplify perfectly and universals that they exemplify imperfectly. This is why, in the course of an abstract discussion of definition in *Metaphysics* VII, Aristotle repeatedly brings in as examples such

10 Cf. Ross (1924, comm. vol. 2, p. 181), who agrees with Natorp's contention that Chapters 7–9 interrupt what would otherwise be a continuous argument from Chapters 1–9 through 10–12 but disagrees with Natorp's view that the interruption shows that *Metaphysics* VII was originally two separate treatises. Ross (vol. 1, p. xxx), however, accepts Jaeger's view that VII 12 is an interpolation, as do Frede and Patzig (1988, vol. 1, pp. 24–26). See also Furth (1988, pp. 114–15).

11 It is an advantage of the present interpretation that it provides an explanation for the location of Chapters 7–9 in the received texts.

items as bronze spheres, snub noses, and human beings; he is determined to give an account that grounds the universal, the definition, in the particular. The formula realized in the bronze sphere, a concrete particular, is the definition of sphere. As Aristotle recognizes, this story ignores the defining formula of the universal artifact type, bronze spheres, and this leads him to investigate the nature of the relation between form and matter in the concrete individual.

After developing and defending the thesis that form or essence is the primary object of definition and thus is primary substance in *Metaphysics* VII, in the closing chapter Aristotle ponders the unity of a concrete particular: Why are these ⟨bricks and mortar⟩ a house? Because the essence of house belongs to them (1041b5–6). Answering this question satisfactorily is important to Aristotle for several additional reasons. One factor is the legacy of the *Categories* account of primary substance. Another factor is the use this legacy has been put to in the attack on Platonic Forms. The unity of the concrete individual figures importantly in *Metaphysics* VII in the critique of Platonism. Another factor is the tension between the epistemological priority of universals and the ontological priority of substantial form. An indispensable premise in the argument for the ontological primacy of species forms over other universals is the thesis that the kind of thing a concrete particular is is more fundamental than are any of its other properties. This belief is justified only insofar as the ontological priority of concrete individuals is granted. Thus it is not surprising that *Metaphysics* VIII and IX are designed to show how the form can be primary substance and the concrete particular remain a unified and genuine substance.

In VII 17, Aristotle approaches the topic of substance from a new starting point by considering the role of substance as principle and cause (1041a6–10). He distinguishes between the cause that makes an object what it is – the cause, for instance, of fire and earth constituting flesh or the cause of the letters *b* and *a* being the syllable 'ba' – and the material elements (fire and earth, *b* and *a*) that are so structured as to be an object of a certain sort (flesh, a syllable) (1041b11–33). This effects a shift of focus from essence as the object of definition to essence as the immanent cause of the nature of the perceptible substance. In the following pages, Aristotle develops the causal account of the relation between the essence and form of a concrete individual and the material in which the form is realized as the relation between an internal actualizing cause and a material potentiality.[12]

12 Lewis (1991, pp. 160–3) finds support for a Fregean interpretation of form as "a function from matter to a compound" in the account of form as principle and cause in VII 17. Although I have reservations about the general theory of compounding that Lewis attributes to Aristotle, Lewis is right to emphasize the functional role of form in the compound.

In VIII 2, in order to explicate the notion of actuality, Aristotle appeals to the different senses of 'is' and finds that there are as many senses as there are ways of composing matter.[13]

Hence it is clear that 'is' is said in many senses. For a threshold is because it lies in such and such a position, and its being means [σημαίνει] its lying in that position, while being ice means having been solidified in such and such a way. And the being of some things will be defined by all these qualities, because some parts of them are mixed, others are blended, others are bound together, others are solidified, and others use the other differentiae, e.g., the hand or the foot. (1042b25–31)

The things that are by common agreement are material objects or their parts (1042a7–11). Nevertheless, even in the ordinary nontechnical sense of stuff, matter is such that describing the matter of an object does not explain why the object is what it is. It would be possible to give a detailed description of the stones making up the threshold in terms of their intrinsic properties. This description would be the same as the one that would be given, were the stones still in the quarry, and it would provide no information about the threshold as such. The threshold is what it actually is in virtue of the mode of composition of its matter, and this holds true of all material objects. The mode of composition may be as simple as mixing or as complex as the functional organization of a living thing. Despite the enormous differences between different modes of organization, Aristotle believes that they all share a common feature, namely, that of being what, at the end of the day, makes a particular concrete individual an individual of whatever kind it happens to be. Because the end that the concrete object is designed to serve, if the object is an artifact, or the end that is realized in the object, if it is a natural substance, determines the mode of composition, Aristotle subsumes the mode of composition under descriptions of the function of the object. The threshold is intended to serve a specific purpose, and so the wood and stones are arranged in a particular way. A structure of stones, bricks, and wood is an individual house just in case it is so constructed as to be a shelter for humans and chattel (1043a16–18).

Returning to the difficult question 'What makes a definition one?' in VIII 6, Aristotle proposes a solution:

But if as we say one element is matter and another is form, and one is potentially and the other actually, the question will no longer seem to be a difficulty. For this

13 Irwin (1988, p. 225) construes Aristotle's task here as one of limiting the range of potentiality and actuality, because there appear to be good reasons to identify substance with potentiality: "But though it is easy to see why form is identified with actuality, it becomes difficult to see how it could be identified with the primary essence or basic subject." It is precisely the identification of form with actuality, I believe, that provides Aristotle's justification for identifying form with substance.

difficulty is the same as would arise if 'round bronze' were the definition of 'cloak'; for this word [τοὔνομα] would be a sign [σημεῖον] of the formula [λόγος] so that the question is, what is the cause of 'round' and 'bronze' being one? The difficulty disappears, because the one is matter, the other form. . . . Of matter some is intelligible, some perceptible, and one part of a formula is always matter, and another part actuality. (1045a23–35)

This passage should dispel any lingering doubts that we might have entertained about the close connection Aristotle envisages between the question about the unity of a concrete substance and definitional unity. The answer to both questions, Aristotle claims, is to be found by appeal to the notions of potentiality and actuality. Aristotle makes some effort to define the latter notions in VIII, but his final account is yet to come. Noting that the terms 'potentiality' and 'actuality' have several senses in *Metaphysics* IX 1, Aristotle first gives a general account of potentiality.[14] In IX 6, he returns to the sense of actuality that is most relevant for understanding substance and begins by contrasting this notion of actuality to that of change.

For every change is incomplete – making thin, learning, walking, building; these are changes and incomplete at that for it is not true that at the same time something is walking and has walked or is building and has built or is coming to be and has come to be, or is being moved and has been moved, and what is moving is different from what has moved. But the same thing at the same time has seen and is seeing, or is thinking and has thought. The latter, then, I call an actuality [ἐνέργεια] and the former a change [κίνησιν]. (1048b29–35)[15]

The distinction drawn here between actuality (ἐνέργεια) and change (κίνησις) appears to be incompatible with Aristotle's analysis of change in *Physics* III 1–3. There, the definition of *kinesis* (change) is the actuality of the changeable qua changeable (201a9–15, b12–15).[16] One strategy for resolving the conflict would be to say that actuality (*energeia*) in the sense defined in *Metaphysics* IX 6 is a special case, and that only in this narrower sense is *kinesis* not an actuality. The mark of a *kinesis* as an actuality in the *Physics* is the realization of a potentiality as potentiality, and in the *Metaphysics* it is having an external product. Some potentialities are such that the potentiality is used up in the course of being actualized and is thus converted to something that stands outside the actuality; for in-

14 See Frede (1994) for a careful study of this topic. Frede concludes that "what counts as a potential F here, in the case of some material with a passive capacity to undergo a change, is determined by what *single* process or change there is which could turn a potential F into an actual F" (p. 190).

15 I follow Bonitz and Ross and many other commentators in accepting 1048b18–35 as genuine. I use the text as edited by Ross. For a discussion of the manuscript tradition, see the notes in Ross (1924) on this passage.

16 When defining *kinesis* in the *Physics*, Aristotle uses two terms for actuality; *entelecheia* is used in the initial definition (201a9–15) and *energeia* appears in a formulation given later (201b12–15).

stance, the house stands outside the act of building, for building, which is a *kinesis*, exhausts the potential of the bricks to become a house (as distinguished from being a house).[17] In the case of intentional action, this product is typically the reason the action is undertaken.

This clarification is helpful but does not completely resolve the problem. The actualization of the visible qua visible would seem to fit the description of a *kinesis* in the *Physics*, but in IX 6, seeing, which just is the actualization of the visible qua visible, is an *energeia* in the narrow sense that is contrasted with *kinesis*. This suggests that Aristotle is implicitly narrowing the conception of a *kinesis* in IX 6 by emphasizing the incompleteness of the activity in this context, whereas in the case of an *energeia*, the potentiality (whether it is a potentiality qua potentiality such as the visible qua visible or a simple potentiality such as the material of a composite substance) is fully realized in the actuality, and in this way the actuality is incomplete. It may prove instructive to label the narrower notions of IX 6, $kinesis_2$ and $energeia_2$ and the broader notions found in the *Physics* III $kinesis_1$ and $energeia_1$. While a $kinesis_2$ falls under the broader notion $kinesis_1$ and an $energeia_2$ falls under the broader notion of an $energeia_1$, the narrower notions do not neatly fall into the categories of complete and incomplete actualities employed in *Physics* III. The *Physics* definition of $kinesis_1$ applies to seeing as an actuality of the visible qua visible but not to the form of the house, because in the second case the *energeia* is not of the materials qua materials but of the materials simpliciter; in the *Metaphysics*, however, the narrow notion of a complete actuality ($energeia_2$) applies to seeing, as well as to *ousia*.[18] Despite the drawbacks to Aristotle's construal of *energeia* in IX 6, why he chooses to emphasize completeness is clear. Armed with a notion of actuality as *energeia*, he can explain the unity of a definition.

One part of a definition is form and the other matter; here too form should be construed as $energeiai_2$. At 1045a35, Aristotle gives 'plane figure' as the definiens of 'circle'. This is an odd example; at best, the definiens is incomplete.[19] The full definition would be 'a plane figure bounded by one line' (*De Caelo* 286b14–15).[20] Aristotle has, however, defended the unity of plane figure elsewhere.

> In a definition one thing is not predicated of another – e.g., neither is animal predicated of two-footed nor this of animal, nor indeed figure of plane (for plane is not figure nor is figure plane). (90b35–37)

17 Cf. Kosman (1969, pp. 40–62).

18 According to *De Anima* II 5, all forms of perceiving are a sort of alteration, but here seeing is given as an example of an *energeia*.

19 Jaeger (1957) brackets the whole phrase (οἷον ὁ κύκλος σχῆμα ἐπίπεδον), citing its omission in Alexander; his reservations may also stem from a worry about the inadequacy of the definition of circle given here.

20 Cf. Euclid, *Elements*, Book I, Definition 15: "A circle is a plane figure contained by one line such that all the straight lines falling upon it from one point among those lying within the figure are equal to one another" (Heath trans.).

'Plane figure' is an obvious case for Aristotle where the definiens is unified in the same way that other composites of matter and form are unified. Generic characteristics are realized through, not destroyed by, specific difference. A figure is no less a figure for lying in a plane. In the (complete) definition of circle, plane figure is the genus. The characteristics of the generic plane figure are realized through the specific difference (being bound by one line) as a curvilinear (περιφερόγραμμον) plane figure, a circle (286b14–15).

A substance is also an *energeia*$_2$; it, too, is a complete realization of a potentiality. What makes this analysis of substance useful to Aristotle is its ready applicability to natural substances. In the strictest sense, only natural beings are substances (1032a19, 1034a4, 1041b28–30, 1043b23). Natural substances are characterized by the possession of an internal principle of change. The form as that which determines the essential characteristics would be the cause of the innate source of change. Biological individuals are paradigmatic substances, and they provide a particularly clear case of the inseparability of the substance from the innate source of motion and change. The soul as the substance, form, and actuality of the body is the origin of all the vital functions the body performs; because the functions include changes of all sorts, from simple alterations (*kineseis*$_2$) to activities (*energeiai*$_2$), their source, while not a *kinesis* of any sort, is akin to a *kinesis* because it is an actuality (*energeia*$_2$).[21] Moreover, the conception of form as the actuality that most completely realizes the potentiality of the matter to be a composite substance offers the greatest promise for resolving the tension between the unity of the concrete substance and the analysis of the concrete substance into form and matter. The unity of the individual substance depends upon its having a functional organization that integrates its various parts, functions, and dispositions. The distinction between form and material components presupposes the existence of characteristics that are properly associated with the material components. By identifying matter with potentiality, Aristotle is able to explain how these characteristics are expressed in the concrete individual without thereby threatening the unity of the individual.

The form that is the substance of the concrete particular is the same *logos* as the one grasped in the definition of the essence of the particular.[22] Because the *logos* is a structural principle, Aristotle can coherently

21 In *De Anima* I 3, Aristotle adduces a number of reasons in support of the thesis that the soul is neither self-moved nor moved by another, i.e., the soul does not undergo any form of motion (κίνησις). However, the definition of the soul as first actuality and its activities as second actuality in *De Anima* II 1 introduces an additional wrinkle, since the notion of second actuality here appears to be the same as the narrow notion of actuality in *Metaphysics* IX 6, but the notion of first actuality here is identified with substance, as is the narrow notion of actuality in *Metaphysics* IX.

22 When the explanatory context is that of the substantial change from log to chest, wood is identified with the enduring substratum (cf. *Met.* 1033a13–23). However, when the

maintain that, although the expression of the *logos* in matter yields a concrete object whereas its expression in thought does not, the *logos* is the same in both instances. The description of the form as *logos* provides the basis for meaning and knowledge; the description of the form as actuality provides the basis for understanding the nature of the *logos*. A particular functional organization is actualized in the material of a living creature; this functional organization is characteristic of the species to which the creature belongs. The conception of form as *logos* and actuality is inter alia Aristotle's device for alleviating the tension between the *Categories* conception of primary substance as concrete individual and the *Metaphysics* conception of primary substance as form. The concrete substance is what it is because its matter actualizes a particular form, and for this reason Aristotle says that the concrete substance is derivative and the form is primary (1029a29–33). The concrete individual is always primary in the order of our cognitive powers; it is the concrete individual that the mind confronts through perception. The concrete individual is not primary in the order of intelligibility, however, because the individual (unlike the form) is subject to generation and decay. Our 'knowledge' of the individual lasts only as long as our perception of the individual does (67a39-b3); thus the proper object of knowledge and definition is the *logos* in and of itself. The unity of the *logos* expressed in a definition is now explicable, Aristotle believes, by appeal to the notion of a potentiality realized through an actuality. A definition consisting of a differentia and genus is yet another instance where a potentiality (a cluster of generic characteristics) is realized through an actuality (specific differentiation).

3 Unity of Substance and Definition

A proper definition expresses the nature of an entity that is one. This construal of definition in *Metaphysics* VII led Aristotle to limit its application to the essences of indivisible species.[23] There is a shift of emphasis in *Metaphysics* VIII to commonly accepted substances, namely, concrete individuals and their parts, and by extension to the meanings of terms in ordinary language. The interest in lexical definition complicates the issue of unity on both the ontological and conceptual fronts.

> Sometimes it is not clear whether a name signifies [σημαίνει] the composite substance, or the actuality or form, e.g., whether 'house' is a sign for the union [κοινοῦ] 'a covering consisting of bricks and stones laid thus and thus', or for the actuality or form 'a covering', and whether a line is 'twoness in length' or 'twoness', and whether an animal is 'a soul in a body' or 'a soul'; for this is the

chest is the object of analysis, the wood is identified with matter that exists potentially in the composite substance (*Met.* 1049a18–24).

23 See Chapter 5, sections 1 and 2.

substance or actuality of some body. 'Animal' might even be applied to both, not as something definable by one formula [λόγῳ], but as related to a single thing [πρὸς ἕν]. (1043a29–37, trans. follows Ross)

Aristotle speaks of what a name signifies and he goes on to list items that we would expect to find in the definition of the terms in question. Thus I have followed Ross in using quotation marks to indicate lexical items. That said, the linguistic items mentioned name composite universals and forms. A composite universal and the corresponding form have different *logoi* because reference determines sense and the referents are different in the two cases. The term ζῷον (animal), Aristotle notes, may be used to refer to the soul (the form of the animal) and to the natural kind animal, which includes a reference to the body. The fact that Aristotle treats both cases as instances of *pros hen* predication underscores his determination to make the form the unifying principle of the composite animal.

The essence is one because it is simple. Concrete substances are composites of form (essence) and matter. Ordinary definitions are generalizations based on concrete particulars and their characteristics. An individual may be thought about in terms of its essence or in terms of its essence embodied. This introduces an ambiguity into the name as ordinarily used, for it may be used of the essence or of the enmattered essence. 'House' is used for both the functional organization (the form) of the materials of a house and for the composite substance. Corresponding to the two uses are two distinct albeit related definitions – the first type of definition states only the essence and the second includes a general description of the materials in which the essence is realized. While Aristotle has no doubt that the first type of definition is required for knowledge, he is less certain about whether the second should be totally discounted by the scientist.[24] The two are closely connected in his mind, because the form as functional organization imposes functional constraints on the material in which the form can be realized.[25] The second type of definition mentions the actual materials in which the functions are realized (cf. 1036b28–32). The functional organization characteristic of human beings need not be realized in flesh and bones, but in actuality it is always realized in flesh and bones (1036b3–7). Definitions of essence are stated using a number of terms, and since from that perspective they are not simple, Aristotle is troubled by the question of unity.[26] Definitional unity, however, is threatened on two fronts in the

24 In the first chapter of the *De Anima*, Aristotle questions whether the natural scientist should consider definitions that mention both form and matter and decides that up to a point they should be (403a25–b12). Cf. *De Partibus Animalium* 640b23–29.

25 Aristotle develops the notion of hypothetical necessity in order to characterize the way in which the form as the determinant of the end product constrains the material; see discussion in Chapter 2, section 5, in this volume.

26 See Chapter 5, sections 2 and 3.

case of the composite treated as a universal. (The concrete individual is a single (composite) substance but it lacks definitional unity.)[27]

Aristotle's solution (found in VIII 6) is to reaffirm the thesis that the unity of the definition is a function of the unity of the object. The parts of the definition of the composite are related as form to matter and the definition of the essence is simply one. The details of this account are fairly fuzzy, but perhaps we can reconstruct the reasoning that supports Aristotle's conclusion. The object of definition is always a universal. The universal, however, may be the *logos* (soul) or the enmattered *logos* (animal). The definition of the soul is one, because the soul is the essence of an indivisible species, and thus its definition contains no extraneous elements. As Aristotle puts it: soul and to be a soul are the same (1043b1–2). A soul just is what it is. The unity of the definition of 'man' like the unity of the composite substance is secured by taking one component of the definition as matter and potentiality. This component describes the matter, flesh and bones, in which the form is realized. The remarkable feature of Aristotle's approach is its comprehensiveness. A single, relatively simple concept, that of the fulfillment of a potentiality in an actuality, allows Aristotle to treat concrete substances, definitions of composite universals, and definitions of essence both as ontological and as intelligible units of one kind or another because they are analyzable (unlike the simples of the *Theaetetus*). The definiens yields an analysis in terms of the differentia and the genus. The concept of the latter is incomplete and is intelligible only as a potentiality that requires further differentiation to yield a complete concept. The mind is able to grasp the concept of the genus and consider it as if it were an independent concept on the basis of apprehending the complete concept (differentia and genus), but the starting point of reflection is of necessity the complete concept as realized in the world. The unity of the definition remains intact because it does not consist of several fully actualized concepts.

Aristotle is now in a position to give a compelling account of the relation between the world of concrete objects, grasped through perception, the world of objects as constructed through language, and the world of objects as understood through the theoretical sciences. At the base, there are concrete substances that are composites of matter and form; more precisely, these concrete individuals are definable essences realized in matter. Concrete objects are apprehended through the senses; they are the basic referents of ordinary language; they are the source of meanings. At the first level of abstraction, there are the meanings of the universal terms that are used to classify the composite substances. Generalized composite substances such as man belong to this level. The definitions of

27 Pace Gill (1989), who argues that the concrete substance is a definable unity and primary substance in Aristotle's considered judgment.

such items reflect their composite nature. At the next level, there are essences that exist in the world as the forms of composite substances and exist in thought abstracted from their material substrata. These essences are the objects of the sciences – or at least of the most abstract sciences. How this works will become clearer if we look at one of Aristotle's favorite examples, 'man' as the name of the natural kind, and '(human) soul' as the essence of the human being and the proper object of the natural science, psychology, that studies the substance of the human being.

One way to spell out the definition of the term 'man' is discussed in detail when Aristotle evaluates the strengths and weaknesses of the Platonic method of division in VII 12. In this discussion, the phrase 'two-footed animal' is cited as the definiens of 'man'.[28] In this definition, two-footed is the final differentia and animal is the genus (1038a8–30). The definition of man qua composite substance is obviously at issue here, since the final differentia is a physical characteristic that could not be explicated without making reference to the human body. Since the final differentia comprehends all of the broader differentiae, for instance, two-footed comprehends footed and terrestrial, the final differentia gives us the form or essence of a particular kind of footed creature, namely, a two-footed one. Moreover, Aristotle's assimilation of the genus to matter suggests that 'animal' should be taken as an abbreviated description of all those characteristics shared by animals. As the final differentia, two-footed gives what would otherwise be merely a list of common animal characteristics a unique structure and renders the whole a single concept, the expression of which is the definiens of 'man'.[29] This definition may be adequate for the needs of ordinary speakers; it is, however, not adequate as the articulation of the nature of the human soul, which is the essence, the presence of which in organic material makes a particular lump of flesh and bones a man (1036b3–4, b11).[30]

The definition of the essence of human found in the *De Anima* is considerably more complicated than the analysis of man as object of definition or composite substance in the *Metaphysics*. The soul is substance as form and actuality, and the body is matter. The type of soul is characteristic of a species of living creatures, from plants to human beings. The most complex type of soul found in the sublunar realm is the human soul. It contains all of the faculties possessed by any other living creature as well as rationality – which is a power belonging only to the human soul. Aris-

28 Aristotle is quite flexible about what he includes in the definition of 'man' for the sake of illustration; in the discussion of division in *Posterior Analytics* II 5, he offers the following definition: animal, mortal, footed, biped, wingless (92a2).

29 Cf. Plato's final putative definition of knowledge in the *Theaetetus:* knowledge consists in the enumeration of the elements plus a distinguishing mark.

30 Aristotle also uses body (σῶμα) for the matter of a human (e.g., *Met.* 1037a5, 1041b7), in this context σῶμα seems to be a synonym for flesh and bones (cf. *Met.* 1041b14–27).

totle says that the rational soul contains the nutritive soul (the constellation of the functions characteristic of all life forms, namely, digestion, reproduction, elimination, respiration), the perceptive soul (the constellation of perceptual capacities, including the individual senses and the capacity to feel pleasure and pain) and the locomotive soul (the constellation of functions involved in self-locomotion) as potentialities. Just as the rational soul contains all the lower types of soul, the perceptive soul contains the nutritive. The three types of soul are hierarchically ordered, as are the life forms that they define.

> The case of the soul is exactly like that of figure; for in the case of both figures and living beings, there is always a series in which each successive term potentially contains its predecessor, e.g., the square the triangle, the perceptive faculty the nutritive. (*De Anima* 414b28–32)

The Aristotelian soul is a complex of nested vital capacities. In certain respects, the relation between the type of soul that is actualized and the ones that are contained in it potentially is analogous to the relation between ultimate and proximate matter and the form that is actualized in the matter. Earth can be an independently existing element, but when it is a component of wood, it exists potentially as the stuff in which the form of wood is realized. In certain circumstances, wood is a composite substance, in others it is the matter of a composite substance. The wood constituting a chest exists potentially in the chest.[31] Similarly, nutritive soul is an autonomous essence in plants and it exists potentially in the perceptive soul of animals (415a1–3). The perceptive soul exists potentially in the rational soul.

The human soul is not many but one, because all the functions belonging to it are integrated into a single whole, the unity of which is a consequence of its being a distinctive form. How this works cannot be explained by a top-down approach.[32] This Aristotle believes was the error of the Platonists. The nature of soul can only be understood through the careful examination of actual life forms. Is human sight different from feline sight? Well, it is and it isn't. The proper object of sight is color. The mechanism is the same: a ratio (*logos*) of light to dark that is transmitted through a transparent medium from an external object to the eye jelly. The *logos* of light to dark is realized in the percipient organ and becomes the basis of a seeing. There are also differences. Some creatures have sharper vision than humans; all other animals have a sharper sense of smell than humans and an inferior capacity for tactile discrimination (*De*

31 When the explanatory context is that of the substantial change from log to chest, wood is identified with the enduring substratum (cf. *Met.* 1033a13–23). However, when the chest is the object of analysis, the wood is identified with matter that exists potentially in the composite substance (*Met.* 1049a18–24).

32 Cf. Gotthelf (1976, pp. 226–54).

An. 421a10–15, *De Sens.* 441a1–3). More significantly, the perception of incidental objects and the various activities of the imagination (*phantasia*), such as dreaming and memory, will be shaped by reason in the human case but not in the case of any other animal – even though *phantasia* and the perception of incidental objects are perceptual functions. That this should be true is, for Aristotle, evidence that rationality gives the other faculties, especially the other cognitive faculties, a distinctive character even though they retain many of the characteristics they have in other nonrational creatures. In an analogous way, the wood of the chest continues to have many of the same characteristics that it had before becoming a chest, but the wood has other characteristics, which it would not have, were it not a chest. The wood has the nature it now has (namely, constituting a chest) because of the presence of the form of chest in it. One way to explain why the chest has certain features that are universal characteristics of wood would be to say that the form of wood is a component of the form of chest in this instance. This is not, however, the way Aristotle describes the situation; the lower-level "forms" are included with the matter realized in a composite substance that has a single form. Because of the presence of the form in the proximate matter (wood), the composite, the wooden chest, is one. In this instance, matter is conceived as a layered series of potentialities, but not form. The wood is the proximate matter of the chest, but the immediate constituents of the wood are also the matter of the chest, and its ultimate matter is earth.[33] Had Aristotle pursued this line as a psychologist, he would have assigned all the vital functions except rationality to the human body and not its soul. This is not, however, what he did in the *De Anima,* where his objective is to give a full description of the soul. The soul contains all the vital functions of the species in question. Keeping all the vital capacities in the form (soul) greatly complicates the issue of definition, for the expression of the form (the essence) required will be equally complex. It also complicates the issue of specifying the matter of the living thing.[34] These drawbacks notwithstanding, it is possible to see how in principle the fact that every biological individual belongs to a species that has a distinctive organization of vital capacities realized in appropriate matter would secure the unity of the definition of the species and the unity of the composite individual. The unity of the definition of the soul as such is also secure because one element in the definition, for instance, rationality, contains all the others as potentialities.

Aristotelian natural sciences primarily employ definitions of essence as embodied, and even geometrical objects are said to have intelligible

33 *Met.* 1049a18–24.

34 Ackrill (1972–3, pp. 119–33) has brought these difficulties to the attention of scholars. I argued that Aristotle has a ready answer to these difficulties in Modrak (1987a, chap. 2).

matter.[35] Aristotle is sharply critical of attempts to eliminate all talk of bodies from natural science.[36] Psychology is a natural science, and the definitions Aristotle offers in the *De Anima* are ones that could be stated in a way that only imposed certain functional constraints on the material substratum, but as stated they typically make reference to the actual organs involved (cf. *Met.* 1026a1–6).[37] In *Metaphysics* VII, by contrast, definitions of essence that exclude reference to matter are emphasized. This apparent shift of emphasis is explained in part by the fact that first philosophy studies objects that are separated in contrast to the objects of natural science, which are inseparable from bodies (*De An.* 403b14–16, 1026a6–19). There is another motivation, however; because the essence determines the structure of the matter, the natural scientist's interest in matter should always be subordinated, Aristotle believes, to the study of essence (*De Part. An.* 640b18–29). Careful descriptions of matter alone will not further the ends of the biologist, any more than they would prove helpful to the metaphysician (cf. 403b12–14). Because the essence determines the character of the physical individual and the character of the composite universal species, the natural scientist considering the embodied essence and the metaphysician considering the essence simpliciter are studying the same object for different ends; and thus Aristotle believes that definitions of essence are the building blocks of the natural as well as formal sciences. The definition of the soul (in the case of living organisms) is more fundamental than (because required for) the definition of the species, and in principle the soul could be described in functional terms that did not make reference to particular matter.

Let us reconsider the definition 'two-footed animal'. In the *Metaphysics,* Aristotle draws an analogy between the genus name, 'animal', and matter. It may be instructive to consider this suggestion anew for, as we have seen, Aristotle's considered judgment seems to be that a human is a composite substance consisting of an ensouled body of a type that is characteristic of humans. The definition of the composite *anthropos* will mention matter as well as form (1045a20–30). Aristotle's shorthand description of the matter of the concrete human in the *Metaphysics* is flesh and bones. Should this description be reinterpreted in light of the description of levels of matter in *Metaphysics* IX 7 and in light of the description of the stages of fetal development in the *De Generatione animalium,* the proximate matter would not be flesh and bones in the ordinary

35 Intelligible matter is mentioned at *Metaphysics* 1036a9–12, 1037a4–5, 1045a33–5. Moreover, the objects of all three types of theoretical science are derived in one way or another from the experience of concrete objects, and thus embodied essences are relevant to all types of science. See Chapter 4 in this volume.

36 See, e.g., *De Caelo* 299a2–16.

37 For a more detailed discussion of Aristotle's handling of definition in the *De Anima,* see Modrak (1987a, chap. 2 and *passim*).

sense of these terms, but rather an organic material enformed by the nutritive, perceptive, and locomotive capacities (cf. 1049a1–2).[38] These capacities are also definitive of the genus animal and thus the same potentialities seem to be realized in the concrete object as in the genus. Parallel descriptions of the genus and the proximate matter of the concrete human are possible. This may well explain why in some places Aristotle speaks as if the matter mentioned in the full definition of a composite substance just is the general description of the proximate matter of the composite (e.g., flesh and bones) and why in other places he speaks as if the mention of the genus of the substance is the material component of the definition.[39] Standard definitions of natural kinds in terms of genus and differentiae challenge Aristotle's account of definition. Aristotle has claimed that the definiens of a proper definition is unified because one element of it is not predicated of another, yet two-footed appears to be predicated of animal in 'two-footed animal'. In order to subsume the genus under the differentiae, Aristotle makes it the material element of the definiens. Since matter exists potentially in the compound of which it is the matter, the genus as matter becomes the common properties that are subsumed under the final differentia. For the same reason that the matter of a composite individual is posterior to the form of that individual, the genus would be posterior to the final differentia.

The nesting of capacities of all sorts and hence the layering of potentialities is a pervasive feature of Aristotle's ontology. It is the strategy he adopts to unify proper definitions and composite substances. There seems to be something prescient, if not right, about Aristotle's approach. Complex organizational structures, especially organic ones, seem to take on a life of their own, which cannot be explained, or can be explained only with great difficulty and many codicils, by appeal to the characteristics of their components. Aristotle urges us to look at what makes a conglomerate a whole and to recognize that the realization of a particular organizing principle in a single organism, artifact, or institution may be quite complex and involve the integration of a number of subordinate systems in the whole. The identification of the (dominant) form (organizational structure) with the function of the system enables Aristotle to conceptualize a complex artifact or organism as an integrated whole.

The object of definition is always a universal of one sort or another. The object of definition in the strict sense is the essence or form. There are different types of definitions. Broadly speaking, there are lexical def-

38 According to *De Gen. an.* 736b5–29, the psychic capacities develop as the appropriate organs are acquired by the fetus, and rationality, which does not have a specific organ, is acquired last. At no time does a fully formed and nonmaimed human lack any of the psychic capacities, nor does organic material that is enformed by the nutritive, perceptive, and locomotive faculties exist on its own as matter.

39 *Physics* 200b7–8; *Met.* 1043b31–33, 1045a29–30.

initions for natural language terms and scientific definitions. The latter, as we have seen, take the form of an analysis of a composite kind or the analysis of an essence in and of itself. As Aristotle says, the definition of animal may be in terms of the soul alone or the compound of soul and body (1043a34–35). The unity of the first type of scientific definition is greater than that of the second; the unity of the definiens in both cases, however, is explained by Aristotle in terms of lower-level potentialities that are realized through the actualized form. To the extent that a lexical definition coincides with the scientific definition of the same object, it will have genuine unity; often, however, the sole sources of unity for a lexical definition are conjunction and convention (cf. 1030a7–11). All three types of definition apply to mind-independent objects apprehended through sense perception. These objects are the primary referents of natural language terms, and the understanding of their essences and relations is constitutive of the various sciences. While not definable, individuals exhibit the same structure as the generalized compound substance. A substantial individual is a compound of form and matter and yet a single substance, because the matter exists potentially and the form actually. Perhaps the greatest advantage of this explanatory strategy is comprehensiveness, for the same factors are relevant to the explanation of unity and intelligibility at different ontological and epistemic levels.

4 Identity and Accidental Sameness

Aristotle makes sameness a criterion for distinguishing among definable unities, universalized compounds of matter and form, and accidental unities. The various senses of 'same' are discussed in *Metaphysics* V 9:

> 'The same' means that which is the same incidentally, e.g., 'the pale' and 'the musical' are the same because they are accidents of the same thing, and 'a man' and 'musical' because the one is an accident of the other; and 'the musical' is the same as 'a man' because it is an accident of the man. . . . Some things are said to be the same in this sense, but others are the same in themselves (*kath' hauta*), in as many senses as that which is one is so; for both the things whose matter is one either in form or in number, and those whose substance is one, are said to be the same. (1017b27–1018a7)

The first case Aristotle discusses is that of accidental sameness. Accidental sameness is of particular interest to Aristotle because it appears to be a case where the referents of two natural language terms are the same but the meanings of the terms are different. This would present an apparent puzzle on the *De Interpretatione*'s theory of meaning. Aristotle gives three examples. In the first, two different definite descriptions asserted in a particular context refer to one and the same individual. Since the same individual may be both pale and musical, the definite descriptions 'the pale' and 'the musical' used in a context where they denote the same individual are said to be the same. In this case, 'the pale' and 'the musical' are understood as 'the pale *x*' and 'the musical *y*' and are said to be the same just in case *x* is the same individual as *y*. Aristotle is quick to point out, however, that sameness of reference in this case is due to the possession of two distinct qualities by the same individual. The meaning of the description is ultimately a function of the property in virtue of which the individual is called pale or musical. Expressions such as 'the pale' and 'the musical' as used by Aristotle have several closely related functions, namely, to refer to the attribute that is present in the individual and by extension to refer to the individual.[40] The latter use is evident in the present categorization of identity statements where the issue is synchronic identity; the former has center stage in the analysis of change in *Physics* I 7.[41] The second case of accidental sameness Aristotle considers is of interest for related reasons. Here, too, the referents of the two descriptions appear to be the same. The second example consists in an indefinite description 'a man' and an adjective 'musical', which are said to be the same because there exists at least one individual satisfying the indefinite description who is musical. (Alternatively, Aristotle may intend to consider a stronger claim here, namely, that any *x* who is musical is a man. The example is too compressed to be certain which reading Aristotle has in mind, but the stronger claim would not raise any additional problems for his theory of meaning.) The third example consists in a definite description 'the musical' and an indefinite one 'a man'. In certain contexts, the definite description picks out an individual satisfying the indefinite description, and under these circumstances the two descriptions refer to the same individual. Again, Aristotle appeals to the difference between the basis for the meanings of the terms, one accident and one substance, to explain how reference works in this case. The use of definite and indefinite descriptions to refer to specific individuals is such that an individual who is one and the same may be the referent of different descriptions. This use has now been shown by Aristotle to be consistent with his theory of meaning.

Aristotle's examples of accidental sameness explicate different kinds of particular identity statements. The second type of identity that he discusses is exhibited by universally true identity statements that assert either that a type of composite substance is the same as itself or that a particular composite substance is the same as itself or that an essence is the same as itself. The fourfold ontology defined in *Categories* 2 resulted in two types of predicates that are applicable to individuals, ones predicating secondary attributes and ones predicating secondary substance.[42]

40 See also Chapter 1, sections 2 and 4, and Chapter 5, section 2.

41 The difference in explanatory context and the close association of the two uses explains why Aristotle uses the same expression, τὸ μουσικόν, for the attribute and the individual. See the discussion of *Physics* I 7 in Chapter 5, section 2 in this volume.

42 See Chapter 1, sections 2 and 4.

This basic division supports the distinction between the two cases just mentioned. Because Aristotle's conception of substance in the *Metaphysics* is one that distinguishes between composite substances, kinds of composite substances, and primary substances (essences), the account of substantial sameness at 1018a5–7 mentions three possibilities.

The difference between accidental sameness and substantial sameness is also invoked in *Metaphysics* VII–VIII. There, the distinction between types of sameness finds expression in assertions such as 'Pale man is not the same as man' (1030a5); 'To be a man is not the same as man' (1043b2–4); 'To be a soul is the same as soul' (1036a1, 1043b2–4); and 'What is predicated in virtue of itself is the same as its essence' (1029b14).[43] These statements presuppose a consistent and interesting notion of sameness that is similar to, but different from, the modern conception of identity. Let us consider three statements:

(a) Socrates = Socrates.
(b) The man wearing a mask = Socrates.
(c) Socrates at time t_1 = Socrates at time t_2.

Statement (a) is tautologous, and Aristotle's reason for accepting it is the same as ours. Statements (b) and (c) are more interesting from both a modern and an ancient perspective. For Aristotle, the reference of the description or name defines an ontological level that must be taken into account in order to establish the truth conditions of the statement.[44] The definite description 'the man wearing a mask' refers to a composite substance, the character of which is explained by appeal to a characteristic (wearing a mask) that belongs to a particular composite substance (a man) (cf. *Met.* 1015b16–27). If 'Socrates' refers to the same composite substance, then statement (b) is true. Statement (b) is a classic example of Aristotle's notion of accidental sameness. This notion seems to cover many of the same cases that today would be labeled cases of contingent identity. Since, however, for Aristotle what makes identity statements of the form (b) true is the coincidence of two distinct characteristics in the same individual, there is at a deeper level of analysis no identity, and thus he will qualify the assertion of (b).[45] To explain transtemporal identity of the sort expressed in statement (c), Aristotle would appeal to the nature of the enduring object. That 'Socrates' refers to a composite substance, the character of which is determined by a particular species essence being realized in a particular body, is the crucial factor for evaluating (c).

43 See the discussion in Chapter 5, section 2.

44 Examples of type (b) figured importantly in sophistic arguments (*Met.* 1026b15–18, *Topics* I 7).

45 The difference between Aristotle's conception of accidental sameness and the modern notion of contingent identity has been much discussed in recent literature. See, e.g., Cohen (1984, pp. 41–65); Lewis (1991, chap. 5); Spellman (1995, chap. 2).

Socrates is a human, and as long as he remains a human, he exists as the same individual, and hence (c) will be true. The statement (b) is true just in case the composite substance is in a certain state; (c) is true just in case the composite individual exists at both t_1 and t_2. The ontological level that is relevant to determining the truth of (c) is the fundamental level of substance (a continuously realized form); the ontological level that is relevant to determining the truth of (b) is the level of composite substance. The critical factor in determining whether the identity asserted by (b) is true is whether the compound *logos* 'man wearing a mask' can be truly predicated of the individual substance denoted by 'Socrates'. Whether the identity asserted by (c) is true will depend on whether the item denoted by 'Socrates' at time t_2 is the same substance as the item denoted by 'Socrates' at time t_1. In both cases (b) and (c), what is at issue in the evaluation of the identity statement is the presence of the relevant *logos* (accident or essence) in a substratum (the individual man or the matter).

In the *Metaphysics,* Aristotle only occasionally makes statements having the form of (a) or (b) or (c); such statements are of marginal interest to him. He is much more interested in generalized expressions of sameness. The statement (d) 'man = to be man', which Aristotle believes to be false on the standard interpretation, is more interesting to him than statements about individuals, because were (d) true without qualification, it would be a first step toward a definition of 'man' (1043b2–4). The meaning of 'man' would be the same as its essence, both 'man' and 'to be a man' would pick out an essence, and the next step for the philosopher would be to determine what the essence was. Similarly, the statement (e) 'pale man = man' would, were it true, explicate the meaning of 'man' by identifying it with a description of a property belonging to a composite substance. The true identity statement, (f) 'soul = to be soul', indicates that soul is an essence (1036a1–2, 1043b2–4).

The false statement of identity (d) and the true statement of identity (f) have the same form, *X* = to be *X;* however, only in the case where a term naming an essence is substituted for *X* will '*X* = to be *X*' be true without qualification.[46] In the case of statement (d) (a statement in which a term for a compound substance is substituted for *X*), further analysis reveals that 'man' is a term for a generalized composite substance consisting of the essence, 'to be a man,' and matter. This is a more complex item than the essence. Nonetheless, one essence figures in the interpretation of both descriptions appearing in the statement of sameness (d). Two different essences are included in the meaning of the accidental unity, 'pale

46 Plato's description of the Ideas as just what they are is an attempt to capture this same feature of essential unities (*Parmenides* 129ae). When one grasps beauty itself (αὐτὸ τὸ καλόν), one knows what beauty is (ὅ ἔστι καλόν) (*Symposium* 211cd).

man', and this can be shown by substituting 'to be a pale man' for 'pale man' and 'to be a man' for 'man'. Since this substitution produces a falsehood, the identity statement is false, if universalized. Since it may be true that there are individuals who are both pale and men, Aristotle introduces the notion of accidental sameness.

Aristotle's treatment of identity statements is strikingly different from ours. For contemporary philosophers of language and metaphysicians, identity statements where different terms (names or descriptions) flank the identity sign raise puzzles about reference and puzzles about opaque contexts. In such cases, truth-preserving substitutions into true statements may not be recognized as true by persons accepting the original statements as true. For instance, Callias may believe that Socrates is a philosopher and not believe that the masked man is a philosopher, even though the identity statement (b) is true, if Callias does not believe that (b) is true. For Aristotle, reference is of interest because he wants to link meanings to extralinguistic objects. This desire leads him to look for privileged descriptions that specify actual natures. This desire is expressed in the classification scheme of the *Categories* and the prominent place assigned to terms referring to substance in the central books of the *Metaphysics*. The search for privileged descriptions, when successful, yields descriptions in which meaning coincides with actual essence. This explains Aristotle's interest in statements (d), (e), and (f), all of which purport to be analyses of terms for basic objects.

5 Forms and Universals

Aristotle explores several ways to develop the analogy between the composite substance and the definition of essence. For him, the importance of the analogy is a consequence of the way in which universals are known. The mind must be able to derive universals from its experience of concrete individuals.[47] These universals must be such that, when fully articulated, they can function as the basic definitions required for systematic knowledge. The story of the origin of universals in experience is retold in *Metaphysics* I 1–2 as an account of the historical development of knowledge. Aristotle places wisdom (σοφία) or metaphysics at the pinnacle of knowledge and describes it as the knowledge of first principles and causes.

> Of these characteristics that of knowing all things must belong to the one having universal knowledge in the highest degree; for he knows in a sense all the underlying particulars. And these things, the most universal, are perhaps the most difficult for men to know; for they are farthest from the senses. And the most ex-

47 See Chapters 3 and 4.

act of the sciences are those which deal most with first principles. (*Met.* 982a21–26; Ross trans.).

In *Metaphysics* IV 1 and again in VII 1, the subject of metaphysics is defined as the study of substance. In the latter, substance is described as prior in definition (λόγῳ), prior in knowledge (γνώσει), and prior in time. In *Metaphysics* VII 4–6, Aristotle establishes that the essence of a substance is identical to the substance. Essence is the proper object of definition, and definitions are universals. In *Metaphysics* VII 15, Aristotle argues that individuals are indefinable.

For this reason, also, there is neither definition [ὁρισμός] of nor demonstration about individual perceptible substances, because they have matter the nature of which is such that they are capable both of existing and of not existing. (1039b27–30; cf. 1040a27-b2)

Aristotle is faced with a challenge: meanings are universal concepts, definitions are of universals, but the primary referents of substance sortals such as man are concrete individuals. To avoid the separation of reference and meaning, Aristotle introduces the notion of a composite universal that is a generalization of the essence and the material substrate of the concrete individual. The concrete object is not definable – except insofar as it is a substance and thus has an essence.[48] In *Metaphysics* VII, the essences of primary objects are the bridge that Aristotle envisages between concrete objects and the first principles of science. Aristotle describes the concrete individual as a *logos* with matter (*logos syn tei hylei*) and the essence as the formula by itself (*logos haplos*).[49] The essence is the *logos* that exists both as an object of thought and in matter. The concrete substance is a composite of matter and form. Since he also identifies forms with essences and makes them the object of definition, it seems likely that the form that is constitutive of the individual is, for Aristotle, the substance and essence of that individual.[50] The form will be definable only insofar as it is not unique to the individual, and thus the form of the individual that is its essence and substance would seem to be the species form.

Although many of the things said in the preceding paragraph would be granted by most recent commentators on the *Metaphysics*, the last statement would be hotly contested. The ontological status of Aristotelian

48 The relation of essence and definition to substance is discussed at 1029b20; 1030b5; 1031a1, 10, 18; 1031b32 and 1039a20.

49 *Met.* 1039b20–27. Cf. 1033a1–4; 1035a22–23. While Aristotle might have used the phrase "*logos syn tei hylei*" to describe the universal definition that mentions matter, he is not using the phrase in this way at 1039b21 for he claims that the *logos syn tei hylei* is subject to generation and destruction.

50 That form is substance is asserted at *Met.* 1028a28, 1032b1–2, 1033b17, 1035b14–22, 1037a29, 1038a26, 1041b6, and 1050b2. The connection between form and essence and/or definition is discussed at 1035a31, 1029b1–3, 1036a29, 1043b1, and 1044a10.

forms is quite controversial today. At least four lines of interpretation can be found in recent literature on *Metaphysics* VII and VIII: (a) forms are unique individuals; (b) forms are particulars because they contain proximate matter or because they are so specific as to have only one instance; (c) forms are a special type of universal; (d) forms are universals.[51] Elsewhere, I have argued that forms are a special sort of universal and will summarize my arguments below.[52]

Aristotle's discussion of essence, definition, universals, and form in the central books of the *Metaphysics* is confusing, to be sure, for he seems both to assert and to deny that forms are universals. More precisely, the account of essential definition makes the object of definition a universal and a substance, a species form exemplified by many individuals, and yet the anti-Platonist arguments deny that universals are substances. Perhaps the most important of these arguments is found in VII 13, where Aristotle repeatedly asserts that no universal is a substance (1038b7–12, 1038b35).[53] If Aristotelian forms are universals, Aristotle seems to be caught in a major contradiction. One uncharitable explanation is to assume that Aristotle mistakenly believes that abstract universals and embodied universals have different logical properties. A far more charitable approach is to point out that if Aristotelian forms are particulars, then they escape the brunt of Aristotle's anti-Platonist arguments. Not surprisingly, several recent commentators have developed this line of interpretation with great care and insightfulness. Another equally charitable solution, however, is to show that Aristotle has good reason to distinguish between his universal forms and the universals under attack in this chapter.[54]

Forms are predicated of matter, and properties are predicated of particulars (1029a21–24, 1038b4–6); this ontological difference, I have argued, provides Aristotle with a way to distinguish between forms and other universals.[55] Because an Aristotelian form is a substance type, which standardly has many numerically different tokens, a form satisfies

51 Among those defending the uniqueness of forms are Frede (1987, chaps. 4–5) and Hartman (1977). Those defending the particularity or specificity of forms include Irwin (1988, chap. 12); and Gill (1989), who argues that forms are so specific as to apply to only one individual. Those defending the thesis that forms are universals include Ross (1924), and Furth (1978, pp. 627–32). Two interpreters who argue that forms are neither universal nor individual are Owens (1963) and Lear (1988).

52 See Modrak (1979, pp. 371–81).

53 This chapter has spawned a veritable industry of articles. See Woods (1967); Lesher (1971, pp. 169–78). The claim that no universal is a substance is also made at 1003a7, 1060b21, 1087a2, a10–15.

54 Woods (1967) proposes a distinction between universals and things said universally in order to show that Aristotle's criticisms in VII 13 are compatible with his conception of universal form. In Modrak (1979), I defend a different approach that distinguishes between a narrow notion of universals, universals$_p$, satisfied by Platonic substances and ordinary properties and a broader notion, satisfied by Aristotelian forms. Anything satisfying the narrower notion is not a substance, according to the arguments of VII 13.

55 See Modrak (1979).

the broad notion of universal required of an object of definition.[56] In the broad sense, a universal is anything (kind, type, property) that has or might have more than one exemplification.[57] Platonic forms and other properties of particulars fall under a narrower notion of universal (universal$_p$); a universal$_p$ not only has many exemplifications but also is predicated of the particulars that exemplify it. When, as in VII 13, Aristotle asserts that no universal is a substance as part of an argument against Platonic forms, he means that no universal$_p$ is a substance. When he claims that the proper object of definition is essence and form and that only universals are definable, he means universal in the broad sense. The fourfold ontology of *Categories* 2 has been modified with the introduction of the distinction between form and matter, but the underlying conception of concrete particulars having properties and manifesting substance types is retained in the twofold conception of the concrete particular as composite substance and the form as substance type and in the twofold conception of the subject of predication as particulars and matter.

Further support for this interpretation is afforded by the identification of the form with the *logos* that exists in matter and is articulated in the essential definition.[58] In a discussion of which parts to include in the definition, Aristotle says,

> A part then may be a part either of the form (i.e., of the essence), or of the compound of the form and the matter or of the matter itself. But only the parts of the form are parts of the formula [λόγου] and the formula is of the universal; for being a circle is the same as the circle, and being a soul the same as the soul. But of the composite, e.g., this circle . . . of these there is no definition [ὁρισμός]. (1035b33–1036a5)

Only parts of the form of the individual will be included in the *logos* expressing the essence, and there will be no definition (*horismos*) applying to concrete individuals. One might argue, however, that since Aristotle had no such device as quotation marks to indicate that the identification of the definiens with the definiendum in an articulated definition of essence is at issue, the received text is more ambiguous than the translation above suggests. Suppose, then, that instead of interpreting this text in a way that takes 'being a soul' to be a constitutive definiens of a definition of essence, we read these identities as assertions that an essence is self-identical, that is, the essence is a soul and the essence is being a soul. Aristotle's claim that the *logos* (now interpreted as essence) is of the universal results in the form's being universal, since form and *logos* have the same parts and hence the same logical structure. On either interpreta-

56 Aristotle compares the form to the arrangement of letters that makes the spoken or written token the word-token it is (*Met.* 1041b11–28; cf. 1035a10–15).

57 Cf. *Met.* 1040a28–b1.

58 *Met.* 1035b16, b32; 1036a5, a29; 1042a17.

tion of Aristotle's examples, the relevance of form and essence to definition (*horismos*) is clear. Were the form particular rather than universal, it like the concrete particular would be indefinable.[59]

But the skeptic might wonder why, if Aristotle distinguishes between types of universals, he does not make this explicit.[60] The answer, I believe, is that Aristotle's term for universal '*katholou*' (literally 'on the whole') is a much more plastic notion, for him, than 'universal' is for modern philosophers. Aristotle uses *katholou* adverbially to mean 'in general' and as a term for collections and wholes made up of parts as well as for predicates applying to a number of particulars. The first adverbial use corresponds to common usage, for *katholou* is a contraction of *kata* (as) and *holou* (whole). The last sense is closer to the modern notion of universal, and it is in this sense that definitions seem to be universals. Aristotle repeatedly reaffirms the connection between definition and universals.[61] The definition of belonging universally in *Posterior Analytics* I 4 mentions characteristics that are also mentioned in connection with strict definition.[62] These include belonging in itself and as such, and holding primarily and in every case. However, the core notion of *katholou* as a predicate applicable to more than one particular also seems to apply to Platonic Ideas and genera, and hence, if these are not substances because they are universals, it is hard to see how the same notion can be applied to essences and their definitions without making them vulnerable to the same objections.

Metaphysics VII 3–12 establish the identity of form with substance and essence and the object of definition. In VII 13, these conclusions are called into question by the arguments against Platonic universals. Acknowledging the difficulty, Aristotle hints at its solution at the end of VII 13 when he remarks that in one sense not even substance is definable and in another it is. In the following chapters, he develops an account of definition as the specification of the formula of the essence that the concrete particular embodies. The formula is general; the concrete particular is an individual. Strictly speaking the formula (*logos*/form) is not said of the concrete particular but of its matter, and this kind of predication is different from the predication of other characteristics of the particular. The groundwork for this theory has already been laid in the preceding chap-

59 Aristotle makes the same point about the imagined circle existing in thought as its concrete counterpart; both are indefinable, and like the latter, the former also contains matter (albeit intelligible matter) (*Met.* 1037a1–4).

60 A similar objection may be raised against the proponent of individual form, for Aristotle uses "*eidos*" for species and form, as well as for Platonic form.

61 At the end of VII 13, after arguing against the thesis that universals are substances, Aristotle worries that this will make definition impossible (1039a14–23); at *Met.* 1040a29–b2, he argues that because the sun is a particular, it is indefinable.

62 As noted in Chapter 2, section 4, the circumscribed notion of *katholou* found in *Posterior Analytics* I 4 is narrower than Aristotle's usual use of the term.

ters. In VII 3, in the course of eliminating the matter of a composite as a candidate for substance, Aristotle identifies matter with what is left once the individuating features are stripped away.

When everything else is stripped off evidently nothing but matter remains. For the others are affections, products, and potencies of bodies, and length, breadth, and depth are quantities and not substances (for a quantity is not a substance), but the substance is rather that to which these belong primarily. But when length and breadth and depth are taken away we see nothing remaining unless there is something that is bounded by them; so that to those who inquire in this way matter alone must seem to be substance. By matter I mean that which in itself is neither a particular thing nor a quantity nor assigned to any other of the categories by which being is defined. (1029a11–21)

Matter so defined is a substratum that does not correspond to a natural linguistic category. The word that Aristotle uses for the material substratum, ὕλη, is not a term ordinarily meaning a substratum about which nothing further can be said. In its most specific and presumably original use, ὕλη means wood; in its generalized sense, it means a material component or substratum. Aristotle abstracts from the generalized sense to describe a notion of substratum that is without positive characteristics. The only way he can talk about this type of substratum is as a potentiality to take on forms.[63] The predication of form of matter is a unique kind of predication, because only in this case is there a subject of predication lacking any characteristic that would distinguish it as a distinct particular; qua subject, matter exists as a mere potentiality.[64] Matter as ordinarily conceived is the constituent stuff of which a concrete particular is made; the chest is made of wood, and the man of flesh and bones. 'Wood' and 'flesh' and 'bones' as ordinarily used have apparent referents.[65] Recognizing this, Aristotle draws a distinction between the use of the same word to pick out a composite substance, for instance, the use of 'wood' for the wood composed of earth and the form of wood, and its use to pick out the material of a composite substance, the chest composed of wood and the form of chest (1049a18–24). In the latter case, Aristotle recommends that the chest be called wooden, not wood, to indicate that the wood as the substratum in which the form of chest is realized exists potentially in

63 Schofield (1972) argues that 1029a10–27 is not a specification of matter but rather an argument to show that if stripping away is the way to arrive at the substratum the outcome will be featureless matter.

64 This is the kernel of truth in the traditional doctrine of prime matter. But it would be a mistake to suppose that because Aristotle defines matter as potentiality, he believes that something exists as an independent entity in reality that fits this description. The basic materials of the universe for Aristotle are the four elements found in the sublunar world and the fifth celestial element, aether.

65 The latter pair, flesh and bones, according to Aristotle, are standardly used of living beings and homonymously used of corpses (*De Generatione animalium* 734b24–31). This philosophical refinement of ordinary usage is also motivated by the consideration of the reference of the term as used in different contexts.

the chest. This linguistic recommendation is motivated by Aristotle's desire to make language display real relations, which in this instance are obscured by the use of 'wood' for the material of which the chest is composed. The chest is not a union of two individuals, a wood-chest; it is one object, a wooden chest.

In short: in different contexts, Aristotle develops a picture of the world, language, and human cognitive capacities that makes the exemplification of universal features by concrete particulars the basis for meaning and knowledge. The concrete substance is a compound of matter and form. Perceptions of the individual prompt (in human beings under favorable conditions) concepts of the compound universal (a generalized notion of the instantiated form and matter) that is the meaning of the name of the individual's kind. Under the best epistemic conditions, a concept of the species form arises; this concept, when articulated, is the scientific definition of the species. The picture is simple and elegant, and the main charge one might bring against it is that it is short on details. The introduction of particular forms to this picture would at a minimum complicate it and at worst be inconsistent with it.

Aristotle does sometimes talk as if forms are particulars. What motivates these remarks, and do they commit Aristotle to a conception of form that is inconsistent with his semantics? With respect to motivation, there are two contributing factors. The first is found in his desire to secure the place of concrete individuals as the source of universals, and the second closely related objective is his desire to undermine Platonism about objects of knowledge. According to *Posterior Analytics* II 19, the ability to grasp the most intelligible objects of all develops out of the capacity for sense perception and the character of the perceptible particular is determined by the universal. This commits Aristotle to an ontology of concrete individuals and universals and to a conception of exemplification that justifies the knower's confidence in universals derived from perceptions. In the *Categories,* the commitment to an ontology of individuals and universals is expressed in the fourfold distinction between primary and secondary subjects and particular and universal attributes.

In the *Metaphysics,* a more epistemically sophisticated version of the same distinctions yields concrete substances whose essences are exemplified by all the individuals belonging to the same infima species and are knowable just as they are in themselves. These essences are now elevated to the status of primary substance, because the essence of a concrete substance makes its matter a substance. This conception resolves the tension between the *Posterior Analytics*' emphasis on universals and the *Categories*' emphasis on individuals. Because Socrates' essence is the essence of a particular human body as well as the exemplification of the essence of human being, Aristotle finds it more natural than we might find it to talk about this essence, this soul, when speaking of Socrates, even though Socrates' soul is the functional organization that he shares with all other human beings. Not only does such talk come easily to Aristotle, but he also intends to emphasize the sameness of the form found here in these bones and sinews and the form articulated in the definition of human being employed by the biologist. The mental image of a circle that a geometer contemplates at a particular time is also an enmattered individual, according to Aristotle, and it is an instance of the circle that is the proper object of geometry (*Met.* 1036a2–9). The imagined circle goes out of existence when the geometer stops picturing it, but this does not invalidate the theorems about circles in geometry because the universal is unaffected. Because the essence of the imagined circle is the same as that of the universal, the geometer is able to use the former to draw conclusions about the latter.

Having defined two types of predication, one where the subject is potentiality and another where it is enformed matter, that is, a composite individual, Aristotle has a good reason to think that essences, species forms, escape the force of his anti-Platonist arguments against universals. A Platonic form belongs to the particular in the same way that any other property belongs to that particular, but this is not true of an Aristotelian form. By defining two different notions of ontological predication, Aristotle has in effect differentiated between a broad notion of universal that can be met by species essences and a narrower notion that does not apply to them but applies to Platonic Ideas, genera, and all more mundane universals.

> Again, in another way the genus seems more substantial than the species, and the universal than the particulars. And with the universal and the genus the Ideas are connected (for by the same argument they are thought to be substances). (1042a14–16)

When Aristotle asserts in VII 13 and elsewhere that universals are not substance, he is explicitly taking aim at such pretenders to the mantle of substance as Platonic Ideas and the genera of species and numbers.[66] In order to argue that none of these universals are substances, Aristotle employs a circumscribed notion of universal without fanfare. Unlike a modern philosopher, who might be discomforted by this stratagem, he does not believe that a single, clearly defined notion of universal is needed. He is content to employ different notions of universal in different contexts.

The feature that Platonic forms share with other nonsubstantial universals is that they are common to a number of different particulars in contrast to substance that belongs only to itself and to that of which it is the substance (1040b21–24). Only in contexts where Aristotle has defined the universal as that which is common (*koinon*) to a number of par-

66 *Met.* 1038b34, 1041a3–5; cf. 1042a15–17.

ticulars does he claim that no universal is a substance.[67] Aristotle chides the Platonists for positing a substantial form that is a one over many (1040b27–30). An Aristotelian form, by contrast, is not a common property shared by a number of actual individuals but a substance type realized in a number of spatially discrete bits of matter, thus producing composite substances that are one in species and essence but many in number.

Suppose the proponent of particular forms concedes that, when arguing against the Platonists, Aristotle may employ a Platonic conception of universal, and that Aristotle does not believe that a form in his sense is a Platonic universal. Several passages remain that lend some support to the claim that Aristotelian forms are particulars. One is VII 15, 1035b25: "The being of house is not generated but only the being of this house." The phrase translated as 'being of' is *to einai* with the dative, and this construction is often used by Aristotle to indicate the essence of the thing named. In the present context, however, Aristotle is contrasting the formula that is neither generated nor destroyed with the concrete embodiment of the formula that is subject to generation and decay, and thus several alternative interpretations are available. Aristotle may, in this context, mean by 'the being of this house' the existence of this house rather than the essence of a house. Or, he may be using the phrase to pick out the form-as-instantiated-here-and-now-in-these-bricks not the form or essence of house simpliciter. Similarly in *Metaphysics* XII 5, when Aristotle argues that the father is the cause of the child not the abstract universal, he is not thereby making the form particular.[68] Here he is concerned to establish that the causes of generation are particular composites, as are the offspring.[69] Aristotle goes on to say:

> And of things in the same species [εἴδει] these are different not by species-form [εἴδει] but because ⟨the cause⟩ of one individual differs from that of another, as your matter and the form [εἶδος] and the moving cause are different from mine, but they are the same in universal account. (*Met.* 1071a27–29)

The context and even Aristotle's phrasing makes the interpretation of this passage difficult. The context is one in which he is concerned to contrast proximate causes to universal causes, and generation provides a particularly clear case. This context lends itself to underscoring the differ-

67 At VII 13,1038b9–12, at the outset of the argument, the universal is defined as that which is common to many; see also VII 16, 1040b21–30.

68 When the issue is biological generation, Aristotle typically emphasizes the role of the composite substance that is the proximate cause of the offspring; cf. *De Gen. an.* 767b29–35.

69 We need look no further than Plato to understand why Aristotle should think he needs to argue that proximate causes are found in the physical world. In the *Phaedo*, for instance, Plato argues that the only causal theory that makes sense is one that eschews explanation in physical terms and invokes only Ideas (100b–103e).

ences between individuals rather than affirming the specific sameness of individuals. Aristotle uses the personal pronoun with matter and the definite article alone with the other two causes, thus emphasizing the contribution of matter to the differentiation of two composites. If Aristotle intends to say that the two individuals differ in form, he confuses matters by using the same word (*eidos*) in several different senses in the same sentence.

In *Metaphysics* VII 6, Aristotle addresses the question of whether each thing and its essence are the same and discusses this question with respect to accidental unities such as pale man and *kath' hauta* entities.

> But in the case of the things said ⟨to be⟩ in virtue of themselves [τῶν καθ' αὑτὰ λεγομένων] is a thing necessarily the same as its essence? E.g., if there are some substances which have no other substances nor entities prior to them, substances such as some say the Ideas are? (1031a28–31)

The chapter ends with a brief discussion of the question about whether Socrates and being Socrates are the same. The initial question with its reference to each thing, the discussion of accidental unities, and the closing remarks about Socrates' essence all contribute to the impression that Aristotle is asking whether the particular is identical with its individual essence. Aristotle argues that even though 'man' and 'pale man' are identical, their essences are different. The only sense in which 'pale man' and 'man' are the same is in contexts where the two terms are coreferential, and thus it seems that the puzzle is about the relation between an individual man described in various ways and his essence. The phrase "being Socrates" (Σωκράτει εἶναι) seems to suggest that Socrates' essence is peculiar to him. Notice, however, that it is logically possible to raise the question of whether Socrates is identical to his essence as a step toward an analysis of the relation between a particular and its essence that makes the latter a species essence. At the end of the day, Aristotle concludes that only in the case of *kath' hauta* entities is the thing the same as its essence. According to VII 4, only species have essences, strictly speaking. This conclusion is consistent with Aristotle's account of the universal in *Posterior Analytics* I 4, and the definition of a species essence would express a necessary truth as required by demonstration. While the mention of Socrates' essence in VII 6 raises the intriguing possibility of unique, individual essences, the treatment of this topic is such that it would also be consistent with the rejection of individual essence. In short, there is no hard evidence for individual essences in VII 6.[70]

Besides these texts, there are certain general considerations that seem to support the attribution of particular forms to Aristotle. Aristotle's reasons for making the form and not the concrete individual the primary

70 Cf. Code (1985), whose careful analysis of VII 6 concluded that the essence of man is identical to man but that Socrates' essence is not identical to Socrates.

substance, it is argued, derive from his desire to explain the diachronous individuation of particulars. Many particulars, especially living ones, are thought to remain the same individual despite the replacement of some or perhaps all of their matter. The cells in the human body are constantly being replaced without this affecting in any way the individuation of a particular human; Socrates is the same man at seventy that he was at twenty.[71] But, as the Greek philosophers were well aware, a similar phenomenon occurs with artifacts; throughout its long career the ship of Theseus is the same ship despite the regular replacement of boards.[72] Something other than the matter seems to explain the survival of the individual over time. Second, there are a cluster of arguments for individual forms drawn from Aristotle's biological theory (including psychology). The form of a living thing is its soul and the soul seems to be peculiar to its possessor. Moreover, the form is the vehicle for the transmission of characteristics from one generation to the next, and here again it looks as though individual differences must be expressed through the transmitted form.

Something more than spatial and temporal continuity seems to be involved in the survival of an individual over time. Suppose the ship of Theseus is ever so slowly transformed into a pier; suppose further that the shapes and sizes of the timbers making up the pier are exactly the same as those previously making up the ship. No one would be tempted to say the pier was the very same individual as the ship. Aristotelian form could be invoked to explain why the ship is one individual and the pier another; the two structures exhibit different organizations of their matter and serve different functions. Since the form accounts for the individuation of the particular, it might seem that the form must be individual. Granted, a unique form would serve this function quite satisfactorily, but is it necessary?

Suppose that what makes the ship a ship and the pier a pier is in each case a form the individual shares with all other particulars of its type. Then it looks as if all ships having the same form and consisting of the same (generic) parts would be the same individual, which is absurd. Suppose we assume, as Michael Frede suggests, that all the planks of the original ship of Theseus have been replaced and another ship made of the old planks; it seems clear both that the ship made of the replaced planks is not the ship of Theseus and that it is a distinct individual.[73] That there are two individuals can be explained by appeal to two instantiations of the same form in different materials, but can the identification of the ship of

71 See Plato, *Sym.* 207de, where Diotima makes this point.

72 Or, to cite a contemporary example: the USS *Constitution* sailed on its 200th anniversary, July 21, 1997. According to news reports, only 15 percent of the ship consists of original materials, yet it remains "Old Ironsides."

73 Frede (1978).

Theseus with the individual made up of new planks be explained on the hypothesis that the form is common? (Frede's solution is to appeal to each ship's unique history and individual form.) The identity of the ship of Theseus can also be explained, however, by appealing to the spatiotemporal continuity of the concrete individual in conjunction with the (common) form. Spatiotemporal continuity is sufficient to explain why the ship of Theseus is the ship made of the replacement boards.[74] Spatiotemporal continuity is also peculiar to the concrete individual, but unlike a unique history, there is little temptation to think that spatiotemporal continuity belongs to the form rather than the concrete individual. A unique history, especially in the case of humans, is quite naturally thought of as a property of the soul and this brings us to the second general argument.[75]

The form of a living being is its soul, and this identification seems to settle the issue in favor of individual forms. It is worth noting, however, that the argument for individual forms seems especially compelling when human souls are at issue. Plants and simple animals also have souls and the view that the plane tree on the right has a unique soul different from the soul of the plane tree on the left is somewhat less persuasive. Aristotle's psychology defines souls in relation to particular species; the human soul is what makes this bit of flesh and bones a human being and the feline soul is what makes that bit of flesh and bones a cat. Nevertheless, the relevance of memory to the individuation of a human being has often been defended by philosophers, and memories are unique and are a feature of the individual's psychic life. This would seem to provide evidence for a unique form. But the evidence is less clear-cut than a proponent of individual forms might hope. Memory, for Aristotle, is a function of the enmattered soul; the concrete individual, a unified composite of body and form, has memories.[76] This being is an individual, and at least part of the reason for saying that Socrates as a child is the same individual as Socrates the aging philosopher is that the latter is intimately connected with the former by memory. What memory individuates, however, is Socrates, not just his soul. Were Aristotle to entertain the conception of a separated soul, such a soul would not possess memory, because memory is a function of the common sense that is a psychophysical power the

74 The philosopher appealing to spatiotemporal continuity alone would have more trouble handling the case where the ship is slowly transformed into a pier, but Aristotle is not this philosopher because he can appeal to a difference in the form shared by all piers and the form shared by all ships.

75 This is not how Frede (1978) develops the notion of a unique history, which he treats as an external individuating factor.

76 *De Mem.* 450a15–b12, 451a15–18. Cf. *Physics* 247a7–13; *De An.* 408b13–18. For a detailed discussion of Aristotle's use of the psychophysical principle in constructing his psychological theory, see Modrak (1987a).

exercise of which requires a body.[77] For Aristotle, appealing to a unique set of memories in order to individuate a particular person is appealing to a unique property of a psychophysical composite and not to a property belonging either to the matter alone or the form of the composite alone. (The relation of form to matter is not additive, and thus the composite has properties in its own right that belong to neither of its constituents.)

The account of reproduction in *De Generatione animalium* is the source of yet another argument in support of particular forms. The sperm is the vehicle for the transmission of species form, but it is also the vehicle for the transmission of the father's characteristics and those of his family. If the semen transmits only form, then it appears that the form transmitted is either individual or specific to a particular family rather than the species. There is a further wrinkle in Aristotle's genetic theory, however: the need to explain the transmission of the mother's characteristics, including her sex and those of her family. Aristotle claims that these are due to the weakness of the transmitted form; its weakness makes it liable to being counteracted and altered by the *katamenia,* the material supplied by the mother. If what is altered is the form, then this is an instance where matter acts on form, which would be inconsistent with Aristotle's understanding of the relation between form and matter.[78] Perhaps Aristotle means that the form is less perfectly instantiated than it might be, because the matter has affected the outcome, the composite. But a similar strategy applied to the case of the transmitted form would locate the transmission of individual characteristics in the semen's role as vehicle rather than in the form itself.

Even an interpreter who is sympathetic to particular forms is unlikely to find unassailable evidence for them here. John Cooper, for instance, after a careful study of *De Generatione animalium* IV 1 and 3, concludes that the forms that are transmitted are at a considerably lower level of generality than species form but seem to lack the specificity of particulars.[79] Aristotle works very hard to bring his acute observations as a biologist under the umbrella of his metaphysics. The difficulty is that making the father the source of the form and the mother the source of the matter hampers his ability to give a satisfactory account of inherited traits. Moreover, there is evidence that, at the end of the day, Aristotle assimilates family-specific traits to other traits originating in the composite. In *De Generatione animalium* V, typical inherited traits such as eye and hair color are as-

77 Aquinas struggles with the issue of individuation of souls prior to the resurrection of the body for precisely this reason.

78 Cf. *De Gen. an.*. V 1, 778b6–7: "For the generative process does not follow the substance but is for the sake of the substance, but the substance is not for the sake of the generative process."

79 Cooper (1988, pp. 14–41).

signed to the material and motive causes and not the formal and final causes. The latter but not the former are species specific (778a33–34).

On balance, there is more reason to believe that the form that is the substance and essence of the individual composite substance is the species form than to believe that the form is a unique individual. The ontology presupposed by this theory is simpler, consisting in composite substances (substance tokens) and essences (substance types), and it fits Aristotle's account of definition and knowledge better. Individuals are indefinable. Were Aristotle to posit individual forms, these would be indefinable ex hypothesi.[80] The *logos* that is the essence of the individual would not be the same *logos* as the *logos* grasped in thought which is a universal. The individual *logos* would at best be an instance of the universal *logos* expressed in the definition. Not surprisingly, most advocates of particular forms have posited a systematic relation between the particular form and the species form.[81] Some proponents of individual forms distinguish the individual form from the composite and thus posit three ontological levels – composite substance, individual form, and universal form – while others identify the particular form with the composite substance.[82] The former is a more complicated picture than the one that results from the identification of Socrates' form with the form of human being, and the latter is difficult to maintain while simultaneously making sense of the distinction between form and matter in the individual.

It seems that in Aristotle's considered judgment the form realized in matter is the same form as the form that is the object of definition. Notice, however, that the impact of positing particular forms on the interpretation of Aristotle's theory of meaning need not be great. If the particular form instantiates a species form, then the story to be told about concrete particulars and meanings will be complicated by the introduction of the particular form but will follow the same lines as the story told about species forms. To explain the signification of general terms, universals are required. Suppose Aristotelian forms are unique individuals, that, for instance, Socrates' form is distinct from Callias's. Of what help will grasping Socrates' form be to understanding ἄνθρωπος or to theorizing about human beings? This cognition will be helpful just insofar as Socrates' form exemplifies a form shared by Socrates, Callias, and all other human beings – or for certain purposes, a form shared by Socrates and all members of a definable subclass of human beings, for instance,

80 At 1040a27–b2, Aristotle argues that unique cosmic bodies, e.g., the sun, are indefinable because they are individuals and that this would also be true of a property said to belong only to that particular body.

81 See, for instance, Irwin (1988, section 142); Hartman (1977); Frede (1987).

82 For these two different lines of interpretation in defense of the attribution of particular forms to Aristotle, see Hartman (1977); Irwin (1988, chap. 12).

adult males. The individual form is not even especially helpful if one wants to explain the reference of a proper name, for 'Socrates' typically denotes the compound of matter and form, not simply the form.[83] In an aside at VII 11 1037a7–10, Aristotle admits that someone might use 'Socrates' to name Socrates' soul (form), but he hastens to affirm the standard use of proper names for the compound of body and soul.[84]

Aristotle's conception of the essence or form as *logos* in the *Metaphysics* provides the ontological support required by his realist epistemology and by his conception of meaning. A basic premise of the epistemology offered in the *Posterior Analytics* is the thesis that the human mind is able to grasp universals that exist in the world as essences and properties of concrete individuals. In the *De Interpretatione,* Aristotle defined meaning by appealing to a mental state that was like the object existing in the world. The *Metaphysics* discussion of essence and definition and the appeal to a common *logos* gives good sense to the seemingly unfortunate claim that reference is determined by resemblance.[85] The definition is like the objects in its extension in that the same *logos* is realized cognitively and materially.

6 Conclusion

The topics under investigation in *Metaphysics* VII–IX are largely determined by Aristotle's desire to offer an ontology that will satisfy the conceptual constraints of a language adequate for the expression of truths and of principles adequate for knowledge. To this end, Aristotle distinguishes between form and matter, between essence and composite substance, between the descriptive content of a definition of essence and the descriptive content of an attribution of an accidental characteristic. The comparison of two sorts of descriptions – the *logos* that is a definition in the strict sense, that is, a definition of a substance, and the *logoi* that attribute other characteristics of one sort or another to a composite individual – is a device for articulating ontological distinctions that support the distinctions required by knowledge. Making forms and essences primary substance and construing forms and essences as universals broadly conceived is a way to provide the right sort of basic ontological objects. These are ones the characters of which can be expressed by universal

83 This is not true if one identifies the particular form with the compound individual substance, as does Irwin (1988, chap. 12), or if one argues that the form of the composite is so specific as to apply only to that composite, as does Gill (1989, chap. 5).

84 Aristotle's worry about the referent of "Socrates" becomes puzzling for a different reason if the particular form just is the composite, for then what Aristotle should have said is that it makes no difference whether "Socrates" is used of the soul or of the composite.

85 See Chapter 8, sections 2 and 3.

principles as required by demonstrative science. Central to Aristotle's project is the resolution of the apparent tension between the primacy of the concrete individual in the world and the role of the universal in language and knowledge. The concrete individual is the object of reference and the determinant of meaning; the concrete individual is also the basis for the apprehension of universals. The meaning of a general term is a concept produced by encounters with individuals having similar features. The concept is both universal and a likeness of the individuals instantiating it. The paradigmatic individual is a substance, not a simple substance, but a composite substance that is the realization of a *logos* (essence) in matter.

This ontological analysis provides the basis for an explanation of different levels of description, all of which connect in a direct way with the extralinguistic world of concrete objects. There are proper names and descriptions of the concrete individual as an individual substance or an accidental unity; these refer to the concrete individual. There are at the next level of description common nouns and general descriptions of the kind to which the individual belongs; these refer to the individuals exemplifying the kind. There are at the next level of description proper definitions of essence (primary substance) and qualified definitions of property essences (of qualities, quantities, etc.); the latter definitions are inferior, because, unlike definitions of substance, they contain added determinants (cf. 1031a1–4). Primary substance is the essence of an indivisible species; it is the species form exemplified by the concrete individual. Socrates is not the same concrete substance as Callias yet both exemplify the same substantial form. Were concrete substances simple substances without structure, the terms and descriptions at the second and third levels, which are the levels required for universals and science, would be without an adequate basis in the world. They would be mental constructs that would have at best only marginal justification. (Plato's critical arguments against a theory of meaning based on reference to physical objects and against knowledge based on perception had shown just how weak the justification would be.) Scientific definitions articulate essences. Linguistic definitions express meanings of ordinary language terms. Many of these terms do not refer to essences. The individuals to which these terms refer are composites of matter and form. The presence of matter provides the basis for synchronic individuation, for spatial and temporal location, and for the many accidental characteristics belonging to the individual. Both with respect to strict, scientific definition and with respect to linguistic definition, Aristotle is in a position to argue that if the analysis of substance and the account of definition in the central books of the *Metaphysics* are right, then there is good reason to accept his account of meaning and knowledge.

In recent discussions of metaphysical realism, a view scathingly called "the duplex view" has been widely discredited.[86] This position conjoins the theses that the references of our words are causally determined by a mind-independent reality and that meanings have a cognitive content. Since the causal mechanisms seem to be independent of the cognitive content, how words hook up with the world becomes baffling. One way to understand our findings about Aristotle's conception of definition is as an answer to this puzzle long before the puzzle was framed. For Aristotle, the character of physical objects is determined by their essences. It is in the nature of such essences to be cognitively accessible, because the very same essences also exist as objects of thought. Since cognitive accessibility is an essential property of an essence of a material object, cognitive content takes precedence over causal mechanisms. The causal mechanisms are not thereby eliminated in favor of a mysterious magical process of cognitive transfer, however, because the causal mechanisms are the analog of matter in the concrete individuals in which the *logos*, the cognitive content, is realized. This is quite apparent in Aristotle's treatment of perception where changes in the material medium, for instance, air, are the causal mechanism for the apprehension of the sensible form, the *logos* of light and dark that is color.[87] In the course of exploring the psychological side of this story in the next two chapters, the details of the cognitive and causal mechanisms involved will be discussed further.

In this and the preceding chapters, we have looked at Aristotle's treatment of ontology and epistemic requirements in *Metaphysics* I, IV, VI–IX, and XIII. No doubt different parts of the *Metaphysics* were written at different times and with different focal points, and thus it is all the more significant that one finds throughout an abiding concern on Aristotle's part to secure the foundations of knowledge and language. He hopes to do this by isolating and explicating the universal principles and characteristics required by the sciences. His goal is to develop an ontology of basic objects that will support the foundational principles of physical science, mathematics, and theology (cf. *Met.* 1025b3–18). Because he believes that the concrete particular is first in the order of human cognition and the universal first in the order of intelligibility, the relation between the world as experienced and the world as known and the relation between ordinary language descriptions of the world and the precise definitions of the specialist are central to his philosophical investigations.[88]

> All humans by nature desire to know. And further the affection for the senses is a sign of this; for even apart from usefulness they are loved for themselves, and the sense through the eyes is valued above all the others. (*Met.* 980a21–24)

86 McDowell (1992, pp. 35–48); McGinn (1982, pp. 207–58).

87 I develop and defend this interpretation of perception in Modrak (1987a, chap. 3).

88 The distinction between what is most accessible for us and what is most intelligible is made in a number of contexts. See, e.g., *Physics* 184a16–21; *N.E.* 1095b1–3.

These are the opening lines of *Metaphysics* I 1, and they are instructive, for here the human impulse toward knowledge is coupled with the capacity to perceive. In the next two chapters, we will look at Aristotle's account of human cognitive capacities and attend to the crucial contribution perception makes to the ability to apprehend universals in thought, since the latter capacity is required for language and knowledge.

PART III

Cognition and Meaning

7

Phantasia and Representation

In *De Interpretatione* 1, no sooner has Aristotle asserted that the mental states that words stand for are likenesses of the *pragmata* of the world, than he dismisses this topic with the words:

This matter has, however, been discussed in my treatise about the soul, for it belongs to an investigation distinct from that which lies before us. (16a8–9; trans. follows Edghill)

The place in the *De Anima* that Aristotle has in mind in the *De Interpretatione* is not easily discovered.[1] Nor is it entirely clear which features of the theory of meaning will or should be explained there. Is it merely the nature of the psychic *pathemata* (internal states) or the likeness obtaining between the *pathemata* and their external correlates (*pragmata*)?

Speech is not mentioned in its own right in the *De Anima* but only in connection with hearing.[2]

Consequently speech [φωνή] is the impact of the inbreathed air against that which is called the windpipe by the soul in these parts . . . what produces the impact must have soul in it and must be accompanied by an act of imagination [φαντασίας τινός] for speech is a sound with a meaning [σημαντικός] and not merely the inbreathed air as a cough is. (420b27–33)

Here the intent is to differentiate between speech and other types of noises produced by the respiratory system. What the passage adds to the *De Interpretatione*'s description is the explicit mention of imagination (φαντασία). Written speech is wholly ignored in the *De Anima*, nor is there any discussion of signification in the *De Anima*. The relation of sign (σημεῖον) to thing signified is broadly construed in the *De Anima* as the relation between any sort of evidence and that for which it is evidence.[3]

1 Beginning with Andronicus, commentators have puzzled over the implications of this reference. See Ross (1924, p. 10); cf. Cooke (1938, pp. 114–15).

2 Not only does the *De Interpretatione* make reference to the *De Anima*, at *De Sensu* 440b27, Aristotle says that speech (φωνή) is discussed in the *De Anima*.

3 While σημεῖον (translated as 'sign' at 16a7) occurs relatively frequently in the *De Anima*,

A brief reference to words as symbols is made in the first chapter of the *De Sensu.* Aristotle remarks that hearing contributes more than the other senses to intelligence but does so incidentally.

For speech [λόγος] is the cause of learning because it is audible, not ⟨because audible⟩ in itself but incidentally, because speech is made up of words [ὀνομάτων], and every word is a symbol [σύμβολον]. [437a11–15]

Sounds do not convey meaning in themselves but only insofar as they are employed as symbols, but the psychic capacity that enables this use is not even mentioned, much less explained in the *De Sensu.*

Voice (φωνή) is frequently mentioned in *Historia Animalium* IV, much more frequently than in the *De Anima,* in fact. In IV 9, Aristotle draws a threefold distinction between noises an animal makes in its larynx, for example, coughing; voice (φωνή) that is voluntary and characteristic of the species; and articulate speech (διάλεκτος). All three are defined physiologically.

Surely the only part of the body with which any animal can utter a voice is the pharynx. . . . Speech [διάλεκτος] is the articulation of voice by means of the tongue. Voice and larynx then produce the vowels and the tongue and the lips, the consonants; of these speech consists. (535a29–32)

Although unwilling to attribute language to other animals, Aristotle is willing to allow (nonhuman) animals to utter sounds, for example, mating calls, having natural significance for other creatures of the same species (536a11–27).[4] Such sounds are instances of voice. Voice requires lungs, windpipe, and tongue. Some creatures, for example, dolphins, have all of these but because their tongues do not move freely, they lack articulated voice. Other creatures, for example, birds, possess articulated voice. Unlike voice, which is species-specific, articulated voice may differ owing to differences in locale or other factors. Control of the tongue is required, and this develops with maturation. Articulated voice is also conditioned by early experiences. Just as the young child must learn to use its tongue and acquire the language of its parents, the young bird raised by foster parents of a different species will develop a different song than it would have, had it been reared among members of its own species (536b11–16).

Even though birds and other animals with mobile tongues are capable of articulated voice, Aristotle attributes language only to humans

it is typically used to introduce an observable phenomenon that Aristotle cites in support of his position; in two passages, it names the imprint in the wax seal (424a20, 435a9) and in another passage a point on a line (427a12).

4 This is also mentioned at *De Int.* 16a27–29. Cf. S. E. *M.* 7.274: "If 'rational' stands for 'uttering significant sounds [σημαντικὰς φωνάς]' we shall be saying that crows and parrots and the like are men."

(536a33–b2).[5] The definition of language as articulated speech does not provide an adequate justification for this restriction. Only if the *Historia Animalium* definition is supplemented by adding the condition mentioned in the *De Anima,* namely, *phantasia* employed in a way that yields significance, does it differentiate between human language and other types of articulated voice. Moreover, since many other animals possess *phantasia* and since for animals of the same species voice is a natural sign of the state, location, and "intent" of another animal, the *De Interpretatione* description seems to apply even to the use of voice by other animals. For instance, a male elephant who has been defeated by another will flee upon hearing the voice of the successful male (610a17). Even in the *De Anima* Aristotle is sometimes willing to treat animal voice on a par with human voice.

> ⟨An animal⟩ possesses hearing that something may be indicated [σημαίνῃ] to it and tongue that it may indicate something to another. (*De An.* 435b24)

From this perspective, the attribution of language to human beings alone appears arbitrary. The only way that Aristotle can avoid the charge of species-centrism is by buttressing the *De Interpretatione* analysis with a description of the psychological basis of language that is such that only humans would be capable of language.

1 Psychological Basis of Meaning

If anything mentioned in the *De Interpretatione* analysis of meaning is explained in the *De Anima,* it must be the nature of the internal states, the *pathemata* (παθήματα), of which spoken words are signs.[6] The term παθήμα and its cognates (πάθος, πάσχειν) do a great deal of work in Aristotle's psychology. '*Pathos*' is the term Aristotle standardly uses for the affective and cognitive states of ensouled individuals.[7] Thinking, perceiving, loving, hating, and remembering are all included under πάθη (*pathe*).[8] The reference to psychic *pathemata* in *De Interpretatione* 1 is no doubt intended to add the internal correlate of a meaningful sound to this list. As employed in the theory of meaning, the *pathema* does double

5 That language is possessed only by humans is also pointed out in the *Politics* at 1253a8–15.

6 Ammonius (26, 1), however, finds the relevance of the *De Anima* in the distinction drawn by Aristotle in III 3 between the νόημα and φάντασμα.

7 At *De An.* 403a3–25, πάθη and παθήματα are used as synonyms in a comprehensive list of emotional responses and cognitive activities; cf. 403b17, 408b26, 409b15.

8 There are sixteen occurrences of *pathos, pathema,* and *pathesis* used as generic terms for psychic states in the *De Anima.* Aristotle uses these terms as synonyms. See, for instance, 403 a 3–20 where, when addressing the question of whether there are states peculiar to the soul or whether all such states are common to body and soul, he uses *pathe* and *pathemata* interchangeably.

duty; it is an internal state, a psychic state of an individual. It is also the vehicle of a meaning shared by speakers of a common language. In the latter capacity, the *pathema* is an intentional state. The psychological state that Aristotle identifies with the 'linguistic' *pathema* must be such that it satisfies both these descriptions; it must also be such that it could be described as a likeness of an external *pragma*.

The question then becomes: With what psychic *pathos* should this internal state be identified? In light of the *De Anima*'s description of speech as sound informed by *phantasia* (420b29–34), the *pathos* in question seems to be a particular use of imagination *phantasia*. Images (*phantasmata*) are *pathe* (427b18).[9] Moreover, among the cognitive activities described by Aristotle, there are few other candidates, and none other is as promising as *phantasia*. Broadly speaking, human cognitive capacities are divided into the capacities of the perceptual faculty of the soul and the capacities of the noetic faculty. The perceptual faculty is exercised in relation to perceptible particulars; the noetic faculty is exercised in relation to intelligible universals. At one end of the cognitive spectrum, there is sense perception and at the other end, the intellection of the most intelligible universals. The perceptual faculty includes sense perception and imagination among its functions. Perceiving is not likely to be the *pathos* at issue. The capacity for perception is possessed at birth and its exercise need not involve prior learning, whereas the acquisition of a language does involve learning. Memory plays a role in the acquisition of a language and memory belongs to the faculty of *phantasia* (450a23–25). Nor does abstract thought, which is at the other end of the cognitive spectrum, seem to fit Aristotle's characterization of the internal correlate of a word. To describe an image as a likeness is unproblematic, but this would not be true of the meaning-bearing *pathema*, were it a purely abstract representation. The same considerations that count against identifying the internal state with an abstract representation also count against severing the link between *phantasia* and sensory representation.[10] (It might be possible to tell a philosophically respectable story about likeness that does not appeal to images by starting from the premise that the same *logos* is realized as an object of thought and a materially realized essence. Whether this strategy, which is suggested by the *Metaphysics*' treatment of *logos*, will work in the context of Aristotle's psychology will be considered in Chapter 8. At first blush, it seems at odds with Aristotle's analyses of thinking and perceiving.) All things considered, that the *pathemata* mentioned at *De Interpretatione* 1, 16a6, are *phantasmata* seems

9 Cf. N. Kretzman (1974, p. 9), who argues that only if the mental impressions mentioned in *De Interpretatione* 1 at 16a3–8 are mental images does Aristotle's claim that mental impressions are likenesses of things have any chance of being true.

10 See Section II.

a likely surmise. If so, Aristotle's reference to the psychological writings is explained, for *phantasia* is discussed at some length in these works.[11]

I have argued elsewhere that *phantasia* is Aristotle's mechanism for handling internal representations.[12] As configured in the theory of meaning, the internal state is an intentional state, a meaning, and at the same time a psychological state. *Phantasia* as a psychological faculty that is a mode of representation would be well suited to be the faculty exercised in language use. The *phantasma,* the sensory content realized as an occurrent cognitive object in an exercise of *phantasia,* is well placed to be a likeness of an external object. The *phantasma* is a consequence of a perception, according to Aristotle, and *phantasia* is one of the capacities falling under the perceptual faculty of the soul.[13] To better understand the character of *phantasia* and the *phantasma,* we should look at Aristotle's general theory of perception. The perceptual faculty of all higher animals, including human beings, consists of the five special senses (the most basic sensory powers), the common sense (the joint operation of several special senses), and *phantasia,* which includes the capacities for imaging, dreaming, and remembering.[14] Each special sense is the capacity to apprehend a particular kind of sensible object, for instance, color in the case of sight or sound in the case of hearing. The sensible object that is the proper object of a sense is defined by a basic pair of opposites, in the case of color by light and dark, in the case of sound by high and low pitch.[15] A particular color is a particular *logos* of light to dark (cf. *Met.* 1070b18–22). Aristotle appeals to a *logos* of sensible opposites in order to give a general characterization of the proper objects of the special senses.[16] Perception is the reception of the sensible form (424a17–28). The sensible form is a *logos* of opposite qualities.

Aristotle's causal theory of perception accommodates the material side of perceptual occurrences without reducing the perceptual process to a series of material changes in the organ and the medium through which the external object acts on the sense organ causing the perception.

11 Not only is *De Anima* III 3 devoted exclusively to the topic of *phantasia,* but also the range of its functions means that *phantasia* is appealed to repeatedly in the *De Anima* and the *Parva Naturalia.*

12 Modrak (1986 pp. 47–69; 1987a); see also Wedin (1988).

13 That *phantasia* always involves a sensory content will be, I hope, clear from the summary below of arguments that I have made at greater length elsewhere (see note 12).

14 In what follows I give a summary account of the functioning of the perceptual faculty of the soul. For a more detailed account, see Modrak (1987a, chaps. 2 and 3).

15 In the case of tactile sensations, the picture is slightly more complicated. At first blush there seem to be numerous pairs of opposites; these, Aristotle believes, can be reduced to two basic pairs (wet and dry and hot and cold) but not one, as in the case of the other special senses (422b17–33, 423b27–31).

16 In the *De Sensu,* the analysis of sense objects is framed in terms of *logoi* of opposite qualities (439b27, 440a23, 440b19, 442a12–17, 442b17–19, 448a8–12). Cf. *De An.* 426a 27–b3; *Met.* 1043a11–12.

He does this by identifying the object actualized in the act of perceiving with a form and a *logos*. The clanging bell causes changes in the air between the ear and the bell, and the medium affects the ear, causing a perception of a clanging sound. The external object causes the changes in the medium that affect the organ and thus is causally connected to the perception, but this sort of causal story, were it the whole story, would not justify the belief that the clanging sound as heard corresponds to anything outside the percipient's head. On the causal story what causes the perception of clanging might have nothing in common with such auditory effects as loud and low. The Greek atomists accepted this consequence, as have many later philosophers, and thus Democritus distinguished between the causal properties producing perceptions and the contents of those perceptions.[17] Aristotle, however, resists all attempts to sever the connections between the world as experienced and the world as it is in itself. The material causal chain is the vehicle for the sensible form that is actualized in the act of sensing. The sensible form, the *logos* of high and low, informs the air that is compressed when the bell is struck, and the same *logos* is realized in the auditory system of the percipient. The clanging is not just how a series of causally connected changes in the air in the bell, in the air extending from the bell to the percipient, and in the air in the inner ear, affects the percipient. The clanging occurs in the world and is simultaneously actualized as a clanging-as-heard in the bell and in the ear (cf. 425b27–426a8).[18] The significance of this picture for an account of meaning is the direct connection envisaged between the content of the perception and the external object of the perception. Since the percipient is connected to the external object not only by a material causal chain but also by the phenomenal features of the object as perceived, there is no gap between the object as conceived (the basis of meaning) and the (external) referent of the term for the object.

Besides the proper objects there are, according to Aristotle, two other types of sensibles:

> But objects of perception are spoken of in three ways; of these we say two are perceived in themselves [καθ' αὑτά] and one incidentally [κατὰ συμβεβηκός]. Of the two, one is proper to each sense, the other common to all. (*De An.* 418a8–11)

> Those that are spoken of as common are movement, rest, number, figure, size; for such as these are not proper to any, but common to all ⟨senses⟩. For certain movements are perceptible by touch and also sight. An object of perception is spoken of as incidental, e.g., were the white thing the son of Diares; for one perceived this incidentally, because this is incidental to the white thing which one perceives. (*De An.* 418a17–22)

17 Democritus, DK fragments B 9 and B 11.
18 Cf. Kosman (1975, pp. 499–519).

The coordinated exercise of several senses is constitutive of the common sense. When perception takes place simultaneously through several senses with respect to the same sensible characteristic, for instance, magnitude, the common sensible is perceived in itself, namely, as a sensible characteristic that is perceptible through different sense modalities. The perception of a common sensible is, nonetheless, dependent on the perception of the proper objects of the senses through which the common object is perceived. The perception of magnitude through sight and touch involves the perception of the color and the tangible characteristics of the object of which the magnitude is perceived. Unlike a common sensible, an incidental object of perception does not directly affect any sense organ. It is apprehended through a sense but not because the object as such (the son of Diares) affects the percipient, but because a certain colored shape does. Nonetheless, the incidental objects are perceived (not inferred); the percipient who has had the appropriate experiences will see the white thing as a particular person, the son of Diares. Although the perception of an incidental object is shaped by learning and memory, it is totally spontaneous for the person having it. By contrast, the person who reasons that the approaching object must be the son of Diares on the basis of various beliefs about him, for instance, that the son of Diares is six foot tall and always accompanied by Callias, does not perceive the son of Diares but judges that the person she perceives is the son of Diares. The perception of the incidental objects, while a case of sense perception, resembles many of the other functions of the perceptual faculty in being a cognition that is constituted by sensible features that are perceptible in themselves. The proper and common sensibles are the vehicles for all other types of perception as well as the vehicles for apperceptual awareness, memories and dreams, to mention but a few of the other functions of the perceptual faculty. Indeed what distinguishes the activities of the perceptual faculty from other psychological activities is the fact that its activities always involve the utilization of sense objects. Colored shapes and other proper sensibles are the vehicles for all perceptions and all other functions of the perceptual faculty, and this fact is the basis for saying that Aristotle makes the awareness of a sensory content the defining characteristic of the perceptual faculty. At the same time, the content of a perception of an incidental object is significantly more complex than the perception of a proper or common sensible, and this explains the modern tendency to treat perceptions of incidental sensibles as judgments. The relative complexity of incidental sensibles is evidence that, for Aristotle, sensory contents may (and often do) represent complex states of affairs.

Like the apprehension of the common objects, reflexive perceptual awareness is also a function of the senses acting together.

Each sense has a special function and a common function. The special function, for example, of sight is seeing, that of the auditory sense is hearing, and similarly with the other senses. But there is also a common faculty associated with them all, through which one is aware that one sees and hears (for it is not by sight that one is aware that one sees; and one judges and is capable of judging that sweet is different from white not by taste, nor by sight, nor by a combination of the two, but by some part which is common to all the sense organs). (*De Somno* 455a13–21)

This is Aristotle's considered judgment about apperception; in *De Anima* III 2 he argues that the proper sense is aware of its own operations. To be aware of seeing, Aristotle reasons, is to be aware of color and hence the reflexive awareness of seeing must belong to sight (425b12–23). A similar argument is offered for assigning the discrimination of differences among sensibles to the perceptual faculty:

Since we judge both white and sweet and each of the objects of perception by reference to each other, by what do we perceive also that they are different? This must indeed be by a sense; for they are objects of perception [αἰσθητά]. (*De An.* 426b12–15)

This passage provides the reason why in the *De Somno* Aristotle assigns the reflexive awareness of sensing to the common sense. Aristotle recognizes that in most cases of perceptual self-awareness a percipient is aware of sensing through several sense modalities at once. At the moment I am aware that I am listening to music, that I am touching a keyboard, and that I am looking at a playground. At a minimum, the objects of which I must be aware in order to be aware of sensing include colors, sounds, and tactile characteristics. In order to explain how we can be simultaneously aware of so many different objects, Aristotle suggests that the senses act as one constituting a common capacity of the perceptual faculty.

The subsumption of apperceptual judgment under the functions of the perceptual faculty is significant for our investigation in that it establishes that for Aristotle the perceptual faculty of the soul is a critical faculty capable of making cognitive discriminations; otherwise the perceptual faculty could not function in this way. This should dispel any tendency on the part of an interpreter to reduce the perceptual faculty of the Aristotelian soul to a bare capacity for sensation.[19] A minimalist conception of perceptual functions would count against the identification of the *pathema* in the theory of meaning with a *phantasma*. Here the character of the *pathema* must be such that it is simultaneously the vehicle for a meaning and a likeness to an external object. Aristotle's broad conception of perceptual activity, by contrast to the minimalist's, holds some promise of providing support for an explanation of meaning that invokes *phantasia*.

19 With better reason, commentators have attributed a minimalist conception of perception to Plato. See, however, Modrak (1981, pp. 35–54); and Laidlaw-Johnson (1990).

What may prove still more significant, however, are two other features: (a) sensory contents are employed in apperceptual discriminations and (b) the sensory content is the realization of certain features of the external world. Colors exist in the world as actual *logoi* of light and dark, and they also exist as potential objects of sight. A color exists as an actual object of perception when it is perceived. Seeing and the actuality of color are one in fact but not in definition (426a2–15). The relation Aristotle envisages between the *pathema* and the external *pragma* is universal and natural. The realization of the sensible features of external objects in perceptions provides a foundation on which to build an account of the relation between *pathema* and *pragma* in the theory of meaning and to explicate the notion of likeness as applied in this context.

The general account of sense perception is presented in *De Anima* II 5–III 2; it is immediately followed by the analysis of *phantasia.* After discussing the ways in which *phantasia* is unlike sense perception and unlike (noetic) judgment, Aristotle concludes that *phantasia* is a psychic activity occurring as a result of sense perception (428b30). Aristotle's analysis begins with a nominal definition: "*Phantasia* is that in virtue of which we say a *phantasma* arises in us" (428a1–2). *Phantasia* is the psychic faculty through which images (*phantasmata*) are presented, stored, and recalled. *Phantasmata,* on Aristotle's account, are sensuous contents (431a15, 432a12); at baseline they are the residual traces of things seen, heard, smelled, tasted, or touched that remain in our perceptual organs and are subsequently brought to consciousness. This feature of *phantasia* is one piece of evidence for the sensory content analysis that I have defended elsewhere.[20]

The sensory content analysis is based on Aristotle's various descriptions of *phantasia;* on it, his core conception of *phantasia* can be stated as follows:

> *Phantasia* is the awareness of a sensory content under conditions that are not conducive to veridical perception.

A sensory content is a complex of sensible characters. In the case of perception and nonveridical appearance, these characters are properties that the external object possesses in relation to the percipient; in the absence of an external stimulus, a sensory content is an internal representation employing sensible characters.

There is ample textual evidence that the object of *phantasia* is a sensory content. The features of the *phantasma* mentioned above support the identification of a *phantasma* with a sensory content, as does Aristotle's statement in the *De Insomniis* that the faculty of *phantasia* (*phantastikon*) and the perceptual faculty are the same faculty but differ in essence

20 See Modrak (1986; 1987a, chap. 4).

(*einai*) (*De Insom.* 459a16–17; cf. *De An.* 432a31–b2). The *phantastikon* is exercised through the same organs as the perceptual faculty. *Phantasia* occurs in organisms that perceive and with respect to those things of which there is perception (428b12–13). Aristotle divides the objects of *phantasia* into the same three types as the objects of perception, namely, proper, common, and incidental objects (428b25–26). The ultimate bearers of perceptual information are the proper objects (cf. 418a24–25), and we would expect the same thing to hold true of *phantasia.* Aristotle's description of both types of *phantasia,* namely, nonveridical appearance and mental imagery, bear out this expectation. The object of perception is (inter alia) a complex of sensible characters that belong to an external object, as is the object of *phantasia* in the case of nonveridical appearances. When an inanimate object seen at a distance appears to be a man (428a14), or when a stranger appears to be one's beloved (*De Insom.* 460b3–13), the object of the experience is presented sensorially; its vehicle is a complex of sensible characters.

In other cases of *phantasia,* such as dreaming or remembering, a complex of sensible characters represents an object not immediately present to the senses. In the *De Insomniis,* Aristotle groups together rational faculties, including *doxa,* and contrasts them to faculties through which sensory characters are apprehended, namely, *aisthesis* (sense perception) and *phantasia,* to argue that a dream is a kind of *phantasma* (458b10–459a22). Dreaming is not to be identified with opining because "we seem to see that the approaching object is white as well as a man [in a dream]" (458b15). Memory is defined as the disposition of a *phantasma* related as a likeness to that of which it is the *phantasma* (*De Mem.* 451a15–16). Not every object of memory is remembered in itself (*kath' hauto*); some are remembered coincidentally (*kata sumbebekos*) (450a23–25). Concrete particulars that were seen, heard, or otherwise experienced in the past are remembered *kath' hauta.* A *phantasma* representing the past experience is the vehicle for the memory of the particular. An abstract object is remembered *kata sumbebekos* when a thinker employs certain sensory features to represent the abstract object in a temporal context.[21]

Up to this point, reasons have been adduced in favor of the first part of the sensory content analysis, that *phantasia* is the awareness of a sensory content. The other clause, namely, that *phantasia* occurs under conditions that are not conducive to veridical perception, is needed to differentiate between *phantasia* and perception, both of which are forms of sensory awareness, and to allow the inclusion of different cognitive activities from illusion to memory under *phantasia.* To make out the differ-

21 This use of the *phantasma* will be discussed at greater length below in connection with the representational role of *phantasia.*

ence between *phantasia* and perception (*aisthesis*), Aristotle implicitly appeals to a distinction between standard and nonstandard conditions.[22] Whether the awareness of a perceptible object in the percipient's environment is an instance of *aisthesis* or *phantasia* will depend upon features of the total situation in which the object is apprehended. These include states of the percipient and states of the external environment. The determining factor is the accuracy with which the external object is apprehended or, more precisely, the likelihood of its being accurately perceived. Sometimes what appears in the distance to be a woman actually is a woman; sometimes it is not. In either circumstance, the experience is an instance of *phantasia* because it occurred under conditions that were not conducive to veridical perception.

The inclusion of cases of perceptual illusion under *phantasia* has led commentators to believe that *phantasia* is involved whenever conditions are such that a perceiver is (or should be) skeptical about the accuracy of a perception.[23] But other roles assigned *phantasia* are such that were *phantasia* chronically unreliable the consequences would be disastrous – as indeed the consequences would be were the *phantasmata* that correspond to terms, deceptive likenesses of extralinguistic objects. The actions of young children and (nonhuman) animals are guided by *phantasia,* and memory is a function of *phantasia.*[24] The sensory content analysis can accommodate these cases as well as cases of illusion. If conditions are such that a veridical perception of *S* is likely to result from the stimulation of the sense organ(s) by *S,* then the awareness of *S* is an instance of perception. The awareness of *S* is an instance of *phantasia* when these conditions are not satisfied; as they would not be were *S* not present, for example, or even though *S* was present if other conditions, for instance lighting, were unfavorable to veridical perception. Since the absence of the object from the immediate environment of the person entertaining a *phantasma* that refers to the object is sufficient to satisfy the second clause of the sensory content analysis, there is no bar to including veridical memories and other reliable cognitions under *phantasia* – as Aristotle does.

The sensory content analysis faces challenges from two fronts: some commentators dispute the sensory basis of *phantasia,* and others dispute the representational function of *phantasia.* Both features are relevant to the explication of Aristotle's theory of meaning. As a sensory content, a *phantasma* would be well placed to mediate the relationship between the

22 Standard conditions include such features of the total perceptual environment as a normally functioning, healthy sense organ and an object within the field of perception of the organ.

23 For an especially clear statement of this position, see Schofield (1978).

24 See *De Mem.* 451a15–18; *De An.* 433b27–28, 434a3–5; *De Motu An.* 702a15–19; *Met.* 980b25–28.

world and the mental state postulated by the theory. If *phantasia* is not a type of representation, it is hard to see how it would contribute to the human ability to use vocal utterances as linguistic signs at all. More needs to be said in defense of attributing a representational function to *phantasia*. It is hoped that the case for describing its object as a sensory content has now been made. To briefly recap the argument for this claim: Aristotle asserts the identity of the faculties of *phantasia* and perception in the *De Insomniis*, and he analyzes *phantasia* in terms of its relation to perception in *De Anima* III 3. Aristotle concludes his account in III 3 with these words:

> If nothing else besides *phantasia* has the features enumerated and this is what we have said, then *phantasia* must be a movement resulting from an actual exercise of perception. (428b30–429a1)

Moreover, *phantasia*, like perception, is exercised in relation to sensible particulars, and *phantasia* is a link between perception and thought. Considerable textual evidence exists indicating that *phantasmata* are sensory contents, and there is no direct textual evidence that would count against this construal of *phantasia*. Typically, commentators arguing for a broader construal of *phantasia* that does not limit *phantasia* to sensory contents base their arguments on the use of *phantasmata* as representational devices.[25] The latter will be discussed below in connection with the issues surrounding sensory representation and its role in the cognitive life of humans. It is, however, worth noting that several functions assigned to the senses are such that the only way to make Aristotle's position intelligible is to grant that sensory characters are the vehicles for the representation of relatively complex states of affairs. This is true both of the description of the incidental objects of perception and the arguments for attributing the reflexive awareness of sensing and other apperceptual functions to the perceptual faculty.

2 Sensory Representation

A visual image of Socrates is an unproblematic example of a likeness of Socrates and a relatively uncontroversial example of a likeness of a man. The puzzle is not about how an image can be a likeness of an external object. The critical questions are: How can an image be a sufficiently powerful representational device to convey linguistic meaning? Can sensory contents in general serve as representational devices? Aristotle's answer to both questions is a resounding yes. One particularly clear illustration is found in *De Memoria* 1. There, the way a portrait represents its subject is compared to the way a mnemonic image represents the original situation:

25 See, for instance, Wedin (1988); Nussbaum (1978).

Just as the picture painted on the panel is at once an animal and a likeness [εἰκ-ών] ⟨of the animal⟩, and though one and the same, is both, yet the essence of the two is not the same, and it is possible to think of it both as an animal and as a likeness, so in the same way we must regard the image [φάντασμα] within us both as an object of contemplation in itself and as an image of something else. (450b21–25; trans. follows Hett)

These remarks show that Aristotle is capable of giving a nuanced account of representation where different cognitions employ the same sensory content. A single object in the world or in the mind is perceived/thought about in a way that generates two distinct mental activities. Perceived simply as a drawing, the painted animal consists in colored shapes that prompt the perception of an animal just as an actual animal seen at a distance is perceived because colored shapes act on the eye and produce the (incidental) perception of the animal. The picture need not be taken simply as a drawing, Aristotle points out, for it can also be perceived in relation to the animal it represents. A viewer may comment, for instance, that the drawing is a perfect representation of a charging boar or an exceedingly poor one. In this case, the stimulus affecting the eye is the same as before but the content of the perception is different. The new content includes the referential relation between the picture and its intentional object; the picture is seen *as* a representation.[26] Similarly, a sensory representation of an object that is not acting on the senses can be taken in a way that includes its intentional object. This is required if an image is to function as the vehicle for memory. Representations depicting particular occasions, things, and objects are characteristic of memories and dreams. We remember what happens on particular occasions such as an afternoon seminar, which individuals were present, where they sat, and what they said. The remembered situation is represented by *phantasmata,* sensory contents of the appropriate sort, that are apprehended in relation to the past occurrence. To remember is to be aware of the sensory content in a particular way, namely, to recognize that it is an *eikon* (likeness) of the past occasion. A parallel account, mutatis mutandis, could be given of how in the case of meaning the *phantasma* associated with a sound refers to an object in the world.

The way that a sensory content functions in memory is similar to the way the sensory content functions in the perception of an incidental ob-

26 Everson (1997, p. 196) finds the difference between perceiving the picture as an animal and as a likeness to be the difference between "those representational items which are likenesses of something real and those that are not." Like Everson, I, too, believe that for Aristotle all *phantasmata* are pictures and those that are perceived as likenesses are perceived as similar to the objects represented by them. I am not convinced, however, that *phantasmata* are for Aristotle ever completely severed from those objects in the world that occasioned the initial sensory experience(s) that caused the *phantasma* to arise. A picture or a *phantasma* of a two-headed creature is not similar to any actual object or past perception, but it consists of parts that are like actual objects.

ject. The content of the perception of the son of Diares is presented by the proper and common objects (the white shape) that are directly perceived. Were two human percipients with normal vision so situated that they both had a clear visual perception of the same person, they would perceive the same colored shape, but they might perceive entirely different incidental objects. The one who is acquainted with the individual would perceive the son of Diares, whereas the other would perceive a tall stranger. The same complex of proper and common objects represents two different perceptible objects. Similarly, the white shape represents the son of Diares as perceived on a past occasion when this sensory content is employed in remembering the past occasion. The content of the memory is more complex than that of the original perception of him for the memory consists of the content of the perception and a reference to the past. Despite the many differences between sense perception and memory, both as described by Aristotle involve the use of sensory contents to represent objects under complex descriptions.

That *phantasia* sometimes is a mode of sensory representation is less controversial than the stronger claim made by the sensory content analysis that *phantasia* always is a mode of sensory representation. Perhaps the best evidence for the stronger claim is provided by Aristotle's demonstration that *phantasia* is not *doxa* (opinion). His arguments turn on the implicit difference between sensory representation and other modes of (human) cognitive activity. According to *De Anima* III 3, both *doxa* and *phantasia* are critical faculties (428a3–5), and both are subject to error (428a19). They differ in that *phantasia* is up to us, while *doxa* is not (427b17–20), and *doxa* carries conviction (*pistis*), while *phantasia* does not (428a20–22). Despite appearances, we need not believe that the sun is only a foot across (428b3–4; cf. *De Ins.* 458b29, 460b18–19). (This argument is no doubt directed at Plato who had defined *phantasia* as the combination of perception and opinion in order to explain illusory appearances.)[27] At 428a18–25, Aristotle argues that *phantasia* and *doxa* must be different faculties because animals possess *phantasia,* but (lacking reason and hence lacking conviction) must lack *doxa.* Were *phantasia* not always a mode of sensory representation, this argument would not establish that *phantasia* is never *doxa.*

Further evidence that the distinction between *doxa* and *phantasia* rests on a distinction between cognitive faculties that are not limited to sensory representation and those that are is provided by the *De Insomniis,* where Aristotle again contrasts *doxa* and other exercises of the rational faculty to perception and *phantasia* (*De Ins.* 458b10–459a22). Dreams consist of *phantasmata,* and thoughts occurring during sleep that are contrary to the *phantasmata* occurring then are not part of the dream (*De Ins.*

27 Plato, *Philebus* 39b; *Sophist* 264a.

462a29). Not only do these distinctions establish the sensory character of the *phantasmata* constituting dreams, they also establish *phantasmata* as representational structures. Were a *phantasma* not a representation, no conflict could arise between it and a thought, which is a representation.

A further bit of evidence that *phantasia* is representational is provided by Aristotle's query at 432a12–13: "But what distinguishes the first thoughts from images?" Lest we think that this query has nothing to do with sensory representation, we should note that it follows immediately on the heels of an argument by Aristotle to the effect that knowledge depends on perception. Aristotle remarks that one must contemplate *phantasmata* (images) when one contemplates, because images are like *aisthemata* (contents of perception) except they lack matter; that is, images occur in the absence of external objects (431a15, 432a9).

That *phantasia* is a mode of representation and that the vehicle of the representation is sensory is well supported by the treatment of *phantasia* in Aristotle's psychological writings. Another role of *phantasia* is emphasized elsewhere – the role of *phantasia* in voluntary movement. *Phantasia* is the faculty that enables (nonhuman) animals, young children, and drunks to engage in goal-directed activity (433a10–12). The birds gather at the empty feeder in a deserted backyard at a certain time of day, not because they see or smell food, but because this is the time when a person usually appears to fill the feeder. Aristotle would explain this behavior as a case where the bird desires an object represented sensorially (food) and remembers a past meal at the feeder; the bird entertains a gustatory image of a succulent seed and has the expectation of future pleasure. Neither memory nor expectation involve rationality in the case of a bird, according to Aristotle, but they do involve *phantasia,* which must do its work employing only sensory contents. Undoubtedly the picture is more complex in the case of human agents; Aristotle, nevertheless, argues from the role of anticipation and memory in action to the claim that the exercise of moral virtue depends upon changes in the perceptual faculty (*Physics* 247a6–14).

A final word should be said about the two passages in the *De Anima* that hint at *phantasia*'s being a form of rationality. Discussing the problems raised by partitioning the soul, Aristotle says that "the faculty of *phantasia* is different from all ⟨of the parts of the soul⟩ in what it is for it to be such, although with which of them it is identical or non-identical presents a problem" (432a31–b2). This worry is prefaced by the statement that the perceptual faculty is not easily assigned to either the rational or the irrational part of the soul. Taken together, these statements support the attribution of representational structures to both faculties, as does the identification of the faculty of *phantasia* with the perceptual faculty in the *De Insomniis* (459a16–17). At 433b29–30, Aristotle differentiates between *phantasia* associated with reason (*logistike*) and *phantasia* associated with perception (*aisthetike*), and he attributes the former to humans but not to other animals. Although important later as developed in Stoic psychology, the distinction between rational and sensory *phantasia* is made by Aristotle offhandedly and not put to further use by him.[28] The topic of *logistike phantasia* will, nevertheless, be revisited in the next chapter. Even if the object of *logistike phantasia* should turn out to be more abstract than the object of *aisthetike phantasia,* this need not prevent *logistike phantasia* from being a form of awareness of a sensory content.

On balance, there is considerable evidence that *phantasia* is a form of sensory representation. *Phantasia,* on Aristotle's account, is an extremely versatile notion – adequate to explain memory, dreaming, and goal-directed voluntary action. The faculty of *phantasia* is the same faculty as the perceptual faculty, although different in essence and definition. Both faculties are realized in the apprehension of sensory contents. In order to distinguish between them, Aristotle appeals to the conditions under which the faculty is exercised. This allows *phantasia* to be a mode of sensory representation that, unlike perception, is not limited to immediate sensory stimuli. The plasticity and the scope of *phantasia* make it a promising vehicle for representations linking uttered sounds to external objects.

3 Likeness and Reference

As a mode of sensory representation, *phantasia* is well placed to be the psychological component of meaning mentioned in the *De Interpretatione.* The psychological state is an effect (a *pathema*), a likeness of an external object, and the meaning of a sound as tokened by a state of an individual mind. A word refers to objects in the world; the mental state as a likeness fixes the reference of the spoken or written tokens of the word. How this might work on the present hypothesis that the mental state is a *phantasma* may be extrapolated from Aristotle's final definition of memory in *De Memoria.*

> What then memory and remembering are has been stated: it is a disposition belonging to an image [φαντάσματος], related as a likeness [εἰκόνος] to that of which it is an image. (451a15–17)

To explain the relation between the image that is the vehicle for a memory and the referent of the image, Aristotle makes the image an *eikon.* By using '*eikon*' as an explanatory term, Aristotle reveals his intent to appeal to likeness as the relation between the image and the past event that the image refers to. The image is able to represent the past event because the

28 For the Stoic distinction between rational and nonrational *phantasia,* see D.L. VII 51; for the importance of this distinction to language, see S.E. *M.* 8.70.

image is like the event. The relation between them is secured by a similarity between sensuous contents; when the event occurred, it affected the percipient through colors, sounds, smells, and so on. Some of these characters are preserved in the image. Consider a simple case, remembering an orange ball. The ball was initially perceived when the orange, round shape of the ball affected the eyes of the person now remembering the ball. Later, when the ball is remembered, the image of an orange, round shape is the vehicle for the memory, which is simply a way of apprehending the image as a representation of the ball as perceived in the past. The orange, round shape of the image is an *eikon* of the orange, round shape of the ball. Of course, the same image might be an *eikon* of an orange or of the sun, and therein lies a difficulty. More generally, the vehicle for a memory is a sensuous image (i.e., a visual, auditory, olfactory, tactile, or gustatory image) and such images seem to resemble many things, yet the object that is remembered by means of the image seems to be unique. In short, resemblance seems insufficient to guarantee that the image refers to the object remembered and no other. In the case of memory, Aristotle might reply that the original experience of the object may have been such that the object as experienced was qualitatively indistinguishable from a variety of other similar objects; it was, nevertheless, a particular ball that was seen, not an orange or the sun; similarly, the memory employing the *eikon* of that ball is about the ball, not about an orange or the sun. When the objection is generalized to include cases of reference that are not as easily connected to an original perceptual experience of a particular object as is a memory, it may prove more troublesome.

The memory image is an *eikon* (a likeness), and it is this feature of the mental state that enables it to refer to a past event. Without that reference, it would not be a memory. The reference of a word depends upon the mental *pathema*'s being a likeness (ὁμοίωμα). Aristotle's choice of ὁμοίωμα as the term for a likeness in the *De Interpretatione* emphasizes the causal dependence of the mental state as likeness on its source; the *pathema* is an ὁμοίωμα, literally that which is made like. In both the *De Memoria* and the *De Interpretatione,* the appeal to likeness explains how the mental state refers to an extramental referent and thus explains how the mental state makes cognizing about the latter possible. The resemblance between the internal state and the external object fixes the referent of the term or the memory and arguably does so in a manner that is natural. I remember the ball because I grasp the relation between the present image and the past perception. I recognize the relation because I recognize that the present image is like the past perception in crucial respects. No longer a matter of convention, the relation between meanings and things meant is naturalized on the hypothesis that the *pathema* is like its object.

Despite this advantage, using the resemblance between a sensory content and an external object to secure reference, not only of the memory image but also of the content that is the counterpart of a term, is problematic. In the first place, the method seems to fit only a limited number of cases. Setting aside proper names, which raise a whole host of problems, consider a relatively easy case – a common noun naming a familiar species of animal, for instance, the term 'dog'. The meaning of 'dog' does not resemble Fido. Aristotle has a rejoinder, however, because he need only claim that the *phantasma* that is the vehicle for the meaning resembles Fido. The *phantasma* refers to Fido and other canines, and the definition of dog specifies characteristics that are apparent in the *phantasma*. The person who hears and understands 'dog' does so in virtue of having a *phantasma* of this sort and recognizing in it some or all of the features that are constitutive of the definition of 'dog'. The difficulty is that while the popular definition of 'dog' might very well consist in perceptible characteristics that a *phantasma* could exhibit, the real definition of dog that the science of biology discovers is unlikely to consist solely in such characteristics. This difficulty would be especially acute in the case of the definition of essence alone, which is more basic than the definition that includes a description of the bodily parts of the animal.[29] Aristotle's considered answer (to be taken up in Chapter 8) is that the *phantasma* of Fido or some other canine may be apprehended by the mind in a way that yields an apprehension of the essence of the species. The same mental state seems to be at one and the same time a meaning and a *phantasma*. It should be admitted, however, that the more attenuated the connection between the mental content and the sensory object that represents that content becomes, the harder it is to tell a story on which likeness secures the reference of the term.

On the other hand, perhaps the problem is not Aristotle's but ours; perhaps we have misdescribed his position. Suppose that instead of associating the meaning with a *pathema*, which is a likeness, we had distinguished between the meaning and the *pathema* and identified the latter with a *phantasma*. The meaning might be represented symbolically in a 'language of thought', which like a text with pictures would be accompanied by a *phantasma* that resembled the perceptible object to which the term applied. This admittedly more familiar picture would enable us to attribute a quite sophisticated theory of meaning to Aristotle. The sticking point is that according to the *De Interpretatione* the word signifies the mental *pathema* that is a likeness of the object. The *pathema* is the only candidate for the internal state that is constitutive of meaning, and the *pathema* is described as a likeness. Turning to the *De Anima*, we found good

29 See the discussion of allowable scientific definitions in Chapter 6 in this volume. Cf. *De An.* 403b7–16.

reason to identify the *pathema* with a *phantasma,* and we found evidence in the *De Memoria* that Aristotle believes that a *phantasma* can function as a likeness that attaches the present mental state to an object in the world. The challenge is to explain how these two pieces, cognitive content and sensory representation, fit together without positing two wholly distinct levels of representation.

4 A Different Reading

Michael Wedin has provided an interpretation of *phantasia* that is at once comprehensive and provocative.[30] If correct in all particulars, it would offer a way out of our difficulty, not available to the proponent of the sensory content analysis of *phantasia.* Wedin and I agree that *phantasia* is Aristotle's mechanism for handling representation and that *phantasia* is closely tied to the perceptual system. We agree that every act of thinking involves *phantasia.* We also agree that Aristotle analyzes thought on a model that is developed in relation to language. Despite these points of agreement, there is a major difference in our understanding of Aristotle's position on *phantasia.* According to Wedin, *phantasia* is a functionally incomplete faculty that is realized in functionally complete mental activities such as thinking. From a modern standpoint, there is much to be said for this approach. It explains the unity of the act of thinking while distinguishing between the mode of representation (*phantasia*) and the content of the thought. What Aristotle actually says, however, challenges a crucial part of Wedin's interpretation.

The distinction between functionally complete and functionally incomplete faculties is central to Wedin's analysis of *phantasia* and thought. A functionally incomplete faculty lacks a proper object and a proper exercise. In this instance, the functionally incomplete faculty, *phantasia,* is a representational capability. This capability is exercised in some manner and is exercised in connection with a particular kind of object, but neither the exercise nor the object count as a proper exercise (actual$_2$ use) or a proper object.[31] A faculty having this character would be without parallel in Aristotle's psychology. Aristotle is too self-critical to introduce an anomalous case without, at least dialectically, challenging its peculiarities, but we find not a hint of such reservations in the *De Anima.* There is, in fact, no direct textual evidence that *phantasia* is not a faculty just like any other cognitive capacity. In the *De Anima* and elsewhere, Aristotle uses

30 Wedin (1988).

31 Wedin (taking notice of Aristotle's distinction between first and second actualities) marks the difference between the exercise of a functionally incomplete faculty and a functionally complete one by using the terms 'actual$_1$' and 'actual$_2$'. An actual$_2$ exercise of a faculty is one that results in a second actuality and is by definition the exercise of a functionally complete faculty.

phantastikon for the capacity to exercise *phantasia,* where the *-tiko* suffix is his standard way of indicating faculties.

The textual case Wedin builds for the claim that *phantasia* is not a functionally complete faculty is based upon there being only one occurrence of *phantaston* (object of imagination) in the entire corpus – at *De Memoria* 450a24 – and even in this instance *phantaston* is not found in all the manuscripts.[32] This argument requires a supplementary argument to the effect that, had Aristotle conceived *phantasia* as a faculty having an object, he would have used *phantaston* to refer to its object and not *phantasma,* which Aristotle does use with some frequency. This, in turn, is supported by the model of cognition that Wedin finds in Aristotle. The model has six elements. In the case of perception, they are (1) perception, (2) that by which perception occurs, (3) perceptual state (*aisthema*), (4) perceived thing (*aistheton*), (5) perceptual organ, and (6) perceiving.[33] Aristotle has terms for all six; in the case of imagination, *phantasma* corresponds to *aisthema,* and no term corresponds to *aistheton.* Hence Aristotle's preference for *phantasma* over *phantaston* when discussing imagination is (according to Wedin) a tacit elimination of a proper object for imagination.

Even if successful, this argument is only as persuasive as the analogy between the perceptual faculty and *phantasia.* But there is a more fundamental problem. The major obstacle to accepting the interpretation sketched above is the importance Wedin assigns the *aisthema.* It is a commonplace among commentators on the *De Anima* that the *aisthema* is marginalized in Aristotle's account of perception. Although Wedin has a number of interesting things to say in response to some of these commentators, one is still left with the nagging suspicion that had the *aisthema* played a central role in Aristotle's theory of perception, he would have used this term more frequently and given a systematic account of its role.[34] In the *De Anima, aisthema* occurs only twice, once in III 7 and again in III 8; it is not found at all in the chapters on perception.[35] A further problem is that on Wedin's account the *aisthema* is both a state of a perceptual organ and an object of awareness; thus it is simultaneously a phys-

32 Not only is *phantasma* (φάντασμα) used much more frequently by Aristotle than is *phantaston* (φανταστόν), but *phantasma* is by far the more common term in other Classical Greek authors.

33 Wedin (1988, p. 30).

34 *Aisthema* occurs more frequently in the discussion of dreams than in any other context (*De Som.* 456a26, *De Insom.* 460b2, 461al9, 461b22); in the *De Anima* (431a15, 432a9) *aisthema* is used to pick out the sensuous content of a perception and is associated with the *phantasma* (cf. *De Insom.* 461b23, *Met.* 1010b33).

35 In both places, Aristotle elucidates the role of the *phantasma* in thinking by saying that the *phantasma* is like an *aisthema* (431a15, 432a12). Were Wedin's account of perception correct, these passages would give us a reason to accept the analogy he draws between the *phantasma* and the *aisthema* and the interpretation he gives of that analogy.

ical and an intentional state. Granted, Aristotle is committed to the physical embodiment of intentional states; however, both ingredients can be accounted for by appeal to the organ and changes in it, on the one hand, and to the object of perception (the *aistheton*), on the other. To posit another entity that mediates the relation between organ and object is unnecessary and not true to Aristotle's descriptions of perceptual processes. But if we reject this model for perception, we have no good reason to doubt that the *phantasma* is the object of *phantasia* and thus no good reason to deny that *phantasia* is a full-fledged faculty. Aristotle's choice of '*phantasma*' for the sensory content that is the object of *phantasia* is probably motivated by his recognition that typically the object represented by the sensory content is not present in the immediate environment of the subject contemplating it by means of a *phantasma*.[36] The *phantasma* represents an external object, but this fact no more undermines its claim to be a proper cognitive object than does the analogous character of color undermine vision's claim to be a faculty.

If we accept, as I believe we should, the analogy with perception, then there is good reason to accept the sensory content analysis developed in the preceding sections. The sensory content analysis explains *phantasia*'s role as sensory representation. The sensory content analysis, moreover, is compatible with our extending the model of explanation that applies to other cognitive faculties to the capacity for *phantasia*. The construal of *phantasia* as sensory representation gives us some insight into Aristotle's remark that "⟨speech⟩ must be accompanied by *phantasia* for speech is sound with meaning" (420b32–33). One advantage that cannot yet be claimed for the present interpretation of *phantasia*, however, is a fully satisfactory account of the cognitive component of meaning. The way out of this difficulty seemingly afforded by Wedin's interpretation is no longer available to us, and we must turn to Aristotle's description of the noetic faculty in the next chapter in hopes of finding a solution.

5 Drawbacks for the Theory of Meaning

In order to clarify the challenge facing the present interpretation of *De Interpretatione* 1, let us suppose that the full story about the *pathema* that mediates the connection between the speaker and the extralinguistic referent of a term is told by the identification of the *pathema* with a *phantasma* (a sensory content). The account of meaning that would result ap-

36 The *-mat* suffix would be appropriate because the *phantasma* would be the internal representation of an external object that resulted from the original perception of the object. It should be noted, however, that Plato uses *phantasma* for certain types of visual illusion, e.g., the appearance of a perfectly proportioned figure produced by a painting with a disproportionately larger top than bottom (*Sophist* 236ab; cf. *Rep.* 602c).

pears to be open to a number of objections. Chief among those that spring immediately to mind are the following.

First having recognized that words are symbols, why would Aristotle make internal representation in this instance imagistic? Sensory contents are, arguably, a much more cumbersome tool than symbolic representations; hence the former might prove to be inadequate vehicles for general notions and complex abstractions. Perceptions are perspectival and of concrete individuals. The visual image derived from a perception of a particular house does not include the visible features of the house that are not perceptible from the vantage point of the percipient. Many of the defining characteristics of the common noun, house, may not be evident in the perception or in the sensory content that represents the house in the percipient's memories of the house. How then can the meaning of 'house' be an internal sensory representation based on previous perceptions of houses? The more abstract the object of the thought, the more limited sensory contents seem to be as vehicles for the thought. Considerations of this sort have led many modern cognitive scientists and philosophers either to reject sensory representation as a component of meaning or to argue that sensory representations must be supplemented by lexical representations involving semantic networks and mental lexicons.[37]

Second, even if the first set of objections can be met, *De Interpretatione* 1 seems to envisage a one-to-one correspondence between words and the *pathemata* that are their cognitive counterparts, but an image seems to possess an open-ended potential for representing complex states of affairs. The holistic character of sensory representation seems at odds with the analysis of meaning into its smallest units. It also raises the question of whether Aristotle envisages a syntactic equivalence holding between the parts of the mental representation of a sentence and the grammatical parts of the sentence and whether any sense can be made of an equivalence relation of this sort if the mode of representation is sensory.

With respect to the first objection, the best strategy would be to explore the possibility that because Aristotle's conception of sensory representation is broad, he is in a stronger position than other proponents of imagistic thinking. In *De Memoria* 1, Aristotle makes a distinction between taking the *phantasma* to represent the object directly, as in remembering a sound, and employing the *phantasma* to represent a universal, as

37 For an especially clear statement of the latter position, see Johnson-Laird (1993), who argues that there are two distinct components of lexical representation, namely, ineffable primitives that are used to construct models of the world depending upon inferences from the context of the utterance about the specific referents of the expressions used (a perceptual mechanism) and something like semantic networks that relate words to each other.

in geometrical reasoning (450a23–5). A geometer might employ an image of a golden triangle in order to think about the Pythagorean theorem, and under these circumstances the geometer's relation to the image would not be the same as that of a person who is using the same image to think about a particular golden triangle. Aristotle, nevertheless, insists that in both cases the image is an integral part of the thought. There seem to be two ways of employing a sensory representation, then, but not, according to Aristotle, two types of representation – one sensory, the other symbolic – if by symbolic representation is meant a form of thought that employs only wordlike mental symbols. Allowing several different employments of *phantasmata* is not enough alone, however, to explain how a sensory representation of one or more individual triangles can serve as the meaning of the term 'triangle'. Just because a representation of a particular triangle can be used to represent any arbitrarily selected triangle does not explain why or how the universal concept or meaning of 'triangle' arises.

Since Aristotle does not work out the details, let us try to extrapolate from his claim that words correspond to *pathemata*. Perhaps the easiest case is that of a term for a natural kind. The internal object that corresponds to the spoken word 'dog' (κύων) might be one or more visual, or auditory, or tactile images of dogs thought about in a way that constitutes a general notion of dog.[38] The notion just is the meaning of κύων and thus a speaker of Greek is able to make general claims using κύων and to apply the term to an individual animal that she is seeing for the first time. This is the crucial (and yet to be adequately explicated) feature of Aristotle's analysis of meaning: the general notion is not reducible to the instantiations of the notion by individuals perceived in the past. Two speakers of different languages in different geographical regions and at different historical moments may use different linguistic tokens to express the same meaning and to refer to individuals belonging to the same kind, for instance, cats. This would not be the case, were meanings restricted to the individuals perceived. Even so, in the case of the lexical meanings of the ordinary language term for dog, there are arguably a variety of meanings, for instance, "domesticated quadruped resembling a wolf" and "hairy animal that barks," that are distinct from each other. The question then arises: How can the meaning of the term be the same for all? While this objection can be generalized to cover the *De Interpretatione* 1 claim that the *pathema* is the same for different speakers – on any in-

38 As we discovered in Chapter 3, Aristotle (*Posterior Analytics* II 19) treats the capacity to form a universal notion on the basis of perceptions of particulars as a primitive human psychological capacity. In Chapter 8, we shall see to what extent the account of thinking in the *De Anima* supports (or fails to support) Aristotle's theory of meaning.

terpretation of that claim – it seems especially plausible on an account that simply identifies the *pathema* with a *phantasma*.[39]

In addition, on the assumption that the meanings of words belonging to other grammatical categories, for instance, verbs and adjectives, are acquired in the same way as those of common nouns such as κύων, the challenge facing Aristotle appears even greater, because the perceptible instantiations of the property referred to would seem to be even less likely to generate a satisfactory meaning of the term. Aristotle might counter that the sensory representation of the state of affairs asserted by a sentence employing the term would be such that it would provide an adequate model for determining whether the sentence were true and in this way would provide an adequate basis for assigning meanings to components of the sentence. This seems to bring us face to face, however, with the question of the correspondence between the mental representations (meanings) and complex syntactic structures, such as sentences, and this brings up the second set of objections to equating sensory representations with meanings.

The second area of difficulty is the poor fit between the holistic character of sensory images and the apparent implication of the account of meaning found in *De Interpretatione* 1 that for every term there is an associated *pathema*. Aristotle remarks in several places that a name by itself asserts nothing (*De Int.* 16a12–15); it must be conjoined with a predicate to make a statement. In a manner analogous to the way that subject and predicate terms combine to form a sentence, simple thoughts combine to form complex thoughts.

> And thus these things, previously separate, are combined, e.g., the incommensurable and the diagonal; and if the thinking is concerned with things past or future, then time is thought of in addition and included. (*De An.* 430a30–b1)

Thoughts, like sentences, are true and false only if they involve combination (430a1–b6). The unity of a composite judgment is mind dependent even when the judgment reflects a truth about the world because the person making the judgment has put subject and predicate together. "But then it is not only false or true that Cleon is pale, but all that he was or will be. That which makes it one, this is mind [*nous*] in each case" (430b4–6).

What needs to be explained, then, is not only how a single spoken or written word is meaningful, but also how complexes of words convey complex thoughts. Unfortunately, when we try to work out the details on Aristotle's behalf, things become rather murky. Suppose a person thinks a quite simple thought, for instance, "Socrates is not sitting beside Alcibiades." Is there a *pathema* that corresponds to each of the words that the

39 Cf. Putnam's (1988) criticisms of the Aristotelian account of meaning.

thinker would use to express this thought – as the summary statement of the theory of meaning in *De Interpretatione* 1 seems to suggest?[40] If so, do these *pathemata* somehow combine to form a complex *pathema* that is the internal state corresponding to the whole thought? When we recall that the vehicle for this thought is one or more sensory representations, the plausibility of the atomic reconstruction just suggested diminishes appreciably. Perhaps Aristotle thinks that even though a single sensory content may as a whole represent a complex thought expressible in a long string of words, were we to reflect upon the contribution of every significant part of the sentence to the meaning of the sentence, we would find that every word or phrase had an internal correlate that shared some feature with the complex sensory content representing the whole.[41] Suppose one were to have the thought, "Callias is a wolf." The internal state might be a sensory content of Callias behaving viciously. If the internal state corresponding to the word 'wolf' is an image of a (canine) wolf, it would not be part of the sensory representation of the complex thought, but it would share a feature with it. Although tantalizing, these speculations, it must be admitted, are just that – speculations. What is clear is that if the vehicle of a judgment expressible in a statement is a single sensory content, then the mind must be able to use that content to represent the different components of the judgment, as well as their combination.

These questions cannot be settled until we look at the other major cognitive faculty, the noetic faculty, the faculty for thought.

40 The *De Interpretatione* (16b22–25) envisages a minimal sense of the copula: "For neither are 'to be' and 'not to be' and the participle 'being' significant of any fact [σημεῖον τοῦ πράγματος] unless something is added; for they do not themselves indicate anything, but imply a predication, of which we cannot form a conception apart from the things coupled." The *Categories* analysis would suggest that the sentence under consideration consists in three significant parts, namely subject, verb, and relation.

41 Words having the force of logical constants (not, and, if . . . then, etc.) would seem to pose a special challenge to such a reduction. At a minimum, Aristotle would need a distinction between meaning-bearing terms and logical functors. He ignores this problem in the *De Interpretatione*, but he does acknowledge the difference between significant and nonsignificant terms in *Poetics* 20 at 1456b37–1457a10.

8

Abstract Thought and Meaning

As a mode of sensory representation, *phantasia* is well placed to secure the reference of a common noun such as cat. An image derived from the perception of one cat resembles other cats. Aristotle's theory of meaning interpreted in light of his conception of *phantasia* faces several challenges, as we saw at the end of Chapter 7. The extension of his theory of meaning thus interpreted to include scientific definition raises additional questions. At best the image of a cat seems to convey minimal information about the essence of a cat, and so it appears to have little relevance for the *logos* that is captured in the real definition and is constitutive of knowledge. The image, moreover, presents as salient characteristics features that may be unique to the individual cat(s) perceived, yet ex hypothesi the mind derives the meaning of the generic term 'cat' from images of individual cats.[1] How the mind grasps the essence remains a mystery, as does how the mind grasps the meanings of the terms that are common names of macroscopic objects.

Aristotle's answer to these puzzles, if he has one, must be found in his conception of thought. The challenge he faces is to give an account that allows *phantasia* to play a crucial role in determining reference while avoiding the pitfalls sketched above. Were he to envisage thinking in a way that forced sensory representation to the sidelines by treating it as little more than a backdrop of moving imagery, sensory representation

1 There is a problem about deriving meanings from perceptions when attention is focused on the actual world. When thought experiments appealing to possible worlds are brought into the picture, the problems are compounded. For instance, let us borrow Putnam's (1988) example of the use of 'water' on earth prior to the discovery of the atomic composition of water and the use of 'water' on twin earth; on earth, the actual but unknown composition is H_2O and on twin earth the actual but unknown composition is XYZ. The reference of the term 'water' is different on earth and twin earth, and if reference is a function of meaning it looks as if there are two different meanings of 'water' that would elude any specification of the meaning on earth or twin earth. Similarly, if the meaning of the term just is the associated image, there would seem to be no way to make sense of the difference between the use of 'water' on earth and on twin earth.

would become irrelevant or dispensable for the activity of thinking. The same outcome would result, were Aristotle to limit thinking to representation in a "mentalese" language. An account of thinking along any of these lines would be highly problematic for Aristotle's theory of meaning. It has become clear in the course of the present investigation that the *pathema* mentioned in the summary account of meaning in *De Interpretatione* 1 does double duty as an intention and meaning and as a mental state that refers to an object in the world by means of resemblance (16a6–8). If the *pathema* is construed as a mere thought, *phantasia* would have no role to play in the explanation of meaning, and Aristotle's making *phantasia* a requirement for language in the *De Anima* would be baffling. Or, if this problem is avoided by making the *pathema* a *phantasma,* the intuitive connection between meaning and thought would be threatened. Aristotle's best strategy would be to attempt to avoid both horns of this dilemma by telling a story about cognition for which the dilemma does not arise. Instead of conceiving sensory and noetic representation as two independent modes of representation, were Aristotle to integrate perceptual and noetic functions, he might be able to bring the cognitive aspect of meaning together with the pictorial character of *phantasia.* The description of the internal state in *De Interpretatione* 1 suggests just such a picture for no sooner has Aristotle described the *pathema* as a likeness, than he speaks of the thoughts (νοήματα) corresponding to speech.

> As there are in the mind thoughts which do not involve truth or falsity, and those which must be either true or false, so it is in speech . . . Nouns and verbs, provided nothing is added, are like thoughts without combination or separation. (16a9–14)

This is not the only passage where Aristotle identifies the structure of language with that of thought. There are, then, two psychic contenders for the role of the *pathema* that makes meaningful utterance possible. The first, *phantasia,* fits the likeness criterion very well. The other, thought, has the requisite structure and hence the precision required. Aristotle might envisage the relation between the two psychic capacities and meaning in a way that makes one or the other more basic: (a) thinking is a way of manipulating sensory contents, or (a') thinking is a way of representing what is presented at a more basic level in *phantasmata,* or (b) thinking is a nonsensory mode of representation that is more basic to human cognition than are sensory modes of representation. Determining which of these pictures is right will not be easy.

1 Thought

Aristotle mentions structural similarities between language and thought when his attention is fixed on the former, but he does not explicate the structure of thought by appealing to that of language. It remains for us to discover whether the relation between *phantasia* and thinking, as he conceives it, is such that it dispels our worries about the limitations of *phantasia* as a vehicle for meaning or compounds them. When Aristotle turns to "the part of the soul by which the soul knows and thinks" in *De Anima* III 4, he emphasizes the similarities as well as the differences between this faculty and the perceptual faculty that had been the focus of his account of cognition up to this point. Both faculties are potentially what their objects are actually; both are brought to full actuality by their objects; both are impassive and activated only by their appropriate objects. All cognitive activities of human beings are exercises of one or both of these faculties. The faculty for thought differs most strikingly from the perceptual faculty in lacking a specific bodily organ that is exercised in thinking; otherwise its character is quite like that of the perceptual faculty.[2]

Because the exercise of the two cognitive faculties is similar in many respects and because the objects of thought are derived from physical objects, Aristotle entertains the hypothesis that the faculties of thought and perception are really a single faculty.

> Since a magnitude and what it is to be a magnitude are different, also water and what it is to be water are different . . . , one discerns what it is to be flesh and flesh either by means of a different faculty or the same faculty differently disposed. (429b10–14)

The faculty that apprehends magnitudes and water is the perceptual faculty. One sees the water and the expanse of the water, but one does not grasp the nature of water or magnitude by employing sight. By thinking about what one has perceived, one comes to understand what its nature is. Yet, significantly, Aristotle does not immediately conclude on this basis that thought and perception belong to different faculties. The query about objects and essences is repeated nearly verbatim a few lines below, but this time Aristotle is describing the relationship between thinking about an arithmetical object and thinking about a geometrical one. The relationship in question is the difference between the cognition of an ideal straight line and the cognition of the essence of straightness.

> Again in the case of abstract objects, the straight is like the snub, for it involves continuity. But the essence is different, if what it is to be straight and the straight are different; let it be duality. One discerns it then by something different or by the same thing differently disposed. (429b18–21)

2 The faculty of thought is "self-starting"; i.e., a subject can think spontaneously about a topic, whereas a subject cannot perceive what is not present in her immediate environment. However, other functions of the perceptual faculty, e.g., remembering, are more under the control of the subject.

By describing the differences between one exercise of thought and another in the same terms as he describes the difference between an exercise of the noetic faculty and an exercise of the perceptual faculty, Aristotle again chooses to emphasize the similarities rather than the differences between these faculties. Thus it comes somewhat as a surprise that although he answers the second question affirmatively, that is, the same faculty, the noetic faculty, differently disposed as geometrical and arithmetical reasoning apprehends the straight and its essence, Aristotle answers the first question about water and its essence negatively.

Several putative explanations of the difference do not bear up under scrutiny. First we might be tempted to think that the difference lies simply in the difference between particulars and universals that is central to Aristotelian epistemology. Water or, more precisely, a particular sample of water that is the object of perception is a particular, whereas its essence is a universal. However, just as the sample is a particular, so is the image of the straight line that the geometer grasps in thought. The natural kind, water, the idealized straight line, the essence of the line and the essence of water, all count as universals, in contrast to concrete instances of water and individual images of geometrical objects. In short, in both cases, the mind apprehends universals on the basis of particulars. A second strategy would locate the difference in the fact that water is a concrete substance consisting of form and matter. The geometer's straight line (although derived by a process of abstraction from observable straight edges) is not situated in the world.[3] Water is situated in the world. The essence of water makes the observable water what it is, but for reasons that are much clearer in the *Metaphysics* than in the *De Anima,* the essence of water cannot simply be identified with concrete instances of water. Water is seen, heard, touched, and tasted; it is apprehended through the senses. Its essence is grasped by thought as a consequence of such perceptions, but the essence is conceptually distinct. Even though this approach seems promising, it too is vulnerable to objection, because, according to Aristotle, the line as imagined by the geometer does have matter, just not physical matter. Why would the difference between physical matter and spatial extension be sufficient to warrant different answers to his twin queries? The difference is that the matter of a physical object exists independent of any cognitive activity; the physical object becomes an object of awareness through perception, but perception plays no role in creating the object. It is possible, moreover, to perceive the particular without comprehending the universal. In the case of the imagined line, the line is created in the act of reflecting on a property that is imperfectly exemplified in physical objects; the existence of the imagined line is de-

3 See Chapter 4 in this volume and also Modrak (1989).

pendent upon the cognitive activity of grasping the universal (the idealized straight line).[4] This is why Aristotle decides that a different faculty is involved in the apprehension of the essence of water than in the apprehension of water, but that the same faculty differently disposed is involved in the apprehension of the line and its essence.

The two queries about how one cognition differs from another suggest that all distinctions among human cognitive faculties fall along a cognitive continuum bounded by the perception of simple, proper sensibles at one extreme and the intellection of the most universal intelligibles at the other. From one perspective, any difference between types of objects results in a difference between types of faculty narrowly defined; arithmetical thinking is different from geometrical thought. From another perspective only logical differences serve to delineate cognitive faculties broadly speaking; the distinction between particular and universal differentiates the two cognitive faculties of the soul. It marks the divide between the activities of the perceptual faculty and those of the noetic faculty. Just as the same rose smells sweet and looks red, the same water has certain sensible characteristics and a particular essence. Just as the distinction between the sense of smell and sight is the result of the difference between odor and color, the distinction between the perceptual faculty and the noetic faculty is maintained by the difference between sensible characters and universals.

The triangle-as-imagined is compared by Aristotle to the triangle as drawn, and both the *phantasma* and the drawing are contrasted to the use of the drawing by the geometer in a proof concerning the abstract triangle (*De Mem.* 450a1–8). This contrast illustrates the difference between the geometer's employment of *phantasia* (a perceptual function) and the geometer's thought about the theorem. Here the difference between faculties is a consequence of the difference between particular and universal objects.[5] Herein lies the crux of the problem for Aristotle's theory of meaning and the postulated relation between a *phantasma* and a meaning. *Phantasmata* seem consigned to the role of representing particulars, but meanings are universals.

Perception, according to *Posterior Analytics* II 19, however, is of the universal, but the articulation of the universal required to comprehend the universal exceeds the scope of perception. From the *Organon* to the psychological and ethical treatises, the close connection between the type of cognitive activity involved in the apprehension of universals and the type of cognitive activity involved in perception is emphasized time and time again.

4 See discussion of the acquisition of geometrical concepts in Chapter 4, section 1.

5 In many different contexts, Aristotle makes the difference between faculties a function of their having different objects. This principle is also emphatically endorsed by Plato (*Rep.* 477c).

It is also apparent that, were a particular sense to be lacking, necessarily some type of knowledge would be lacking, which it would be impossible to acquire, since we learn through induction or through demonstration. Demonstration depends on universals, and induction on particulars, and so it is impossible to contemplate universals except through induction . . . and not having perception induction is impossible. For perception is of particulars. (*Post. An.* I 18, 81a38–b6)

And in a similar vein Aristotle writes in the *De Anima:*

Since there is no subject [πρᾶγμα] that exists separately, so it seems, apart from magnitudes which are objects of perception, objects of thought [νοητά] exist in perceptible forms, both the objects that are called abstract and those that are states and dispositions of perceptible objects. (*De An.* III 8, 432a3–6)

As this passage makes clear, all objects of thought are presented by means of perceptible forms. Although not explicitly differentiated from the objects of physics here, the most universal objects of all, that is, the objects of first philosophy, would surely be included by Aristotle, were he pressed for a clarification.[6] The universal exists as an object of thought, because it exists in some sense in the objects of perception. That this should be so is crucially important to Aristotle's epistemology and his account of meaning. Why it is so requires further exploration.

2 Sensory Representation and Universals

Phantasia is Aristotle's device for internal sensory representation, and thus we would expect *phantasia* to play a crucial role in linking universals as thought to particulars as perceived. This expectation is met in the *De Anima.* When Aristotle wants to minimize the dualistic strain in his account of thinking, he appeals to *phantasia* (403a8–10); when Aristotle objects to the Platonic compartmentalization of human cognitive functions, the faculty for *phantasia* is said to pose a major obstacle to the division of the soul into rational and irrational faculties (432a31–b3); when Aristotle wants to explain practical decision making that involves the application of universals to particular situations, he mentions *phantasia* (433b27–29). Immediately after asserting that *noeta* (intelligibles) exist in sensible forms, Aristotle discusses the role of *phantasia* in thinking (432a7–14). Since the representation of universals cannot be reduced to the mere apprehension of a sensory content, Aristotle must find a more indirect link. Sensory representation can play an important role in the representation of universals, but only if a *phantasma* is taken as a token of the type that is the proper object of the noetic act.[7]

6 For further discussion of the empirical basis of metaphysics, see Chapter 4, section 3.
7 In this section, I shall summarize arguments that I have made in much greater detail in Modrak (1987a, chaps. 5 and 7; 1989, pp. 121–39).

Any perceptible individual will exemplify many types, some essentially, some accidentally. Socrates is not only a human being, he is also a two-footed, tame animal; he is also an animal and a living thing. Socrates is often a pale thing, toward the end of his life, an old thing, and so forth. Because Socrates is a member of all the classes involved, an exemplification of all the universals under consideration, the perception of Socrates and the retained *phantasma* of Socrates can serve as the basis for the apprehension of these universals.[8] The *phantasma* is a representation of a sensible particular, which is a token of a number of types, and the more abstract representations represent the types exemplified in the *phantasma.* The relation between species, genus, and higher-order universals consists in the degree of abstractness with which the features of the particular are conceptualized (cf. *Met.* 1075a1–3). Many more of Socrates' characteristics are disregarded when we use a *phantasma* of Socrates to represent the universal, living thing, than when we use it to represent the species, human.

Thinking is a way of comprehending or representing the object presented sensorially through perception or *phantasia.* The individuating features of an object are salient when the object is the object of a perception or *phantasia.* The features the individual shares with other tokens of a particular type are salient when the *phantasma* of the individual is the basis of a thought about the universal. To apprehend the essence of water is to conceptualize a blue, fluid patch in a particular way; it is to represent water in terms of its essential properties. Similarly, if Socrates is perceived as short, snub-nosed, and balding, the *phantasma* of Socrates employed in thinking about the essence of human beings would include (some of) these idiosyncratic characteristics, but the thought would ignore them. To grasp an intelligible form is to reinterpret the content of an appropriate *phantasma.* Nevertheless, the *phantasma* is a necessary component of the thought. Just as in the extramental world, essences inhere in matter, essences-as-thought inhere in the *phantasmata* that serve as their material substrata. The *phantasma* is caused by the external object, an embodied form, and serves as an internal model of the external object. In the mind, the form of the object is realized as the object of thought. Universal features realized internally as the objects of mental activity demarcate a distinct kind of mental activity, namely, noetic activity as distinguished from perceptual activity.

As the vehicle for the internal representation of the embodied form, *phantasia* is indispensable for thinking. Yet because Aristotle is deeply committed to the distinction between embodied forms, whether physical or mental, that are particulars and forms that are universals, he worries that the distinction between the *phantasma* and the thought will break down.

8 Thinking about Socrates can even yield the notion of an indivisible unit and hence provide the basis for the foundations of arithmetic (cf. *Met.* XIII 1078a23–26).

But what will distinguish the first thoughts [νοήματα] from images [φαντάσματα]? Neither these nor even any other thoughts are images, but they do not occur without images. (*De An.* 432a12–14; cf. *De Mem.* 450a13)

As described, the *noema* and the *phantasma* are conceptually simple, and the mind refers both of them to the same object. The *noema* just is the apprehension of the universal that is exemplified in the *phantasma*. Apprehending the universal as such is a particular way of grasping the content of the *phantasma*. The *noema* cannot occur without the *phantasma* because the *noema* is a particular construal of the object presented sensorially by the *phantasma*. The *noema* is distinct from the *phantasma* because the *noema* is a distinct way of representing the object in terms of its universal features.

Thinking about the universal by employing a *phantasma* of an exemplification of that universal results in a mode of representation that is not limited to specific objects (as are the senses) and that enables its possessor to manipulate concepts, draw inferences, and conceive of abstract objects and imaginary ones. Aristotle sometimes juxtaposes a belief and a perceptual state: for example, the belief that the sun is huge is contrasted to the visual appearance that the sun is small (*De An.* 428b1–4). Were sensory and noetic representation not distinct ways of employing *phantasmata*, it would not be possible for the same subject to use one mode to represent the other. When our beliefs contradict illusory appearances, hallucinations, or dreams, we are simultaneously representing the same object in two incompatible ways. Abstraction also involves the separation of the intelligible from its basis in the physical. Sensory contents are employed symbolically in thinking about abstract objects. Aristotle remarks that the geometer uses the image of a line in the same way she uses a drawing of a line (*De Mem.* 450a1–9).[9] The geometer ignores particularizing features such as size in order to treat the drawing as an arbitrarily selected instance (*Met.* 1078a16–20). Similarly, an image (when used to facilitate reasoning about a type) is treated as a representation of a token of the type under consideration, and the thinker ignores the characteristics that are peculiar to it. Sometimes this use is the result of conscious effort, as when the scientist struggles to differentiate between the essential and accidental features of a species. But at a more basic level, it is simply a consequence of having human cognitive powers; we experience the world through perception as consisting in kinds of objects, and we use linguistic signs of universals to name these kinds and to describe the world as experienced.

Our ability to use sensory representations of the same object in a variety of ways is exploited by Aristotle to explain memory in *De Memoria* 1 and to give an empiricist account of mathematical knowledge in *Meta-*

9 How the mind might use visual representations to conceive geometrical objects is discussed at greater length in Chapter 4, section 1.

physics XIII. It would serve him equally well in giving an account of meaning that fits the synopsis in *De Interpretatione* 1. For the challenge is the same in every instance, namely, to explain how an image or a particular as presented in perception can be used to refer to something else. In the case of memory, the reference is to the past event, now no longer accessible through perception but accessible through memory. In the case of mathematical objects, the reference is to a universal exemplified by the image or drawing of an individual. In the case of meaning, the reference is to a universal concept that licenses the application of a universal term to the object represented by the image. In the first two cases, Aristotle explicitly points to the ability of the cognitive agent to use a picture, an image, or a concrete individual as perceived in either of two ways. The agent may simply attend to the picture, image, or concrete particular as it is in itself with reference to nothing else, or the agent may attend to it with reference to something else. The picture is seen as a representation of a particular individual and judged as a good or poor likeness (450a21–27); the straight edge of the panel is apprehended as a representation of the straight. In the third case, the language user hears a sound and attends to it as a token of a linguistic type. To understand this token is to grasp the type. The latter operation depends upon the language user's having access to a universal that is not peculiar to the speaker's natural language but is a common feature of human languages (16a5–8). Because *phantasmata* originate in the action of external objects upon cognitive agents, those objects as represented in *phantasmata* are the basis of meaning, just as they are the basis of memory and higher-order reasoning.

Another constitutive capacity of thought is the ability to draw inferences. This capacity also requires the manipulation of *phantasmata,* and yet at the same time, it seems to depend on the possession of a language. Aristotle makes no attempt to derive the capacity for reasoning from the ability to apprehend universals – although a case could be made that a creature lacking universal concepts would be unable to draw inferences. The ability to reason discursively is (like meaningful utterance) a uniquely human phenomenon.

> And this is the reason why ⟨an animal⟩ is not thought to have belief [δόξαν] because it does not have belief based on inference [ἐκ συλλογισμοῦ]. (*De An.* 434a10–11)

> While many of the other animals possess memory, none so to speak of the known animals possesses recollection except man. The reason is that recollection is as it were a sort of inference [συλλογισμός τις]. (*De Mem.* 453a7–11)

Belief is one of the functions of the noetic faculty that can be false; nevertheless, to have a belief is to hold a position on the basis of evidence of one sort or another. Only human beings are able to recognize and articulate the connection between a proposition and the evidential basis for that proposition. The crucial feature is not truth, but the cognitive process itself, which enables us to recognize the logical and conceptual relations obtaining among ideas. At one level – the one most immediately accessible to consciousness – this operation involves linguistic symbols. The question is what sort of representation is involved at the base level. A system of representation that is more versatile than mere sensory representation is clearly required. Yet inference, like the apprehension of universals, also involves the manipulation of *phantasmata,* as is evident from the description of recollection as both a search for a *phantasma* (453a15–16) and a kind of inference.

Aristotle describes a deliberative process that involves the manipulation of *phantasmata* and the deliberate construction of one *phantasma* out of many.

> Perceptive [αἰσθητικὴ] *phantasia* then, as has been said, belongs also to the other animals, but deliberative [βουλευτικὴ] *phantasia* belongs only to rational animals (for whether to do this or that, is already the work of the rational faculty; and it is necessary to measure by one; for a person pursues the greater and so must be able to make one out of many *phantasmata*). (*De An.* 434a7–10; cf. 431b6–8)

Some inferential processes, namely, recollecting and deliberating about practical matters, issue in cognitions that are functions of the perceptual faculty: in memories and judgments about particular objects in one's immediate environment. The rational agent, in contrast to other agents, must be able to stand back from his or her immediate sensory representations and manipulate them in accordance with some general strategy aimed at bringing about a desired result, for instance, becoming thinner by refusing food. The ability to do this involves the peculiarly human capacity to use sensory representation in a way that issues in judgments employing universals. Other animals are trapped by the immediacy of perceptions, imaginings, and desires; they are not able to deliberate about courses of action or attempt to recollect a forgotten bit of information, because they cannot distance themselves from their occurrent sensory representations. To deliberate, to reason about *phantasmata,* to manipulate ideas, to apprehend universals, to abstract mathematical objects, to construct proofs, to achieve insights – these are activities that exceed the cognitive powers of creatures possessing only the perceptual faculty because their execution requires a flexible and powerful mode of representation. Language seems just such a mode of representation, but the *De Interpretatione's* description of it makes language dependent upon our having a prelinguistic mode of representation. The basic mode of representation cannot be linguistic. In our search for the basic mode of representation, the only candidate for which textual evidence has been found is *phantasia.* Not only is *phantasia* mentioned in connection with language, but the two distinct activities of the rational faculty, namely, the apprehension of universals and the ability to draw inferences, require the presence of appropriate *phantasmata.*

Aristotle does not explain precisely how this works, but he does give us some clues. In the discussion of memory, he assigns the *phantasma* two functions: to be the object of *phantasia* and to be the bearer of the object of the memory. Memory is also assigned two roles: belonging in itself to the perceptual faculty and belonging incidentally to the noetic faculty (450a15–16). When the object of the memory includes an object of reason, as when we remember not only learning the Pythagorean theorem but the content of the theorem, it is remembered incidentally (*kata sumbebekos*). Aristotle is here envisioning three cognitive possibilities, all of which at base are cognized *phantasmata.* Memory proper occurs at the second of the three possible cognitive levels, for memory requires that the *phantasma* be taken as a representation of a past experience; memory as incidental to an act of thought occurs at the third level, where the *phantasma* is taken as a token of a universal. This cognitive continuum illustrates both the capacity of a *phantasma* to represent a complex state of affairs (the past experience remembered) and the difference between taking a *phantasma* to represent a particular object or event and using a *phantasma* in a way that yields a universal concept.

Even though noetic representation is a distinct form of representation, it requires a sensory content.[10] The human mind is able to transform the apprehension of a *phantasma* (a sensory content) into the understanding of a universal. The concrete particular, a composite of matter and form, acts on the mind through the senses. Perceptions give rise to *phantasmata* that represent particulars. The *phantasma* may be experienced as a complex of sensory characteristics; this is sensory representation. Or, the *phantasma* may be used to think about the form of the entity; this is noetic representation. Or, to put the point in another way: the human mind grasps the form embodied in a concrete particular by recognizing the form as displayed in the sensory representation of the particular (432a3–14). Just as the form exists in matter, the form is thought about in sensory contents. Embodied forms (concrete substances), when perceived, cause the formation of *phantasmata* in the human mind that model the embodied forms. Because *phantasmata* have the same structure as the concrete substances bringing about perceptions, the forms of substances are accessible to the mind. The intelligible forms are in the sen-

10 Since noetic representation is the symbolic use of a *phantasma* (a sensory content), one might describe it as a rational form of sensory representation, and this in effect is what Aristotle does by distinguishing between simple *phantasia* and mental acts that are not possible without *phantasia* and by modifying '*phantasia*' with '*logistike*' (433b29). Believing that the ability to use reason is reflected in all the cognitive activities of mature humans, the Stoics declared that all the *phantasiai* of rational beings are *logikai* (D.L. VII 51).

sible forms (432a5), and as a result, in the favored cases, the intelligible forms are realized in the mind and expressed in real definitions.

Human cognitive processes actualize features of the world, and features of the world are preserved in cognitions. In order to capture this phenomenon, the model of cognition found in the *De Anima* makes the features that are realized cognitively the very same features as the ones that are realized materially. The same sensible characters are found in the *phantasma* and the concrete particular. The same *logos* is found in the intellection of the essence and in the concrete particular. The relation between the *logos* and the sensible characteristics in the particular is duplicated in the relation between the intellection of the essence and the *phantasma* that is the vehicle for the essence. The *logos* realized in thought is the form of the external object. The *phantasma* that is the material substratum of the thought represents the *logos* as enmattered in one or more of its concrete exemplifications. The parallelism between mental structures and physical ones supplemented by Aristotle's causal theory of cognition avoids the actual occurrence of cases where the perceptible qualities of samples of two different natural kinds are identical but their essences are distinct. Not only does this parallelism secure knowledge claims, but it can also be invoked to explain the dual function of the *pathos* underlying meaningful utterance. Meanings are universals that at the base level make reference to and are likenesses of extralinguistic particulars.

Thought cannot be reduced to sensory representation. It is best construed as a property that humans possess that is for them the natural outcome of having the ability to represent objects and states of affairs sensorially (cf. *Post. Anal.* 100a13–14).[11] The paradigm objects of noetic representation are real essences that, like the concrete particulars represented sensorially, exist in the world. The use of a *phantasma* as an arbitrary token of a specific type of object enables the mind to apprehend the essence of any object of that particular type. Were the apprehension of the essence identical to the sensory apprehension of the *phantasma*, (nonhuman) animals would be able to recognize essences and other universals. On the other hand, were comprehending the essence purely an exercise of the noetic faculty, then Aristotle would be on shaky ground when he insists that the essence is, necessarily, a feature of a physical object.[12]

11 An emergent property is a property E such that there are lower-level properties $p_1 \ldots p_n$ that are necessary but not sufficient for property E and that there is no other property p_{n+1} at the same level as $p_1 \ldots p_n$ that is sufficient singly or jointly with $p_1 \ldots p_n$ for property E. If $p_1 \ldots p_n$ are properties belonging to the perceptual faculty and E the possession of rationality, then $p_n + 1$ cannot be being human that is at the level of E, even though this property conjoined with $p_1 \ldots p_n$ would be necessary and sufficient for E.

12 I am using 'physical object' in a broad sense to include both material objects and immaterial realities that are known on the basis of their observable effects (e.g., unmoved celestial movers).

Aristotle conceives the relation between the two types of representation in a way that makes sensory representation integral to noetic representation and thus the perception of concrete particulars is required for the intellection of universals.

3 Answer to the Puzzle

At the end of Chapter 7, we were puzzled about how to bring together two rather different notions, both of which apparently described the *pathema* required for signification in the *De Interpretatione,* namely, meaning and likeness. Simply identifying the *pathema* with a *phantasma* seemed to leave little room for meanings that were universals. The content of the *pathema* seemed to exceed the scope of the *phantasma,* a complex of sensory characters representing a concrete particular. However, simply identifying the *pathema* with a meaning left us puzzled about its character as a likeness.

In *De Interpretatione* 1, Aristotle refers to the inner state as a *pathema,* not as a *logos* (meaning) or a *phantasma,* and this may be an intentional gloss. The vagueness and the indefinite scope of the term '*pathema*' allows room for both meaning and eidetic representation. By using *pathema,* Aristotle emphasizes the passive character of the mental state. The *-mat* suffix indicates a state that is the result or effect of an action.[13] The source of the action is presumably the object (or one like it) that the *pathema* resembles. Calling the *pathema* a likeness of an external object is consistent with the *De Anima's* assigning *phantasia* an essential role in the use of language. Perceptible features of the external object are realized in the activity of perceiving, and these features are preserved in the *phantasma.* A meaningful utterance signifies the *pathema,* however, and thus surely the *pathema* is also the meaning of the utterance or inseparable from it. In light of the peculiarity of this stance, we would be well-advised to review the reasons for attributing it to Aristotle.

The identification of the *pathema* with a *phantasma* has considerable textual support (as we discovered in Chapter 7). Aristotle mentions *phantasia* in connection with meaningful sounds (420b31–33). *Phantasia* is the awareness of a sensory content that originates in perception, and thus there is a perfectly straightforward way to understand how a *phantasma* could be the likeness of an object in the world. The evidence supporting the claim that the *pathema* must be in some sense a *logos* is more indirect, but nevertheless considerable. Sounds are significant because they make reference to the world. Words and sentences (significant sounds) are used to convey information. Even when what is heard produces a visual image in the hearer, it typically does so in the context of a language that is shared by the speaker and the hearer, and typically the hearer is able

13 Smyth (1920, §841).

to state in words what the utterance signified. With lots of fancy footwork, a philosopher might be able to explain this phenomenon on a picture theory of meaning that construed all utterances as merely external speech acts corresponding to internal images. This approach is not taken by Aristotle, who claims that every significant expression has a *logos* (1030a14–15). He standardly appeals to definitions (*logoi*) construed as linguistic items to explicate the use of words and expressions. Claims made in the *Organon* about words and statements make it abundantly clear that significant sounds are definable and their definitions are *logoi*. The primitive statements of a science include definitions.[14] These definitions refer to objects or properties that exist in the world or ones that are derived from such objects. The account of essential definition found in the *Metaphysics* also supports the interpretation on which the *pathema* is a meaning, as does the identification of the substantial form with the embodied *logos* that is expressed in the essential definition. A final consideration in favor of equating the *pathema* with the possession of a *logos* is the fact (according to Aristotle) that in the sublunar realm only humans possess rationality and use language.[15] Aristotle does not attempt to show that the latter is a consequence of the former, but a defense of this position probably would not strike him as necessary, since the common meanings of *logos* as word and reason assimilate the two notions.[16]

Aristotle's conception of noetic activity and its relation to *phantasia* provides a way out of our dilemma. The apprehension of an intelligible form is a particular use of a sensible form. In order to see how the story about meaning that Aristotle does not bother to tell might go, let us exploit a familiar Aristotelian example. Let the word 'cloak' mean a light-complexioned human. One or more visual perceptions of a human having a light complexion produce a *phantasma* of a light-complexioned human. This *phantasma* is apprehended in a way that yields a general conception of a light-complexioned human. This conception just is the definiens of cloak.

Because noetic representation is the use of *phantasmata* as symbols, Aristotle is able to construe the role of *phantasia* in meaning in a way that retains its sensory character without gutting his account of meaning. The image of Fido is apprehended as a token of a type of animal and is thought about in a way that issues in the meaning of the term 'dog' or in the understanding of the essence of dog. While both the meaning and the essence can be expressed in an adequate natural language, there is not a 'mentalese' language that is symbolic in contrast to eidetic. Because

14 Arguably, there are no primitive statements that are not definitions. See Chapter 3, section 2.

15 *Hist. An.* 536a33–b2; *Politics* 1253a8–15.

16 The way that the various meanings of *logos* are exploited to advantage by Aristotle will be discussed below.

phantasia is a sensory mode that can be put to two different uses (*De An.* 434a5–10), the *pathema* signified by a word can be both a likeness and a meaning.[17] Aristotle calls the use of *phantasia* to represent sensible particulars, *aisthetike,* indicating that this use is simply an exercise of the perceptual faculty of the soul (the *aisthetikon*). He calls the use of *phantasia* by rational creatures that makes 'one out of many' *bouleutike* (434a7), to indicate that this use involves the capacity for deliberation (*bouleusis*). *Bouleusis* is a function of the noetic faculty of the soul. The human mind is such that it can think a sensory content in a way that results in the symbolic use of the sensory content. The exercise of this cognitive ability yields the universals required for language and knowledge. This use of *phantasia* is also glossed by the term *logistike* (rational) (433b29).

At what stage does the exercise of the capacity to think about universals employing sensory representations of concrete particulars become a function of training and inclination? Aristotle does not say. It is pretty clear that the initial formation of simple, universal concepts is a natural outcome of having a human's capacity for generalization and comprehension. The infant begins to categorize male and female persons at an early age and mistakenly takes her concepts of male and female as the meanings of the terms 'father' and 'mother' (184b9–14). At a later stage of linguistic development, the child is able to use many of the terms of its native language as signs of the meanings assigned them by speakers of the language. As a consequence of cumulative experience and further education, a speaker in the favored cases comes to employ a natural language term as a sign of the essence of the object in question. The cognitive process involved in the acquisition of a language and in the apprehension of essences is characteristic of human minds. Although it involves the successive reinterpretation of a sensory content that ultimately yields a universal concept corresponding to a real nature, the process is not driven by a conscious reinterpretation of the sensory representation; rather, it is a process that will take place given appropriate conditions of experience, training, intellectual acuity, and historical situation, just as perception is a cognitive process that will take place under appropriate conditions without conscious effort on the part of the percipient. Humans are by nature language users.

The object the geometer employs in thinking about a geometrical figure has a specific magnitude, Aristotle says, even though the object the thought is about does not (450a1–4). In *De Interpretatione* 1, Aristotle describes the *pathema* as a likeness. Both passages raise the question of the role resemblance plays in the representation of universals. Aristotle dis-

17 The dual role of *phantasia* in human cognition no doubt explains why Aristotle argues against the division of the soul into a rational and irrational part on the grounds that it would be difficult to assign the perceptual faculty to either part (432a30–31).

tinguishes between sensible and intelligible forms and makes the former the vehicle for the latter; to clarify his position, let us define two ways in which a mental state may be a likeness. The first (resemblance$_1$) is fairly straightforward: the *phantasma* resembles$_1$ the external object of which it is the image by sharing certain sensible features with it; in Aristotelian terminology, the sensible form is realized as the cognitive object. The red ball as remembered is (typically) represented as red and round.[18] The second (resemblance$_2$) is a more attenuated notion of likeness: when the *phantasma* is employed in a way that enables it to represent a universal, it resembles$_2$ by representing general features manifested by the object of which it is the *phantasma*. The image of a round object employed in thinking about the geometrical object, circle, resembles$_2$ the abstract notion by exhibiting features that are common to all circles. Whether this picture is more unwieldy than one appealing wholly to symbolic representation will depend at least in part on how the rest of the story is told. Moreover, if pressed to defend his position, Aristotle would no doubt cite a further advantage of his account. It avoids certain skeptical worries that would not be avoided were the vehicles of meaning, just like the spoken words, conventional signs, or were the relation between the internal state and the external object left unexplained. To appeal to resemblance, Aristotle would contend, is to appeal to a nonarbitrary relation having its source in the nature of things; in this case, it is to appeal to features that are shared by the internal state and the external object, and this naturalizes the relation between internal signs and the external objects to which they refer.

The meaning, as it turns out, is a way of thinking the content presented in the *phantasma*. The *pathema* mentioned in the theory of meaning is a *phantasma* employed by the mind to yield a *logos*. The *logos* is the meaning of the utterance. The tension between the *pathema* as a *phantasma* and the *pathema* as a meaning is resolved, and Aristotle's willingness to shift from *pathema* to *logos* in the *De Interpretatione* is explained.[19] *Logos* is his term for the formula that expresses the meaning of a significant word or expression.[20] There are ordinary language definitions and technical definitions of essence. All are *logoi*, but only the latter are proper definitions (*horismoi*). Used in this way, *logos* indicates a linguistic expression or a

18 The object of introspection is red and round. This is not to say that the mental image has the physical characteristics that would produce a perception of red and roundness on an external percipient who had access to the states of the heart. The second actuality of the sensible form is realized only in the percipient, and it is this actuality that is preserved in the image.

19 See Chapter 1, especially sections 2, 3, and 7.

20 *Logos* is easily one of the most overworked terms in the history of Ancient Greek philosophy. From Heraclitus to the Stoics to the Church Fathers, *logos* is used to describe the most fundamental ontological principle. Aristotle uses *logos* variously for term, sentence, definition, premise, formula, form, principle, speech, and rationality.

thought. The sensible form is also described by Aristotle as a *logos*, a *logos* of opposite sensible characteristics.[21] That Aristotle chooses to use *logos* for cognitive objects as different as sensory contents and meanings is all the more striking when one considers that, for Aristotle, there are only two types of cognition broadly defined. Every exercise of either the perceptual or noetic faculty of the soul is the realization of an object that Aristotle calls a *logos*. The role of the *logos* is the same in both cases; it affords an analysis of the object. An object-as-perceived is not simply red, for instance, but a particular ratio of light to dark. A term-as-thought is not simply a word, 'cat', for instance, but a particular notion of a small, domesticated feline.

Less frequently, but significantly, Aristotle also uses *logos* for the immanent form, which is the substance of the concrete individual.[22] There is a counterpart to this use of *logos* in the case of perception, namely, the *logos* of opposites that is in the external object of perception. By using *logos* for the form that exists independently of human cognitive activity, Aristotle makes it clear that, on his view, both intelligible and perceptible characteristics have a mind-independent existence. Aristotle repeatedly asserts that the cognitive object (noetic or perceptible) is the same as its (external) object. The term *logos* is well-suited to name the structural principle that exists in matter and in cognition.

When (in the case of understanding a term) the internal state is the recognition of an essence, the mental object is the same *logos* as the *logos* embodied in the external object and modeled in the *phantasma*. Under these conditions, the *logos* qua cognitive object, which is a meaning, arguably resembles$_2$ the object to which the uttered sound refers in that the essence (*logos*) of the external object is the same *logos* as the one grasped in thought. Under ideal circumstances, using the *phantasma* of a concrete particular as a representation of a token of a certain type enables the thinker to recognize the essence that is characteristic of the type. In such cases, the *pathema qua phantasma* is like (resembles$_1$) a token of the type, and the *pathema* qua meaning is also properly described as a likeness (a resemblance$_2$) of the *logos* realized in the concrete token.

A word, unlike other sounds made by living creatures, is what it is precisely because it has a meaning. By employing *logos* for both speech and definition, Aristotle expresses the necessary connection between the two notions. Making statements is fundamental to language and truth, and thus Aristotle uses *logos* for what is asserted by a sentence. He traces meaning, assertion, and truth back to states of mind. The sameness of the faculty and its object is captured by the common use of *logos* for the faculty of reason as well as the content of thoughts. Finally, the use of *logos* for

21 See the discussion of the *logos* doctrine in Modrak (1987a, chap. 3).
22 See Chapter 6, section 1.

form and formula enables Aristotle to describe the substance of a physical object and the real definition of the substance as the same entity. This said, Aristotle's use of *logos* lacks the precision that we modern philosophers value. By using the same term (*logos*) with related meanings, Aristotle has, at best, produced a suggestive picture of the connections between cognitive states and the world, between meaning and reference. The world is intelligible because, independent of human minds, it is so structured as to be accessible to human minds. The accessibility depends upon the possibility of realizing in perception and thought the same structures as are found in the world.[23] What better term to use to capture this fact (for Aristotle) than *logos*, with its ordinary language use for words and meanings?

The present construal of the meaning-bearing *pathema* also explains why Aristotle is confident that only humans have the capacity to use language. An uttered sound only has meaning in the strict sense if the creature for whom the sound is a sign is able to represent the meaning of the sound to itself. This requires the possession of the noetic faculty as well as the perceptual faculty. Nonhuman animals lack the former and hence do not grasp a *logos* as the result of hearing the sound. Many other animals, however, are able to recognize characteristic sounds as signs because hearing the sound issues in the sensory representation of some object, for instance, its young in distress (cf. *Pol.* 1253a11–14).

Interpreting the *pathema* in this way also provides some insight into what Aristotle's answer would be to one of the other puzzles discussed above, namely, the apparent conflict between the holistic character of *phantasmata* and the analysis of sentences into meaningful terms and phrases.[24] Words (names and verbs) are the significant units of speech, yet meaning is determined by reference. The context provided by the sentence in which the term occurs determines the reference of that occurrence of the term. Thus Aristotle makes sentences the basic semantic unit; sentences, not terms, are the bearers of truth. These features of Aristotle's analysis of language suggest that the meaning of a term is a function of the sentences in which it occurs.[25]

What is presented in perception, Aristotle believes, are not isolated sensible qualities but rather combinations of sensible characters that present complex objects and relations to the percipient. Through a window I see the children playing in the school yard, and this visual perception of a complex state of affairs leads me to reject the hypothesis that it

23 Motivated by puzzles raised recently about externalism and the explanatory role of mental contents in behavior, modern philosophers have adopted various strategies from internalism to accounts that appeal to mental models that simulate structures similar to things in the world. See McGinn (1989) for one such account.

24 See Chapter 1, section 3; Chapter 7, section 5.

25 See Chapters 1 and 2.

is bitterly cold outdoors. Instead of a string of *phantasmata* fixing the reference of each term occurring in a sentence, it seems far more likely that Aristotle would envisage a single *phantasma* employed in the thought and verbalized in the sentence expressing the thought. In order to give a perspicuous account of truth, Aristotle conceived sentences in a way that resulted in the meaning of the whole sentence taking precedence over the meanings of the words occurring in it. By assigning the *phantasma* a necessary role in meaning, Aristotle would be in a position to exploit the holistic character of images for the sake of his semantic theory. Similarly, a strategy is now available to make psychological sense of Aristotle's comment that the verb signifies something but not a *pragma* (*De Int.* 16b19–23). A verb uttered in isolation is understood by means of a thought employing certain *phantasmata.* For a thought to use a *phantasma* as a representation of a *pragma,* however, there must be some sort of closure. The world consists in objects standing in various relations. The reference of a name can be understood in terms of an object, presented through a *phantasma,* but a verb can only be understood in relational terms. When a name and a verb are combined to form a complete thought (sentence), there is a complete state of affairs to be presented by means of the *phantasma* expressed in the thought.

The *logos* embedded in matter and in the *phantasma* provides the basis for the analysis that finds in the *phantasma* a structured whole. The articulation of the *logos* in thought and in speech is simultaneously the expression of a single nature or a particular state of affairs and the analysis of that nature or state of affairs into conceptual parts. The relation between the meaning of the sentence and the meanings of the terms occurring in the sentence has a counterpart in the relation between the *logos* as the object of thought and its conceptual parts.

4 Synopsis

In this chapter and in Chapter 7, we followed Aristotle's suggestion that the compressed description of meaning in *De Interpretatione* 1 should be interpreted in light of the psychological treatises. His theory of cognition (we found) provided the key to understanding how the mental state signified by a word can be both a *logos* and a likeness of the physical object to which the word refers. The *pathema* (internal state) is a *phantasma* employed by the language user to represent a *logos.* The *logos* is a meaning as grasped by an individual. The *logos* is common to a number of speakers, because that particular *logos,* although associated with a particular sound of a particular language, is the *logos* (account) of a type of external object (substance, quality, relation, etc.). Instances of the type are accessible by other persons speaking the same language or another language. The *phantasma* is caused by an external object and is a likeness of the external object; it resembles that object in a straightforward, sense-based way (resemblance$_1$). Because the relation between the mental state and its object is straightforward and natural, how the word (or sentence) refers to an extralinguistic object is easily explicated. The *logos* (meaning) is the apprehension of the *phantasma* in a way that yields a universal concept. In the favored cases where the meaning captures essential features of the external object, the *logos* as meaning corresponds to the *logos* as structural principle of the external object. This correspondence (resemblance$_2$) explains the relation posited on Aristotle's theory of meaning between the mental states of language users and the external world. Aristotle's theory of meaning, interpreted in light of his ontological and psychological theories, meets one crucial test of adequacy; it affords an explanation of meaning and reference and the relation between the two.

Aristotle's cognitive theory also provides a way to explain how, as a matter of psychological fact, meanings are determined by the external world. That this should be so is, as we discovered in Chapters 1–4, assumed – by Aristotle's analyses of statements, truth, necessary truth, and science. The belief that the world is intelligible is fundamental to Aristotle's philosophy from the *Organon* to the later writings. In the *Metaphysics,* especially in the central books, Aristotle explores the ontological requirements of knowledge. The intelligibility of changing and corruptible objects is explained by appeal to a real distinction between unchanging essences and corruptible materials. A *logos* (form) is realized in matter, and thus realized it constitutes a particular object; and the same *logos* is realized in the mind thinking about the object. To understand an essence (form) is to be in possession of a real definition. In the psychological context, the ontological distinction between primary substance, form, and composite substance, which consists of the form realized in a particular body, has a counterpart in the intellection of the essence of a concrete individual and the perception of the individual. Because the form determines the essential characteristics of its physical realizations, the noetic faculty is able to use an image of a particular physical realization to think about the essence. The essences realized in perceptible particulars not only determine the character of the immediate objects of observation but are also shared by all other individuals of the same type. The human observer perceives the concrete object, which is an embodiment of a species-specific essence. The language user grasps universals on the basis of the patterns exemplified by particulars and uses the words of his or her language as signs for universals. The knower grasps the essence as such and is able to use the image of the concrete object to think about the essence.

9

Conclusions

This short chapter has two objectives: to review the interpretation of Aristotle's theory of meaning developed in this volume and to consider whether his theory of meaning can successfully answer philosophical challenges of both ancient and modern origins. The treatment of these topics will of necessity be brief and selective. The intent, especially in the case of modern theories, is to provoke discussion, not to settle questions that would demand a much more thorough investigation than is appropriate here.

1 Pulling the Threads Together

De Interpretatione 1 offers a terse explanation of meaning:

> Spoken words then are symbols of affections of the soul [τῶν ἐν τῇ ψυχῇ παθημάτων] and written words are symbols of spoken words. And just as written letters are not the same for all humans neither are spoken words. But what these primarily are signs of, the affections of the soul, are the same for all, as also are those things [πράγματα] of which our affections are likenesses [ὁμοιώματα].

To understand this description, I have argued, we must interpret each of its parts within the context provided by Aristotle when he discusses the issues surrounding signification, ontology, and psychological processes. In Part I, Aristotle's conception of meaning and reference was explicated within the logical and ontological framework of the *Organon*. There the basic entities are simple subjects and their characteristics. For language and logic, the basic items are simple subjects and predicates. For epistemology and ontology, the basic units are simple substances and their properties and relations. Throughout, Aristotle assumes that the basic categories of language – knowledge and reality – are structural equivalents. Chapter 1 established that *De Interpretatione* 1 gives a summary of a promising theory of meaning that meets certain minimal requirements for a semantic theory. It provides an account of reference. The meaning of a particular term is the result of a relation obtaining between an internal state of the language user(s) and the external object(s) to which the term applies. The *Categories* classifies the entities to which terms refer according to basic ontological type. The question was then raised whether Aristotle was committed to a more populous ontology than that of the world of ordinary objects and their properties; he was not. Words refer to real objects and their characteristics. Chapter 2 turned to other semantic properties, namely, truth and necessity. Sentences making assertions about extralinguistic objects are true just in case the asserted state of affairs corresponds to the actual state of affairs. Assertions are necessarily true (according to Aristotle) if the asserted state of affairs corresponds to an unchanging state of affairs. Both the correspondence theory of truth and the Aristotelian conception of necessity are consistent with and buttress the *De Interpretatione* theory of meaning. A similar conclusion about the epistemic importance of reference to mind-independent objects was reached in Chapter 3. There the relation between word and object was situated in the broader background theory of the requirements for definition and the knowledge of basic concepts. Inter alia, the exposition of a body of related propositions constituting a particular discipline requires axiomatization. For each science, according to Aristotle, there is a set of basic objects, the definitions of which are first premises. Chapter 4 developed this line of interpretation further by examining the semantic requirements of the three types of theoretical science (metaphysics, physics, and mathematics). Although the theoretical sciences have different basic objects and first premises, the primary definitions of all three refer to physical objects or their properties, or in the case of abstraction, to objects derived from them.

In Part II (Chapters 5 and 6), we probed Aristotle's ontology of substance in the *Metaphysics* to determine whether it met the ontological requirements of his semantic theory and epistemology as described in Part I. In the central books of the *Metaphysics*, Aristotle ultimately identifies the basic objects (primary substances) with forms that are realized in matter and are apprehended by the mind. The existence of stable, extramental, and intelligible objects is critically important to Aristotle's explanation of meaning and knowledge – for reasons that are clearly stated by Plato in the *Theaetetus* and accepted by Aristotle. The distinction between nominal and real definitions in the *Posterior Analytics* is developed further in the *Metaphysics* to make the real definition the expression of an essence of an extramental object. Meaning requires an intelligible essence; knowledge requires a unified essence (to block a potential regress of basic objects). Aristotelian forms have the requisite character. Forms exist in the world, make physical objects what they are, and are accessible to human minds. The ability to apprehend forms is the source of the definitions of essence that are fundamental to Aristotelian science; it is also the basis for Aristotle's picture of language, in which terms have empirically based meanings. In the favored case, the meaning of a term for a natural kind will be the articulation of the species form that is realized in the individuals belonging to the kind.

At that point, the only issue remaining to be addressed in order to explicate Aristotle's theory of meaning was the nature of the mental state, the *pathema*, that is, a likeness of the external object. In Part III (Chapters 7 and 8), we turned to the psychological writings in order to answer this question, and we found the explanation in Aristotle's conception of internal representation. *Phantasia* (imagination) is mentioned by Aristotle in connection with human language, and the *phantasma* (image) seems well-suited to play the role of a likeness of an external object. *Phantasia* is the cognitive ability to use sensory contents to represent objects. These representations include representations of objects in the subject's immediate environment (when conditions do not favor veridical perception), or representations of objects that were perceived on a prior occasion, or representations of objects that are constructions out of sensory contents that were previously acquired. Appealing to Aristotle's conception of representation by sensory contents, it is much easier to make sense of his claim that thoughts refer to objects because they resemble them. Socrates' thought is about the tree because the sensory content employed in thinking about the tree is like the tree as perceived. The picture becomes more complicated, however, when Socrates' thought is not about the plane tree he is sitting under but about the universal features of plane trees. Aristotle's explanation (found in *De Anima* III 4–8) is to attribute to humans the ability to employ *phantasia* in a way that allows the subject to apprehend universals. *Phantasia* presents sensory individuals, but the rational faculty uses these presentations to think universals. This cognitive ability is what distinguishes human beings from other sentient creatures and distinguishes language users from other creatures employing species-specific sounds. In view of the full range of human cognitive capacities, it is possible to interpret likeness in Aristotle's theory of meaning in a way that is much less problematic than the simple imagistic interpretation initially canvassed in Chapter 7. An enriched notion of likeness is the result of interpreting its semantic role in light of Aristotle's treatment of thought. Likeness in the context of meaning need not be restricted to the sensory likeness between a concrete individual and its image but includes as well the likeness that exists between an essence as an object of thought and the same essence as a nature in the world. For Aristotle, one type of likeness need not exclude the other; the sensory element is always present in thinking, but the employment of the *phantasma* may be such that the individual is subsumed under the universal.

Happily, the interpretive strategy adopted in the preceding chapters has yielded results. First a central text, *De Interpretatione* 1, 16a3–8, which has baffled commentators from the ancients to our contemporaries, has been explicated in a way that leaves Aristotle with a defensible and interesting theory of meaning. Second, my interpretation clarifies Aristotle's conception of the relation between the terms of ordinary discourse and the terms employed in scientific reasoning. It is impossible to understand Aristotle's frequent appeals to ordinary language in support of his technical claims or to understand the importance he attaches to essential definition in the central books of the *Metaphysics* without understanding the relation he envisages between ordinary discourse and scientific discourse. Third, the cogency of Aristotle's empiricist and realist conception of the objects of knowledge depends upon a certain conception of the acquisition of the basic categories of language. The results here lend further support to the empiricist interpretation of the final chapter of the *Posterior Analytics,* which has been defended by several recent commentators, including me. Fourth, my interpretation has shown why Aristotle believes his brand of empiricism is consistent with realism not only about the objects of reference but also about the objects of knowledge, even though the latter have (he believes) many of the characteristics of Platonic Ideas.

In a word, the pieces of the puzzle are now in place. Language and knowledge are possible, because the world is intelligible and human cognitive abilities are such that perceptions and thoughts refer to extramental objects and express the same structures as the extramental world. It is time to take the measure of Aristotle's theory of meaning. Do its strengths outweigh its weaknesses, or conversely? These questions will be briefly addressed from both an ancient and a modern perspective.

2 The Ancient Perspective

Does Aristotle succeed or fail to meet the objectives he might reasonably have set for his theory of meaning? One way to measure his success is to consider the problems bequeathed him by Plato. In the *Cratylus* (and elsewhere), Plato makes a strong case for the thesis that (a) meaning depends on reference and successful reference depends on stable objects. From this conclusion, Plato argues for the claim that (b) real natures are known by the mind alone.[1] Aristotle accepts (a) but rejects (b) in favor of reference to extramental objects having real existence. In *De Interpretatione* 1, Aristotle gives a synoptic statement of his own theory offered as an alternative to Plato's solution to the problem of meaning.[2] When this ellipti-

1 Plato, *Cratylus* 440a–c, *Theaetetus* 157b.

2 Aristotle does not mention Plato in *De Interpretatione* 1, but the language in which his theory is framed includes many of the same terms as the *Cratylus*'s critique and he makes distinctions that block the dialogue's conclusions. See discussion of this point in Chapter 1 in this volume.

cally stated theory of meaning is supplemented by material drawn from his discussion of the relation between existents and predicates and the character of substance and cognitive function, the contours of his view come into focus. As we have discovered, within this broader context Aristotle has all the elements he needs to tell a persuasive story about how signification and reference work.

By and large, the same semantic and epistemic considerations that led Plato to Ideas led Aristotle to realism and empiricism. Aristotle recognizes and exploits the fact that many of Plato's arguments for independently existing Ideas are arguments for realism about objects of knowledge, and he recognizes that the conclusions of these arguments (despite Plato's employment of them) are neutral with respect to whether an idealist or materialist account is true of the reality that exists independent of human minds.[3] This neutrality, of course, does not support materialism any more than idealism, but Aristotle believes that materialism is more consistent with ordinary cognitive experience. A world of concrete objects is presented through our senses and is represented in our prephilosophical reflections about the world. The grounds for questioning this picture of reality are conceptual, and conceptual arguments, Aristotle believes, must be truly compelling to give us an adequate justification for doubting the evidence of our senses and untutored thought. In the central books of the *Metaphysics* (and elsewhere), Aristotle argues persuasively on conceptual grounds against the theory of Ideas. Far from providing stable objects of reference, the Platonic theory of Ideas, Aristotle argues, gives rise to regresses and other complications that would undermine reference and make impossible meaning and knowledge. In short, although there are good reasons to be a realist about the objects of language and knowledge, there are no compelling arguments forcing one to choose Ideas over material objects, to choose Platonic rationalism over Aristotelian empiricism.[4]

A skeptic might challenge Aristotle's optimism about knowledge by pointing out that Aristotle standardly assumes that there is an extramental world of objects. Without a proof that such a world exists, the skeptic claims, there is no reason to believe that this assumption is justified. The evidence Aristotle cites, indeed the only evidence he can cite, in favor of his position are beliefs and perceptions, and their claim to be veridical is open to skeptical attack. Occasionally, Aristotle offers a bad argument for his position, arguing, for instance, that we have just as many senses as there are types of thing to sense (*De An.* 424b22–425a13). Mostly, he re-

3 Here I am using 'materialism' in the broad sense that is consistent with accepting the reality of the properties of concrete objects and of their natures (forms).

4 Neither Platonic rationalism nor Aristotelian empiricism should be confused with the more familiar, seventeenth-century forms of rationalism and empiricism, which were more extreme forms of rationalism and empiricism, respectively.

lies on commonsensical arguments against skepticism and pragmatic considerations in favor of realism. Such arguments are unlikely to sway the skeptic, but Aristotle may succeed in shifting the burden of proof to the skeptic to show that skepticism about the external world is more rational than realism.

Aristotle frames his theory of meaning with an eye to the tension between conventionalism and naturalism that is brilliantly drawn by Plato in the *Cratylus*.[5] Aristotle's answer is that written and spoken words are conventional signs, but meaning and reference are to be explained by universal cognitive states referring to extramental objects. Aristotle agrees with the dialogue's Cratylus that a natural relation between word and object is required and that resemblance is the best candidate. Unlike Cratylus, Aristotle looks for resemblance not between sounds and things, but between an inner state and an external object. Despite making sensory representation a necessary component of cognitive activity, Aristotle resists the reduction of the inner state to a mere complex of sensory characters that resembles the object as perceived, and he expands the notion of likeness to include the relation between an essence as the content of a thought and the same essence realized in matter. Within the context of the problem of meaning as framed in the *Cratylus,* the benefit of this approach for Aristotle is great. Plato's strategy had been to display the advantages for the theory of knowledge of positing a natural relation between meanings and the world and then to conclude with the suggestion that only the immediate nonverbal intuition into the real natures will do. Aristotle blocks the dialogue's outcome by giving a naturalized account of reference that does not isolate language and perception from the understanding of reality. Aristotle also has the wisdom to resist the reduction of meaningful words or phrases to meaningful vowels and consonants, as well as the reduction of truth-functional sentences to truth-functional words or phonemes and phones.

The *Cratylus* develops one strand of a debate that predates Plato; what is at issue is whether change that is an inescapable feature of the natural world and of human artifacts, including languages, is inimical to understanding. Should philosophers attempt to accommodate the experience of change in the theories they advocate or dismiss observable changes as mere appearances that are not part of an underlying, unchanging reality? The debate dates back at least as far as the pre-Socratic philosophers, Parmenides and Heraclitus. As both Plato and Aristotle realize, this debate has consequences for the theory of meaning. Aristotle constructs an account of language and knowledge that accommodates the epistemic requirements for universality, stability, and permanence and the changing

5 See Chapter 1, section 1.

reality of the world of objects as perceived by human beings, as well as the conventional character of language.

Plato often appeals to the contrast between image and reality. Physical objects are described as images of Ideas, and in the *Cratylus* the relation between linguistic representations and reality is also described in these terms.[6] This contrast is typically invoked to disparage the image's epistemic importance. The image may be useful as a stimulus to inquiry and learning, but unqualified knowledge is the immediate understanding of reality. The physical world is the real world for Aristotle. Yet he, too, describes the relation between the object and the internal state signified by the word in terms of likeness. This description is, or might be thought to be, weaker than the description he gives of the relation between the percipient and the perceived object and the thinker and the thought. In the case of perception and intellection, the relevant form (perceptible or intelligible) is realized in the cognitive agent. Formal identity of this sort is a specialized notion that is found in Aristotle's mature works, which include the central books of the *Metaphysics* and the *De Anima*. Formal identity is too technical and narrow a concept to be used to explain reference, and thus it should come as no surprise that this notion is not employed by Aristotle in the summary statement of the theory of meaning. In addition, by using the term ὁμοιώματα (likenesses) Aristotle is in a position to explain reference by means of a familiar and natural relation. Likeness, as Aristotle construes it, would not exclude formal identity, and likeness is a broader notion that can be extended to ordinary meanings and nominal definitions. Aristotle has no desire to require the ordinary person to have scientific knowledge in order to speak Greek or any other natural language. Since formal identity is a special case of likeness, the theory of meaning also applies to the use of a term in scientific discourse. On Aristotle's picture of the relation between words and the world, it is easier to understand the role played by words in learning and the articulation of knowledge claims.[7]

Undoubtedly one of the greatest strengths of Aristotle's theory is its internal coherence. Within the context provided by his theory of human cognition and his conception of being and truth, Aristotle offers a theory of meaning that is as flexible and comprehensive as possible. This theory meets the requirements of his epistemology, and it enables him to answer the objections raised in the *Cratylus*. Aristotle establishes that it is possible to give an account of a natural language that allows for the conven-

6 *Republic* 476c, 510d, 529c–e; *Parmenides* 132d; *Symposium* 211a–c; *Phaedo* 74a–e; *Cratylus* 439a–b; cf. *Phaedrus* 250a–d.

7 This is a topic that Plato's Socrates puts aside as too difficult to understand at the end of the *Cratylus* (439b).

tional and dynamic aspects of language without destroying its capacity to express timeless truths. With respect to coherence and comprehensiveness, Aristotle's handling of these topics is without parallel in the ancient world.

3 The Modern Perspective

Comprehensiveness and coherence are also strengths from a modern standpoint. In other respects, Aristotle's position appears more problematic. To attempt to summarize the literature on meaning and reference appearing even in the past two decades in a few pages would be foolhardy. In the discussion below, I shall concentrate on several well-discussed examples in contemporary literature that purport to show that meanings and other intentional states have wide content. These same examples also seem to raise certain puzzles about whether linguistic behavior and other psychological phenomena can be explained scientifically and seem to lend credence to global skepticism. Any psychological state the attribution of which posits a relation to something external to the mind has wide content. My desire for a cold glass of water on a hot day has wide content as it not only consists in my inner state but also refers to the desired external object. Psychological states as ordinarily conceived typically have wide content; however, arguably, theoretical rigor requires descriptions of psychological states in terms of narrow content. The proponents of narrow mental content argue from the advantages for the philosophy of mind of having closure and being able to specify necessary and sufficient conditions for mental states.[8] Definitions, for instance, are construed as mere notational devices.[9] Computational-representational models of mental activity posit psychological states with narrow content in order to construct formal models of mental processes. Not all modern philosophers are in agreement here, however, and some have argued that an adequate account of mental activity cannot be given that eschews psychological states with wide content. Here again, Aristotle's position seems to combine features claimed by opposing parties in the modern debate.[10] Like proponents of narrow contents, Aristotle believes that psychology is a branch of naturalistic inquiry and that the explanatory models employed in psychology should satisfy the same norms

8 For an especially clear defense of this approach to the study of language, see Chomsky (1992, pp. 205–31).

9 The formalist conception of definition contrasts sharply with Aristotle's conception of real definitions and perhaps even with Frege's conception of definition. For an interesting discussion of Frege's position, see Horty (1993).

10 McDowell (1994) defends a Kantian approach to mental content that is rather close to Aristotle's position in that the base level of cognition (sensibility) is a product of receptivity, impressions caused by the world on our senses, and yet at the same time has conceptual content.

as those employed in the other natural sciences. Notwithstanding, Aristotle's theory of language and mind are such that he is clearly committed to wide contents. Like the critics of internalist accounts of mind and meaning, he believes that states of perceiving, thinking, and understanding meanings are intrinsically connected to the external world. Is Aristotle's conception of content the same as that of the proponents of wide content today? If so, is it vulnerable to the same criticisms?

A good place to start would be with an examination of Aristotle's view in light of Hilary Putnam's argument to show that "meanings ain't in the head."[11] More precisely, Putnam offers a thought experiment designed to show that psychological states do not determine extension. Suppose there is an exact replica of our world (twin earth) with the exception of the chemical makeup of a fluid that twin earthians who speak English call 'water.' My twin and I have exactly the same beliefs about the fluids we call 'water' and the same perceptions of this fluid. It is fun to swim in, quells thirst, and so forth. The molecular structure of what my twin calls 'water' is not H_2O; it is XYZ. My twin and I, despite having all the same perceptions and the same beliefs about what we call 'water', mean something different by 'water'. Our psychological states are the same, but the extension of 'water' is different in our worlds. Should I visit twin earth and become aware of this difference, I might say when I return to earth, what twin earthians call 'water' looks and tastes just like water, but it is not water but twater.

While Aristotle would not appeal to counterfactual situations to make the case for wide content, his theory of cognition does provide a way to make the distinctions required to articulate Putnam's example and unpack it. At the level of sensory experience, my twin and I have the same experience of the two different fluids. We may share the same nominal definition. At the level of essence-as-apprehended, we have different experiences. If we each grasp the real definition of the fluid that we call 'water', we have different mental contents. When either one of us uses 'water', the meaning is a resemblance$_2$ of the referent of water in our world; it is formally identical with the substance we perceive. If that substance is XYZ, then that is the concept we employ. Meanings for Aristotle are in the head because they are in the world. The structure of our psychological states are like those found in the world because the latter cause the former. However, because there are different levels of understanding, different speakers may have a weaker or a firmer grasp on the meanings of their terms. On Aristotle's picture, meanings have wide content, but his cognitive theory allows for internal states that, because they are formally identical with independently existing essences, could be analyzed in themselves, that is, as if they had narrow content only. This would be seen

11 Putnam (1975).

as an advantage by those who believe that to frame an adequate linguistic theory or give a scientific account of psychological states intentional states must be construed narrowly. It is unlikely, however, that Aristotle would have thought it wise to thus restrict theories about language and mind.

Aristotle has an explanation ready to hand for the similarities and differences between the cognitive states of speakers of English on earth and those on twin earth. This explanation treats the difference between nominal and real definition as unproblematic for an Aristotelian proponent of wide content, but arguably this distinction is not unproblematic. Suppose I have only the nominal definition of 'water' and suppose further that the nominal definition does not include the identification of water with H_2O.[12] Because I possess the nominal definition of water, I am able to communicate with other speakers of English about water.[13] My (earthly) twin who is a chemist knows what the chemical composition of water is. She would have the essential definition, and so on Aristotle's theory 'water' appears to have different meanings for us. But Aristotle accepts something like the causal theory of reference and on the causal theory of reference our beliefs about water have the same reference (they are about a natural substance that is essentially H_2O in the actual world), and hence the meaning of the term should be the same for both of us. Aristotle's best strategy would be to argue that my twin's understanding of the meaning is not radically unlike mine but rather is a far more sophisticated and adequate conception of the fluid we both call 'water'.[14] The meaning, whether construed by me according to a nominal definition or construed by her according to a real definition, is a likeness. My internal state is like the external fluid that has caused my many perceptions of water. Her internal state is like the external fluid in the strongest possible sense, as her thought is formally identical with the essence of water.

Many other questions are raised by this thought experiment that cannot be easily answered. Do I intend to ascribe the essence of water to the fluid I call 'water' even though I am ignorant of that essence? Or do I intend to ascribe just those features that are common to the nominal definition and the essential definition? Since the concept I consciously employ when I use 'water' is expressed in the nominal definition, do I know what I mean? If meaning determines reference and my thought refers to the fluid in the world that (as a matter of fact) has a particular essence,

12 In the case of water, one might argue that the linguistic definition does include the formula expressing its chemical composition; if so, water would be exceptional in this regard as the majority of speakers, who are able to use the names of natural kinds appropriately, would be hard pressed to identify many natural kinds in terms of such formulas. Cf. Putnam (1975, p. 228).

13 Cf. Burge's (1979, pp. 82–5) argument that the meanings of many, if not all, of the words of a natural language are or could be incompletely understood.

14 See Chapter 5, section 3.

then arguably my self-knowledge is limited.[15] If I do not know the essence of water, I cannot know that I am thinking about water. In order to counter this objection, Aristotle would no doubt invoke the fact that I have a nominal definition of water to explain that in one sense I do know that I am thinking about water and in another sense I do not know because I do not grasp the essence of water.

Realism about the objects of knowledge and belief is all of a piece with the view that mental states have wide contents. Our best theories, Aristotle believes, are about the extramental world and are true because they correspond to the extramental reality. Aristotle is a semantic and epistemological realist who is untroubled by skeptical worries. Yet modern philosophers have insisted that realism makes skepticism intelligible, and some would say inevitable. If intentional states such as meanings and beliefs have wide content and in addition the world exists independently of the mind, then the suggestion that thinkers are in no position to discern the difference between true and false belief, between genuine knowledge and putative knowledge, gains credibility. Aristotle does not attempt to meet this challenge head-on; he is content to assert that our minds are capable of grasping real natures and to tell a story explaining how our minds do it. The story begins with meaning as likeness, the modeling by the mind of structures that exist external to it. Likeness includes but is not limited to formal identity. When a proper object of perception is realized in a percipient or an essence is realized in a knower, the object realized in the subject is formally identical with the extramental object (the perceptible quality or real nature).

Perhaps Aristotle would see the force of the skeptic's argument were he to reflect upon the case of the brain in the vat (another much-discussed modern conundrum). Suppose you are a brain in a vat that has certain experiences – for instance, perceiving that the room is warm – because your brain has been electronically stimulated in a way that produces these beliefs. Under these conditions, none of your beliefs would be caused by the objects that they seem to be about, for instance, the temperature of the room. Indeed, since it is possible that we are all brains in a vat, global skepticism seems warranted. Aristotle would probably dismiss this puzzle in much the same way that he handles the suggestion that our waking experience is really a dream (1011a6–8). He responds that no ordinary, sane person has this worry, although lovers of argument may entertain it. Nevertheless, the brain in the vat does raise a question that is relevant to his cognitive theory. Aristotle constructs a theory of human cognition where a natural relation (resemblance) secures the reference

15 This objection can be generalized to any speaker who is not omniscient, with the consequence that a speaker cannot know that she knows the meaning of the terms she uses; at best, she knows that she is able to competently employ her language to communicate with others who are also competent in the use of that language.

of a thought to the world. However, since a causal process produces the cognitive state, which is the end result of the process, it appears that our mental contents might not correspond to a mind-independent reality. Aristotle grants this possibility for individuals; the feverish person's physical state explains why his perceptions are delusional, yet Aristotle refuses to generalize from the individual case to global skepticism, as he puts it, to those people who do "seek a reason for things for which no reason can be given" (1011a12–13). Individually, we err, yet as a species we get it right more often than not (993a30–b4). Aristotle finds the hypothesis that the structures of the world act on the mind through perception and reflection producing understanding of the essential features of the external world more compelling than any alternative proposal. He does not, at the end of the day, have an answer for the philosopher who finds global skepticism more compelling.

Even if willing to accept broad contents for mental states, a modern philosopher will certainly balk at Aristotle's conception of mental representation. Modern philosophers, by and large, have been very unwilling to assign visual or auditory images (or sensuous images of any sort) any significant role in thought, and they have made symbolic representation the principal mode of representation in their theories of human cognition. From this perspective, Aristotle's unwillingness to replace eidetic representation with symbolic representation at the base level of mental activity seems to deprive him of a device for representing meanings and other abstract objects.[16] Many modern philosophers will see this as making the project of explaining meaning and other complex operations of the mind impossible. The best way to save Aristotle's capsule theory of meaning, these philosophers would argue, would be to posit a mental language that employs a purely symbolic mode of representation. Equipped with that notion of a mental language, he would be better able to defend the thesis that the same essence is grasped in thought as exists in matter.[17] Aristotle would not be persuaded by these considerations. The advantages of the modern approach would be more than offset for him by the fact that any account of meaning along these lines would sever the natural connection between the mental state and the world. Aristotle believes that there would be no reason in the nature of things (i.e., no nonconventional or nonstipulative reason) why a representation of *X* by a sign that bore no intrinsic relation to actual *X*'s would be a representa-

16 To sample the type of arguments given by philosophers of mind for a base level of representation that makes no use of imagery, see Block (1981). Sensory representation as Aristotle envisages it is a much more versatile form of representation than modern notions of eidetic representation. See Chapter 8, section 2.

17 Arguably, since Aristotle has a notion of representation that allows for internal structure, he does envisage a kind of mental language. Cf. Fodor and Pylyshyn (1988, pp. 803–8).

tion of *X* rather than a representation of *Y*. The approach that he adopts forces the mental state to have an intrinsic natural connection to the external world.

The amount of controversy today surrounding the correct resolution of the issues discussed in this section attests both to the difficulty of the questions asked by modern philosophers of language and to the difficulty of formulating a broad account of language and ontology of the sort found in Aristotle's writings. Aristotle emphasizes different issues than the issues emphasized today, and we cannot find answers to all of today's quandaries in his theory of meaning. Nevertheless, Aristotle's account of mental representation and reference and his conception of nested cognitive levels suggest directions that might still be fruitfully explored. In Aristotle's theory of meaning, similarity is a natural relation between a mental representation and an external object; it is also a semantic relation that obtains between an articulated sensible or intelligible form and the physical realizations of the form. Another promising strategy can be found in Aristotle's handling of the relation between linguistic meanings and scientific definitions. Here he envisages a nesting of concepts where the experiences that determine the linguistic meaning also present the essence that is subsequently articulated in the scientific definition. This approach might be used to resolve the apparent conflict between externalism and self-knowledge.[18]

4 Final Thoughts

What should we conclude about the strengths and weaknesses of Aristotle's theory of meaning? It will not satisfy modern philosophers looking for a theory of meaning in terms of necessary and sufficient conditions, nor will it satisfy those looking for sharply drawn distinctions matching those of modern philosophy.[19] That said, what Aristotle accomplishes is impressive. His concern is to present an account of language that allows humans to use words to articulate and communicate knowledge about the extramental world. He achieves this by carefully constructing an account that speaks first, in the *Categories* and *De Interpretatione*, to the relation between words and objects, then, in the *Posterior Analytics*, sets out the requirements for knowledge of the world, and then, in the *Metaphysics*, gives an account of a suitable ontology. As Aristotle suggests in *De Interpretatione* 1, to understand the psychological basis of intentional

18 For other attempts to resolve this puzzle, see Bilgrami (1987); Burge (1988); and Davidson (1967).

19 For instance, the distinction between verificationist accounts of truth such as Carnap's and the correspondence theory of truth is sharply drawn today. But as we discovered in Chapter 2, section 2, Aristotle is a proponent of truth as correspondence who, nevertheless, invokes norms of rationality to defend logical laws in *Metaphysics* IV.

states, we must turn to the psychological treatises. There we find an account of perception and thought that supports the *De Interpretatione* description of meaning in terms of likeness and the *Posterior Analytics* account of the origin of universals. Both accounts presuppose the existence of a psychological capacity for processing sensory contents in a way that yields the understanding of universals. Aristotle locates this capacity in the character of *phantasia* and its role in thought, and this brings the account full circle and explains why *phantasia* is required for signification.

Taken as a whole, the picture that has emerged is remarkably coherent, simple, and even elegant. Nevertheless, it must be admitted that if we turn to Aristotle hoping to find a rigorous theory of meaning, we will be disappointed. Even after we have culled from the corpus the context in which Aristotle would situate his cryptic description of meaning, we find an account of meaning that is remarkable for its breadth but not for its detail. Once again we are brought up short by Aristotle's willingness to paint in broad strokes and to leave the details to posterity. But surely that is part of his appeal.

Select Bibliography

Ancient Authors

Editions of Aristotle

Categories and *De Interpretatione*

Minio-Paluello, L. 1949. *Aristotelis* Categoriae et Liber De Interpretatione. Oxford.

Prior and *Posterior Analytics*

Ross, W. D. 1964. *Aristotelis* Analytica Priora et Posteriora. Oxford.

Topics and *Sophistici Elenchi*

Ross, W. D. 1958. *Aristotelis* Topica et Sophistici Elenchi. Oxford.

Physics

Ross, W. D. 1950. *Aristotelis* Physica. Oxford.

De Caelo

Allan, D. 1936. *Aristotelis* De Caelo. Oxford.

On Generation and Corruption

Joachim, H. 1922. *Aristotle:* On Coming-to-Be and Passing-Away. A revised text with introduction and commentary. Oxford.

De Anima

Ross, W. D. 1956. *Aristotelis* De Anima. Oxford.

Parva Naturalia

Ross, W. D. 1955. *Aristotle:* Parva Naturalia. A revised text with introduction and commentary. Oxford.

Parts of Animals

Peck, A. 1937. *Aristotle:* Parts of Animals. Loeb Classical Library. Cambridge, Mass.

Generation of Animals

Lulofs, H. J. Drossaart. 1965. *Aristotelis* De Generatione Animalium. Oxford.

Metaphysics

Frede, M., and G. Patzig. 1988. *Aristoteles,* Metaphysik Z, 2 vols. Text, translation, and commentary. Munich.

Jaeger, W. 1957. *Aristotelis* Metaphysica. Oxford.

Nicomachean Ethics
Bywater, I. 1894. *Aristotelis* Ethica Nicomachea. Oxford.

Editions of other ancient authors

Alexander of Aphrodisias
Hayduck, M. 1981. *Alexandri Aphrodisiensis.* In *Aristotelis* Metaphysica Commentaria. Berlin.

Ammonius
Busse, A. 1895. *Commentaria in Aristotelem Graeca,* vol. iv. 4–5. Berlin.

Diogenes Laertius
Hicks, R. D. 1925 (1972 reprint). *Diogenes Laertius* Lives of Eminent Philosophers, 2 vols. Loeb Classical Library. Cambridge, Mass.

Plato
Burnet, John. 1900–1907. *Platonis* Opera. 5 vols. Oxford.

Modern Authors

Ackrill, J. 1963. *Aristotle's* Categories and De Interpretatione. Clarendon Aristotle Series. Oxford.

———. 1965. "Aristotle's Distinction between *Energeia* and *Kinesis,*" in *New Essays on Plato and Aristotle,* edited by R. Bambrough, pp. 121–41. London.

———. [1972–3] 1979. "Aristotle's Definitions of *psuche.*" *Proceedings of the Aristotelian Society* 73: 119–33. Reprinted in *Articles on Aristotle,* vol. 4, *Psychology and Aesthetics,* edited by J. Barnes, M. Schofield, and R. Sorabji, pp. 65–75. London.

Alston, W. 1993. *The Reliability of Sense Perception.* Ithaca: Cornell University Press.

Anscombe, G. 1956. "Aristotle and the Sea Battle, *De Interpretatione,* Chapter IX." *Mind* 65.

Anscombe, G., and P. Geach. 1961. *Three Philosophers.* Oxford.

Balme, D. M. 1972. *Aristotle's* De Partibus Animalium I *and* De Generatione Animalium 1. Clarendon Aristotle Series. Oxford.

———. 1987. "Aristotle's Use of Division and Differentiae." In *Philosophical Issues in Aristotle's Biology,* edited by A. Gotthelf and J. Lennox, pp. 69–89. Cambridge.

Barnes, J. 1969. "Aristotle's Theory of Demonstration." *Phronesis* 14: 123–52.

———. 1994. *Aristotle's* Posterior Analytics. 2d ed. Clarendon Aristotle Series. Oxford.

Berti, E. 1978. "The Intellection of Indivisibles according to Aristotle, *De Anima* III, 6." In *Aristotle on Mind and the Senses,* edited by G. Lloyd and G. Owen. Cambridge.

———, ed. 1981. *Aristotle on Science: The Posterior Analytics.* Proceedings of the Eighth Symposium Aristotelicum. Padua.

———. 1996. "Does Aristotle's Conception of Dialectic Develop?" In *Aristotle's Philosophical Development: Problems and Prospects,* edited by W. Wians. Lanham, Md.

Bilgrami, A. 1987. "An Externalist Account of Psychological Content." *Philosophical Topics* 15.

Block, N., ed. 1980. *Readings in Philosophy of Psychology,* vol. 1. Cambridge, Mass.

———. ed. 1981. *Imagery.* Cambridge, Mass.

Bolton, R. 1976. "Essentialism and Semantic Theory in Aristotle: *Posterior Analytics* II, 7–10." *Philosophical Review* 85: 514–44.

———. 1985. "Aristotle on the Significance of Names." In *Greeek Philosophical Society: Language and Reality in Greek Philosophy,* pp. 153–62. Athens.

———. 1987. "Definition and Scientific Method in Aristotle's *Posterior Analytics* and *Generation of Animals.*" In *Philosophical Issues in Aristotle's Biology,* edited by A. Gotthelf and J. Lennox, pp. 120–66. Cambridge.

Brunschwig, J. 1979. "La forme, prédicat de la matière?" In *Etudes sur la métaphysique d'Aristote, Proceedings of the Sixth Symposium Aristotelicum,* edited by P. Aubenque, pp. 131–66. Paris.

Burge, T. 1979. "Individualism and the Mental." *Midwest Studies in Philosophy* 4: 73–121.

———. 1988. "Individualism and Self-Knowledge." *Journal of Philosophy* 85.

———. 1992. "Philosophy of Language and Mind: 1950–1990." *Philosophical Review:* 3–51.

Burnyeat, M. 1976. "Protagoras and Self-Refutation in Plato's *Theaetetus.*" *Philosophical Review* 85: 172–95.

———. 1981. "Aristotle on Understanding Knowledge." In *Aristotle on Science: The Posterior Analytics,* Proceedings of the Eighth Symposium Aristotelicum, edited by E. Berti. Padua.

Charlton, W. 1970. Aristotle's *Physics: Books I and II.* Clarendon Aristotle Series. Oxford.

Cherniss, H. 1935. *Aristotle's Criticism of Presocratic Philosophy.* Baltimore.

Chomsky, N. 1992. "Explaining Language Use." *Philosophical Topics* 20: 205–31.

Code, A. 1976. "The Persistence of Aristotelian Matter." *Philosophical Studies* 29: 357–67.

———. 1985. "On the Origins of Some Aristotelian Theses about Predication." In *How Things Are,* edited by J. Bogen and J. McGuire. Dordrecht.

———. 1986a. "Aristotle: Essence and Accident." In *Philosophical Grounds of Rationality: Intensions, Categories, Ends,* edited by R. E. Grandy and R. Warner, pp. 411–39. Oxford.

———. 1986b. "Aristotle's Investigation of a Basic Logical Principle: Which Science Investigates the Principle of Non-Contradiction." *Canadian Journal of Philosophy* 16: 341–8.

Cohen, M. 1984. "Aristotle and Individuation." *Canadian Journal of Philosophy* 10: 41–65.

Cohen, M., and I. Drabkin. 1948. *A Source Book in Greek Science.* Cambridge, Mass.

Cooke, H. 1938. *Aristotle* On Interpretation. London.

Cooper, J. 1985. "Hypothetical Necessity." In *Aristotle on Nature and Living Things,* edited by A. Gotthelf, pp. 152–67. Pittsburgh.

———. 1988. "Metaphysics in Aristotle's Embryology." *Proceedings of the Cambridge Philological Society* 214: 14–41.

Dancy, R. M. 1975. *Sense and Contradiction.* Dordrecht.

Davidson, D. 1967. "Knowing One's Own Mind." *Proceedings and Addresses of the American Philosophical Association* 60.

———, and G. Harman, eds. 1972. *Semantics of Natural Language.* Dordrecht.

DeMoss, D., and D. Devereaux. 1988. "Essence, Existence, and Nominal Definition in Aristotle's *Posterior Analytics* II 8–10." *Phronesis* 33: 133–54.

Dennett, D. 1981. "True Believers." In *Scientific Explanation,* edited by A. Heath. Oxford: Clarendon.

Diels, H., and Kranz, W., eds. 1952. *Die Fragmente der Vorsokratiker.* 10th ed. Berlin.

Donnellan, K. 1966. "Reference and Definite Descriptions." *Philosophical Review* 75: 281–304.

———. 1968. "Putting Humpty Dumpty Together Again." *Philosophical Review* 77: 203–15.

———. 1972. "Proper Names and Identifying Descriptions." Reprinted in *Semantics of Natural Language,* edited by D. Davidson and G. Harman. Dordrecht.

Dover, K. 1971. "Socrates in the *Clouds.*" In *Socrates,* edited by G. Vlastos, pp. 50–77. Garden City.

Driscoll, J. 1981. "EIDH in Aristotle's Earlier and Later Theories of Substance." In *Studies in Aristotle,* edited by D. J. O'Meara, pp. 129–59. Washington, D.C.

Dummett, M. 1978. "Frege's Philosophy." In *Truth and Other Enigmas.* Cambridge, Mass.

Everson, S. 1997. *Aristotle on Perception.* Oxford.

Ferejohn, M. 1991. *The Origins of Aristotelian Science.* New Haven, Conn.

———. 1994. "The Definition of Generated Composites in Aristotle's *Metaphysics.*" In *Unity, Identity, and Explanation in Aristotle's Metaphysics,* edited by T. Scaltsas, D. Charles, and M. Gill, pp. 291–318. Oxford.

Fodor, J. 1984. "Observation Reconsidered." *Philosophy of Science* 51: 23–43. Reprinted in *Readings in Philosophy and Cognitive Science,* edited by A. Goldman, 1993. Cambridge, Mass.

———, and Z. Pylyshyn. 1988. "Connectionism and Cognitive Architecture." Reprinted in *Readings in Philosophy and Cognitive Science,* edited by A. Goldman, 1993. Cambridge, Mass.

Frede, D. 1970. *Aristoteles und die 'Seeschlacht'.* Hypomnemata, Heft 27. Göttingen.

Frede, M. 1978. "Individuen bei Aristoteles." *Antike und Abendland* 24: 16–29. Reprinted and translated in *Essays in Ancient Philosophy,* chap. 4. Minneapolis.

———. 1981. "Categories in Aristotle." In *Studies in Aristotle,* edited by D. J. O'Meara (*Studies in Philosophy and History of Philosophy,* 9). Reprinted in *Essays in Ancient Philosophy,* chap. 3. Minneapolis.

———. 1987. *Essays in Ancient Philosophy.* Minneapolis.

———. 1994. "Aristotle's Notion of Potentiality in *Metaphysics* Θ." In *Unity, Identity and Explanation in Aristotle's Metaphysics,* edited by T. Scaltsas, D. Charles, and M. Gill. Oxford.

———, and Günther Patzig. 1988. *Aristoteles, Metaphysik Z' Text: Übersetzung und Kommentar,* Bd. 1–2. München.

Furley, D. 1985. "The Rainfall Example in *Physics* ii 8." In *Aristotle on Nature and Living Things,* edited by A. Gotthelf. Pittsburgh.

Furth, M. 1978. "Trans-temporal Stability in Aristotelian Substances." *Journal of Philosophy* 75 (1978): 627–32.

———. 1985. Aristotle's *Metaphysics: Books VII–X.* Indianapolis.

———. 1988. *Substance, Form, and Psyche: An Aristotelean Metaphysics.* Cambridge.

Gill, M. L. 1989. *Aristotle on Substance: The Paradox of Unity.* Princeton.

Gold, J. 1978. "The Ambiguity of 'Name' in Plato's *Cratylus.*" *Philosophical Studies* 34: 223–52.

Goldman, A. 1979. "What Is Justified Belief?." In *Justification of Knowledge: New Studies in Epistemology,* edited by G. Pappas. Dordrecht, Holland.

———. 1986. *Epistemology and Cognition.* Cambridge, Mass.

———. 1988. *Empirical Knowledge.* Berkeley and Los Angeles, Calif.

———, ed. 1993. *Readings in Philosophy and Cognitive Science.* Cambridge, Mass.

Gotthelf, A. 1976. "Aristotle's Conception of Final Causality." *Review of Metaphysics* 30: 226–54.

———. 1987. "First Principles in Aristotle's *Parts of Animals.*" In *Philosophical Issues in Aristotle's Biology,* edited by A. Gotthelf and J. Lennox. Cambridge.

———. 1991. "Division and Explanation in Aristotle's *Parts of Animals.*" Society for Ancient Greek Philosophy.

Graham, W. 1975. "Counterpredicability and per se Accidents." *Archiv für Geschichte der Philosophie* 57: 182–7.

———. "States and Performances: Aristotle's Text." *Philosophical Quarterly* 30: 117–29.

Granger, H. 1981. "The Differentia and the Per Se Accident in Aristotle." *Archiv für Geschichte der Philosophie* 63: 118–29.

Grene, M. 1963. *A Portrait of Aristotle.* Chicago.

Hartman, E. 1977. *Substance, Body, and Soul: Aristotelian Investigations.* Princeton, N. J.

Hintikka, J. 1973. *Time and Necessity.* Oxford.

———. 1977. *Aristotle on Modality and Determinism.* Amsterdam.

Horty, J. 1993. "Frege on the Psychological Significance of Definitions." *Philosophical Studies* 72, edited by M. David.

Horwich, P. 1995. "Meaning, Use and Truth." *Mind* 104: 355–68.

Irwin, T. H. 1982. "Aristotle's Concept of Signification." In *Language and Logos,* edited by M. Schofield and M. Nussbaum, pp. 241–66. Cambridge.

———. 1988. *Aristotle's First Principles.* Oxford.

Joachim, H. 1922. *Aristotle on Coming to Be and Passing Away.* Oxford.

Johnson-Laird, P. 1993. "The Mental Representation of the Meaning of Words." In *Readings in Philosophy and Cognitive Science,* edited by A. Goldman. Cambridge, Mass.

Kahn, C. 1973. "Language and Ontology in the *Cratylus.*" In *Exegesis and Argument,* edited by E. N. Lee, A. P. D. Mourelatos, and R. M. Rorty. Assen.

———. 1981. "The Role of *Nous* in the Cognition of First Principles in *Posterior Analytics* II 19." In *Aristotle on Science,* edited by E. Berti. Padua.

———. 1992. "Aristotle on Thinking." In *Essays on Aristotle's De Anima,* edited by M. Nussbaum and A. Rorty. Oxford.

Ketcham, R. 1979. "Names, Forms and Conventionalism: *Cratylus* 383–395." *Phronesis* 24: 133–47.

Kirwan, C. 1971. *Aristotle's Metaphysics: Books Γ, Δ, and E.* Clarendon Aristotle Series. Oxford.

Kneale, W. 1962. "Modality de Dicto and de Re." In *Logic, Methodology and Philosophy of Science,* edited by E. Nagel, P. Suppes, and A. Tarski. Stanford.
———, and M. Kneale. 1962. *The Development of Logic.* Oxford.
Kornblith, H. 1993. "Our Native Inferential Tendencies." In *Readings in Philosophy and Cognitive Science,* edited by A. Goldman. Cambridge, Mass.
Kosman, L. A. 1969. "Aristotle's Definition of Motion." *Phronesis* 14: 40–62.
———. 1973. "Understanding, Explanation and Insight in the *Posterior Analytics.*" In *Exegesis and Argument,* edited by E. N. Lee, A. P. D. Mourelatos, and R. M. Rorty. *Phronesis* supp. vol. 1. Assen.
———. 1975. "Perceiving That We Perceive: *On the Soul* III, 2." *Philosophical Review* 84: 499–519.
———. 1984. "Substance, Being, and *Energeia.*" *Oxford Studies in Ancient Philosophy* 2: 121–49.
Kraut, R., and T. Penner, eds. 1989. *Nature, Knowledge and Virtue: Essays in Memory of Joan Kung.* Edmonton.
Kretzmann, N. 1971. "Plato on the Correctness of Names." *American Philosophical Quarterly* 8: 126–38.
———. 1974. "Aristotle on Spoken Sound Significant by Convention." In *Ancient Logic and Its Modern Interpretations,* edited by J. Corcoran. Dordrecht.
Kripke, S. 1972. "Naming and Necessity." In *Semantics of Natural Language,* edited by D. Davidson and G. Harman. Dordrecht.
Kung, J. 1978. "Can Substance Be Predicated of Matter?" *Archiv für Geschichte der Philosophie* 60: 140–59.
Laidlaw-Johnson, E. 1990. "The Combined Doctrine of Knowledge: An Interpretation of Plato's Epistemology." Ph.D. diss., University of Rochester.
———. 1997. *Plato's Epistemology. How Hard Is It to Know?* New York.
Lear, J. 1980. *Aristotle and Logical Theory.* Cambridge.
———. 1982. "Aristotle's Philosophy of Mathematics." *Philosophical Review* 91: 161–92.
———. 1988. *Aristotle: The Desire to Understand.* Cambridge.
Lennox, J. 1987. "Divide and Explain: The *Posterior Analytics* in Practice." In *Philosophical Issues in Aristotle's Biology,* edited by A. Gotthelf and J. Lennox. Cambridge.
Lesher, J. 1971. "Substance, Form and Universal: A Dilemma," *Phronesis* 16: 169–78.
———. 1973. "The Meaning of *Nous* in the *Posterior Analytics.*" *Phronesis* 18: 44–68.
Lewis, F. 1982. "Accidental Sameness in Aristotle." *Philosophical Studies* 42: 1–36.
———. 1991. *Substance and Predication in Aristotle.* Cambridge.
Lloyd, G., and G. Owen, eds. 1978. *Aristotle on Mind and the Senses.* Proceedings of the Seventh Symposium Aristotelicum. Cambridge.
Lorenz, K., and J. Mittelstraus. 1967. "On Rational Philosophy of Language: The Programme in Plato's *Cratylus* Reconsidered." *Mind* 76: 1–20.
Loux, M. 1979. "Forms, Species, and Predication in *Metaphysics* Z, H, and Θ." *Mind* 88: 1–23.
McCall, S. 1966. "Temporal Flux." *American Philosophical Quarterly* 3.
McDowell, J. 1992. "Putman on Mind and Meaning." In C. Hill, ed., *Philosophical Topics 20: The Philosophy of Hilary Putman,* 1992: 35–48.
———. 1994. *Mind and World.* Cambridge, Mass.

McGinn, C. 1982. "The Structure of Content." In *Thought and Object,* edited by A. Woodfield, pp. 207–58. Oxford.

———. 1989. *Mental Content.* Oxford: Basil Blackwell.

McKirahan, R. 1992. *Principles and Proofs. Aristotle's Theory of Demonstrative Science.* Princeton.

Mansion, S. 1976. *Le jugement d'Existence chez Aristote.* 2d ed. Louvain.

———. 1981. "La Signification de l'Universal d'après An. Post. I1." In *Aristotle on Science: The Posterior Analytics,* edited by E. Berti. Padua.

Matthews, Gareth B. 1982. "Accidental Unities." In *Language and Logos,* edited by M. Schofield and M. Nussbaum, pp. 223–62. Cambridge.

———. 1989. "The Enigma of *Categories* 1a20ff and Why It Matters." In *Nature, Knowledge and Virtue. Essays in Memory of Joan Kung,* edited by R. Kraut and T. Penner. Edmonton.

Mayr, E. 1974. "Teleological and Teleonomic: A New Analysis." *Boston Studies in the Philosophy of Science* 14: 91–117.

———. 1982. *The Growth of Biological Thought. Diversity, Evolution, and Inheritance.* Cambridge, Mass.

Mignucci, M. 1981. "ὡς ἐπὶ τὸ πολύ et Nécessaire dans la Conception Aristotelicienne de la Science." In *Aristotle on Science: The Posterior Analytics,* edited by E. Berti, pp. 173–203. Padua.

Modrak, D. 1979. "Forms, Types and Tokens in Aristotle's *Metaphysics.*" *Journal of the History of Philosophy* 17: 371–81.

———. 1981. "Perception and Judgment in the *Theaetetus.*" *Phronesis* 26: 35–54.

———. 1985. "Forms and Compounds." In *How Things Are,* edited by J. Bogen and J. McGuire. Dordrecht.

———. 1986. "Φαντασία Reconsidered." *Archiv für Geschichte der Philosophie* 68: 47–69.

———. 1987a. *Aristotle: The Power of Perception.* Chicago.

———. 1987b. "Aristotle on How We Think." *Proceedings of the Boston Area Colloquium in Ancient Philosophy* 2.

———. 1989. "Aristotle on the Difference between Mathematics and Physics and First Philosophy." In *Nature, Knowledge and Virtue: Essays in Memory of Joan Kung,* edited by R. Kraut and T. Penner. Edmonton.

———. 1991. "The *Nous*-Body Problem in Aristotle." *Review of Metaphysics* 44: 755–74.

Moravcsik, J. 1967. "Aristotle's Theory of Categories." In *Aristotle: A Collection of Critical Essays,* edited by J. Moravcsik. Garden City, N.Y.

———. 1973. "The Anatomy of Plato's Divisions." In *Exegesis and Argument,* edited by E. N. Lee, A. P. D. Mourelatos, and R. M. Rorty, *Phronesis,* supp. vol. 1. Assen.

Morrow, G. 1970. "Plato and the Mathematicians: An Interpretation of Socrates' Dream in the *Theaetetus* (201e–206c)." *Philosophical Review* 79: 309–33.

Mueller, I. 1970. "Aristotle on Geometrical Objects." *Archiv für Geschichte der Philosophie* 52: 156–71.

Nussbaum, M. 1978. *Aristotle's* De Motu Animalium. Text with translation and notes. Princeton, N.J.

Owen, G. [1960] 1986. "Logic and Metaphysics in Some Earlier Works of Aristotle." In *Aristotle and Plato in the Mid-Fourth Century,* edited by I. Düring and

G. Owen, pp. 163–90. Proceedings of the first Symposium Aristotelicum. Göteborg. Reprinted in *Logic, Science and Dialectic: Collected Papers in Greek Philosophy, G. E. L. Owen,* edited by M. Nussbaum, pp. 180–99. Ithaca, N.Y.

———. [1961] 1986. "Tithenai ta Phainomena." In *Aristote et les problèmes de méthode,* edited by A. Mansion, pp. 167–90. Louvain. Reprinted in *Logic, Science and Dialectic: Collected Papers in Greek Philosophy, G. E. L. Owen,* edited by M. Nussbaum, pp. 239–51. Ithaca, N.Y.

———. 1965. "Inherence." *Phronesis* 8: 97–105.

———. [1975] 1986. "The Platonism of Aristotle." *Proceedings of the British Academy* 50: 125–50. Reprinted in *Logic, Science and Dialectic: Collected Papers in Greek Philosophy, G. E. L. Owen,* edited by M. Nussbaum, pp. 200–220. Ithaca, N.Y.

Owens, J. 1978. *The Doctrine of Being in the Aristotelian Metaphysics.* Toronto.

Palmer, M. 1989. *Names, Reference and Correctness in Plato's* Cratylus. New York.

Pellegrin, P. 1987. "Logical Difference and Biological Difference: The Unity of Aristotle's Thought." In *Philosophical Issues in Aristotle's Biology,* edited by A. Gotthelf and J. Lennox, pp. 313–38. Cambridge.

Penner, T. 1987. *The Ascent from Nominalism.* Dordrecht.

Pettit, P., and J. McDowell. 1986. *Subject, Thought and Context.* Oxford.

Prior, A. 1953. "Three-Valued Logic and Future Contingents." *Philosophical Quarterly* 3: 317–26.

Putnam, H. 1975. "The Meaning of 'Meaning.'" *Minnesota Studies in the Philosophy of Science* 7, edited by K. Gunderson, pp. 131–93. Minneapolis.

———. 1988. "Meaning, Other People, and the World." In *Representation and Reality.* Cambridge, Mass.

Quine, W. 1969. "Epistemology Naturalized." In *Ontological Relativity and Other Essays.* New York.

Robinson, R. 1969a. "The Theory of Names in Plato's *Cratylus.*" In R. Robinson, *Essays in Greek Philosophy.* Oxford.

———. 1969b. "A Criticism of Plato's *Cratylus.*" In R. Robinson, *Essays in Greek Philosophy.* Oxford.

Ross, W. 1924. *Aristotle: Metaphysics,* vols. 1 and 2. Oxford.

Russell, B. 1956a. "On Denoting." Reprinted in *Logic and Knowledge,* edited by R. Marsh. London.

———. 1956b. "Lectures on Logical Atomism." Reprinted in *Logic and Knowledge,* edited by R. Marsh. London.

Schofield, M. 1972. "*Metaph.* Z.3: Some Suggestions." *Phronesis* 17: 97–101.

———. 1978. "Aristotle on the Imagination." In *Aristotle on Mind and the Senses,* edited by G. Lloyd and G. Owen. Cambridge.

———. 1982. "The Dénouement of the *Cratylus.*" In *Language and Logos,* edited by M. Schofield and M. Nussbaum. Cambridge.

Sedley, D. 1991. "Is Aristotle's Teleology Anthropocentric?" *Phronesis* 36: 179–96.

———. 1996. "Aristotle's *De Interpretatione* and Ancient Semantics." In *Knowledge through Signs: Ancient Semiotic Theories and Practices,* edited by G.Mannetti, pp. 87–108. Brussels.

Sim, M., ed. 1995. *The Crossroads of Norm and Nature. Essays on Aristotle's Ethics and Metaphysics.* Lanham, Md.

Smith, R. 1989. *Aristotle Prior Analytics.* Translation with introduction, notes, and commentary. Indianapolis.

Smyth, H. 1920. *Greek Grammar.* Cambridge, Mass.

Sorabji, R. 1980. *Necessity, Cause and Blame. Perspectives on Aristotle's Theory.* Ithaca, N.Y.

Spellman, L. 1993. "Naming and Knowing: The *Cratylus* on Images." *History of Philosophy Quarterly* 10: 197–210.

———. 1995. *Substance and Separation in Aristotle,* chap. 2. Cambridge.

Stich, S. 1990. *The Fragmentation of Reason.*

Waterlow, S. 1982a. *Nature, Change and Agency in Aristotle's Physics.* Oxford.

———. 1982b. *Passage and Possibility: A Study of Aristotle's Modal Concepts.* Oxford

Wedin, M. 1973. "A Remark on *per se* Accidents and Properties." *Archiv für Geschichte der Philosophie* 55: 30–35.

———. 1988. *Mind and Imagination in Aristotle.* New Haven, Conn.

———. 1993. "Nonsubstantial Individuals." *Phronesis* 38: 137–65.

———. 1997. "The Strategy of Aristotle's Categories." *Archiv für Geschicte der Philosophie* 79: 1–26.

Wheeler, M. 1995. "Real Universals in Aristotle's Organon." Ph.D. diss., University of Rochester.

Whitaker, C. 1993. "An Analysis of Aristotle's *De Interpretatione.*" Diss., Cambridge University.

———. 1996. *Aristotle's* De Interpretatione: *Contradiction and Dialectic.* Oxford.

White, Nicholas. 1971. "Aristotle on Sameness and Oneness." *Philosophical Review* 80: 177–97.

———. 1972–3. "Origins of Aristotle's Essentialism." *Review of Metaphysics* 26: 57–85.

———. 1986. "Identity, Modal Individuation, and Matter in Aristotle." *Midwest Studies in Philosophy* 11: 475–94.

Wians, W. 1996. *Aristotle's Philosophical Development. Problems and Prospects.* Lanham, Md.

Williams, C. 1982. *Aristotle's De Generatione et Corruptione.* Clarendon Aristotle Series. Oxford.

Wimsatt, W. 1972. "Teleology and the Logical Structure of Function Statements." *Studies in the History and Philosophy of Science* 3: 1–80.

Woods, M. 1967. "Problems in *Metaphysics* Z, Chapter 13." In *Aristotle,* edited by J. Moravcsik. Notre Dame.

———. 1974–75. "Substance and Essence in Aristotle." *Proceedings of the Aristotelian Society* 75: 167–80.

Author Index

Subject Index

Note: The most important treatments of topics are given in bold type.

Index Locorum

OTHER ANCIENT AUTHORS

LaVergne, TN USA
01 October 2010

199160LV00003B/23/P